"Makes the case that 'soft pow_____ ___ ___ ___ _ foreign relations and in life."   *_ily Press*

"Argues that etiquette and small matters of cultural nuance play a huge role in functional politics." —*New York Times Book Review*, "New & Noteworthy"

"Fascinating. . . . An informative and often charming primer on a little-known—but vital—government post."   —*Kirkus Reviews*

"A treasured friend and a trusted colleague. I can't imagine anyone who has been a greater public servant."   —Hillary Clinton

"An interesting and well-written account of the role of protocol in modern diplomacy. Marshall's stories and lessons, drawn from years of experience, are entertaining and valuable in navigating everyday life."

—Henry A. Kissinger

"Protocol—the rules that govern professional, government, and social interactions—may be the very reset we need. These practices aren't dependent on your wallet size or where you come from, your skin color or your nationality—rather, protocol is something we all can get behind, and once you read this, it will jog your memory and reintroduce you to the connectivity necessary in order to move collectively as the better human beings we long to be. My thanks to Ambassador Capricia Penavic Marshall for this book. Give it to everyone you meet, for birthdays, weddings, and elections. It can only help."

—Whoopi Goldberg

"Working with Capricia during the Obama administration was nothing short of wonderful! Her guiding hand and innovative methods laid the foundation for our successful diplomacy on the world stage. Through amusing and touching anecdotes, many of which we shared together, Capricia details the superpower of protocol, a power that helped foster an environment conducive to many of President Obama's successes."

—Valerie Jarrett, former senior advisor to Barack Obama
and author of *Finding My Voice*

"Capricia Penavic Marshall was an extraordinary chief of protocol, and she has now written an extraordinary book on how international protocol actually works, and how it can work for every business and person. I cannot recommend this book highly enough."

—David M. Rubenstein, cofounder and co–executive chairman of the Carlyle Group and author of *The American Story*

"Capricia is the ultimate master in the art of protocol. As a first-generation American woman, she brilliantly manages the cultural nuances of consequential public- and private-sector engagements. Reading her book, I have learned a lot, I have laughed a lot, I have enjoyed every page."

—Christine Lagarde, president of the European Central Bank

Protocol

Protocol

THE POWER OF DIPLOMACY
AND HOW TO MAKE IT WORK FOR YOU

CAPRICIA PENAVIC MARSHALL

ecco

An Imprint of HarperCollins*Publishers*

PROTOCOL. Copyright © 2020 by Capricia Penavic Marshall. All rights reserved. Printed in the United States of America. No part of this book may be used or reproduced in any manner whatsoever without written permission except in the case of brief quotations embodied in critical articles and reviews. For information, address HarperCollins Publishers, 195 Broadway, New York, NY 10007.

HarperCollins books may be purchased for educational, business, or sales promotional use. For information, please email the Special Markets Department at SPsales@harpercollins.com.

Ecco® and HarperCollins® are trademarks of HarperCollins Publishers.

A hardcover edition of this book was published in 2020 by Ecco, an imprint of HarperCollins Publishers.

FIRST ECCO PAPERBACK EDITION PUBLISHED 2021

Designed by Michelle Crowe

Library of Congress Cataloging-in-Publication Data has been applied for.

ISBN 978-0-06-303223-1 (pbk.)

21 22 23 24 25   LSC   10 9 8 7 6 5 4 3 2 1

To my mother and father:
Thank you for the curiosity of difference, appreciation of all, and desire to
reach beyond. And for your loving belief in me.

CONTENTS

INTRODUCTION

I f I told you there existed a single negotiation tool that would reduce confusion, stabilize an arbitration, strengthen your relationships, and give you the advantage, you would certainly want to learn it and use it. Protocol—the rules that govern professional, government, and social interactions—does all of this, and more. As someone who used protocol to fuel successful agreements between world leaders in my four years as chief of protocol for the Obama administration and eight years in the Clinton administration—and between dinner party guests and during grade-school auction meetings—I can say with authority that protocol is a legitimate superpower.

Today, governments and businesses are challenged by a revolving door of crises—some new, like cyber hacking, and some age-old, like pandemics. How leaders react is more important than ever. Economic sanctions and harsh reprimands may address the politics of the day, but these penalties alone are shortsighted. When the crisis has passed, what are you left with? A damaged long-term relationship and weakened leverage.

The guidelines and tools of protocol, such as building and maintaining bridges of understanding, are imperative, especially during these moments of crisis. When we neglect them—particularly with those countries and businesses whose economies are intertwined with ours—we cut off our nose to spite our face. The remedy to our global challenges must provide dual purpose: to be potent and curative. Herein lies the power of protocol.

Our codes of conduct are endangered in all realms of life. In the halls of our government and in public discourse, protocol has been blatantly ignored, resulting in chaos and stalled progress; in business, protocol is underused, either out of neglect or because people do not understand its importance; and in personal relationships, we have become less willing to engage civilly. This is all to our demise. The rules of social behavior matter so much that when they are not adhered to, the fallout—in the form of cultural offenses, logistical misunderstandings, and missed opportunities to connect—can lead to a business deal destroyed, a family gathering gone wrong, or even war between nations.

What exactly *is* protocol? Protocol is a set of guidelines for social behavior, a framework for how to interact and communicate. In our personal lives, we have protocol for everything from walking (stay to the right on the sidewalk) to celebrating (invitations and toasts). In business, protocol can dictate seating (the CEO sits at the position of power), greetings (a strong handshake kicks off an introduction), and dress code (suit and tie or jeans and sneakers). And in government, protocol initiates the wheels of diplomacy, laying out a road map for every exchange, big or small, between diplomats and leaders. From the pomp and circumstance of arrival ceremonies to the seating for a bilateral, relationships are built and agreements are made within the defined and carefully curated structure of protocol.

Why is it so important to have a framework for diplomacy, guidelines for international greetings, or a process for exchanging gifts? Does it really make that big a difference if you serve food prohibited by a guest's culture or bungle a toast with a German or Japanese client? Or if you sit in the wrong seat at a social dinner or board meeting? I can't reiterate enough that it does. And not simply because you've "breached protocol" or "broken a rule." *You have created a slight instead of conferring respect. You have put up an obstacle to connecting instead of moving swiftly along the intended path. No matter what your goal is in an interaction—to persuade someone to see things your way or to leave that person intrigued and wanting more—you first have to make a connection, and you cannot do that to the best of your ability without the elements of protocol.*

When you ignore a cultural norm or mangle a title, the infraction goes deeper than the surface—it affects the emotions of the participants and the tenor of their exchange. Getting a South American colleague's title wrong can make her feel diminished, meaning there is no longer an equal playing field for the interaction. Ignoring the hierarchy in a group of Asian colleagues and addressing the middle manager before the CEO sends the message that you did not care to learn about their cultural norms and that you have a disregard for their professional identities. Suddenly, what was to be a productive flow of communication and ideas becomes a slowed or even stalled interaction, with stops and starts and detours. You may also have unintentionally given rise to misperceptions about your own character and intentions, or introduced unnecessary defensiveness and confusion into the exchange. Not being savvy about the rules of engagement can also affect *your* performance: You may become more hesitant; not wanting to offend, you may withdraw into yourself and fail to make the critical connection you need.

Protocol also keeps us in line. Polite, civil behavior is the glue of a successful society. Kind and respectful exchanges have healthier outcomes. When we interact with people in a welcoming, dignified way, we are encouraging communication rather than shutting it down. And depending on our position and visibility, we are sending out signals for how others can and should behave. For governments, businesses, and personal relationships, our best chance of creating strong and enduring partnerships lies in understanding our counterpart and connecting with him or her. Even when your goal is mostly to persuade—as it often is in diplomacy or business—getting that edge begins with forging or enhancing a relationship. We must learn who the other person is sitting across from us and also share who we are. We have to respect differences and find common ground. If we don't, someone else—another country, another business, another individual—will step in and do it instead. There's not a single nuclear summit, business meeting, or personal interaction that can't benefit from the tools of protocol and diplomacy.

When I entered the position of chief of protocol in 2009, I was step-ping into a profoundly historic role, inheriting wisdom that had evolved over more than a thousand years. Protocol, in both its role and its ety-mology, has ancient roots. The word *protocol* is the combination of the ancient Greek words *protos* (first) and *kollao* (glue). In other words, it is something "glued first," a reference to the first sheet of papyrus that would come at the beginning of an official missive. Quite literally, pro-tocol means setting the stage for engagement.

The ancestors of our modern-day protocol officers (the diligent staff who work for and travel with the chief) were Greek heralds who would be sent to other city-states to make contact with ruling parties during wartime or to scout a future journey for a formal delegation. Heralds were guaranteed safe passage, even by a warring state, because of pre-sumed protection by the gods (a qualification that I am sure many a pro-tocol officer or ambassador today would appreciate). A herald returned with the preconditions for a short-term visit from an envoy. Envoys made frequent journeys to other city-states, but, unlike our modern ambassa-dors, they did not remain in a foreign land for an extended period.

Thereafter, the development of diplomatic protocol was tied closely to the evolution of Western Europe. In 1648, the Peace of Westphalia—a series of treaties between Europe's warring factions—created something we twenty-first-century folks take for granted: territorial sovereignty, meaning each leader was given complete governing control over his rec-ognized territory. Foreign ministries and ambassador corps then arose across the continent to represent their territories and interests, traveling to and from the various nation-states.

But without rules governing these encounters, the gatherings resulted more often in drama than diplomacy. The jockeying of emerging pow-ers in the seventeenth and eighteenth centuries—rife with hierarchical rivalries—threatened to disrupt peaceful foreign relations at every turn. Even the seating for a formal dinner (which ambassador would get the coveted seat of honor nearest the host?) or the order of carriages for a ceremonial procession became charged. These decisions held dire conse-quences, for any slight against an ambassador reflected how his sovereign was viewed by the host country.

Things reached a fever pitch in 1661, when war nearly broke out due to a mishap in the order of carriages in England. On a crisp fall afternoon, the city of London was set to welcome the new Swedish ambassador to present his credentials to His Majesty Charles II, King of England. As was the tradition, the Swedish ambassador's carriage would directly follow King Charles II's carriage to Whitehall Palace, followed by other countries' carriages. It was common then for ambassadors from other nations to attend each other's ceremonies, with the notable exception of Spain and France, who were constantly vying for power and sought to avoid situations where one might one-up the other. But on this day, both ambassadors—the Spanish ambassador and the French ambassador—had been sent by their respective kings to take up the position directly behind Sweden's carriage, signaling that their country was the most powerful. Without a set of rules to determine the precedence order, it seemed they would have to battle it out—literally. The streets were packed with onlookers to see how the dispute would unfold; tensions were so high that His Majesty forbade any citizen of helping one side or the other (under threat of death). Midafternoon, the Swedish ambassador boarded his carriage, and at that precise moment the French and Spaniards launched a bloody attack for the coveted position. Spain gained the upper hand—and ultimately the privileged spot—by arriving very early and reinforcing their horses' reins with chains to prevent them from being cut loose from the carriage. Several people were killed and many injured during the brawl. The Spaniards' victory was short-lived, as a few months later they had to publicly apologize and grant the French eternal precedence to avoid an all-out war. (History buffs: you can find more details in Samuel Pepys's diary entries at Pepysdiary.com.)

Clearly, the diplomatic system needed a stabilizing force for the status conscious. The Vienna Congress of 1815, a convention of European powers to restructure the continent after the overthrow of France's Napoleon, provided such an opportunity. One outcome of the Congress, the Vienna Regulation, created an unbiased system for precedence. (The State Department website defines the presiding rule well: "Envoys of equal title would be ranked according to the date and hour that they presented their credentials to the government that accredited them for service.") These objective reasonings took favoritism (and royal battles) out of the picture. Precedence order remains a firm tenant of protocol today. The Vienna Regulation also created a system for treaty signings: French alphabetical order by country name, establishing a system all countries still follow.

As transportation became easier in the twentieth century, heads of government were able to interact directly instead of only sending emissaries for negotiation. With more in-person, leader-to-leader diplomacy, new components of protocol emerged—arrival and greeting ceremonies, presentation of gifts, toasts—and implementing these facets required that an official from each country orchestrate the many moving parts: thus, the chief of protocol was born. In the United States, the first official chief of protocol, James Clement Dunn, was appointed in 1928. US presidents and most world leaders had preferred having a man standing in (quite literally) for the president on official occasions, until Shirley Temple Black (yes, *that* Shirley Temple) broke the gender barrier in 1976. I must mention, as well, that today chiefs of protocol operate with a huge amount of support from an entire staff made up of excellent officers from several career tracks: career civil servants (federal employees on a permanent track); foreign service officers (commissioned members of the diplomatic personnel system); and political appointees (appointed by the president or secretary). I took great pride that neither President Obama nor Secretaries Hillary Clinton or John Kerry could tell who in our office was one or the other, confirming that our team was united and collaborative.

With new modes of communication and expanding policy areas, protocols must continually evolve. The changing nature of protocol—and the importance of all countries being on the same page—is why I organized the first ever Global Chiefs of Protocol Conference in 2012 at the US State Department, with over seventy-seven countries and one hundred chiefs attending (some countries have two chiefs of protocol). During three busy and wonderful days, we exchanged best practices and ideas and developed a blueprint for the future. (I believe my ancient Greek predecessors would have approved.) All the participants signed a declaration of goals and accomplishments and agreed to meet biennially.

I'm thrilled that they have kept this commitment, having met in 2014 in Seoul, Korea, and two years later in 2016 in Abu Dhabi, UAE.

The convening was a highlight of my career. It brought together people from all edges of the globe who had the same passion as I did for the use of rules, traditions, and tools to create bridges of understanding and advance foreign policy goals. I learned that many of my counterparts had family histories similar to my own, ethnically diverse upbringings that drove their aspiration to serve in ways that would cross borders, blend cultures, and find shared pathways to prosperity.

———

I AM THE DAUGHTER OF TWO IMMIGRANTS, a Mexican mother and a Croatian father. Together my parents achieved the American dream, but they each suffered their own hardships before meeting on a blind date in Cleveland. My mom, Refugio—which she never went by, adopting instead the name of Mary to assimilate—arrived as an infant in the United States from Guadalajara, Mexico, with her mother, Guadalupe, and her father, Gambino. My grandma, whom we called Nonny, was promised to Gambino at the age of sixteen, and she committed to a new life in Cleveland, Ohio, where Grandpa's family owned a basket-weaving company. From the moment they emigrated, they discovered that realizing *their* American dream would be a challenge. Gambino left my Nonny shortly after their arrival to raise four children (including two adopted daughters, Lucianna and Emily) on her own. Mom spoke only Spanish until the age of five, when the school informed Nonny (who had changed her name to the American-preferred Rose) that her children would be sent home if they did not learn English. Thereafter, my mom never spoke Spanish again, a sadness that she and her sisters, Rose and Lupe, and brother, John, felt deeply; their mother so longed to speak with them in her native tongue, but being "American" won out.

What was lost in language was made up for in food. I was raised on the staples of traditional, made-from-scratch Mexican meals—mole, tamales, corn tortillas—lovingly cooked by my mother and Nonny, whom, as the matriarch of a line of strong women, I strove to emulate. We lived with her in one-half of a small duplex home for part of my childhood while my father was growing his residential construction business, and I'm forever grateful for her example: coming to this country so young, not speaking the language, and being an incredible single mother. She was my hero.

My father's journey to the United States from Yugoslavia (currently Croatia and Bosnia-Herzegovina) was a greater struggle. At twenty-six, Dad was posted to the Yugoslavian army to fight for a communist government he didn't believe in. In the early 1950s, President Josip Broz Tito's regime was engaged in a forceful unification of the many ethnicities of the region. The Penavic name was quite prominent in the village of Listica (now known as Široki Brijeg), but by the late 1950s, the government had confiscated all of his family's property and money. They were living penniless and cramped in a small building that they shared with extended family members.

My father wanted a future with opportunities, so he escaped from the army. He began his migration—about 360 miles on foot—to where an uncle was living in Austria. The journey took him several long, hard months. When he heard dogs barking, he assumed the worst—that the army was on the hunt for deserters (he would have been tortured had he been captured)—and he threw off his scent by crossing streams and dropping pepper in his path. (As a child, I remember him teaching me to drag my coat behind me so vicious dogs couldn't jump up and bite me.) When he finally made it to Austria, his uncle contacted a Croatian friend in the United States, a lovely elderly woman, Olga, who sponsored my father's citizenship, becoming a lifelong family friend. Arriving in Cleveland in 1961 with the equivalent of $4 in his pocket—and with no career or family—he sought out *his* American dream.

When we were growing up, Dad shared with me and my exceptional brother, Frank (Frankie), the hardships and joys of his life in his small village, and he strove to keep beloved elements of his culture alive for us. Soccer season started in May, and every Sunday we would head to the Croatian club to watch a game and sit at long communal picnic tables eating lamb and pork straight from the roasting spit while watching the adults drink rakija and sing the folk songs of their homeland. When I was eight, my brother and I traveled with our parents to Croatia and met my *baba* (grandmother) and *dida* (grandfather) at the blue iron gates just off the narrow dirt road that led to their tiny home. Grandma's house was conjoined to two older stone-and-wood homes, one of which my father grew up in. Her home, the "modern" one, had just two rooms, which still lacked indoor plumbing. The outhouse was past the pigs' pen about a hundred yards away, along the path by the field of tobacco plants. I was stunned. Dad grew up not just poor, but really poor. But as the days unfolded, I realized that this was just a different manner of living and that he was rich in many other ways. The care each family took of their neighbor, the ritual of cooking a meal together all day, and the custom of singing the Ganga, a style of vocalized storytelling from one mountaintop to the next—it was a beautiful life.

As an adult, I was able to reflect upon the sacrifice and determination it took for him to escape. I feel both deep pain for the hardships he went through and enormous pride for how he overcame the odds. His recent passing makes these reflections more poignant. His large, swollen, weather-cracked hands told the tale of my dad. He died doing what he loved most: building. Not only was he a builder by profession, but he spent his life building a future for me, my brother, and our children: Cole, Bella, Francesca, and Anthony.

Although my parents believed in the American dream, their day-to-day life as immigrants in the United States in the 1960s and '70s was tough, and they didn't always feel welcome. Dad, mainly due to his thick accent, endured being called a DP—the slur stood for "displaced person," the derogatory label du jour for immigrants. And my mom and grandmother were often scoffed at or completely ignored when they shopped at the local grocery store. I sometimes sensed their anguish of discrimination, which they hid fairly well from me and Frankie, but I have carried it with me ever since, never wanting anyone to experience the sting of not belonging, the isolation of feeling separate and being made to feel less than. Yet through every indignity, they held their heads high, and instead of shunning their past, they embraced it even more, weaving my Croatian and Mexican heritage within our home lifestyle and sharing the rich stories of their ancestors.

My parents were determined to pave a better path for my younger brother and me, giving us opportunities that they didn't have. I am not sure how they did it on their meager earnings as a drywall hanger and grocery clerk, but my parents were thrifty (Mom loved a good yard sale) and found a way for us to grow up in neighborhoods next door to people who had so much more education and earnings. The "more" wasn't meant to make us feel inadequate; it was intended as a window of possibilities. What else was there in the world for us to strive for? My parents knew they could take us only so far, and the rest was up to us. My brother and I felt it. We were driven.

Because of my parents' incredible journeys and their strong belief in the opportunities afforded by this great country, I grew up with a sacred gratitude for America's freedoms. Our country's democratic ideals held a supremely honored status in our family of immigrants, a reverence I carried with me around the world in my role as chief of protocol. As the first person to greet world leaders on behalf of the president (one of the many thrilling duties of the position), I shook every leader's hand infused with an unwavering belief in our country's goodness. My parents' hard-won achievement of the American dream was a driving force in my career in government, where I was honored to practice and preserve the etiquette, cultural tools, and soft power influencers of diplomatic protocol. At the core of my role was something so innate and familiar, something critical and wonderful I'd been witnessing and doing since I was a small child: building bridges between cultures and people, no matter the odds.

Shortly after I left my privileged post at the State Department and began working with businesses, global advisory boards, nonprofits, and individual clients, I was taken aback—perhaps naively—by the void of information about codes of conduct and a lack of understanding about how potent they are. When I shared my insights, people were eager to learn about the unique strategies they could bring to their business or personal interactions to bridge cultural divides and influence the outcome of their engagements. "Please write a book!" was the refrain I heard over and over at meetings, dinner parties, office kitchen breaks . . . and so I have.

What lies within these pages is not only an instruction manual on proper etiquette for business and social exchanges—which are critical influencers, as you'll see—but a big reveal (I'm taking you behind the curtain!) of the many subtle yet powerful adjustments that help you connect with your counterpart and affect the outcome of exchanges: room decor choices that can alter the thinking and feeling of participants; the power of the right venue to support your goal; and how to use food, gifts, and language to move the needle. What I learned in my two senior-level positions in government—White House social secretary and United States chief of protocol—was that there are ways to do things smartly and persuasively, rather than just checking things off a list. You can go through the motions or you can take every advantage of the dozens of opportunities to strengthen your relationships and position.

Today, a fast-paced international landscape requires that we execute critical operations and make important decisions within limited windows of time and opportunity. One slipup can cost a corporation millions, and an unintended insult can set back a pivotal relationship. Every moment and interaction count. Arming yourself with these tools to bridge the cultural divides and influence the outcome of your engagements gains *you* the advantage. Through almost two decades of advising our great nation's leaders, the power of protocol has not let me down.

I know it won't let you down, either.

Protocol

THE HIDDEN SUPERPOWER OF PROTOCOL

As I sprinted past the sparkling infinity pool that reflected the blue Pacific Ocean just beyond it, I made a mental note to return one day to the Esperanza Resort. The delicious Mexican cuisine which reminded me of my grandmother's cooking, the view of waves so perfect they looked photoshopped, the arched diving cliffs of Los Cabos, Mexico—the setting was pure paradise. But sun and surf were the furthest things from my mind. I was preoccupied with policy details and protocol checklists. The following day, Russian President Vladimir Putin and President Barack Obama were scheduled to meet here for the first time as presidents for the 2012 G20 global economic summit. The stakes could not have been higher: two superpowers discussing the roiling conflict in Syria, nuclear arms control in North Korea and Iran, as well as counterterrorism measures. The United States was officially hosting this bilateral (a meeting between two countries), and as US chief of protocol, it was my job to make sure that every interaction between the presidents went exactly as planned. I felt like I was playing matchmaker for the most important first date of the decade. I was energized but also quite nervous: This was diplomacy at its most extreme and formidable.

I raced past a couple of Secret Service agents huddled together, earpieces in, serious looks cemented in place as they reviewed the day's schedule, and descended the spiral steps to the lower level of the resort, where the meeting room awaited. Although the aboveground facilities were stunning, this bilateral was not about elegance but functionality, and I had a very specific list of must-haves. It was my job to give my president and his team subtle advantages to meet their diplomatic goals. Room size, decor, seating arrangement, table setting—these "tiny" details mattered far more than most people realize.

From the moment the meeting was placed on the schedule, our office had been liaising with President Obama's foreign policy team to understand our country's key objectives and how I could assist in tipping the negotiation scales in favor of success. Bilaterals with Russia are always a high-wire act. Of all the leaders that President Obama met, President Putin was the only one who saw negotiations as a zero-sum game. In other words, for one side to win, the other side had to lose. This meeting was especially critical given that a month earlier, President Putin was perceived as having snubbed the United States by not accepting an invitation to attend the G8 summit at Camp David (he sent an emissary, Prime Minister Dmitri Medvedev, instead). Tomorrow was about resetting the relationship and rebalancing the power dynamic. But first we had to get the train out of the station, onto the tracks, and moving in the right direction. It wasn't the best starting point for cooperation, but I've always loved a challenge, and this one would require all my protocol tools to pivot the power in our direction. I knew we needed an intimate setting that would compel these strong leaders to face each other and tackle the volatile topics at hand.

I focused first on how to arrange the room. Asel Roberts, a senior US career protocol officer, highly respected for her understanding of the subtleties of diplomacy and her work ethic, and whose friendship I value, had arrived earlier in the week and sent me photos and videos of the space. But seeing the setting in real life was the ultimate test. I felt the adrenaline surge just before I entered the room. I loved this moment, the reveal of the blank canvas where I could paint the picture for diplomatic success (I have a flair for the dramatic). I stepped through the room's narrow entryway. Hmmm . . . it was a bit too tight. This was where the introductions would begin, and I knew that my president liked ample personal space. It wasn't a deal breaker, but it was a check in the negative column. Things would have to get really cozy, really fast.

I walked in and noticed, approvingly, that the low ceiling height was just about right. People in rooms with lower ceilings tend to think more concretely than those under higher ceilings, which seem to prime people to think more abstractly. Tomorrow the Russian and American leaders and delegates would be hammering out a lot of specifics, so a lower height was ideal. I was also relieved that the overall space was small and spare—the hard policy objectives on the table would be the focus. There was just enough space to fit the countries' flags at one end, the main table in the middle, and a curtained entrance at the other end to allow for the discreet movements of the stewards of the presidential food service, aka US Navy mess (the wonderful US Navy food service staff work in the West Wing and travel with the president on every overseas trip). The room was also set up with security concerns in mind: hard walls on three sides (one wall can have windows, and the principals' backs are never against the windowed wall) and no wide-open spaces that would be difficult to secure.

Next up, the table, which needed to perform a dual role of large enough and small enough. That is, large enough to fit the twelve key delegates—six Russians and six Americans—but small enough to create closeness: all the better for looking each other straight in the eyes. We found one that fit the bill and centered it in the room. The windows had been blacked out for security reasons, so the room was dark. Too dark. We needed to avoid an oppressive feel, so the protocol team and I went on the hunt for standing lamps. I also noted that we needed white and green flower arrangements (locally grown, as a nod to our host country) for nondistracting table decor. And I stipulated they be unscented—we couldn't afford an allergic reaction. We clipped the stems to lower the height so they wouldn't block sight lines and ran them down the center of the table for a streamlined effect. The flowers also softened the vibe, which was more than just a decorative trick: Greenery has a well-known relaxing effect. One of our primary jobs in protocol is to make our visitor feel welcomed, so while we wanted President Putin to sense the weight of the meeting, we also wanted the room to have a bit of a Zen quality, especially since the meeting was anticipated to be long and intense. Additionally, it was rumored that President Putin had hoped Secretary of State Hillary Clinton would not be in attendance . . . but she would (and she should). She had recently criticized his country's election process as being unfair, and he had accused her of inciting violence during the elections. Her presence would likely irk him—all the more reason to create an inviting atmosphere.

I'd requested that nibbles of local breads, cookies, spreads, and nuts be available. I learned in my first year on the job that a hungry diplomat is not a happy diplomat and never again underestimated the power that sharing food had on mood and relationships. The stage was perfectly set. All that was left was for the presidents to arrive.

THE NEXT DAY I woke up with the sun, as is my custom (from my earliest days as a child, my mother would flick on the light in my room and state, "The sun is up and so should you be!"), and did some actual sun salutations on my balcony, courtesy of my travel DVD player and P90X Yoga DVD—my extremely fit cardiologist husband got me hooked. This style of power yoga calms me and gets my blood pumping, the perfect mind-body warm-up for such a day. Between poses, I caught glimpses of President Obama walking along the beach, his security detail hanging back a bit, giving him some privacy since the ocean provided a safe perimeter. Apparently, he also had a pre-meeting ritual for getting his head in the game.

I put on a cotton sleeveless dress with a bolero jacket—green, in keeping with the colorful customs of our host country (fashion diplomacy in action)—and slipped into my four-inch platform heels (with gel inserts for comfort), which gave me confidence and made briefings with my six-foot-one-inch boss less of a neck-craning exercise. I then headed out to go over every last detail with Asel and the White House team . . . a dozen times. I am obsessive, that day more so with so much on the line.

Finally, it was game time. At 10:30 a.m. I was stationed outside the front of the resort awaiting the Russian motorcade, as the meeting was due to start at 10:45. To my right stood the Russian protocol officer, a new junior man who was jumpy and perspiring, quite unlike his predecessor, who had been elegant and highly professional. At 10:50 I started getting antsy too. At 11:00 I knew something was off. I looked quizzically to my counterpart for an answer. His response was a shrug, and thereafter he avoided my stare. I glanced at my watch for the umpteenth time—11:05 now. President Putin was officially late, seemingly on purpose. A diplomatic power play meant to throw the US delegation off kilter? Perhaps. The delay was annoying, but I wasn't unduly worried. Our team was prepared despite this delay. At 11:10 I finally received a nod from security agents indicating the Russian motorcade was approaching. I spotted the lead car and got the tingle in my fingers that I always feel right before a greet. The limo door opened and out stepped President Putin. He had on the reserved face I would get to know well—not warm, not cold, all business. In my pumps I was nearly eye to eye with him, something I was suddenly very conscious of (he reportedly requested that women visiting the Kremlin avoid wearing heels).

I stretched out my hand for the inaugural handshake. As the chief of protocol, my hand was always the first extended to visiting presidents, prime ministers, kings, and queens as the official representative of the president for our invited guest. This simple gesture always gave me goose bumps, for it symbolized the bridge between two leaders and two nations. On this day, as on many times before and after, and always with a surge of pride, I said: "On behalf of the president and of the United States government, welcome, Mr. President." Then I shook hands with his minister of foreign affairs, Sergey Lavrov, whom I had met several times before and with whom I had a cordial rapport.

I led President Putin, Minister Lavrov, and several others from his delegation, along with his security detail, down the narrow spiral steps, treading carefully and holding the banister. When we arrived at the bilateral room, I reached for the Russian interpreter to make sure he was right next to his leader. I was afraid he'd get lost in the shuffle. Interpreters tend to be reserved and are often forgotten until the last moment, which I've never understood because they are so critical. Misunderstand one word and suddenly an agreement is in jeopardy.

President Obama was standing in the doorway. He towered over everyone, but it wasn't just his height that gave him a special presence: His self-assured, relaxed stance conveyed a confidence; his smile was just right—friendly but not too eager—and there was a glint of anticipation in his eye. He was in the zone. The US delegates were behind him in the room, half-hidden. After greeting President Putin with a handshake, President Obama began introductions of his delegation and stepped aside, presenting Secretary Clinton. "You remember Secretary of State Hillary Clinton?" Immediately my eyes diverted to Hillary—how would she present herself, considering everything that hung in the balance? She greeted him with her most dignified, diplomatic expression and handshake, instantly setting a respectful tone. There was a clear pause in everyone's movements, then President Putin, who seemed to express a hint of surprise on his face upon seeing the secretary, responded in kind, greeting her in a similar dignified manner. It felt like we were frozen for minutes in anticipation, but in reality the moment lasted barely a blink, the drama of diplomacy.

Introductions resumed and then everyone took their seats.

I pasted myself against a wall behind the Navy stewards' curtain for a minute longer than usual to ensure that everything was going as planned, an imperative for such a historic meeting. The stewards were preparing to serve coffee and tea (they never missed a beat). Discussions had begun. Everything was in order. I squeezed back out through the door just as my phone started buzzing about the next meeting. I left feeling confident we had done everything we could to set the stage for success.

Two hours later, when everyone exited the room, I could tell by their faces that it had likely gone well. The photos taken of the meeting also tell the story: the two men, looking each other squarely in the eyes, appearing alternately serious, relaxed, and smiling. Did they walk out of the meeting arms linked? No. Nor was that expected. But for a kickoff meeting between these two leaders and countries facing a number of hurdles, we'd done our job. The joint press statement (the official statement for the press corps detailing the meeting results) highlighted the positives. President Putin mentioned that they had found "a great deal of common ground," including on Syria, and thanked President Obama for the United States' assistance in helping Russia join the World Trade Organization. President Obama announced that the two agreed to work together to solve regional conflicts, highlighting Syria. As we know now, Syria deteriorated. But at that time, the meeting was generally considered a success, laying a solid groundwork for future engagements. Diplomacy is always a long game, a sustained effort over time that builds on itself. On this day, protocol had helped ensure this was a promising first step. I'd also learned that when things did not go well, President Obama would let me know what had not worked. Today, he flashed me that winning smile.

———

THE RESULTS WERE QUITE DIFFERENT a year later, when I witnessed the cold, unproductive reunion between the same two leaders at the G8 summit at the Lough Erne Resort in Northern Ireland. The Russians were hosting the meeting between the two leaders this time, and it was a study in contrasts. When you host, you select everything from the venue to the manner of seating to the format of the engagement. To be fair, the political climate was tenser: The situation in Syria had worsened, and the United States had just accused Syria's president, Bashar al-Assad (an ally of Putin), of using chemical weapons. But the environment the Russian team set up did not do anyone any favors. It only reinforced the political distance between them.

When I arrived at the venue, I turned to Asel, who was again our protocol officer assigned to this summit, with a look of horror. "I know!" she confirmed. We knew the meeting space was precast for disaster. The first mistake: They had chosen a huge open tent, a space that would swallow up the leaders and delegates. The lighting was bleak, offering no warmth to the room's ambience. It all felt so stark. The chairs had been placed side by side with only a tiny side table between them (a style we refer to as "fire-side chat"), an uncomfortable configuration in this instance for a few reasons: First, it prevented a more direct face-to-face conversation. The placement of the chairs would allow only a three-quarter view of the other's face, making the conversation strained (Google the photos and you'll see the effects). Second, because the room was large and sparse, there was only empty space in front of them to look at . . . awkward. And although the chairs were a good selection, the table was too low to serve the leaders well (though sometimes protocol has to work with what's available). In addition, this was a hard configuration for such a long meeting. (There are times when this seating style works well—I describe such an instance in chapter 8.) Finally, we noted no food or water was to be served. The only saving grace: The venue had been carpeted, which I knew added a bit of warmth and, research has shown, primes a person to feel more relaxed, compared to a hard surface. Still, the carpet couldn't make up for all the other jarring elements. No matter what advice Asel offered (one of her superpowers: she speaks Russian fluently) to the Russian protocol officer—the same young man I'd met in Los Cabos—he ignored her, either because he didn't care or wasn't aware of how the configurations would affect the diplomatic moment.

Would the lack of protocol, the inattention to all the details we painstakingly implemented in Los Cabos, affect the meeting? The outcome answers the question. It did not go well. Their body language quickly grew tense, and it was obvious that neither leader was able to assert his position. But there was nothing we could do; this was their meeting. I hoped that the chill would thaw as the meeting progressed, but it didn't. Photos showed the two presidents leaning away from the other, uneasily, or facing forward, staring at the carpet. The joint press statement was not as positive as the previous year, and the men barely glanced at each other as they addressed reporters' questions. Putin emphasized the disagreements and defended President Assad's regime. President Obama's remarks were more measured, but he echoed their divergent perspectives on Syria. This second meeting, which could have capitalized on the prior year's momentum and moved the relationship forward still, had stalled. Protocol, along with a promising result, had disappeared.

———

DURING MY TIME IN GOVERNMENT, first as social secretary for the Clinton administration and later as chief of protocol for the Obama administration, I witnessed how a culturally appropriate greeting—a bow, a handshake, or a nod—signals respect and a willingness to engage, and how a misstep can convey the opposite. I learned that the pomp and circumstance of an arrival ceremony isn't just an eye-popping spectacle to impress a visiting leader; it also serves as a shrewd welcome mat, priming participants to take the engagement seriously. The etiquette of a state dinner—from the seating plan to the table setting to the toast—consists of a language that literally brings people to the table and gives them a blueprint for engaging. Protocol facilitates progress, and, when used well, it can make the difference between success and failure.

When I left government for the private sector in 2013, I knew I wasn't leaving the world of protocol behind. Protocol—and the need for it—is everywhere. Like an off-duty police officer who can't help but case her surroundings after hours, my expert eye spotted diplomacy hits and misses all around me. When I hosted extended family for the holidays, I saw the very same dynamics of State Department dinners playing out at my dining room table. Parent meetings for school fundraisers, brainstorming sessions with clients, mentorship moments with young employees looking for their next steps—in all these situations I found myself drawing on my unique skill set to connect person A with person B and to entice both parties to find the common ground or come to an agreement. I was also recruited by many a friend and colleague to rubber-stamp the details of weddings, work retreats, graduations, and more. Nearly every time I showed up to a dinner party, the host or caterer would pull me into the kitchen or dining room to review the evening's itinerary, table setting, and seating plan. They weren't hosting world leaders, of course, but friends and family deserve the best, and everyone wants validation and to execute a successful event.

We are all engaging in diplomacy and relationship building nearly every day. Most of us aren't brokering world peace, but every negotiation hinges on being able to connect with your counterparts and persuade them to see things a little more from your perspective. In essence, we're all participating in our own little "summits" with workplace colleagues, family, friends, or our children's teachers. The same tools of protocol that shape world events have the power to persuade the Putins and Obamas in your life. Whether you're pitching a new client, hashing out a fair estimate with a roof contractor, or refereeing a tense interaction at a family reunion (sometimes the hardest kind of diplomacy!), managing the hidden forces in these situations can give you the power of protocol and diplomacy.

PROTOCOL:
AN OWNER'S MANUAL

Whenever I was asked what I did for living, I'd get a blank stare when I told them, followed by the inevitable, "So . . . what—exactly—*is* protocol?" It's a question I fielded from government interns on up to presidents (yes, even them). The short answer: Protocol is a set of rules that govern behavior. Different industries have unique protocols for all sorts of things. Hospitals have protocols for performing an X-ray; the military dictates protocol for who gets a salute and who initiates it; a restaurant has protocol for how to handle a diner's complaint.

The longish answer: In government, protocol is the framework within which diplomacy takes place, the structure that houses the dignitaries as they have the crucial conversations and negotiations that affect the people they represent. The preeminent expert and one of our country's most extraordinary chiefs of protocol, Selwa "Lucky" Roosevelt, who served President Ronald Reagan from 1982 to 1989—and who wrote a book on the topic (*Keeper of the Gate*)—defines protocol as "the rules that govern the conduct, as opposed to the content, of our international relations." In other words, protocol is more concerned with *how* something is said and done versus *what* is said.

While government protocol certainly encompasses codes of conduct, such as greeting etiquette and flag decorum, it's more expansive than rule following; it also creates a fertile environment for successful interactions. My friend Larry Dunham, who was an assistant chief of protocol under three successive administrations, explains that a protocol expert "must anticipate problems and distractions before they occur, have an understanding of cultural differences, and know how one's appearance and body language convey signals." I often think, if protocol were an organ in the governmental body, it would be the brain, making sure neurological signals are firing properly and that all organ systems are operating at peak performance.

Diplomacy, often another head scratcher, is engaging with other countries in order to achieve a foreign policy objective. Whether our country is looking to strengthen an alliance, address a grievance, or find a solution to a shared problem, you need diplomacy to seal the deal. That's the textbook version. Another way of thinking about diplomacy is on a more human level. I've heard some very smart diplomats liken diplomacy to building relationships. Vice President Joe Biden, a master of diplomacy, boiled it down to this when he spoke at the opening of the Penn Biden Center for Diplomacy and Global Engagement in 2018: "All politics is personal in the conduct of foreign policy." One of the great diplomats of our time, Secretary Clinton, defines it as "the process by which you try to reach out to others in pursuit of an increased under-standing and try to resolve matters between you and your countries." She adds for extra measure: "And as Winston Churchill said, it beats war." So when two leaders or delegates meet, they embark on the dance of diplomacy, and protocol sets the rules for that two-step. Depending on their relationship—new friends, old buddies, or frenemies—and the policy goals, that dance can be an easy, lilting waltz or a fiery tango.

On a practical level, protocol—and its behind-the-scenes prep work—allows the work of diplomacy to take place. For every peace treaty signed, someone scouted the location, set up the room, and provided the paper and pen (you wouldn't *believe* what goes into prepping the pens, which are unique to each president and often gifted after the signing as historical mementos). For every state dinner, someone designed the seating chart to ensure that dignitary A was placed next to dignitary B in the hopes that topic X would come up for discussion. The granular details of protocol may seem insignificant in the big picture, but if they're mishandled, chaos can result. When the finer points are attended to, participants may not fully realize why a meeting is unfolding so wonderfully. They will, however, sense a feeling of accomplishment that propels them to continue the work at hand.

Beyond providing a road map for behavior, there's a broader—and universally applicable—purpose to protocol, one that became clearer to me the more time I spent watching world leaders negotiate and executing the preparations that facilitated those negotiations: **Protocol allows you to pivot your power.** It's that secret weapon that can tip the scales in your direction, that one- or two-degree shift that makes all the difference. How do you pivot the power? By focusing on the mighty engines that fuel diplomacy: bridging and persuading.

THE TWIN ENGINES OF PROTOCOL:
BRIDGING AND PERSUADING

Protocol—at the White House or at your house—has a number of important functions, but there are two overarching goals of *diplomatic* protocol: to **bridge** and to **persuade**. Bridging—establishing a connection with your counterpart—and persuading—convincing others to see things your way—are at the heart of any fruitful negotiation. Nearly every gesture, procedure, or strategy in my grab bag of protocol tools was in service to one or the other, and often to both.

I found myself leaning on this pair of principles to make dozens of tiny and towering daily decisions. Whether I was crafting the menu for a head-of-state luncheon or determining whether it would be advisable to allow President Obama to participate in a host country's cultural ritual, applying this dual litmus test—does it help forge a connection or exert influence?—always steered me and my boss in the right direction.

During a state visit to Beijing in 2009, I was faced with an unusual quandary involving a noodle. We were in the middle of an intimate dinner at the historic Diaoyutai State Guesthouse, the Chinese government's Camp David, which was reserved for very special meetings. The two leaders were discussing economic challenges over a delicious dinner of traditional Chinese prawns and other delicacies. Halfway through the meal, our lead protocol officer, Penny Price, a long-serving State Department employee—she is quiet yet commanding and well respected by our Chinese counterparts—arrived next to me with President Hu's chief of protocol. He inquired, impromptu, if President Obama would participate in the cultural ritual of group noodle making with his leader. He explained that this was a custom in China designed to bring people together, and that it was important for this first meeting.

On the road, the last word on scheduling changes was Reggie Love, the president's trusted adviser. So I made my way toward him (those of us not at the main table were squished together in the back hallway) and outlined the request. He paused, then asked if the president *really* needed to do this, as it wasn't on the official agenda.

I fell back on my two protocol principles: Will this bridge or influence? I knew that it would do both. It was clearly important to the Chinese or they would not have asked. And to have the US president participate in one of their culinary traditions would show a willingness to understand their culture and please the participants. I remembered as a child the great joy I felt when my friends from St. Ann's grade school and I sat around my grandma's rickety steel kitchen table in her tiny home in Cleveland, Ohio, happily devouring her fresh, homemade tortillas with picadillo and mole. They didn't seem bothered or confused by her broken English—they were won over by her traditional recipes. I empathized with the longing to connect through food, and I'd learned from years of traveling around the world with First Lady Clinton that breaking or making bread with others is one of the most effective ways to bridge cultures. Sharing culinary traditions taps into the emotions, piercing the veil of the culture in a way that policy conversations can't.

One of the most difficult aspects of my job, and for anyone in the president's circle of advisors, was to step in and say *yes* when you sensed the president was leaning toward *no* . . . or vice versa. This was also my first foreign trip with President Obama, and I was still finding a rhythm with him and the staff. But my job—my *value*—was to guide him on cultural matters of protocol. (Having served a previous president, I had learned that those who go along to get along are valueless.)

I then explained to Reggie and our team that the president really *should* do this. I knew I had to explain why directly to President Obama. I walked over to where he was seated and whispered, "Excuse me, sir. The noodle-making portion of the evening means a great deal and I strongly encourage you to participate." President Obama looked at me quizzically with an expression I would grow to recognize as his "What?!" look—one eye squinted, the brow over the other eye furrowed—and I could practically see the thought bubble forming over his head: You think this is a good idea? But he didn't say that. He simply said, "Okay, let's make the noodle."

It *did* make a difference. Everyone was smiling as they stood shoulder to shoulder, with the chef in between the leaders, while they began to bounce a small piece of dough in their hands and watched as it stretched from a ball to sinewy lengths across the room. As the dough progressed in becoming the first course of the meal, more staff from both delegations joined in the line to catch the ends of the growing noodles to prevent them from dropping to the ground, all the while laughing hysterically and truly enjoying being a part of this cultural experience. Long noodles are often served as a very special dish in China as a symbol of longevity. The message the Chinese were conveying about this relationship: We intend for this international friendship to last. Suddenly, it wasn't just the Chinese on one side of the table and the Americans on the other side—it was a unified effort and an emotional moment that shifted their relationship. The atmosphere, which had felt stifled, now became more relaxed.

SOFT POWER, SUPERPOWER

I was not, of course, the first person in the history of the office to use the connective and influential magic of protocol to fuel successful diplomacy. I was operating on principles that have been building diplomatic bridges for centuries, and I held firmly to the institutional wisdom passed down from chief of protocol to chief of protocol. I was also guided by the polisci philosophies du jour, concepts discussed regularly at State Department meetings run by Secretaries of State Clinton and John Kerry.

The diplomacy approach in vogue during my time in office was referred to as "soft power," a term minted in 1990 by Joseph Nye, former dean of Harvard's Kennedy School of Government. Soft power is any tool that influences by attracting and enticing, as opposed to forcing.

Put another way, soft power is getting the other side to want what you want, rather than strong-arming them to do what they *don't* want. It's carrots, not sticks. The tools of soft power are often cultural resources like food, language, sports, dress, art, and music. Having beef-free menu options for Indian delegates, whose religion reveres cows, shows respect (and plants the seed that they should do the same for you); addressing Indian ambassadors with a traditional "namaste" greeting says, "I took the time to learn your dialect," which earns you admiration; wearing a country's national color shows a willingness to participate in their customs, as Duchess of Sussex Meghan Markle did in 2018 during her visit to Tonga. She wore an embroidered red dress as an homage to the country's flag.

We've all used some version of soft power in the workplace, dating, parenting, and beyond. Having a chilled bottle of Sancerre to serve your oenophile neighbor when she delivers your accumulated vacation mail? Soft power. Inviting an international client to a Major League Baseball game so he can experience the thrill of America's favorite pastime and feel a connection to our culture? Soft power. A cynic may be thinking, Isn't that just good old-fashioned manipulation? No. Manipulation doesn't take into account the health of the relationship and is only concerned with what you can get out of it; soft power is about recognizing the need for a relationship, developing it through cultural connections, and creating a bond that will last and be beneficial to both parties.

Hard power, as you may guess, is using tactics that coerce, such as military strength—or a show of it—as well as economic sanctions or co-opting of natural resources. Hard power forces a country or dignitary to do what she doesn't want to do. The United States' fight against terrorism or trade embargoes against Cuba and Iran entailed hard power.

And to get you fully up to speed on international diplomatic strategies, there's *smart power*, a newish term—also coined by Nye and popularized by Secretary Clinton—that refers to the combo platter of soft and hard power approaches, as well as tactics that don't fit neatly into either bucket, such as social media, which can be used to influence or coerce (many heads of state have their own Twitter accounts). Smart power also refers to the application of ingenuity and creativity in diplomacy, a code phrase for breaking out of a rote way of thinking: How can you use personal and intellectual skills, cultural resources, economic investment, and more to build sustained trust and solve problems?

A potent smart power tool that has been building diplomatic bridges for decades: people-to-people cultural exchanges, which advance international engagement and rebuild American goodwill around the world. These global networking programs enhance understanding through academic or professional engagement, offering the exchange of ideas and experiences between students and professionals of different cultures. Lee Satterfield, deputy chief of protocol during my tenure, uses this same concept in the private sector at Meridian International Center, where she's executive vice president and chief operating officer. "Similar to our efforts in the State Department, at Meridian, we harness the smart power of global leadership exchanges to build bridges between people of different cultures and provide leaders in business, trade, philanthropy, academia, and the arts with opportunities to exchange perspectives and collaborate on solutions to shared issues."

The Office of Protocol was all about soft and smart power, and the tools were chosen as carefully as a surgeon selects instruments for an operation. When a state visit was approaching, I was briefed by the national security team on the policy goals—maybe it was to show renewed commitment or to reset an unsteady relationship. To develop an air-tight protocol plan, I asked dozens of questions. "Ahem, excuse me, but can you summarize our goals? What are we attempting to highlight? Do you have insights into the visiting dignitaries' expectations? So sorry to bother again . . . can you explain that further?" There were a few exasperated sighs, but the answers outweighed them.

Then I huddled with the greatest protocol staff ever to determine the best game plan for this leader's visit. Should we suggest that the president offer our visitors a stay at the Blair House—the president's official guesthouse—to help them feel honored and embraced by the United States, joining a list of iconic guests, including Charles de Gaulle, Nelson Mandela, and Queen Elizabeth II—any of whom we could highlight for the visitor, depending on policy goals? What gift could we select that would show commitment to an issue about which they felt passionately? Or would a special meal at a unique place help the relationship blossom? Equally important, how could we dig deeper to find the human connection? Even with the right processes in place, diplomacy is ultimately about human interaction, how each of you feels about the other. If you don't find the personal pathways—discovering who they truly are and revealing who you are—you'll never gain the trust you need for success.

Soft power tools for protocol generally fall into three buckets:

Communication Tools, including greetings, language, cultural IQ, and gestures

Physical Tools, such as setting, decor, food, gifts, and dress

Mind-set Tools, or attitudes, that enhance diplomacy, like being flexible and using empathy

For each engagement, the protocol team spent months selecting the just-right combination from the various options, tailoring the tools to the countries, delegates, and policy goals. Each of these tools can be a power pivot on its own, and I cover every approach in the following chapters so you can adapt the strategies for your own business and personal summits. When combined, they have an even greater effect, coming together like instruments in an orchestra, playing the symphony you want your counterpart to hear.

LEARNING CURVES

My start in the Office of Protocol was an educational process for me and my colleagues on the temperament and style of the administration. Some of the White House staff were not strong believers in the power of protocol, and "protocol, shmotocol" was a refrain I sometimes heard. Understandably, they were focused on the top-line items on the nation's wish list in 2009: restoring the economy—we were in the middle of the worst recession since the Great Depression—and extricating ourselves from two protracted wars. I knew that to change their sentiment, I needed to assure the president.

Luckily, I received help from a person who had incredible influence over President Obama: his wife. First Lady Michelle Obama joined forces with me in my early weeks to turn the president's attention in my direction before meetings with foreign dignitaries. He was constantly being briefed by a team of people and finding an opening to give him a protocol rundown felt like getting a bartender's attention during Friday happy hour. The First Lady instinctively got the importance of cultural IQ, that doing and saying the right things with foreign dignitaries helped you connect on a level that went beyond policy details.

When she saw me waiting patiently to give her husband my quick prep, she'd often nudge him. "Barack, Capricia needs you to listen to her for just a few minutes," she'd say, pulling him over gently. He would then turn toward me, put a hand on my shoulder, look down at me with his kind eyes, and say, "Okay, Capricia, go." I'd then run down the top dos and don'ts. In addition, our protocol staff always prepared thorough cultural memos that I handed off to his team well before the meeting. I'd prep the president on seating arrangements by providing him with one of our homemade "face books," with a picture of each leader and delegate and the phonetic spelling of the name beneath to avoid a language offense.

After his first few months in office, where a few protocol elements did not go as planned—resulting in negative press and diverting attention from his foreign policy agenda—he embraced the briefings and often asked for quick reminders before a bilateral. Even the ceremonial aspects were of greater interest to him. On our 2010 state visit to India, he was greeted with a stunning arrival ceremony with majestic horses and decorated elephants in New Delhi and an evening event with the prime minister featuring an orchestra on camelback. Aside from the wow factor, its intention—honoring guests with the best a country has to offer—was not lost on him. He turned to me at the end of the arrival ceremony and said, "Capricia, can we maybe get some horses for our arrival ceremonies at the White House? Or some elephants? What do we have going on?"

He was half joking, but I picked up on his meaning: What can we do to make our visitors feel as special and entertained as I feel right now? (I did inquire with the Military District of Washington about bringing horses to the South Lawn, and was met with an emphatic *no*, since the noise of the crowds and the flash of the cameras were likely to spook the horses, leading to trampling and anarchy—not a good look for an American welcome.) Every day throughout my time in the post I kept his intentions at the forefront of my mind as we planned his global engagements, making sure each felt special.

WHEN PROTOCOL GOES AWRY

I sometimes found that it was easier for people to understand protocol's influence when it was executed poorly because the fallout was obvious. The press is always looking for a story, and a protocol misstep is red meat. One problem with a protocol gaffe is that it can hijack coverage that should be focused on more substantive policy issues. This has happened to every US president. They're human and make unforced errors, but unlike the rest of us, their gaffes get broadcast across the planet: President Trump returned the salute of a North Korean general at the 2018 summit in Singapore (presidents are not required to salute members of the military, and he was criticized for showing respect to a lower-ranking member of an adversarial country). When President George W. Bush greeted Chancellor Angela Merkel by giving her a seemingly unwanted shoulder massage, some press outlets debated whether the display was merely chummy or amounted to inappropriate behavior (as no one else at the table—all male—received a massage). And—horror of horrors—during a state visit to the UK in 1977, President Jimmy Carter kissed Queen Elizabeth II on the mouth. (On. The. Mouth.) Of the incident, she was famously quoted as saying, "I took a sharp step backwards—not quite far enough."

Worse than a breach that only takes over the news cycle: a protocol omission or misstep that offends a dignitary—or even a whole country. Not covering your head when visiting a mosque, playing the wrong national anthem, standing on the wrong side (or in front) of a leader—I'd witnessed all of these things cast a pall and mar relationships. In fact, I myself committed a protocol error of the highest order.

On September 24, 2010, leaders from the Association of Southeast Asian Nations (ASEAN) gathered in New York City for their second ever US-ASEAN Summit. President Obama was hosting the leaders at the Waldorf Astoria hotel to discuss economic issues. Our protocol team had been working twenty-four/seven on meetings for both President Obama and Secretary Clinton for UNGA (United Nations General Assembly), which was also happening that week. To say we were exhausted was an understatement.

Before the main ASEAN event began, I was in meet-and-greet mode behind a curtain, placing each delegate in proper precedence order (precedence is the officially recognized order by which heads of state and government are organized). Out front, camera crews from around the world were in position. A long table, with flags positioned behind the principals' table, lay in wait. President Obama and the leaders filed out to their places.

I assumed I would have a breather before my next task, but as the president stood to make his opening comments, a flurry of messages began popping up on my BlackBerry (the preferred smartphone of choice back then). Ominously, Natalie Jones, assistant chief of ceremonials, whose composure and attention to every detail I greatly admire—and who should have been out front—suddenly appeared by my side. "Capricia, we have a problem." This was a woman who didn't ruffle easily, but her voice was shaky. "It seems the Philippine flag was hung upside down, and social media and the press are already picking up on it," she said. My heart stopped. Not only was this a fundamental disrespect to their country—flag protocol is one of the top priorities a host country is expected to execute perfectly—but in this case the visual sent a very specific message: In the Philippines, an inverted flag signifies that a nation is in a state of war.

I turned and spotted a group of top-level officials from the National Security Council and State Department heading toward me like Mack trucks speeding down a highway, which only verified my fear: This was a *huge* deal. They arrived and idled. "Capricia, we need to speak with you immediately," one of them said with concern. I followed them to a holding area outside the ballroom, my stomach gripping, my face getting hot, the blood rushing to my brain, which was racing. How had this happened? We have protocol in place to avoid this very thing! They immediately began peppering me with some of the same questions: How could this have happened? How can we fix this? How can our president go into a meeting with President Aquino after this? Apparently, President Obama was planning on discussing an important issue with Philippine President Benito Aquino immediately after the opening statements. He would now be entering his negotiation at a deficit.

This was a fireable offense, but I had to shake off the fear and focus on the fix. I knew immediate action was necessary and asked them to give me a beat to determine exactly what had happened. I found the protocol point person, who was visibly shaken, and we viewed it on a camera monitor. Although the flag wasn't actually hung upside down, it *appeared* to be so because it had been reversed, the front facing backward and the back facing forward; because of the way it was slung, the red stripe—which should be at the base—was on the top.

I gathered the protocol team and explained that this wasn't just bad, it was *really* bad because of the subsequent meeting between our president and the leader of the Philippines. Before heading back to the State Department team, I consulted with my close confidante, Ali Rubin. Ali served as chief of staff in the protocol office and had quickly become the go-to person when there was any emergency. She speaks frankly and with sound judgment, and she understood the enormous spotlight we were under. When a moment like this hit (thank goodness not often), I depended on her counsel. "Trace it to the source," she advised, so we quickly walked through the details of our prep and the missing link became clear: Unbeknownst to me, the flag duty had been delegated to non-protocol staff who, seeing we were barely swimming above water, offered to help. The protocol staff all knew the rule—three pairs of eyes were to review the flags, *always*. This was my rule, and first and foremost, I laid the blame on myself for not being the final set of eyes. "We'll discuss this at our evening wrap meeting," I told her. "Let's switch gears and focus on our next events. We still have a long day ahead." I had a dozen things I wanted to say to the team, but for now, I had a raging fire to extinguish.

I returned to the national security team awaiting my answers. I explained how it had happened, took full responsibility, confirmed it was an honest mistake, and told them I would immediately apologize to both President Aquino (through his ambassador) and to President Obama. I suggested our embassy issue a formal apology stating that it was unintentional. They agreed this was the best next step.

"Capricia, time to step up," I told myself as I headed to the high-security, triple-curtained area off to the side of the ballroom, where the president and his staff gathered between meetings. "Mr. President, may I have a word?" I said as I approached him. I bowed my head and with heartfelt gravity said, "Mr. President, sir, I cannot begin to apologize enough for the inadvertent mistake I made with the Philippine flag. I am so sorry for putting you in this position." His response was typically cool and kind—"I appreciate that, Capricia, and it's okay now, it's all good." But I knew he also understood how serious it was by his concerned look, which telegraphed: But we gotta make it right. And I left to do just that. I also apologized to a senior member of the Philippine delegation, who was extraordinary in his kindness and understanding. I will never forget that moment and the impact of forgiveness.

Still, I worried all day: Had we, the United States, been forgiven? I asked the National Security Advisor, General Jim Jones, whether there had been an uncomfortable moment between Presidents Obama and Aquino during the bilateral and whether the flag issue had been discussed. Jim is one of the most genuine people—belied by his towering and stern military stature—and he looked down and assured me warmly that everything was fine. He didn't reveal any details, except to say that it was a near miss. Relief washed over me. I suspect that because we'd immediately accepted responsibility and acted swiftly to right the wrong, we'd moved it off the table before it gained any traction. Still, I was physically ill for the rest of the week, partly because I felt so terrible that I'd let my president down, and partly in anticipation of getting the ax, which thankfully never fell. I recently spoke to Jim about this incident, as it has weighed on my mind for years. He affirmed that we'd handled it properly, but that there would have been serious consequences had we not: "Flag protocol is one of the easiest things to get wrong. In this case, apologies to the principals were made and the situation was rectified. The presidents understood that this was a simple error and it affected nothing in their discussions. However, had the mistake not been discovered and corrected, the Philippine delegation could have thought it to be an intentional slight rather than a simple mistake."

The incident was a huge teaching moment for me and the team, most of whom were beyond consolation, for they understood how offensive this could be to the Philippine people and how it might sour negotiations between the delegations. I held our evening wrap-up in my room and had a few nibbles waiting. I then dove into the postmortem. Several protocol team members jumped in to say it was their fault. (In this moment of anxiety, the silver lining was that we were a team that did not throw each other under the bus but instead stood in front of it.) I reminded them that we should never defer our talent to others. Our officers were the experts in protocol, and there was no way another department could possibly know the ins and outs (and upside downs) as well as we do. Lee, my best friend and omniscient counselor, whose keen administrative skills served us so well, tapped me after the meeting and advised that we institute flag protocol trainings for the whole team and all new on-boards through the Military District of Washington, which were put into place immediately.

I also recognized that this was a young team of talented people and that this international incident presented me with a huge mentorship opportunity. I had to lift them back up to boost their self-esteem because we still had a lot of work ahead of us that week. "The good: We were quick in response, accepted responsibility, and sincerely requested forgiveness—this was proper follow-up and the best we could do. We now have to file it away and move on." These words were as much for my benefit as for theirs: I tend to put my guilt on a film loop, repeating the issue over and over in my head, even when having received a presidential pardon.

I was blessed to have a brilliant team of professionals with me throughout my tenure in protocol. I depended upon them as much as I believe they looked to me for leadership. We operated cohesively as one seamless unit, even though there were a multitude of backgrounds. From those who had served for years, like the late Dean Lewis—whose twenty-plus-year career at State made her our sage counsel—to my youngest intern, Thomas Corrigan, a fellow Clevelander, a consummate professional, and a brilliant writer (and my youth-truth barometer who joined me later at the Adrienne Arsht Latin America Center at the Atlantic Council), I was surrounded by clear counsel, creative energy, and absolute dedication. We were all there to serve at the pleasure of the president and secretaries, and did so with duty and honor to country first.

THE EVERYDAY DIPLOMAT

You may not hold a nationally elected office, but everyone has some skin in the protocol game. The tools of protocol can help you pivot the power in any situation, whether it's the boardroom, the PTA, or your own dining room. In the business world, companies' bottom lines have suffered by ignoring protocol, and failing to build a bridge with a culture or customer can damage reputation. In 1994, McDonald's UK printed two million to-go bags for Happy Meals bearing the flags of all the teams in World Cup Finals, which McDonald's was sponsoring. Great marketing idea, right? Unfortunately, the company hadn't done their research when it came to Saudi Arabia. The Saudi flag shows the image of the *shahada*, a declaration of faith from the Koran that is one of the five pillars of Islam, and great care must be taken in displaying it. Printing it on a paper bag filled with fast food and tossing it in the trash was the equivalent of taking the American flag and stomping on it. Muslims everywhere were offended. (McDonald's apologized for the error and discontinued the bags.)

For those working nationally or locally, using protocol tools can help fuel negotiations. When the right structure is in place, people sense they are in good hands and are primed to forge important interpersonal connections. I'll give you an example from my consulting life. In 2018, I was hired to develop a protocol for Bloomberg Philanthropies' Global Business Forum (GBF), an extremely high-level gathering in New York City of over seventy heads of government and over two hundred international, top-ranked CEOs to solve global economic issues related to trade, innovation, and sustainability. Through my lens, I was looking at bridging two huge cultures: private business and public government. In addition, Bloomberg Philanthropies—whose egalitarian leader Michael Bloomberg insists that everyone call him Mike—was a culture in and of itself, worldly yet relaxed. I needed a framework that facilitated the nexus of C-suite executives and heads of state while still conveying the host's "Hey, I'm just Mike" vibe.

I achieved it by mapping out a detailed blueprint in the tradition of diplomatic protocol. (I also partnered with smart and gifted Bloomberg executives Maia Johnson and Nancy Cutler, who understood the business's culture and the importance of protocol.) I began, as always, by identifying the goals: to show respect and cultural sensitivity, to allow tightly timed interactions to flow seamlessly, and to punctuate the importance of the forum in an elevated yet unpretentious way. And although Mike is the former three-term mayor of New York City, this was not a Big Apple moment; it was an international event that should feel global.

Food diplomacy was top of mind for this global gathering. I affirmed with the Bloomberg team handling the caterers and food suppliers that the menu would hew to international cultural and religious codes: Did we have beef-free options for the Indian attendees and pork-free choices for the Israeli guests? Would there be familiar Middle Eastern foods for those delegations? The menus were perfect. I then personally reviewed each and every invitation that was drafted by their correspondence staff to affirm all honorifics were correct and that we did not unintentionally state something in the body of the email that may be offensive to a particular culture.

I didn't have control over the venue—the elegant Plaza Hotel had already been booked (a lovely choice save its scarcity of public restrooms on the main floor—*always* confirm the number of restrooms before you book an event to ensure the total is sufficient for your guest list)—but days before the event I was able to make over conference rooms depending on the goals of each meeting. I called in former protocol officers Carl Gray and Nick Schmit, who had served for years with me and knew instinctively the protocol processes we were hired to execute. We kept things unadorned—per the Mike mantra and as instructed by Nancy—but made small changes to elevate the experience and facilitate the critical business at hand. In a meeting where an official document would be signed, we traded out smallish, unimpressive tables for larger, elegant ones that would accommodate both parties; we covered tables with crisp white tablecloths and staged them with refined signing pens. To make a room photo-worthy, we angled a table at the edge of the room instead of having it planted in the middle to allow for depth in the photo; we swapped utilitarian seats for stylish chairs to reflect the importance of the moment.

Days before the event, I prepped the Bloomberg arrivals team with "face books" and had them practice the pronunciations of attendees' names so they could recognize and greet each leader properly (soft power of language in action!). I also had the team double-check titles and names on all printed material so they wouldn't risk offending a country's leader or a CEO, which can make someone feel diminished and less open to negotiation.

We rehearsed the route for moving dignitaries from point A to point B efficiently so participants could focus on the crucial conversations they'd come so far to have instead of worrying about where to be next. On the day of, I stationed people at various stops and had them use walkie-talkies and secure messaging apps so each point person knew when a leader was headed their way. (I hate bulky walkie-talkies.) And I made sure (triple sure!) that every country's flag that flanked the entrance was properly hung so all heads of state felt respected from the moment they walked through the door. Each small element was a piece of the bigger whole, like individual notes blending together to create the perfect soundtrack. The event was a success. The crowning moment of the day was when Mike addressed the event staff, expressing deep gratitude for the success and then receiving the thumbs-up from Maia and Nancy with the best compliment: "See you next year!"

If any one of these elements is missing it can imperil a business relationship or compromise a goal. Misstating names and bungling language can leave an impression that a deal isn't being taken seriously. When NBA champ Stephen Curry's business team met with Nike executives in 2013, they were hoping to renew his endorsement contract and court him as the face of their new athletic shoe. Unbelievably, according to an article by ESPN.com, a Nike official reportedly mispronounced his name throughout the meeting, calling him Steph-*on*, which happens to be Steve Urkel's alter ego in the popular TV sitcom *Family Matters*. Then a PowerPoint slide went up with another NBA player's name, Kevin Durant, under an image of Curry. More than a glaring typo, it signaled that the company hadn't prepared and may not have been fully committed to Curry. Shortly thereafter, Curry signed with Under Armour, infusing billions into their bottom line.

A lack of appreciation of cultural differences can also thwart profits and growth. When Home Depot launched in China in 2006, they neglected to research the Chinese buyer, who does not often engage in do-it-yourself projects. And because middle-class home ownership is relatively new in China, they aren't familiar with fixer-upper projects, preferring to follow easy Western-style decor blueprints, like the Ikea model, which is doing well there. By 2012, Home Depot had shuttered all its stores in China.

Using protocol in your personal relationships can be just as transformative. Everything from a handshake to an invitation to a housewarming party to a thank-you note is a framework for connecting, a diplomatic dance among friends, relatives, and parents. Soft power tactics can give you an edge when appeasing neighbors who are frustrated with your noisy home renovations (after mine, I delivered plants to all my neighbors as an apology) or dealing with play-date politics. The subtle gestures and touches of decorum—the centerpiece on the table at your family reunion dinner, the gift you bring to an anniversary party, the way you pace a holiday cocktail party—can influence interactions and help you meet your goals.

Take the rite of passage of high school graduation. The official school commencement is wonderful, but what you do as a family can imbue the milestone with extra meaning. There's nothing wrong with a simple celebration (something I keep telling myself, since I did the bare basics for my son's party). But introducing a few subtle yet special elements can elevate a fun party to a next-level event that's memorable for guests and communicates to your graduate what you wish for him as he flies the nest. (Then you can let your children and their friends go off and have their own celebration.)

For example, have your graduate be the greeter at the door, welcoming guests and looking them in the eye while they shake hands—social pointers I've impressed upon my son since he was five—to make attendees feel appreciated and move your grad into an adult role. You can loosely carve out roles for a few toast givers that reflect their relationship with the grad, perhaps signifying an ongoing mentorship role. Ask a grandparent or aunt to share what they would tell their former eighteen-year-old selves. (If you're feeling really industrious, you can use the occasion to teach your graduate how to give a thank-you toast—turn to page 222 for pointers.)

Your gift can speak volumes, too. In diplomacy, gifts are an indicator of the intimacy of the relationship, an opportunity to show honor and a desire to deepen the partnership. After serving in my chief of protocol role, I have never looked at a present the same way again. Yes, most grads want cold hard cash, but in the coming years they'll also value a present with personal significance. My friend Mary Streett's mother, Sue, gave her the most special memento when she graduated from law school: a frame containing a photo of Mary surrounded by portraits of her great-grandfather, grandfather, and father—all attorneys—in black and white. I'm sure that each time she looks at it she feels the camaraderie and pride. (For secrets to giving the perfect gift—plus how not to get outgifted—turn to chapter 10.)

I was reminded recently of the deep, connective power of protocol during one of the most difficult, significant events of my life: my father's funeral. My dad passed away in February 2018 after a sudden fall. I got the call while I was driving from Los Angeles to Palm Springs for an event at the Sunnylands estate, the Camp David of the West. I answered to hear my husband, Rob, tell me the bad news: Dad was in the hospital and I needed to get home as soon as possible. My father had fallen four years earlier, as well, causing blood to encapsulate his brain. At that time, I'd raced to Cleveland and didn't return home for almost three months, often sleeping on a cot in the hospital next to my dad while he slowly regained both his memory and ability to walk. The extraordinary team of doctors at University Hospital gave him four more wonderful years. But this time the fall had been too much for him to take. I headed home immediately, desperately hoping for the same recovery. When I arrived at the hospital, my mother, who now had a deep sadness in her eyes, lovingly embraced me. She sat huddled next to my sister-in-law, Dyane, and my brother, Frank (who was my rock during this time—Dad would have been so proud of him), and told me the hard news: Dad wouldn't recover, and I had to say goodbye.

I knew that we had to honor my dad not only in Ohio, but also in his hometown of Široki Brijeg, Bosnia and Herzegovina (formerly Croatia)—two services for his two homelands. The mass and reception in Chardon, Ohio, was mainly family, but friends from Cleveland and DC made it through the horrible lake-effect snows, including former Croatian foreign minister Miomir Žužul and his lovely wife, Tatjana. President and Secretary Clinton—who also personally called my mother—as well as President Obama and President Kolinda Grabar Kitrović, of Croatia, wrote poignant letters of condolence to my mother and me, honoring my father, the man who first taught us about the importance of democracy, hard work, and believing in your dreams. I know my father beamed down with pride while his grandson Cole sang "Amazing Grace" as we processed down the aisle and as his granddaughters, Isabella and Francesca, read passages to honor him. After the service, we toasted my father with one of his favorite drinks, *loza*, a strong grain alcohol that my cousin Heather brought. His Excellency Žužul spoke, reminding the gathering what Dad stood for: a struggling immigrant who had made a home in this great nation, and who experienced both hardships and joys along his path.

Planning his tribute in Croatia allowed me to bridge his life in the

United States back to the fig fields of his home and the family and village he left. Although he escaped that home years before, he never forgot it. Creating a ceremony with a reception for the entire village to attend offered us all the opportunity to reflect, grieve, and begin to heal—together. Working with my dad's brother, Ivan, and my cousin Tontika's daughter, Cristina (who learned perfect English from watching American television shows), we planned a mass in his honor in Croatian, with ten priests participating.

Our family then visited the graves of my grandma (*baba*) and grandpa (*dida*). And to top off the tribute in full-on Frank Penavic–style, I held a reception at his favorite local restaurant, Borak, near the clear, clean Lištica River, with his favorite waiter, a Penavic too, of course. Gathered with many generations of Penavics—eating Dalmatian ham, Istrian prosciutto, a wonderful fried bread called *uštipci*, *peka* (a meat-and-veggie dish baked under a domed iron lid), and local *rakija* brandy—helped me feel closer to him and them. His cousin Branko offered the first toast, followed by many others, saluting my father with reverence and admiration. As I sat among everyone, with my husband and son by my side, I thought about all the presidents, prime ministers, and royalty I'd had the honor of greeting, the international partnerships I'd facilitated through protocol and diplomacy. I was so grateful that those experiences had prepared me to honor my beloved father like the majestic man he was in this most important of ceremonies: remembering his life and creating enduring connections among those he loved.

2.

THE ETIQUETTE ADVANTAGE

A few years ago, I attended an annual holiday dinner event at Cafe Milano, a premier DC Italian restaurant, hosted by a person of great accomplishment. Around each of the tables was a mix of governors, members of Congress, senior executives of various businesses, gallery directors, and other notables of DC society. The toasts were about to take place, and then there was that awkward moment: everyone looked to the tabletop—which was jammed with cutlery, plates, and glasses—to find their glass. Instinctively, I quickly lifted the glass on my right and, as is my habit, lightly touched the bread on my left to "mark it," relieving the other guests of the ever-present quandary of "Which is mine?"

The man seated next to me said, somewhat indignantly, "Why did you just touch my bread?" I explained it was positioned to my left so it was mine, but he begged to differ. I didn't want to embarrass him in front of the group, so I acquiesced. Then someone else jumped in (thankfully!) and said, "I'm sure the former chief of protocol knows which bread is hers." He glanced at me with a slightly curious look, and I took the opportunity to share with the table the lesson I use to help my son (and *many* adult friends) navigate tabletop etiquette: Create an okay sign with both hands. The left hand will look like a *b*—bread—and the right hand will form a *d*—drink. Voila! A collective "ah" came from my tablemates, though the man to my left said nothing and continued to eat my slice, leaving me breadless for the evening (and I love Cafe Milano's crunchy bread!).

In government, etiquette—the conventional rules that govern social interactions—is built into many of the protocols. Official state luncheons and dinners are plated according to proper table etiquette (White House butlers train all members of the protocol team); invitations to White House events are labeled according to proper envelope etiquette; attire is always specified for an event, whether it's black tie, cocktail, or casual. In fact, etiquette is so critical to diplomacy that the Office of Protocol has a whole department, the Ceremonials Division, that is devoted to the minutiae of social conduct and ceremonies.

Why is etiquette so important? My answer is the same whether I'm making the case for it in a diplomatic setting or at the family dinner table: Etiquette provides expectations for how everyone should interact— it's a road map for behavior that makes connections easier and telegraphs meaning. Proper etiquette can land you on the right side of a tricky social interaction or, if it's bungled, can introduce unnecessary confusion. We participate in etiquette every day, often without thinking about it . . . and sometimes wishing we *wouldn't* have to think about it. Most people view etiquette as rules made up long ago for how civilized people should greet, meet, and eat. And they are that, on the surface. The framework of table etiquette organizes and keeps a meal from devolving into *Lord of the Flies*.

But beyond the obvious and practical purpose of etiquette lies a hidden world of communication and leverage. Like an emoji, etiquette is a code that transmits intention and feeling. A firm handshake is an invitation that says, "I'm a friend not a foe" or "Game on" (as before a debate). Using a proper title—monsignor, madame, officer—bestows respect and reinforces a person's role in society. Gestures also communicate history: The fist and palm salute used in China as a salutation for special occasions likely got its start centuries ago as a show that neither hand held a weapon, and that the "fighting" fist (usually the right) was being held back by the palm: I come in peace.

Etiquette—and its cousins, ritual and ceremony—also gives outsiders the opportunity to become a part of the culture by participating in the agreed-upon codes of conduct. When I was six, my mother enrolled me in a Miss Manners course at our local community center. She insisted that I learn the proper way to stand and walk "like a lady." I wore a fancy yellow knit dress, a style in keeping with the little-lady attire of the times, and diminutive white gloves, and I embraced each week's lesson, whether it was resetting the table over and over according to the diagram or walking gracefully with my child's purse on my arm, a white-woven pillbox style that I adored. As for proper walking—keeping my head up and gaze forward—it never quite materialized. But that didn't matter; I was so grateful to have some standard operating procedures to help me avoid embarrassment. Looking back, I believe my mother never wanted me to feel out of place, hoping that I would become more accepted and not hindered by economic or racial prejudice.

The beauty of social codes is that they serve all these functions—acceptance, history, intention—while being a seamless part of the scenery, operating subtly in the background, like an undercover operative. Manners are a form of soft power. Well-executed etiquette in government, business, and personal relationships can influence dealings and open doors.

THE RESPECT EFFECT

Etiquette is always whispering something, but one of its most fundamental messages is basic respect. When you engage in social niceties—especially when you make the effort to learn another culture's etiquette—you're honoring your counterparts, and as a result they become more open to collaborating. Etiquette taps into "the respect effect," a term coined by business personality Paul Meshanko in his book of the same title, and a principle grounded in research on how the brain responds to workplace situations. One study in the *Journal of Business Ethics* found that employees who felt respected by their managers—through a variety of treatments including politeness and attentive listening—were more motivated and had improved performance compared to those who didn't feel as respected. Study coauthor Niels Van Quaquebeke points out that showing respect is different from simply "being nice or polite." Respectful treatment includes exhibiting fairness, demonstrating trust, and taking subordinates seriously. The respect effect also works in a 360-degree circle, laying the groundwork for strong connections with managers and peers.

Etiquette also defines who we are . . . or aren't. Social codes of conduct signal where we fit into the scheme of things. At a staff meeting, you can usually spot the CEO because she traditionally sits in the chair at the head of the table. In business introductions, the person with a higher status offers his hand first to the person of lower status. Most royals around the world, from Africa to Asia to Europe, are *not* to be touched—unless they extend their hand first. Perhaps no other country is as well known for etiquette of status as the United Kingdom and their monarchy. Royal rules of behavior—from those governing walks (Prince Philip must walk several paces behind his wife, the Queen, at all official functions) to sitting (you must not sit until the Queen does, and stand when she enters the room)—leave no question as to their elevated social perch. (I binge watched Netflix's *The Crown* and felt that the rules of the monarchy were practically a character in and of themselves.)

In 2011, I had the thrill of personally meeting Her Majesty, Queen Elizabeth II of the United Kingdom of Great Britain and Northern Ireland, at Buckingham Palace, during President Obama's state visit. Per royal protocol, I was careful not to touch Her Majesty. But assisting with her purse is also clearly forbidden, a red line I nearly crossed when I attempted to relieve her of her top-handle Launer handbag (her preferred brand) before she stepped onto the palace lawn for the arrival ceremony with President and Mrs. Obama. (My habit when I was White House social secretary and chief of protocol was to ask women if I could unencumber them by holding their bags during these official moments.) Immediately, the palace protocol official stretched his arm in front of me with the urgency of an MI6 operation and, in a firm whisper, stated, "Do not touch the bag." I quickly stepped back and asked *why*. With his arm still up, barring any further movement, he simply repeated, "We *never* touch the bag." It had not occurred to me that Her Majesty kept total sovereignty over her purse. Regrettably, I couldn't stop myself from asking the burning question on the minds of many a monarch enthusiast: "What's in the bag?" He looked at me with horror. "We don't know what's in the bag; we just *never* touch the bag." (I've since learned that her handbag might be more than a catchall for lipstick and mints, as she may also use it as a signal for her aides: placed on the table, for example, it might indicate she's ready to leave in five minutes. And she allegedly carries a mobile phone to chat with her grandchildren.)

Other rules of engagement include not speaking to her unless she speaks first and never turning your back on her. These edicts aren't arrogance—they are part of what make the queen *the Queen*. Otherwise, she would not command the status necessary for a monarch from her citizens. I discovered a great deal more about her later that evening. I understood that Her Majesty's usual custom is to retire after the dinner, but she instead mingled with the guests at the post reception by herself—she keeps her own counsel. I was in conversation with a few colleagues, when I turned around briefly and saw *her* walking our way. She wasn't hard to miss in her white silk crepe evening gown and one of her many glittering tiaras (the imperial crown is reserved for coronations and the annual opening of Parliament). Per my custom, I backed up against the wall, thinking she wanted to pass by, but instead she stopped right in front of me and, still holding a purse, an elegant evening version, in the crook of her arm—tapped me with her finger lightly on the shoulder. "Good evening. Who are you? I have seen you everywhere throughout the day." Awed by the moment, I was slow to respond. My brain went into overdrive. "The Queen just touched and spoke to me!" I took a breath to relax, reminded myself not to touch the purse, then straightened my shoulders and introduced myself. "Good evening, Your Majesty, I'm Capricia Penavic Marshall, President Obama's chief of protocol." She responded, "A very hard job indeed, well done." I could tell by her tone and expression that she, of all people—a woman whose life is governed by rules—empathized with my role and genuinely approved. Then she moved on through the crowded reception, acknowledging guests with a slight nod of her head, making our verbal engagement all the more meaningful.

ALL TOGETHER NOW:
RITUALS AND CEREMONIES

When social codes become more elaborate and symbolic—unfolding in stages and requiring choreography—you've waded into the waters of ritual and ceremony. Rituals are often performed as a group, whereas etiquette is usually (but not always) enacted one-on-one. (I sometimes think of etiquette as a mini-ceremony between two people.)

The bells and whistles of a ceremony—the public grandeur of an arrival ceremony or the decorated festivities of a birthday party—say, "You're special!" But there's more to pomp and circumstance than adulation. When performed as a group, rituals have measured psychological and social benefits. The shared rites of a funeral service help alleviate grief, as I discovered firsthand with my father's recent memorial. A sport team's pregame chant motivates players and fans.

EVEN CEREMONIES THAT DON'T CARRY a specific function can have a positive influence. To find out how group rituals affected subsequent interactions, psychologists in New Zealand gave several small groups a set of motions or chants and then measured the results. They found that those who moved or chanted together at the same time were more cooperative with one another when playing a game that involved risk and money compared to those who moved or chanted out of time. As study coauthor Paul Reddish explains, when a group's goal is synchronicity—and the members *perceive* that synchronicity—a positive feedback loop develops, heightening a group's cooperative tendencies. Perhaps going line dancing or taking a Zumba class with clients or coworkers isn't merely fun—it's a smart strategy.

One of the most rewarding ceremonies I had the honor of arranging was the laying of the wreath at our nation's Tomb of the Unknown Soldier at Arlington Cemetery, where several unidentified service members from our country's major wars are interred to represent all those who are missing and unknown. Many countries hold a similar ritual to honor their unidentified military dead. In our country, the president lays a wreath on the tomb on Veterans Day, a custom that originated in 1921 when the first unidentified US soldier, who died in France during World War I, was buried at Arlington.

Visiting leaders also often lay a wreath at the tomb as part of their official state visit and/or pay a visit to the grave of a former president. In such cases, the chief of protocol stands in for the president. I was honored to escort many a leader and royal into the historic tomb, including—and I mention this for all the royal followers out there—the UK's Prince Harry in 2013, who was incredibly charming and humble, even in the face of throngs of girls taking his picture. (He also visited the grave of a soldier who had died in Afghanistan, where Prince Harry served two tours of duty.)

The symbolism and connective power of the ritual was never lost on me. When a host country invites a visiting leader to participate, it offers the nations a way to engage that goes beyond conversations and policies. No words are spoken, no treaties are signed, but the nations are cementing a bond nonetheless. The host country shows trust by inviting the visitor to be a part of a sacred ceremony, and the guest shows honor by participating.

The wreath-laying ritual is especially meaningful when the leaders are commemorating a war fought side by side as allies, acknowledging a shared history of sacrifice, such as the poignant tribute in 2010 by Secretary Clinton and South Korean President Lee Myung-bak when they laid a wreath at the Korean War Veterans Memorial to observe the sixtieth anniversary of the start of that war. President Myung-bak was honoring the nearly forty thousand US soldiers who died (including eighty-two hundred missing in action) when the United States answered South Korea's SOS after it was invaded by communist North Korea. I've spoken to Secretary Clinton about the importance of these shared tributes and their profound effect on diplomatic relationships. "Participating in rituals is evidence that you recognize the humanity, suffering, and experiences of a country," she told me. "You are making connections, both personal and collective."

So much preparation goes into a wreath-laying ceremony—it's a military protocol and they have scores of rules governing the timing of movements—but it doesn't always go as planned. In November 2011, President Obama was invited by Australian Prime Minister Julia Gillard to lay a wreath at their war memorial: the United States and Australia have a strong history of friendship, and Australians fought alongside Americans in several wars, including the war in Afghanistan and World War II. The wreath had been in water to keep its red, white, and blue flowers—chosen for our country's flag colors—fresh for the ceremony. Minutes before the arrival of the president and the prime minister in the memorial room, an embassy aide lifted the wreath from its box to place it on a tripod stand, and the entire bottom half—its floral foam backing soaked to the point of instability—disintegrated and dropped to the ground with a loud splat, leaving only the upper portion intact. Wet leaves, flowers, and green foam spread out on the slick marble floor. The aide stared in shock at the mess, frozen in fear. Nobody moved. Everyone shot each other the same glance: Are *you* going to do something about this? But since it was *our* wreath that we were presenting to the Australians, it was on us to fix it. I took the undamaged portion, laid it down carefully on the marble floor and bent over (unwittingly directing my entire backside to the press corps) to collect the stems of greenery and flowers that were salvageable from the pile spattered across the ground. Quickly, I attempted to cover the hole of the missing lower arc with the fallen twigs and leaves, layering and securing them as best I could to re-create it.

The president's advance person was now at my side. "Two minutes until the leaders arrive, Capricia," she warned urgently. I continued Operation Wreath Rescue at a furious pace. "One minute." My work was starting to pay off—the wreath looked almost presentable. "Thirty seconds." Done! I placed the rehabbed wreath on the tripod stand, brushed the rest of the debris under a bench with my foot, and took my place in the delegation line just as I heard the clicking of the prime minister's heels on the entryway marble. I glanced over to catch the gaze of Valerie Jarrett, the president's most senior and trusted adviser, who was encouraging my efforts throughout and offered a consoling smile with a crossed-fingers signal. We all held our breath as two soldiers carefully (oh so carefully, for they had witnessed the wreckage!) took the wreath from the stand and placed it over the tomb. I willed the petals to hold and they did. President Obama then knelt down and laid his hands on it (rarely do leaders actually lift and lay the wreath themselves, perhaps for reasons we'd just witnessed). Veterans honored. Embarrassment averted.

Not surprisingly, one of the press outlets reported on the botanical blunder. But I considered this a minor stumble compared to what could have been the bigger story: the president laying a hot mess of a wreath on the memorial tomb, which could have had lasting repercussions: One of the official talking points for the president's visit was to discuss an increase in the United States' military presence in Australia as a counterbalance to China's growing military strength. This ceremony was directly connected to the diplomacy of the day. It would have been beyond poor form to diminish a time-honored ritual so tethered to present-day dealings.

ETIQUETTE AND RITUAL IN BUSINESS

While in government I'd gained a profound understanding that micro-moves, gestures, and social rules speak volumes and can affect the tone and outcome of an interaction. In my private-sector consulting work today, I encourage all my clients to pay extra attention to the etiquette and ritual aspects of work, whether they're hosting a meeting or attending a business lunch. Greetings, gestures, and other codes of conduct are critical assists in making your shot, that extra something that quietly elevates an interaction so your counterpart feels appreciated and open to teaming up.

To be clear, etiquette doesn't always need to be extra formal, and it should be adapted depending on the environment. You don't need to set the conference table for a casual working lunch with a dessert fork, bread plate, and a name card—that's over the top. But you can do a little something to elevate the experience. Cloth napkins properly folded and placed atop real plates instantly make attendees feel like someone took the effort. What can you do to make guests feel special?

In addition to the basic etiquette of civilized society—don't speak loudly on your phone in public, do eat with your mouth closed—the work-place has its own MO. Over the years, I've watched with a cringe as people botch moments that are critical when establishing a new connection, either because a person isn't adhering to prevailing etiquette or because the evolving communications and tech landscape is lacking well-defined protocols. Luckily, the missteps are all easily avoidable with a little awareness. These are my nonnegotiable SMART Rules that I impressed upon the staff in every office in which I have worked and which I advise my clients today to follow. (I do a deep dive into international business etiquette, table manners, dress code, gestures, and greetings in upcoming chapters.)

THE FIVE SMART RULES

1. **S—Shake hands.** Shake hands with *everyone* you meet for the first time (unless you have a cold, in which case you should nod and explain your circumstance). Keep it firm (but not crushing), look the person in the eye, hold it for about three seconds, the ideal amount of time, according to science. Any longer is awkward; any shorter can make you look indifferent. (Handshakes are pretty much de rigueur worldwide, but they do require some adjustments depending on the country. Turn to page 371 for a useful guide.)

2. **M—Meet and greet like a pro.**

   FOLLOW PROPER PRECEDENCE. Name the most senior person first: "President Obama, may I introduce to you the ambassador of Singapore." Then reintroduce the lower-level person to the senior-level person (this gives everyone a second chance to remember names and pronunciations). If people's positions are relatively equal, I give precedence to the person who seems the eldest, out of respect.

   STICK WITH FORMAL TITLES. Address colleagues, managers, and subordinates by their formal names—Mr. Garza, Ms. Johnson— until they tell you it's okay to use their first name. (Thank you, Sister Rosemary from the Beaumont School for impressing this upon me!)

   ASK IF YOU FORGET A NAME. If there's no work-around (such as listening to someone introducing themselves), I politely—and apologetically—ask the person to refresh my memory, as the greater sin is to bungle a name. *Pro tip:* To recall new names, tell yourself a rhyming story—e.g., Mary took the ferry to the dairy. It sounds corny, but it works.

KNOW WHEN TO SIT OR STAND. Stand when a person arrives to a small business meeting that's underway; others will follow your cue. If it's a larger group, however—six or more—I stay seated, as it can be disruptive for so many to get up. If the newcomer circles the table to greet everyone, I will stand, however (I'm not a fan of the subtle power play of someone hovering over you while you're sitting). I maintain the practice of standing when a government person of high rank (a cabinet secretary or Speaker of the House) enters a room.

3. **A—Ace elevator and door etiquette.**

   IN THE ELEVATOR: Move to the back if your floor is a high level. Push the button for others as they join you if you're standing near the panel. Step off so people behind you can exit, then step back on. Allow elderly folks and your boss to hop on first.

   AT A DOORWAY: If you're there first, hold it for either gender; it's just good manners. If a man insists on holding a door for me, I let him, as it's always more awkward to insist on opening it myself. (It's a door, not a marriage proposal.)

4. **R—Restrict interruptions.** With the ever-increasing pace of technology and communications, interruptions are becoming more common. But a culture that tolerates disruption is bad for business: Employees who report frequent interruptions have higher rates of exhaustion. And error rates double after interruptions, according to a study by researchers at Michigan State University. Here's how to minimize intrusions:

   RETHINK THE POP-IN. New hires, in particular, are guilty of sticking their head in a colleague's office or cubicle to get an immediate answer to a question. "Hope I'm not bothering you . . ." does not give you carte blanche to bother (and, by the way . . . you just did). Knock and ask permission. If it's urgent, send a text or email with a request to see them asap.

AVOID PHONE FELONIES. Keep your phone on mute or vibrate and don't place it on the table at an office or lunch meeting; it signals that you're not giving your boss/client your full attention. If you're expecting a super-urgent call, let your companions know in advance (then excuse yourself if the call comes in). Caveat: When traveling internationally, follow the cues of your host. In Spain and Italy, for example, people may keep their phones out, answer calls during meetings, or text under the table. In other countries, such as Japan, however, it's rude to speak on your phone when strangers are around.

HEAD OFF HEADPHONE OFFENSES. Wearing headphones is a great way to signal that you shouldn't be interrupted. However, always remove them completely when having an in-real-life conversation: The half-off position signals you are being bothered. Ditto earbuds.

5. T—Thank people and wrap up properly.

BE A GRACIOUS HOST. When ending a meeting that you're hosting, escort the person to the exit. It makes your guest feel taken care of and ends the meeting on a gracious note.

BE AN APPRECIATIVE GUEST. If you're the invitee, always send the handwritten thank-you note in addition to the thank-you email after an important meeting; emails get lost in a cluttered in-box and the notes are *always* appreciated.

DON'T GHOST. If introductions were made via email or text and you're closing out the exchange, always reply, even to say, "No, thank you" or "Not now but we'll be in touch." Ghosting— vanishing from a thread or exchange when a reply is expected—is becoming increasingly acceptable in the business world, especially among younger employees. I've even heard colleagues describe it as "an effective strategy to leverage a relationship." This is flat-out wrong and rude. You wield more power when you interact with basic respect to avoid possible offenses, allowing you to easily reestablish that connection if need be.

Then there are the behaviors that can be adapted after you get a sense of how things are run. When etiquette isn't clear-cut, start out playing by the traditional rules (dressing more conservatively, for example, or using formal titles) and pull back based on circumstances and as you get to know the people and culture. On a generational note: The older the person, the more likely that he will expect you to stand on ceremony. Codes of conduct shift over the decades, so what might be acceptable for a twenty-five-year-old would not be for a fifty-five-year-old (and vice versa).

If you're in the position to establish or tweak office etiquette, be sure everyone is aware of why changes are happening—perhaps you've made it okay for employees to bring cell phones to meetings as long as they're on mute, or you've changed the protocol for which employees are invited to senior-level meetings. If you don't provide a full explanation for the change, people may fill in the blanks on their own and misinterpret your intentions.

This heads-up policy applies to presidents too, and when protocol and etiquette changes aren't explained, confusion results. When I first entered the position of chief of protocol, President Obama's team wanted to keep ceremonies simple and chose to eliminate some of the more formal elements of a head-of-state arrival ceremony, such as flags lining the south grounds and the military band. It's a president's prerogative to break with tradition and bring his own style to the office. However, these very obvious changes were confusing to our foreign visitors, who understood the value and expected the full pomp and circumstance. I explained to our staff that the purpose of these ceremonial elements was to begin a visit with the right tone and that they allow the visitor to immediately feel welcome and respected; ultimately, the administration saw the advantages of doing so and gave the green light to these integral elements.

One of the toughest lessons all presidents must learn is how to inhabit the office as the president of the United States and not just as an individual. The symbolism, etiquette, and ceremony of the position become part of who you are. You're no longer just Barack Obama, George H. W. Bush, Bill Clinton, Jimmy Carter, or Donald Trump; you are *President* Obama, *President* Bush, *President* Clinton, *President* Carter, *President* Trump, and certain traditions mark you as such. President Carter, for example, insisted on carrying his own luggage to show he was a man of the people. No problem, right? Well, it may have confused delegations during international travel—was this the president of the United States, the man hauling his own suitcases?

Over the last couple of years, I've noted that a visiting leader has sometimes stood or sat to the left of President Trump, in opposition to the traditional protocol, which dictates you offer your visitor the position to your right as the seat of honor. I understand that President Trump has stated he feels this protocol should be fluid. However, if that change is not communicated to the leader's delegation and to the world at large, particularly the citizens of the visiting country, the assumption may be that the change is either a mistake—which causes discomfort and confusion—or a deliberate signal that could convey a shift in attitude or policy.

ETIQUETTE IN SOCIAL SITUATIONS

Etiquette can be equally influential in the personal realm, despite the fact that our relationships are less formal. We are always forging connections—with friends, family members, parents at our kids' soccer games, the cable rep helping us restore internet service—so etiquette *always* carries sway.

Serving as social secretary for the Clinton White House, a position that required a near-maniacal dedication to social Ps and Qs, I became a walking encyclopedia of etiquette know-how. In the Clinton administration, the job required planning not only official social events—holiday festivities, teas, dinners—but *any* event held at 1600 Pennsylvania Avenue, including press conferences and policy announcements. The role would have been a tall order even if it had been confined to social gatherings. It wasn't unusual for the Clintons to invite thousands of people to a summer picnic. And on any given day, there was some event going on in virtually every room of the White House. Led by the talented team of Kim Widdess, Sharon Kennedy, Laura Schwartz, Emily Feingold, Sarah Farnsworth, and Eric Hothem—plus interns and the most amazing volunteers (especially Tutty Fairbanks and Debby McGinn)—the office was busy around the clock with menu planning, guest-list pruning, seating chart drafting, and invitation sending: we oversaw a staff of full-time calligraphers—this was before email invitations were a regular thing (the White House does sometimes use email invitations, a practice that caught on during the George W. Bush administration).

Cutting my etiquette teeth in this job would have been brutal had I not been shadowing my predecessor, Social Secretary Ann Stock, during my time as special assistant to the first lady. Ann was brilliant at the job, and watching her operate gave me a solid understanding of what was required and how to pull it off with efficiency and grace. I also received priceless advice and support from all the former social secretaries, no matter the administration. They were all incredibly helpful and invested in my success, and I loved carrying on the tradition of many of their best practices: Letitia "Tish" Baldrige, Jacqueline Kennedy's social secretary and the "doyenne of decorum," insisted on no open-toe shoes in the White House, a rule I adhered to; the impeccably poised Gahl Hodges Burt, President Reagan's social secretary, taught me you can set the tone of an event with a winning guest list; and the elegant and candid Bess Abell, President Johnson's social secretary, who brought some serious fun and sass to the job, warned me about "the begged invite" with this cautionary tale: She was in the final prep stages for a state dinner for the king of Norway when she received an urgent phone call from a colleague. His wife was dying of cancer and her last wish was to be invited to the dinner. The event was at capacity, but Bess felt so terrible for him that she immediately went to President Johnson and got permission for two more dinner guests. A year later, lo and behold, she ran into the man . . . and his extremely healthy wife.

I also had a deep bench of social fairy godmothers: Ann Jordan (whom I met through her niece and my dear friend Ann Walker Marchant, and her legendary husband, Vernon Jordan), whose charm, humor, and signature phrase "bless your heart" helped her navigate any social situation with grace; and her friends, the trifecta of Ann Hand, Ellie Trowbridge, and Buffy Cafritz. These women are the grandes dames of the DC social scene and they, along with a few savvy friends from New York City, like Liz Robbins, stepped in and offered me their counsel on dressing (hit up the New York sample sales), accessorizing ("Every social secretary should own a nice pearl necklace"), and socializing, giving me an insider's essential background on who's who in Washington, DC.

Their guidance, combined with the rules of etiquette I learned from my mother, aunts, and Miss Manners (aka Judith Martin), have served me well, and now I've become the social fairy godmother to those in my circle. Once you've been a social secretary, you are always the go-to person, receiving emergency texts and calls or getting pulled aside during dinner parties, holiday get-togethers, and galas. And I love it.

In general, you can't go wrong when you operate from this golden principle: Be gracious to everyone. Making others feel special has always brought me great joy, and it's so easy. Send a surprise flower arrangement to let someone know you're thinking of her; be the one to start off a toast to a person who is rarely recognized for his talent and good work; bring out the good china and cocktail napkins for a neighborhood event; remove your sunglasses when speaking to someone. All these efforts, big and little, indicate that you care. Executing the little touches with panache and avoiding the faux pas can be your greatest tool in making a connection stronger.

For more specifics on all things etiquette—as well as answers to some of the social etiquette questions that flood my phone and in-box (for example, how to handle a no-show RSVP, the proper response when a guest breaks an item in your home or vice versa, or how to handle someone who wants to vape in your home), turn to A Handbook of Protocol and Etiquette, page 369.

3.

CULTURAL IQ:
WHO IN THE WORLD ARE YOU?

Whenever I stepped off *Air Force One* in some far-off country and scrambled to get into the motorcade—always an ordeal since I carried several large bags that contained everything I needed "just in case"—there was a moment on the tarmac when I would pause to take in the smells, sounds, and landscape of this new country. I relished that discovery of something new and special, like a peek into a present that I was about to receive. The motorcade then zipped away, to either the hotel or more often to our first location, as the president and secretaries of state liked to hit the ground running.

My next observation was always perplexing. En route, I would see billboards for Kentucky Fried Chicken and McDonald's or announcements for the arrival of Beyoncé in concert. The music in our cars was always American—from the 1970s or '80s, some good Fleetwood Mac or Lionel Richie ("All Night Long" seemed to be a favorite). The contradictions fascinated me: Countries with such different values and customs from those of the United States—including those that hold us in low regard as a society and stage protests against our government—still devoured so many aspects of our culture.

All countries export an identity, and it's rarely the full picture. What arrives overseas through the media and consumer market may exaggerate aspects of a culture, positive or negative. (Or it may be totally on point, as in the case of Beyoncé!) Furthermore, what plays well in one country can play poorly in another, depending on *their* values. Every foreign visit offered me an opportunity to color in the stark black-and-white images that counterparts held of us, to correct misperceptions and celebrate the legitimate aspects of our culture that they embraced. It was imperative to present the best and most accurate version of America.

Conveying your character and goals *accurately* is a key element of successful diplomacy in government and business. And to do this well requires self-knowledge: Who are we as US citizens? Even within our own country we have a varied tapestry of what it means to be American, often based on our own religious affiliation, ethnic origins, family values, education, political affiliations, and more. We are all hyphenated to some degree. Identity can change over time, especially as we open ourselves up to new experiences, but like factory settings on a new TV or phone, we all have presets. And when we come to a negotiation, all of these presets—our biases, characteristics, and style of interacting—are along for the ride.

Now here is where it gets really interesting: Knowing your presets well, understanding how those traits are interpreted by those outside your group, resetting those presets if need be, and then communicating who you are *smartly* is a power pivot and can give you an edge in any interaction. Identity branding is a form of cultural intelligence—the ability to collaborate with people who think and act differently from ourselves—and it was a big part of my job as chief of protocol. In addition to digging deeper into other cultures to learn their customs, I had to consider how they were reacting to me, in all of my Americanness, and which of my presets to retain or recalibrate in order to move the ball down the field.

In the business world, companies do this all the time in the form of branding—they create and convey an identity to connect with consumers who will, hopefully, want to share in that identity via a product or service. In social relationships too, self-knowledge and strategic sharing is pivotal. What part of you do you want to reveal to make the connection? Finding the points of intersection help pave the way for successful diplomacy and relationships.

AMERICA THE BEAUTIFUL—SHOWCASING WHO WE ARE

What does it mean to be American? What are our most attractive national qualities? And how can we leverage those to bolster relationships? These were questions that we, the protocol staff, asked ourselves regularly. Early on in my post, Secretary of State Hillary Clinton had directed the entire State Department staff to think about ways to raise our game. How could we use every tool of diplomacy, especially soft power, to strengthen ties to foreign diplomats?

I embraced this mission, and so did the entire protocol staff. I worked with a variety of outside experts in different fields who volunteered to help us brainstorm ways to use cultural resources, tapping people like José Andrés, the talented Spanish-American chef and humanitarian; David Adler, an events guru and CEO of BizBash media; and John Sykes (cofounder of MTV and president of Entertainment Enterprises for iHeartMedia). Most important, I set up one-on-one meetings with my predecessors. At the top of my list: Selwa "Lucky" Roosevelt, the "dean" of the former chiefs of protocol, who's held in high regard throughout Washington, DC, for her superior judgment and grace; and Lloyd Hand, the chief of protocol to President Johnson, and his lovely wife, Ann, who have been valued advisers and friends to me. What worthy programs had my predecessors launched that they felt should continue administration to administration?

Our office was basically promoting America, and we had to figure out how best to inform diplomats about our country's values and assets in ways that went beyond the traditional and below the surface. Many foreign ambassadors posted to the United States go on to serve in influential posts in their own countries—Croatia's ambassador to the United States was elected president in 2015, and Egypt's ambassador to the United States was appointed minister of foreign affairs in 2014— so establishing a stronger attachment to our country and people is an enormous win in the long game of diplomacy and the essence of smart power.

To that end, we launched the Diplomatic Partnership Division (DPD), whose programs all had one thing in common: to share our cultural resources smartly in order to forge stronger diplomatic and personal connections. (It also offered me more time with the diplomatic corps community, people I admire so much.) After some trial and error, I proudly rolled out three new programs and reinvigorated a fourth: (1) The State of the Administration Speakers Series, a recurring Q&A with top administration officials whom the ambassadors may not otherwise meet, such as Rahm Emanuel. Back then the president didn't tweet his every thought, so having his right-hand man—a funny, tell-it-like-it-is chief of staff—download the Obama mind-set was imperative to hear. (I credit Lucky and Lloyd with the inspiration for this program, since they strongly advised me to offer the diplomatic corps opportunities to engage with members of the administration.) (2) The Diplomatic Partnership Roundtables, which brought together the diplomatic corps in smaller groups to discuss regional issues or other challenges with US government officials. This included roundtables with the US ambassador to a foreign country, that country's ambassador to the US, and business leaders who had a stake in relations between the countries. We launched these curated brainstorming sessions because, in reality, it was rare to have all these stakeholders together—and even more unusual to have a closed-door, off-the-record meeting with a loose agenda that allowed them to discuss new approaches and have an open dialogue. (Former chiefs Evan Dobelle and Abelardo Valdez—both of the Carter administration—and Donald Ensenat of the George W. Bush administration all suggested this style of engagement.) (3) The Cultural Exchange Program, which gave us new and creative ways to have meaningful interactions within international diplomatic circles. One of my favorite engagements: the Taste Of . . . Program, a wonderful show-and-tell that took place at Blair House during state visits between DC schoolchildren and the children from the visiting country's US embassy. The children learned how to cook local dishes and dance traditional dances, and eagerly compared notes on everything from sports to dress to school-day routines.

Scholastic came to cover the events for its viewers and readers so that children across America could also get "a taste of" the world outside our borders. (Both former chiefs for President Clinton, Molly Raiser and Mel French, advised on having more cultural activities.)

And then there was Experience America, one of the crown jewels of the DPD, which was launched before my arrival by my immediate predecessor, Nancy G. Brinker. When I landed in the job and reached out to Nancy for big-picture guidance, she invited me to her fabulous apartment in the Ritz-Carlton Residences to fill me in. I was a bit nervous: She was beyond elegant and had a reputation as a force of nature. Nancy not only served as chief of protocol under President George W. Bush, but she had been an ambassador to Hungary and had founded the Susan G. Komen organization in the name of her sister, who had passed away from breast cancer. She could not have been more gracious, and we bonded instantly as mothers of only sons. (Her invaluable mom advice: Bring your child into your work life; it's a great learning opportunity and makes them feel a part of the experience.) On the business front, she clearly had one objective: to tell me about her genius (my word, not hers) innovation, the Experience America program. I knew immediately we had to formalize this unparalleled program so it wouldn't suffer the fate of previous endeavors at the State Department, which typically ended when their chiefs of protocol exited the position. (Happily, this one is still going strong.)

EXPERIENCE AMERICA WAS DESIGNED to take foreign ambassadors and their spouses outside the Washington, DC, bubble and introduce them to the best of the best of America, with the ultimate goal of showcasing the beautiful diversity of our nation and people. I agreed with Nancy that a foreign diplomat wouldn't fully "get" us only by meeting with DC insiders, who often have a reputation for being out of touch with the rest of the country. We wanted diplomats to experience our nation not just as government operatives but as visitors curious to learn more about the *real* America, and then to use that knowledge to strengthen bonds between our countries. The thrill for a diplomat to find a piece of themselves in a small corner of America—a diaspora of Irish in Anchorage, Alaska, or the infusion of French culture and food in New Orleans—reinforced how diverse a country we are and how welcoming we are to the world.

Experience America also offered ambassadors the opportunity to take full advantage of their postings. An ambassador posting to the United States is usually the highest placement within the diplomatic corps, and making useful connections in our country was critical to their success. As a former ambassador, Nancy knew that bringing diplomats to all corners of our huge country and introducing them to unique communities, businesses, and organizations could lead to opportunities that would help deliver that success.

One of Nancy's trips brought ambassadors from forty countries to Texas to showcase the hometown of then-President George W. Bush and to help inform them of his decision making. Any personal insights we could give these diplomats about the leader of the free world were pearls of wisdom these diplomats could take back to their home country's dignitaries. Seeing where our forty-third president lived for much of his life—an amiable, family-oriented community—would help guide them in their diplomacy negotiations. The ambassadors were given a tour of the Bushes' Crawford ranch and met with leaders in the tech and clean-energy realms, discovering that President Bush, while governor, pushed renewable energy policies, leading the state to become number one in wind-generated energy in the country (and heralding his presidential commitment to fund renewable energy). They also met with leaders in the health-care realms, such as the world-renowned MD Anderson Cancer Center in Houston, where Nancy herself had been treated for breast cancer.

Similarly, the first Experience America trip the DPD team and I planned was to Chicago to offer insights into President Obama and Secretary of State Clinton, both of whom hail from the Windy City. We also took our diplomats to Atlanta, where they learned about our civil rights movement; Los Angeles, home of the country's (and the world's) entertainment industry; New Orleans, the birthplace of jazz and a city with a deep understanding of disaster relief; rugged Wyoming, where the diplomats went "wild" over the Wild West lifestyle and pioneer history; Little Rock, Arkansas, where ambassadors were treated to the finest southern hospitality, including a reception hosted by Arkansas native President Clinton himself; and Alaska, home to glaciers, forests, lakes, and some of our country's indigenous communities. Each trip was chosen to highlight aspects of our national character and flavors. The local hosts, usually a private-public partnership, shaped the visit, from the businesspeople we met to the museums we toured to local citizens who hosted our visitors in their homes for intimate dinners. Everyone loved it. When the delegates climbed onto the bus the following day, they were bursting with stories about the details of the residents' houses, jobs, and upbringings, and the neighbors they met—and, of course, the food. On each trip I made the rounds to every dinner (speedily, as I only had an hour and a half to hit anywhere from five to eight dinners!) and raised a glass to everyone, experiencing what our visitors did: the distinct regional accents, the local cuisine, and the inquisitive comments ("So what do you eat in Kazakhstan? What are the royals of Monaco *really* like?").

There were so many extraordinary moments, but the trip to Atlanta in 2010 stands out as being unexpectedly profound. After visiting the CNN studios (where the Kosovo ambassador informed the crew that the global map they flashed daily on the screen was missing his country—it was quickly rectified the next day), we toured the Martin Luther King Jr. Visitor Center and heard civil rights champion Representative John Lewis speak about our country's devastating history of slavery and the rise of the civil rights movement. He shared his experience marching alongside Martin Luther King Jr. and spoke passionately about the importance of nonviolent revolution and of looking back on our legacy of achievement in the face of present-day struggles.

After his speech, the South African ambassador to the United States, Ebrahim Rasool, who had served time in jail as a youth along with Nelson Mandela for similar "crimes," spoke. "Your country's example helped me continue to fight against the apartheid in our country, to find strength in our darkest hour," he said. There was not a dry eye in the house. This was the impact moment. We all felt the emotional bond between these two men and the connective potency of their shared history.

History is an incredible tool for unification, a soft power resource we should tap more often. We are all interested in origin stories. How did a country or a business or a person become what they are now? This journey of transformation fascinates people and offers a unique way to feel connected. The Atlanta visit also underscored a counterintuitive truth, one I practice to this day in all my travels and interactions: Don't gloss over the darker parts of your history. We wanted the diplomats to see the underbelly of our country's racist history. Trying to sweep that under the rug would have been a missed opportunity to address a core piece of our national identity. What marks a country or business or person is not only the successes but also the struggles and the response to those challenges.

Guess who else was "experiencing America"? Me. I was in a unique position to tune in to the staggeringly different qualities of Americans and observe how those traits were viewed by our international visitors. This education was an extension of what I experienced abroad: understanding who we are through others' eyes and learning to hone my choices when interacting with dignitaries. There are so many qualities that define us, but the following four play a key role in diplomacy and international business. Anyone doing business overseas or with foreign colleagues here in the United States can benefit from understanding how these attributes are viewed by others and how they can be calibrated to bridge and persuade.

1. The Transactional American

"Just do it!" Nike's successful ad slogan could easily be America's: We get stuff done. Quickly. Our transactional style of business—a laser-focused intentionality on closing the deal efficiently and without much sentimentality—is an American signature. We are the land of opportunity and have encouraged a go-get-it MO since we became the ultimate start-up in 1776. Our country's accelerated prosperity over centuries has created a stable risk-and-reward environment, and our capitalist policies have encouraged entrepreneurship. The United States ranks number one in venture capital invested, and we have a healthy and continued growth of start-ups. This can-do climate has created a business style that is transactional and clipped enough to keep up with a steady pace of progress and a "what's next" eagerness.

In addition, because we don't have the same level of class consciousness as some other countries, it can be easier for the average Joe or Josephine to make connections—doing a deal is less dependent on a person's social standing and bloodline and more about the actual business at hand (although who you know can still be a factor). As a result of a fairly democratized landscape, we don't engage in as much "getting to know you" preliminaries (What do your parents do? Where were you born?) as some other countries before getting down to business. The American business climate is fast-paced. We work more hours a year than many countries and have no mandatory minimum vacation days, unlike other advanced countries—and over half of us don't use up the days we do get!

This bottom-line style is super productive when everyone's on the same page. But the breakneck pace can come off as abrupt in cultures where courtship is expected before the engagement. (Our incessant drive forward can also prove to be shortsighted. Case in point: Facebook's now-defunct motto "Move fast and break things!") A few years ago, I consulted for a US-based company that had recently expanded overseas to Europe. I was brought in to help guide them in best practices for international relations and strongly recommended that the in-country team—those employees based overseas—do business in the MO of the country in which they were operating, not the MO of the US headquarters. Otherwise, they would have a harder time communicating with colleagues raised in that culture. The company then made the advantageous decision to allow their foreign teams on the ground to brand and operate the company according to each country's culture—for example, changing the outward-facing company name to incorporate the national language and hiring and partnering with locals. It was a strategy they'd already utilized within the United States and had found successful. They understood that regional differences matter in the States, that customers respond more positively to a business whose name and brand reflects local attitudes and climate (using words like *friendly* or *sunny*, for example, in marketing materials for regions where those attributes are valued). They just needed to apply this same cultural understanding globally.

But like any business engaging internationally, challenges arose. One of their European partners was managing things more quietly and playing their cards close to the vest. The US home team interpreted this behavior as lax. I was able to explain to the American executives why the international division acted in this manner—it wasn't laziness but a cultural business norm—and how we could advise them to ramp up their efforts without coming off as "American big-footing," an approach that is frowned upon in many countries.

In international diplomacy, we encounter these differences all the time, but because we have protocol, the framework helps us all follow the same path and there are fewer cultural missteps. Most leaders don't just cannonball into a bilateral with their own way of doing things— changing the format of the meeting, insisting upon press in closed-door sessions, raising issues that were pre-agreed to be off the agenda, or bringing along an extra delegate after a pre-negotiated number of attendees—because *protocol* dictates the rules of engagement. Intentional practices set the pace and allow for expected moments of cultural exchanges. There are introductions to be had, anthems to be played, and local ceremonies that present our values and identity.

Even on presidential trips, however, unforeseen challenges can eclipse protocol, allowing cultural biases to break through and presets to take control. In November 2010, President Obama was invited for a state visit to India. We were all very excited about the trip, although there was some concern that many details of the schedule had not yet been shared by the Indian counterparts. When we landed in Delhi, I met with Shilpa Pesaru, the senior protocol officer whose in-depth knowledge of the culture and acute judgment served the office well. She let me know that all our protocol interests were being addressed as expected, but that the press team had urgent concerns. It seemed we lacked a final schedule of the president's press movements, including the location and format for press interactions—many of the details that the advance staff would usually receive well before we arrived. They were growing more desperate by the minute. In an effort to assist, I immediately requested a meeting with the Indian chief of protocol to get clarity, and I invited staff from our delegation so they could ask questions as well. We all huddled in a small room next to where our leaders were holding their first bilateral. A young press aide, who was understandably anxious to find out which press events were open to reporters, began to fire off questions in a familiar American manner. I could see that my Indian counterpart was getting annoyed and began ignoring her. The nature of those I'd encountered in India, especially in government, was polite yet formal, and there was an expectation that such meetings have a certain pace and protocol—formal introductions were important, as was the custom that lower-level staff's interests be represented by senior members in the room. This young woman's urgency and forwardness went against their MO.

I understood the young woman's reason for being dogged. I'd been in her shoes, getting constant pings on my phone from higher-ups asking for updates. But her insistence was being read as arrogance and impatience. I kept shooting her looks to slow down but couldn't catch her eye. So I made a split-second decision to pause the meeting and pull her out of the room. I knew that if I returned on my own and adopted a patient and deferential manner, I could elicit the information she needed. I told her it would be more productive if I went back in solo. (She too sensed the tension, but I don't think she understood why my Indian counterpart stopped responding to her questions.) I returned alone, and my instincts paid off: I was able to procure what she needed. She later expressed relief that I had stepped in, and I explained to her that India's pace—and specifically this government representative's pace—was more moderate and steady than our usual one hundred miles per hour, and that they placed a premium on formalities.

To keep a brisk manner from reading as impatience or entitlement, I advise a few things:

- **Take the temperature of the room.** You want to get a sense of the people across the table so you can adjust your style. If they're fidgety, their anxiety may be high, and you should take a calmer approach. If they appear to be disengaged, ask them questions to reengage. If they cut you off, they may be feeling impatient or annoyed. It's best to address this head-on by saying, "Let me cut to the chase here."

- **Take a beat mid-conversation.** You don't have to react to everything immediately. Let what they've said sink in and use the pause to your advantage. I've found that because people are uncomfortable with a pause, they feel compelled to fill the silence, which gives you insights into their thinking.

- **Turn the tables.** Get them to give you more intel on what they are seeking by asking questions that focus on them and their issues. This slows things down so they can recenter, and so can you.

2. The Chill, Cool American

The American attribute of a relaxed and confident vibe isn't necessarily the norm in other cultures. On the spectrum of decorum, Americans generally veer toward the informal end, and as a result we are viewed as easygoing and not uptight or rehearsed. This self-possessed nature can be a big benefit in negotiations, putting the other party at ease while still transmitting assuredness. The flip side: An overly relaxed air can come across as arrogance or disinterest, so the informality factor has to be carefully calibrated.

No one epitomized classy cool like President Obama. His nickname, No-Drama Obama, stuck with him throughout his two terms. President Obama also has an intrinsic rock-star quality. I (and everyone else) felt this at global summits. Each delegation had their own air when they entered the convening space—it all felt a little like the scene from Martin Scorsese's movie *Gangs of New York*, each group's identity set by the stride and vibe of their leader (without the intention of wanting to bloody each other to the death, of course!). The purposeful walk of the French and the all-business hustle of the Brazilians contrasted with the excitement of the non-G20 countries, who were invited to the summit for the first time. We—the Americans—had a glide and vibe set by our self-assured, laid-back president. The president's walk, a cross between a swagger and an effortless stride, had a confident cadence that we all tried to adopt as we trailed him. (I had to take three strides to his one, not easy in four-inch heels.) From the moment he stepped out of the Beast, the moniker for the presidential limo, a spotlight seemed to shine on him: The US president had arrived.

His quick-to-form smile was also part of his charm and could put anyone—dictators, talk-show hosts, journalists—at ease. President Obama had an inherent ability to feel at home with anyone, and because his capacity to connect was nearly effortless, you knew it was authentic. I observed this natural assuredness with President Bill Clinton as well, who, with his saunter, inclusive nature, and thoughtful gaze, emitted a relaxed confidence. Both Presidents Bush, as well, displayed an "I got this" air. President George H. W. Bush was always a cool customer—former CIA usually are—and President George W. Bush, in addition to his guy-next-door quality, had a certainty that radiated. There is something about being the American president and the weight of the role that makes the shoulders broader and bigger.

I witnessed President Obama's serene nature serve as a tool for smart diplomacy, and on more than one occasion his measured manner made my job easier by sweetening the bitterness of a tense exchange. In April 2010 our delegation flew to Prague, where Russia and the United States were set to sign the New START (Strategic Arms Reduction Treaty) bilateral agreement, which had gone through several iterations (not all of them successful). The Czech Republic (or Czechia as of 2016) was playing an important supporting role by serving as host country. When a third-party country hosts, they want to shine in their role and do not want to be sidelined on the world stage. The Czech staff had prepared an elegant engagement, but due to the high stakes, their nervousness was palpable. I don't blame them: The United States rolls boldly into every country with our huge delegation, and our counterparts are sometimes taken aback, instinctively putting up barricades—doors, gates, and even bodies!—to manage the influx of officials.

But on this day, the hurdles were over the top. President Obama himself barely made it through the doors to the Prague Castle, the presidential offices where the bilateral meetings and signing were taking place. I attached myself to him like glue in order to get through. But our interpreter—the nicest, most genteel man—had the door to the bilateral room slammed in his face. I turned around and looked at my Czech protocol counterpart with absolute shock, only to see him defiantly look away. He was a novice who was clearly working hard (as the sweat on his brow showed), but he took his job—determining who got in and who did not—too far and didn't think through the consequences. I loudly whispered my protests about needing our interpreter, and President Obama immediately noticed that I was having trouble getting my counterpart to see the logic in admitting the interpreter. The president very coolly turned to the Czech president, Václav Klaus, who had escorted us to the bilateral room—and who had his own interpreter with him—caught his gaze, looked at the Czech interpreter, and then flipped a look toward me trying to pry the door open. Without saying a word, he conveyed, "We will have a hard time talking to each other without *my* interpreter." President Klaus immediately acknowledged the fuss and strongly nodded toward my counterpart, who took that as a directive to let the interpreter enter. It was President Obama's calm demeanor that unleashed the tension and allowed common sense to prevail.

His ability to maintain a cool head—I never once saw him lose his temper—was a balm even among his own staff. One afternoon, while I was waiting for the president and Secretary Clinton in the Outer Oval Office (a small reception room with two desks and computers), I saw a couple of staffers grow extremely nervous when Secretary Clinton read aloud some information prepared by their policy aides that she ascertained wasn't fully accurate. Time was short—this was for an important and imminent foreign policy announcement—so the staff went into a frenzy. You'd think we were at a Broadway show of Bob Fosse for all the jazz-hand waving going on. They all frantically checked their Black-Berries, but President Obama simply took the level-headed secretary's hand and guided her over to the Outer Oval, where Brian Mosteller, the president's director of Oval operations (and a reliable and perfectly styled aide), handled a multitude of details for the president on his computer. (There are no computers in the Oval Office, in part because of security concerns but also the Oval is meant to be ceremonial in appearance—computer monitors, cords, and modems would diminish this effect.) There, at Brian's computer, the president and secretary—the two biggest geeks in the government—sat down and nerded out over the details to figure out the proper data and language. President Obama's calm reaction took the moment from DEFCON 1 back to normal status. I wasn't at all clear on the policy details, but the moment stayed with me: A cool head can win the day.

When a nonchalant vibe is employed deftly, it's a game changer and takes the edge off an anxious situation. But the danger of American "chill" is that it can come off as impolite, depending on the culture. To keep a laid-back demeanor from reading as rude, keep these pointers in mind:

- **Perfect your posture.** Choose a moderately relaxed posture that indicates both attentiveness and comfort. A too-relaxed posture when sitting—slumped back into a chair, for example—can signal disinterest or disrespect. Studies show that the more positively a person feels about a conversational partner, the more he will lean forward, whereas someone who doesn't respect his conversation partner appears super relaxed.

- **Watch your quirks.** When we become too comfortable, we may revert to the automatic behaviors we engage in when we're not on guard: hair twirling, tapping a pen, chewing gum, or even picking up your phone as a crutch. Aside from being distracting, these behaviors can appear outright rude.

- **Mind your language.** A comfort with informality and trendy terms can open the door to language that might come off as disrespectful, exclusionary, or confusing. Stick with polite and universal terminology.

3. The Loud, Proud American

America was founded on the idea of individual freedoms. The ability to worship, vote, work, love, and learn the way we choose—and knowing we are a beacon to other countries striving for those same freedoms—is an envied way to live. Our Constitution affords Americans the right to create the lives we dream of (recognizing that many still lack opportunities), so it's no wonder we carry a fierce national pride. I truly believe we are the greatest country in the world, especially since I witnessed the transformative power of American ideals in my family and upbringing. During my entire career in government, but especially as chief of protocol, I walked into every interaction practically on steroids about how fabulous our country and its inhabitants are. Our loud, proud, and ruggedly individualist nature is gritty and great, and it's one attribute that makes us so exceptional. To be clear: I'm speaking about the loud and proud national characteristics that lie at one end of the pride spectrum. At the other end is the to-be-avoided-at-all-costs "ugly American," the culturally insensitive and arrogant stereotype who uses foul language and annoys everyone around him. I live by Michelle Obama's famous line—"When they go low, we go high!" Wise words for all situations.

Despite the obvious benefits of being confident and proud, we Americans should sometimes tread lightly. On the international diplomatic stage, I found that tempering my outspokenness helped keep relationships with counterparts balanced so I wasn't necessarily the dominant force. To be clear, you shouldn't be inauthentic or censor what makes you uniquely American. Some of the unedited parts of my personality were the reasons I was able to make such strong connections. The trick is to be aware of those traits and soften the edges if need be. The framework and decorum of protocol helped me color within the lines, but I also relied on a couple fail-safe strategies to avoid any perception of stepping on toes:

- **Be curious.** One way to positively channel outspokenness is to express curiosity. Ask about food practices, dress, and other cultural traditions. And participate in those traditions when invited: Make the Chinese noodle or wear the national costume if it's offered. Try the unusual dish—I've eaten shark-fin soup (now outlawed in many states), blood sausage (yum!), and whale fat (curiously chewy) in the name of diplomacy. Showing interest also demonstrated to foreign dignitaries that I cared about the relationship beyond the veneer of the job. Asking about an ambassador's children or family vacation moved the relationship to another level. Curiosity is in my DNA, and I was truly interested to learn more about them, but I was also aware that these questions opened up a door to a deeper connection, and it was in these personal connections that I often found my greatest successes.

The master of using curiosity to bridge cultural gaps was President Bill Clinton. His sense of service drove him to listen compassionately so he could understand people's needs. His ability to connect—and to make you feel like you were the only person in a room of two hundred—was legendary, and due in great part to his insatiable interest in other people's stories. During my time as social secretary, more than once I found myself running around an event looking for him, only to discover him in the kitchen or the back hall, sitting with the cooks, cleaning staff, or waiters, drinking in the details of their lives, nodding his head and saying, "You're from where? I know folks from there—do you know so-and-so? They are good people, right?" He used these collections of stories to make points about what people from around the country and the world were thinking and experiencing.

- **Be human.** You can be proud, but don't let that stop you from admitting foibles or sharing humanizing stories. Ambassadorial postings to the United States are the ultimate posting for other countries, and many arrive in DC excited but nervous, afraid to make the wrong move. I embrace that I am a bit of goofball and sometimes have the biggest laughs at my own mistakes and misunderstandings—and welcome others to do so at my expense as well. When I admitted that I, too, had spent a whole day walking around with smeared eyeliner or with my skirt zipper down—or that I had also experienced the highs and lows of life's rites of passages—they were able to relax a bit and relate to me. The woman who was giving them the rules for how to behave in this country was much more approachable when she stumbled, too.

  An inability to be anyone other than who I am seemed to be

a trait that was useful in my post. One year during the United Nations General Assembly, President Obama hosted the traditional reception for the chiefs of state and heads of delegations at the American Museum of Natural History in New York City. All went well until the departures. We always have an assigned entry and departure point for the US president, separate from other dignitaries, and halted the movement of all guests while the president is entering and departing. This lull usually lasts only a minute or two, but that evening, there was a hitch.

I was in the midst of bidding farewell to every head of state, and the departure line suddenly stopped with President Mwai Kibaki of Kenya standing in front of me. I shared with him that the pause would only be a moment and asked if he'd had a good evening. He assured me he had and we exchanged a few more niceties. Then we waited, and waited . . . and it got *awkward*. One minute became two became three. Suddenly, his staff was at my side—four very tall and very unhappy men—asking me what was going on. I scooted over to talk to the United States Secret Service (USSS) agent at the door. He told me that the president had made a stop at the men's room. Well, I certainly couldn't share *that* with the president of Kenya, so I returned to say it would be just a moment longer and flew into storytelling mode with the objective to distract. I told him of my first trip to Kenya with a college boyfriend to meet his family: the bustling markets, the freshly caught fish, and—oh!—how we enjoyed the moonlight on the beaches of Mombasa. The president wanted to hear more about the relationship—how we met, what we did, what happened to my ex-beau. He was completely enraptured and I think a bit disappointed when the USSS finally signaled that the path was clear and he could depart. Not only did my story alleviate any awkwardness, but I made a great connection with him. When I saw him later in the week, he reminded me that I needed to finish the story!

- **Avoid taboo subjects.** It's fine to recount a funny or self-deprecating story that will help you connect, but don't tread into the territory of anything too private, such as sexual or medical matters. In addition, I do not mention political stories that would offend or launch a discussion that can go wildly out of control. I also get up to speed on the cultural taboos of each country so I don't broach a topic that they deem off-limits.

4. The Generous American

When Hillary Clinton was First Lady, her guiding principle for international trips was simple and pure: Where there are needs, we will come. When we traveled to New Delhi, India, in 1995, she made sure we planned a visit to one of Mother Teresa's orphanages. The facilities were incredibly crowded, but there was no shortage of love and attention being given to the children. Hillary had learned of orphanages' great deficiencies and brought as a gift for Mother Teresa items that would meet their most pressing needs. American businesses were asked to donate medical kits, toys, and school supplies for the children. Mother Teresa was incredibly moved by Hillary's thoughtfulness and Americans' open hearts and hands.

I can attest that virtually all countries on the planet are gracious and make visitors feel special. And yet, I believe Americans' brand of generosity is unique. For one, we are generous hosts. For centuries America has been the receiver of "huddled masses yearning to breathe free," as the Statue of Liberty's plaque testifies. Although immigration is a hot-button policy issue right now (to put it mildly), the fact remains: The United States has more immigrants than any other country in the world (although as of 2018 we lost our top spot as the global leader in refugee settlement to Canada, according to the Migration Policy Institute); nearly 14 percent of our population, or 44.5 million, is foreign-born (a steady increase from 5 percent in 1970).

We're also philanthropic. In 2018, Americans ranked number four in charitable giving in the world, according to the Charities Aid Foundation (CAF), and almost 60 percent of Americans reported donating money to a charity, helping a stranger, and/or volunteering time in the previous month. This brand of philanthropy is somewhat unique to America, growing out of our democratic belief—and spelled out in the Constitution, the supreme law of the nation—that everyone has equal rights, that improvement for one is improvement for all. But the very concept of philanthropy is mysterious to some countries. Take Thanksgiving, for example, where we devote a day each year to giving thanks and ensuring that everyone has a delicious meal and someone to share it with. Reserving a day for generosity and charity is not the norm in many other countries.

After a few discussions with various ambassadors during my time in office, it became clear how confusing the ideals and traditions of Thanksgiving were. So working with local restaurants and historians, Ali Rubin, the most innovative of diplomats, designed an annual event for the foreign diplomatic corps at Blair House that would tell not only the story of our country's day of thanks, goodwill, and delicious traditional dishes, but our long-standing customs of philanthropy and volunteering. (Interesting fact: American philanthropy surged during the industrial revolution, when American titans of industry accumulated huge wealth and reinvested it in education, science, and the arts, seeing it as a "payoff" for a better society in which to live and do business. As the middle class became more prosperous, charitable giving moved beyond the scope of the wealthy.) She worked with the chef to showcase each dish with descriptions of the foods' significance and history, and I spoke about the importance of the holiday and our philanthropic history. All of our foreign ambassadors and their families appreciate these insights and the delicious introduction to one of our nation's most unique celebrations.

So with such a generous national spirit, what could possibly go wrong when Americans practice generosity with other cultures? The answer lies in perception. Generosity is viewed differently in each nation, though there are commonalities. A fascinating 2015 study of several countries (Austria, China, Denmark, Turkey, Russia, the United Kingdom, and the United States), found that it pays to be nice . . . but not too nice. Led by Nicholas Epley, PhD, a psychologist and author of *Mindwise*, the study asked participants to read a story where one man was given a sum of money and told he could share any amount with another man. People from different countries read three different renditions of the story: In some versions the man shared it equally; in other versions he shared more or less than half. Participants were then asked to rate the man's traits related to warmth and competence.

Some of the results were what you'd expect: The more generous, the more likely the man was rated as warm. However, two countries stood out for their differences: In China, giving *all* was viewed as more favorable than giving half; and in Turkey, giving all was actually rated more *negatively* than giving half. Dr. Epley theorizes, "Perhaps in Turkey, giving everything is seen as suspicious, as if you might be trying to manipulate the other person." When it came to competence, giving more than half was viewed as *less* competent in most countries, with the exception of China, where giving more than half was seen as more competent: Asian cultures, compared to Western ones, prize traits like generosity that serve the group versus traits like independence that benefit the individual. "In China, more giving implies you have a bigger social network, and the more you give, the more you get, and the more you can get done," says Dr. John Flower, director of China Studies at Sidwell Friends School of Washington, DC. Gifts, he explains, are ways to build and maintain social connections in a society that values the collective over the individual. The takeaway: Unless you are exceedingly familiar with a culture and can fine-tune your generosity, a good rule of thumb is to simply be fair, period.

In diplomacy, you certainly want to show graciousness. But you don't want to be so generous that the other side feels they "owe" you something. Favor swapping is common in politics, but it's frowned upon in diplomacy. Instead, the goal is to find common ground—you're all on the same ship, whether it's sinking or floating. The negotiation should be about how to keep it afloat and sail forward together.

In business and personal negotiations, don't stifle your natural tendency to be kind and generous, but do be aware of these pitfalls:

- **Avoid an overly lavish approach; it can backfire.** The person you're targeting may see right through it, or your colleagues may pick up on it, causing them to suspect a hidden agenda. We've all been in meetings where one person is fawning over another and you want to say, "Enough!"

- **Beware of over-the-top generosity,** which can be misinterpreted as pity. Your international counterpart is proud and will feel shamed if they sense pity versus generosity.

- **Be authentic.** When you give a gift or a compliment, try not to make it seem dutiful, as in "I'm just doing this because it's what I was told to do." People pick up on that right away. Instead, embrace the meaning and the spirit of the gesture and demonstrate a desire for a true connection.

CREATING A BUSINESS IDENTITY

In the same way that traits unite and define a country, a business's brand and culture define it and unite the employees. In fact, many businesses operate as mini-countries, each with their own languages (acronyms, buzzwords), customs (hour-long lunch breaks, silencing phones in the office), ethos (transparency, teamwork), and national costume (dress code). So much goes into shaping a business's outward-facing identity (brand) and inward-facing identity, or what's called organizational culture, aka the shared thoughts and behaviors of a staff. And just as in international diplomacy, knowing who your business is, how it is perceived, and how you *want* it to be perceived will give you a leg up.

The most successful businesses have put a lot of effort and resources into developing and sustaining a strong identity. This is particularly true for a company's organizational culture, a concept that used to sound esoteric or unproven but which is now a main focus for those that want to be at the top of their game. Businesses with a strong, definable culture show higher profits compared to companies with a weak or vague culture, according to James Heskett, PhD, a professor of business logistics at Harvard Business School and author of *The Culture Cycle*. Why? In general, a strong culture engages managers and staff, which results in lower turnover; high turnover costs a company in terms of recruiting, hiring, training, and client interaction (clients don't love having to get to know new contacts repeatedly). It's important to note, however, that the *quality* of the culture matters as much as its robustness. Heskett uses Southwest Airlines as an example of a strong, positive culture. As Forbes.com has reported, Southwest's emphasis on employee recognition programs and instilling company values has led to an extremely low voluntary turnover rate.

Whether you're the CEO, a midlevel manager, or an entrepreneur, you can strengthen your business's or team's identity and culture—or your own individual brand—by honing the following cultural traits.

- **Define your ethos.** Which values do you or does your company embody and want to communicate to employees, customers, shareholders, and the world? Internally, do you want employees to be curious and questioning? Or to follow established protocol to a T? Do you want your structure to be hierarchical or more egalitarian? The stronger the identity, the easier it is to quickly telegraph what you stand for, and to know which new policies and projects to implement: Either they align or they don't. This is true for your clients as well. "I think the best brands, and the ones I look to for inspiration, have a point of view, they aren't trying to be everything to everyone," says Audrey Gelman, cofounder of The Wing, an all-women coworking and social club with thirteen locations in seven cities and growing. "Sometimes that means being comfortable with the idea that your product might not be for everyone. For us, I don't think you can credibly speak to millennial women without getting into conversations about politics and feminism. If you want access to that demographic's pocketbook, then you need to wade into the issues they are passionate about in an authentic way."

  The ethos can be company-wide or be confined to a division. The technology giant Oracle has acquired dozens of companies over the decades, all of which have had their own cultures prior to being a part of the parent company. Oracle smartly allows some of those acquisitions to retain the parts of their culture that were instrumental in their success. "When Oracle purchased Datalogix, which is now part of Oracle Data Cloud, . . . they gave us a lot of freedom to continue the practices that have allowed us to attract and retain top talent," says Michelle Hulst, formerly of Datalogix and now Group Vice President Marketing and Strategic Partnerships, at Oracle Data Cloud (ODC). One of those policies—unlimited vacation days, which aligns itself with the ODC's commitment to employee empowerment and trust (as in "we trust you'll get your job done no matter how many vacation days you take")—has been adopted company-wide due to its success.

- **Hire a culture officer as part of your HR team.** Because culture is so pivotal to employee retention and productivity, some companies have created roles devoted to office culture. ODC created a "culture department" whose officers' jobs are all about maintaining ODC's culture while also aligning with the broader culture at Oracle and other acquisitions. "Each business that gets added to ODC has its own personality that it needs to operate efficiently, and everyone has an allegiance to their brand. How do you pull all those together in a melting pot that serves the bigger business? That's what our culture officers are focused on," says Hulst. Sometimes officers will split their time between divisions, offices, or even cities in order to get to know all the moving parts and cross-pollinate. They may create central hang-out spaces or offer classes (wine tastings, yoga) to get employees to mix outside their division.

  Culture officers also play a big role in the on-boarding process, helping new hires ease into the workplace. And they may also serve as "diversity officers," ensuring that gender and racial diversity is paid attention to. I'm constantly amazed at the number of big start-ups, especially in the tech space, that haven't put policies in place from Day 1 to ensure discriminatory behavior isn't tolerated. Having these best practices spelled out early—by a culture officer or HR Department—can nip costly and damaging issues in the bud.

- **Create shared experiences around company values and identity.** If charitable giving is an important company value, offer employees time off to volunteer, host a blood drive on site after a recent disaster, or offer matching funds for an employee's charitable giving. If respect for the past or traditions is a key part of your company's ethos, arrange for museum discounts or off-site day trips to memorials. Even the US military, which is often seen as strict and "all business," creates experiences for team building and unit cohesion by having recruits participate in communal activities that build historical identity, such as visiting military memorials or cemeteries.

  At the Atlantic Council, where I hold the position of ambassador in residence, closing the gap between generations and fostering a non-ageist environment is a company priority. Through a program developed by Fred Kempe, CEO and president, along with Paige Ennis, a dear friend whose years of executive training and management guide the council, new and younger staff are offered key operational roles in the council's major events and global convenings. This opportunity exposes the younger team members to the council board members, partners, and senior government—as well as to private-sector participants—allowing them to see firsthand the power of assembling communities of influence. These experiences also galvanize the team around the council's mission and allow them to deepen their own professional networks.

- **Embrace diversity.** Diversity in the workplace is a driver of innovation and profits, according to a recent landmark study by McKinsey & Company. Their 2018 analysis, "Delivering through Diversity," looked at data from more than one thousand companies covering twelve countries. They discovered that companies that had a greater share of women and racial composition in leadership positions performed better financially. Some key findings: Companies in the top quartile of gender diversity were *21 percent more likely* to have above-average profits; companies in the top quartile for racial diversity were *33 percent more likely* to have above-average profits, with the figure jumping to 43 percent for companies with diversity at the board of directors' level. (The reverse was true, too: Companies in the bottom quartiles for diversity had less likelihood for above-average profits.) Why does diversity equal success? In part because more diverse companies are able to attract better talent and offer clients a more varied range of experiences, leading to higher customer satisfaction. (I discuss the challenges of Negotiating While Female in chapter 15.)

4.

CULTURAL IQ: *WHO IN THE WORLD ARE THEY?*

We were about halfway down the receiving line at the Blue House in Seoul, the residence of the president of South Korea—where I was presenting top US officials to our hosts—when I spotted a protocol offense in the making. During the introductions, the South Korean and US delegates were exchanging business cards, a ritual that serves as a prelude to meetings in many countries and almost always in Asian countries. I was scrutinizing every move of our delegates, as this 2012 visit was incredibly important. Presidents Obama and Lee Myung-bak were to discuss trade issues and nuclear security—including North Korea's long-range missile tests and increasing aggression—so all protocol processes had to be in perfect form. The Koreans could not be disrespected in any way. Yet suddenly, there it was: a red light, double siren alert that my trained eye detected, an error that could begin a downward spiral. One of our most senior officials was presented with a business card; he took it with one hand and never looked at it, instead keeping eye contact and chatting, as is our American custom. He should have pointedly looked at the card, though that wasn't the end of the world. But then he made a gesture to place it in the back pocket of his pants, and I felt like the entire scene went into slow motion as I lunged toward him to stop the train wreck.

In South Korea, the art of business card exchange is a serious matter, and placing a card in the seat of your pants would be interpreted as sitting on the person's identity—literally and figuratively. Approaching from behind, I lightly grabbed the US official's elbow to stop him and whispered that he needed to look at the card for a moment and respectfully place it in his jacket's breast pocket. He did exactly that, disaster averted, and later thanked me—he'd read the protocol memo, but that detail had slipped his mind in the moment.

Without that intervention, the visit may well have suffered. We were in South Korea and a cultural misstep of this magnitude certainly could have tainted the South Korean's opinion of our delegate—here was someone in a top position who had mishandled an important cultural norm—and the fallout would likely have carried over into the talks, changing the tenor of the negotiations. It might even have led the South Korean delegate to ice out the US official in subsequent meetings. After all, diplomats had been known to walk out of bilateral meetings because their name was misspelled on a tent card.

As free trade finds its way into all corners of the globe, it's critical for Americans to recognize that not everyone does business the way we do. We're no longer the world's only economic superpower, and we can't expect others to play only by our rules. Many people globally are raised to understand that being successful in the world requires sensitivity to cultural differences, and the lessons start young for a number of nations: a median of 92 percent of primary, middle-school, and high-school students in European countries learn a foreign language, compared with 20 percent of American students, according to research from the Pew Center. The scales are tipping, and we have to find ways to play nicely in the international sandbox. More and more, it's expected that *we* learn *other* cultures' codes of conduct. It's also the smart thing to do.

Understanding the basics of another culture is a power pivot. Not only does it make communication easier, but it signals respect and an openness to creating an authentic connection. Plus, being schooled in the rules of engagement allows you to focus on the substance of a meeting: You can be more creative and flexible if you're not worrying about missing a cue or getting a gesture wrong. Perhaps most important: Cultural

IQ legitimizes you as someone worthy of negotiating with—you take their norms seriously, therefore you are a serious-minded potential partner. This, frankly, is where a lot of American businesses go wrong. I hear all the time, "Oh, yes, we're a global company," but then I discover they haven't taken any concrete steps to learn how other cultures think, behave, or do business. As a result, they haven't made adjustments to operating procedures that would help them forge strong partnerships abroad. Just as damaging as a lack of cultural IQ is the message they're sending, even if it's unintentional: "My way or the highway." A much better foundation for a successful global partnership is taking the time and performing the actions to create successful international engagements.

DO YOUR HOMEWORK

In international dealings, preparation is king. I did loads of research before trips or hosting visitors stateside, gathering intel on specific cues and traditions that would elevate each meeting. *Pro tip:* Email or make a call to the US-based foreign embassy of the country you're traveling to or hosting—embassies are always thrilled to share cultural details, and they often have the most up-to-date information, since customs can shift quickly, especially when there is a change in leadership. (Visit the State Department website, www.usembassy.gov, for phone numbers and email addresses.) Beforehand, I also perused the biographies of foreign dignitaries and watched some TV shows to get up to speed on their popular culture. I did this not only because I enjoyed it, but also because I found you can learn cultural norms and colloquial phrases by binge-watching, for instance, a telenovela. And while the whole world knows Beyoncé, it thrills another country when you reference one of *their* rising pop stars. I also familiarized myself with the latest news from their countries so I knew which subjects would engage them and which to avoid.

My eight culture-code crackers are the same ones that anyone doing business with another country should zero in on before a meeting. (For an expanded tip sheet, turn to page 374.)

1. Greetings

Shake hands, bow, nod, or curtsy? It depends on the country, your gender, *their* gender, and their position—and it's critical to get it right. Aside from hitting the perfect first note, a proper greeting can do damage control. We tend to make snap judgments about a person's trustworthiness and competence within seconds of looking at him, research finds. Psychologists call this thin-slicing, and we all do it. The good news: If a blink-of-an-eye impression is negative, you can recalibrate and create a positive impression based on subsequent interactions. The greeting is your first opportunity to override a negative snap judgment. The host country almost always initiates the greeting, so if you're visiting, wait until they make a move, and then follow these rules:

- **Handshakes.** As the world becomes more Westernized, the handshake has emerged as the universal greeting in most countries upon first meeting. The grip-and-grin has been around since about 2800 BC, when historians believed it symbolized a transfer of power from a God to an earthly ruler. It may also have been used to show that you weren't hiding a weapon in your sleeve, according to Pakistan's protocol chief, who shared his region's history of social norms at our first Global Chiefs of Protocol Conference in 2012 at the State Department. You can't shake a hand if you're clutching a cloaked dagger.

  The rule of thumb is to use a Goldilocks approach: a comfortably firm clasp that's not too tight and not too loose. You may need to adjust it depending on the country, so follow your host's cues. For example, in Asia, the grip is soft and lax, and some only use the tips of their fingers to shake. (Turn to page 371 for a country-by-country guide.) As you're shaking, lean in a little to show a welcoming vibe. And sorry, lefties, the whole world shakes with the right hand. Even left-handed presidents—Barack Obama, Bill Clinton, George H. W. Bush, and Ronald Reagan—greeted heads of state with their right hands. Some presidents put a personal spin on the shake. President Trump's handshake, coined "the Trump tug," attempts to pull his counterparts into his zone and hold them there, sometimes leading to a bit of a tussle, most notably with France's President Emmanuel Macron. The two seem to be sawing a log at times!

Also key: looking the person directly in the eye while shaking, which reinforces the emotional connection and helps you remember the person. (Important caveat: In Asia, keep your eye contact minimal and gaze soft.) And when "shaking" the hands of royals around the globe, Africa and the Arab world included, if they offer their hand first, you should lightly grasp the fingers (not the entire hand) while executing a slight nod.

- **Bows and Nods.** Before a visit to the UK, a US government aide asked me whether the president would bow before the Queen. "Certainly not, and do you know why?" The aide shook his head. I responded: "1776!" We fought hard so that an American president would never yield position and power before any sovereign again. A slight nod of the head is all that's required.

  In 2009, bows became the focus of a high-level international visit. President Obama was in Tokyo for the first leg of his inaugural Asia trip to meet with the Japanese prime minister and emperor. I had flown ahead to his next stop, a state visit in China (which was shaping up to be extra challenging) and had prepared a cultural memo for the president on all things Japanese, including pointers on greetings: a reminder that this is a culture that bows to their emperor, but that a US president should not; and once the emperor extends his hand, it is appropriate to shake.

  For nearly every other person, a bow *is* the appropriate greeting for an emperor. It confers respect and humility, and the lower the bow, the more devotion you are showing. However, because President Obama is a chief of state, there should be no demonstration of superiority or inferiority between them.

The day President Obama met with the emperor, I received a call from the lead US protocol officer in Japan with the grave report: "Capricia, the president bowed. What should we do?" There was really nothing we could do. I pulled up video of the incident to see for myself. He shook the emperor's hand when it was extended, held on—good form—and then bent at the waist, down, down, down. It was a cringeworthy moment. I felt mortified for him and was determined we would have no issues during his next leg of the trip.

When the delegation arrived in China, David Axelrod, the president's senior adviser, asked me, "Where were you?" I knew he was referring to the bow. He then laughed and said wryly, "Maybe we could say he dropped his keys and was looking for them." We both knew a media moment was about to hit. As expected, it made the next day's news: A *Los Angeles Times* writer quipped "How low will he go?" And conservative commentators used the moment to push the narrative of Obama as anti-American, with one blogger even calling the gesture "treasonous." This is one reason protocol matters—the importance of this first meeting between two great leaders was completely overshadowed by one misstep. In the president's defense, he was instinctively being respectful and humble. He's always shown reverence for his elders, a custom I believe he learned during his childhood in Indonesia. And the bow was probably received well by the emperor and not viewed as harshly by the Japanese, whose culture prizes deference to elders and humility in general. Behind closed doors, his "faux pas" may have helped discussions along. Against the backdrop of dramatic changes in the region, the United States was shoring up its Asian alliances. A show of humility in a country whose recent election had overturned an almost unbroken streak of fifty years of a single ruling party (and whose posture toward the United States was uncertain) likely enhanced the status of our country with the Japanese.

- **Curtsies.** Female Americans are not advised to curtsy for British royalty for the same reason that men should not bow . . . 1776.

Instead, a slight nod is standard for both men and women. That said, it's usually forgivable if you do curtsy. In fact, I have it on good authority that the Queen rarely gets offended with etiquette errors (unless you're generally being socially insensitive) and that it's the court historians who take offense.

One caveat: While it's not a problem if a private citizen can't resist a curtsy, visiting US government employees should not do so. Alas, not everyone in public service can refrain from the compulsion to curtsy. A former US diplomat curtsied so low before a visiting prince that it set off alarm bells in the media and in political circles, requiring damage control from the State Department, who had to issue an explanation that the curtsy didn't have political implications. The curtsy was meant out of great respect, but the optics did not play well in the press. UK citizens, on the other hand, usually curtsy to their sovereign, as do most other European countries where royals rule. (If you're curtsy curious, turn to page 372 for a how-to lesson.)

- **Kisses.** Perhaps nothing causes as much confusion for Americans as kiss logistics. Do you turn the other cheek? Do you actually put lips to cheek? (Usually not, especially if you are wearing lipstick.) Cheek kisses are generally reserved for social meetings, but in some countries, you may encounter them in a business setting, even upon the first meeting, and particularly if you're a woman.

  Peck primer: Start on the right—meaning your right cheek to theirs—except in Italy, Portugal, and Croatia, where you begin on the left. In business settings, you generally don't touch cheeks—you simply mimic the movement—whereas in social situations you may lightly touch cheeks. And there is no puckering or smooching sounds, nothing that's emotive or romantically suggestive. From there, it depends on the country as to how many rounds you go, and it's best to ask a local for guidance. Generally, in most Latin American countries, it's one cheek; in many Central European countries it's two; and in most Eastern European countries and Russia it's a triple-cheek kiss. Even within countries there are differences. In nations with diverse ethnic cultures, like Brazil, the number of kisses varies region by region and city by city. In the Middle East, kissing is not a common greeting in business, though it is practiced among family and friends (though not between members of the opposite sex). In Africa, cheek kissing is common, and it varies by country. For example, in South Africa, people may be more likely to kiss *on* the lips than the cheeks if they know each other well. (See page 375 for a more specific guide on kisses around the world.)

If this sounds confusing to you, it was to me, too! Luxembourg's ambassador to the United States would regularly rib me when he would come in for the third and I was caught unaware. "Capricia, remember, it's three," he would remind me in his deep voice. Getting a kiss wrong is usually forgiven; attempting nothing at all is the true offense, so go for it if you see your host moving in. But if they don't initiate it, err on the side of not making a move.

I've noticed in the last decade that cheek kisses have found their way into the American social language. I was hyperaware of this when I recently attended a social function after a root canal and felt my gum burn each time someone brushed the side of my face. An uptick in globe-trotting or perhaps a higher number of immigrants living in the United States might be the reason kissing is catching on. Or maybe people have figured out it's the most sophisticated way to disguise the fact that you can't remember someone's name.

2. The Business of Business Cards

South Korea isn't the only country where I had to closely monitor business card presentations between delegates. Many countries prize the art of the business card exchange. In Japan, the ritual is called *meishi koukan*, and it is as choreographed as a ballet and as important as the opening bell of the stock market. The Japanese—as well as the Koreans, Chinese, and Taiwanese—consider the business card a reflection of a person's self. Without a proper exchange, no business can occur, and if it's bungled, the relationship is in peril.

Immediately following the greeting, people of the highest rank exchange cards first, generally with the visitor presenting the card with both hands and the receiver accepting it with both, as well. (If you don't have both hands free, offer with your right and accept with your left, except in places such as India, Africa, and the Middle East, where the left hand is considered unclean.) It's a good idea to have cards printed with your information in the language of the host country on one side and your country's language on the other, and to use a heavier stock so your card is durable (but not so heavy it resembles a credit card). And bring *a lot* of them—you will be giving out many. When you receive a card, take a moment to look at both sides of it and express appreciation for being given one before carefully placing it in your suit breast pocket or your handbag.

3. Preliminaries and Pacing

- **Preliminaries.** Americans tend to separate their socializing from business. At meetings, we generally like to dive into the agenda and may view a lot of chitchat as a time drain. We're not alone in our directness. Germans, for example, are even less prone to small talk, preferring to stick to a strict agenda.

  In many other countries, however, small talk isn't so small—it's your main port of entry to the business landscape. So is sharing a beverage and light snack before talking profit margins. In Latin America, Brazil, the Middle East, India, and Africa there is skepticism about people who do not get to know one another. I so enjoy discussing cultural norms with the immensely talented staff at the Adrienne Arsht Latin America Center, including Director Jason Marczak, Associate Director Roberta Braga, and former Associate Director Katherine Pereira. From our discussions—and from my travels to Latin America—I've learned that personal relationships are key to doing business, and it's common for potential clients to invite you to their home before sealing the deal. Latin cultures are usually quite social, so you might talk about personal matters for an hour before business is brought up. And because many businesses in Latin America are family-owned, there is extra emphasis on family engagement. In return, once you have that trust, they take you at your word and transactions become less formal.

In most African countries, personal relationships are so key to doing business that you may want to hire a local guide to facilitate introductions, says J. Peter Pham, PhD, vice president and director of the Africa Center at the Atlantic Council, who also serves in the State Department as special envoy for the Great Lakes Region of Africa. "Being introduced to a business contact by someone who already has a relationship with them greases the skids." If you don't have a mutual contact or in-the-know guide, use the first meeting simply to get to know your counterpart and don't broach business unless your new acquaintance initiates the discussion, advises Dr. Pham. Wait until the second meeting to talk shop. As I traveled around the world, I began to appreciate these built-in, get-acquainted moments. They forced the pace to slow and enabled the players to relate to one another on a personal level. Think of social bonding not simply as an obligatory step but as a real opportunity to strengthen your relationship.

- **Pacing.** The timeline for business deals in other countries may be more prolonged than in the United States. Americans are the multitasking short-order waitresses serving dozens of rushed customers at lunch hour, whereas many of our international counterparts are the tuxedoed waiters calmly choreographing a three-hour dining experience. Our zippy pace works in part because most US businesses operate fairly independently from the government. In countries where the government is more involved in business—such as China, Turkey, some African nations, or the Middle East—it's common for deadlines to be set further down the road.

Japan in particular has a specific process, but not necessarily because of government red tape. In a society where consensus is the foundation of business, each team member weighs in, a practice called *nemawashi*. The process starts by informally making a proposal, then getting a lot of input from those involved, particularly those of higher rank—often through one-on-one conversations or small group meetings—and then solidifying support. *Nemawashi* protects the decision-making process of a business or organization from disagreement or lack of commitment. Hence, you often need multiple visits to show you are serious about the relationship and project. Similarly, in Latin America, where many businesses are family-owned, each family member may be consulted before a business decision is made.

A note about schedules: In America, it's common to hop onto work email at 10 p.m. or to check in with colleagues on weekends or vacation. In many other countries, such as Germany and Brazil, this is verboten. Workweek schedules also vary around the globe. In the Middle East, the workweek is generally Sunday to Thursday. In Spain, Greece, Italy, the Philippines, and some Latin American countries, they may observe "siesta" from 1 or 2 p.m. until 3 or 4 p.m., though the tradition is fading in urban areas.

4. Precedence and Hierarchy

My first state visit as chief of protocol was to China in 2009, a country where precedence and hierarchy should not be ignored. The meeting between President Obama and President Hu Jintao—their first as chiefs of state—was highly anticipated, with big issues to discuss, including trade imbalances and Iran's nuclear program. Staff from President Obama's advance team had arrived in Beijing early to pin down the particulars, and when I arrived a few days later, I found them despondent. The president's agenda still had too many TBDs on it. We only had a general blueprint for the visit but no specifics from the host country, such as which delegates were invited to key meetings and the format of the state dinner. This was unusual but I suspected there was a logical reason. I was fortunate to have with me Penny Price, a career protocol officer whose years of diplomatic expertise stood her in high esteem, especially in China. She had things as well in hand as possible, knowing that the Chinese would negotiate certain details only with me, as was customary for a culture that imposes great importance on rank. I asked Penny to request a meeting with our counterparts on my behalf and to advise that I would be available according to their schedule (a gesture of respect). She quickly booked the meeting.

Penny and I invited a US presidential advance person to accompany us. On our way to the meeting I explained to him: "Your first exchange is always the most important; you are setting the tone of the visit, confirming we will all work well together. It is important that we get to know one another, and understand why they declined your request to meet." We arrived at the government offices, and I started by asking the senior member of the Chinese protocol team—in the affirmative and without judgment—"What can we do on our side to get clarity about the visit? How can we assist in making this visit a success for us both?"

Without hesitating, she fully detailed the plans and could not have been more helpful. We understood from the exchange that their protocol team would not meet with our advance people because they didn't understand where they fit into the protocol hierarchy. Due to the high level of this visit, hierarchy was at the forefront, and a meeting with me, the chief, was essential. It was just as I suspected. We were in their country, so we followed their lead.

Hierarchy and precedence are central components in diplomacy. To get it wrong is an insult to the individual and the country they serve. Even in business interactions, ranking carries much more weight in other countries than in the United States. A person's title, stature, wealth, family connections, and age can determine the pecking order. It's important to learn the hierarchical ladder so you don't accidentally cross cultural norms. All this said, it's also critical to treat each person, from the busboy on up to the CEO, with the same cultural courtesies. My life's motto: You will never go wrong if you show grace and kindness to everyone. Here are the most common hierarchy protocols in international diplomacy and business negotiations:

- **Entering the room and greetings.** The senior-most person usually enters first followed by the next most senior person and so on. There are a few exceptions, oftentimes age-related. In Japan and Germany, for example, the eldest high-ranking person often walks in first. Greetings follow the same order. Usually the person of the highest status of the host country extends their hand first.

- **Titles.** In America, people are quick to go by a first-name basis after the initial introductions. The same is true in places like Brazil, Iceland, and Canada (once you're invited to do so). Not so in many other countries. In Germany, titles and last names are used throughout the meeting and possibly at subsequent meetings. In most Latin America countries, India, Africa, and the Middle East, titles are also important and seen as part of a person's identity. Using "Doctor" before the person's first or last name, for example, signals you value their education and expertise. "In African countries, you would never address someone by their first name, even after getting to know them, unless they give you permission," says Dr. Pham, who suspects this might have something to do with being a person of color. "It's my theory, based on years of working in Africa and with Africans, that because of the tragic history of colonialism and the fact that they have had to combat racism for so long, many may view overfamiliarity from new acquaintances as an indication of condescension if not outright disdain," says Dr. Pham, who always uses people's full titles, including "Engineer" and "Doctor" unless someone says, "Call me Naomi" or "Call me Peter."

- **Seating.** The most senior-ranking person from each country should sit at the center of the long edge of the table, not at the head, which is more often the case for social dinners. This allows him or her to be easily heard by everyone and vice versa. The next senior-most person should sit to the right and then to the left, and so on.

Interpreters usually sit next to the person they're speaking for. But if they're sharp—or if the visit is more of a social one—they can sit directly behind their client. (I discuss more about strategic seating in chapter 8; there's an art to it, and you should play musical chairs depending on your goals.)

- **Decision-making.** In countries where hierarchy is alive and well— such as India, China, and Russia—decisions are often made only by those at the top. In these places, it can benefit you to bring your senior staff to speed deals along. And in a country like Japan— despite their egalitarian and consensus-building decision-making process—hierarchy still plays a role in how business is conducted. Michelle Hulst, group vice president of Cloud Data at Oracle, uses hierarchy in her international dealings. "At Oracle, the culture is not hierarchical, but in Japan, we'd be at a disadvantage if we didn't respect levels of hierarchy," she explains. "Even though people on my team a few levels down could have handled negotiations with a prospect recently, I attended the initial meeting as a shortcut. If not, they may have thought we didn't see their value as a partner."

  Alternatively, in countries where personal relationships are important—such as in Latin America, Asia, and Africa—hierarchy might take a back seat to familiarity; try to bring someone who already has made inroads, or an even an embassy official who can be a go-between.

5. Religious Customs

Ask whether there are any adjustments for religious observances or national holidays. They will appreciate that you asked, especially if you drop some cultural knowledge to show that you're already tuned in. Query these issues, at minimum:

- **Fasting days.** Fasting is traditional for certain times in Judaism (including Yom Kippur), Christian and Christian Orthodox religions (especially during Lent, the forty days before Easter),

Buddhism (such as for full-moon days), and in Islam, particularly during Ramadan. The majority of Muslims fast for Ramadan, and many practitioners abstain from food and drink from sunrise until sundown, which means business breakfasts, lunches, and early dinners are out of the question. (This is also the case for most Muslims in the United States, where 80 percent report that they fast.) Muslims often dine with families and friends after sunset to break the fast—this meal is called iftar—so it's best not to schedule a post-sundown client dinner, either. (In DC, however, it's common for ambassadors to host "break the fast" dinners, and I'm happy to report they are insightful and delicious.) Even meetings during non-mealtimes are best saved for after Ramadan, if possible. If you absolutely must set a meeting, schedule it for as early in the day as possible, as workdays end early.

In the Office of Protocol, we paid special attention to the rules of Ramadan when we engaged with Muslim diplomats. Still, it could get confusing. In 2010, Ramadan fell during a September visit by Jordanian King Abdullah II bin Al Hussein, President Hosni Mubarak of Egypt, and President Mahmoud Abbas of the Palestinian Authority for the Middle East peace talks. We planned to serve them beverages and nuts and other nibbles at sundown. But the question was, *when* exactly? We didn't want to offer them food after an all-day fast at the wrong moment.

The leaders were in the White House Blue Room that evening with the Egyptian ambassador to the United States and other Egyptian dignitaries, where we were holding them before entering the Old Family Dining Room for dinner. Several waitstaff were hovering outside the room with the snacks on a plate, ready to go, waiting for my nod to enter. For twenty minutes I fielded whispered inquiries ("Should we serve them now?") and frantically checked with my sources, each of whom was giving me a different answer. I was told by the protocol team that the fast should break at 7:38 p.m., the US Naval Observatory's time for sundown. But an expert from the National Security Council who was with us announced it was 7:30. The Egyptian ambassador, Sameh Shoukry, an extraordinary diplomat whose advice I never regretted following—and who was later appointed foreign minister—offered yet a third time, 7:40, with an explanation. I went with his time, as he shared that the Egyptian embassy, as do most Muslim countries' embassies, has an official iftar time so they can counsel others throughout the country who call for the precise time.

- **Dress.** Dress like the locals when visiting places of worship, something you may be invited to do as part of a cultural tour. Loose clothing that covers most of your body (shoulders, upper legs, chest, neck, midriff) is expected in most houses of worship. To enter a mosque, women should wear a head covering, such as a scarf. Men may sometimes be asked to cover their heads as well, and similar standards would apply in a traditional Jewish synagogue. A head covering—or at the very least a shoulder covering—may also be recommended for women for certain Catholic churches. *Travel tip:* A large scarf is a must-pack for women and can serve so many purposes, including covering the head, shoulders, and arms or as a waist wrap or sari, which may be required for certain Hindu and Buddhist temples. In mosques, shoes will need to be removed, so heed Mom's advice and check to make sure your socks are without holes before you leave the hotel.

6. The Diplomatic Rainbow

Specific colors hold different meanings in some countries, so pack accordingly. Red means passion and power in the United States; in China it signals luck, joy, and celebration. In America white is worn for weddings; in many Asian countries white is worn at funerals. You can see how paying attention to color when it comes to clothing, decor (such as flowers), and gifts can boost or torpedo a relationship.

First Ladies and royalty know this well. Michelle Obama regularly used color as a tip of the hat to a country. During the 2009 state visit from Indian Prime Minister Manmohan Singh and his wife, the First Lady brilliantly pulled off a saffron-colored brocade dress (saffron is one of the hues in the Indian flag). Catherine, the Duchess of Cambridge (Kate Middleton), is also known for colorful fashion diplomacy, wearing just-right colors and prints on international visits, such as the deep green sparkling gown she wore on her 2019 visit to Pakistan, a nod to the green in the Pakistani flag. (She also chose a dress bearing a poppy print on a trip to Bhutan in 2016—the blue poppy is the country's national flower.)

Most presidents are also very color- and fashion-conscious. President Obama wore a traditional Indonesian batik shirt in teal, red, white, and black—dominant colors in their culture—during his 2011 visit to the country. (Not only was it a tip of the hat to his hosts but likely reminded him of his childhood there, and of his mother, who wore and collected batik pieces.) President Clinton was all about ties, sometimes matching the color of his necktie to a country's flag colors and drawing attention to it, asking us all to take note: "You like my tie? You know what it means?" On a trip to Denmark in 1997—the first sitting US president to visit that country—he donned a bright red tie in tribute to Denmark's red-and-white flag. And he wore a vivid blue tie to Greece in 1999 in keeping with their flag's blue hue.

Color IQ can even help keep your business out of the red. When United Airlines took over Pan Am's Pacific routes in the mid-1980s, they initiated a first-class service out of Hong Kong and gave white carnations to personnel and passengers. Unfortunately, in that part of the world, as I've already noted, white flowers symbolize death and misfortune—not the concepts United wished to emphasize on its flights! The airline quickly switched to red carnations, which carry much more positive connotations in Hong Kong and the surrounding region. (Turn to page 377 for advice on dressing in flying colors.)

7. Personal Space

I'll never forget the classic *Seinfeld* episode where Elaine's boyfriend stands uncomfortably within an inch of Jerry's face while talking, leading Jerry to dub him a "close talker," and giving viewers a name for space-invading conversationalists. In 2014, New York City launched a campaign to discourage subway riders from "manspreading" (sitting with knees splayed far apart) in an effort to create more room on crowded trains. Personal space is, well, personal. I've seen presidents lean away instinctively in conversation with another head of state when nose to nose. Americans like their space. We practically have a dotted line indicating "do not cross" where our zone begins and someone else's ends. In other countries, there are no such boundaries, resulting in an intimacy that can feel awkward—even aggressive—to Americans, never mind that the intent is to express friendship.

Knowing cultural space limits can help you avoid sending the wrong message or misinterpreting someone else's. A fascinating 2017 study published in the *Journal of Cross-Cultural Psychology* offers guidelines for wiggle room: Researchers found that the amount of space people were comfortable with when speaking to a stranger ranged from an intimate thirty inches (in Argentina) to a far-off fifty-three inches (in Romania). In general, people in the Middle East, Eastern Europe, and Asia prefer more distance, whereas those in South America, the Mediterranean, Russia, and Ukraine like to keep things close. Countries in North America, Northern Europe, South America, Africa, and Indonesia fall somewhere in between.

The best gauge: Tune in to space cues sent by your host. If you feel alarmingly close, don't pull back sharply, which can come off as rude. Instead, do what I dub the "Hmm . . . Step Dance": Shift slowly from side to side as you are listening, moving back ever so slightly as you say "hmm" to acknowledge a point. No one will be the wiser.

8. Facial Expressions, Gestures, and Body Language

Most of the time, President Obama's long legs were an asset, giving him a towering, commanding presence. But they proved a liability in the Middle East and Asia. In this area of the world, showing the bottom of your shoe is an insult, and to sit with long crossed legs and keep your soles out of sight takes agility. President Obama tried to honor this practice, but his legs were so long that it was hard to do. "I'm trying, Capricia," he'd say when I'd gently remind him. Middle Eastern and Asian cultures consider the bottom of the shoe to be unclean and lowly, since the sole is the lowest part of the body. (It was no accident that when an Iraqi journalist wanted to express displeasure at President George W. Bush during a press conference in Baghdad in 2008, he threw a couple of shoes at him.)

In addition to sole goals, the following are the nonverbal cues I advised dignitaries to keep in mind for foreign visits:

- **Smiles.** Smile and the world smiles with you, right? Not always. One of Russia's most well-known proverbs loosely translates to "Laughing for no reason is a sign of stupidity." It's best to ask someone in the country you're visiting how to approach smiling, but there are some general rules to follow.

  In most Western, democratic, industrialized countries, a smiling person is seen as honest and friendlier and more intelligent than someone who isn't smiling, research finds. However, in countries where a lot of corruption exists a smile does not increase a person's perceived honesty, according to a study by social psychologist Kuba Krys at the Polish Academy of Sciences. In addition, where the economy and future may be unpredictable and people are less comfortable taking risks, smiling can make you seem less intelligent, explains Krys.

  (Flip to page 379 to see where in the world grinning is winning.)

- **Gestures.** In 1992, President George H. W. Bush visited Australia and held up two fingers to make a V peace sign—palm facing inward—as his limousine drove through the streets of Canberra. Without a word, he unintentionally offended every onlooker he passed. Down under, a peace sign with the palm toward the body is the equivalent of giving someone the middle finger in the US. The same is true in the UK, New Zealand, and Ireland. A thumbs-up sign in Iraq translates to "Up yours!" The okay sign is *not* okay in France, where it is commonly used to signify "zero." If you aren't fluent in a country's sign language, it's best to be hands off and use words instead. Be careful with emojis, too, if you're texting a colleague. (For a handy round-the-world guide, turn to page 375.)

- **Body Language.** That grand sweep of the arm you use at staff meetings to make a point? It can backfire in Japan, where large movements with the hands and arms can be seen as impolite. Sitting with your legs or ankles crossed in the United States is good form, but doing so in many Asian and Middle Eastern cultures can be seen as too informal—it is preferable to sit with feet flat and legs together. Nodding yes actually signals no in certain countries, such as Greece, Albania, and Bulgaria. The best way to model appropriate body language is to study your host and mimic his or her movements.

MICRO-CULTURES WITHIN US BUSINESSES

You don't need to cross an international border to encounter a foreign culture. Each business within your home country—even departments with the same company—are mini-worlds with unwritten protocols: meeting and seating etiquette, dress code, body language, office lingo, and organizational culture. When you embark on a new job or workplace collaboration, it's critical to take the temperature and acclimate. The negotiation begins the minute you step off the elevator. Remember, people will thin-slice you based on your appearance and your facial expressions. They will note whether you're dressed for their office culture. And they will certainly recall if you flub a greeting or their name or title. A savvy executive can gain the upper hand by decoding the cultural nuances, and an assistant can move up the ranks more quickly by learning the office shorthand right away.

I did *not* do any of this in my first internship while in law school, and it cost me a job. I was prim and proper and walked the line, appearing only when asked for. It seemed that in a buttoned-up law firm, this was the way to go. But what I'd neglected to do was leave my cubicle and get the vibe of the office. Although it was a conservative Cleveland law firm, the office culture was more collaborative and casual than I gave it credit for. I became the ghost intern, the one who was never seen. I didn't build relationships or participate in an active way with the associates who could have placed me on cases and projects that would have helped me stand out to the hiring board. Not surprisingly, I did not get a job offer.

These are the elements I advise clients to suss out as they begin a new business relationship or position in order to make the right impression:

- **Seating.** Where do the assistants sit relative to the senior staff? If the assistant or intern is in the corner taking notes and not at the main table, the company may rely heavily on hierarchy.

- **Meeting MO.** Who runs the meeting? Is it always the boss or is the baton passed, depending on the agenda? Are agendas prescribed and followed strictly, or are they looser, allowing anyone to pose questions that are tangentially related?

- **Dress Code.** Do casual Fridays allow a switch from a suit to khakis and to ditch heels for flats? Or is it carte blanche to wear ripped jeans and Birkenstocks? Do staffers who meet with clients have a different dress code than behind-the-scenes folks? A good rule of thumb: Model your dress after one of the senior-most people in the office, since she is an ambassador for the company and an example to others.

- **Language.** Do people use colloquial phrases and share personal stories? Or are meetings and interactions focused and all business? Is everyone on a first-name basis?

- **Office Setup.** What does the decor and layout say about the culture? Open offices, with cubes or communal tables, tend to be more informal and team-based than offices where most folks have offices. Brightly colored walls—or chalkboard or cork walls—reflect a company that values creativity. A company that displays products from years gone by or portraits of founders and CEOs signals an emphasis on tradition and history.

Best Resources

There's only so much you can glean by observation, so you'll also want to actively seek out information by reading the employee handbook and contacting the HR Department. In addition to the usual suspects (dress code, vacation policy, sick days), you should bring up these three issues when meeting with HR or your direct manager:

1. **How should I address the CEO?** Some bosses prefer Mr. Mrs., or Ms., whereas others want to be called by their first name (even by interns) or a nickname.

2. **What are the office hours and schedule?** If there's a strict schedule, arrive a bit early (figure out when your manager arrives and then get there fifteen minutes earlier) and stay until your manager leaves, if possible.

3. **What are the metrics of success at this company/in my department?** Find out what the company values and how you can chart your trajectory to meet those definitive marks.

Another savvy way to decode office culture: Ask a local. Take an assistant or colleague out to lunch and start to build bridges of your own. Don't be afraid to query things in the early days, when it's expected that you'll have questions as the new girl or guy. The one caveat I'd offer: You don't want to reveal your inexperience to someone who might use it for their own benefit down the road, so start with innocuous basics like "What's the lunch culture around here?" until you build a relationship with someone you trust to ask questions that tread into office politics ("What's the best way to get on Sally's calendar for a last-minute request?").

When I left the White House in 2001 and entered the private sector for the first time, I worked for a media start-up helmed by three tenacious and accomplished women: Toni Cook Bush, who is now the executive VP and global head of government affairs for News Corp; Sophia Collier, who founded Soho Natural Soda and is an investment wizard and incredible artist; and venture capitalist Chula Reynolds, one of the most clever and insightful people I know. I felt like a fish out of water the first few weeks, learning the ins and outs of private corporate culture (though the hustle of a start-up environment was familiar—it felt like the high-adrenaline pace of a political campaign). There weren't a lot of us on staff, so we all chipped in with basic tasks. At a meeting, someone asked me to compile an Excel spreadsheet for a region of the country we were targeting. "Absolutely, no problem!" was my response. My inside voice said, How the &*$# do I create an Excel spreadsheet? I hadn't dealt much with computers in my government job. I realized then that the younger staffers who had made life so wonderful for me in the White House had also been a crutch, as I'd relied on them to work their tech magic for me. (To this day I advise clients to learn tech skills themselves to keep up instead of always farming it out to assistants.)

I asked a lovely woman, Linda Rickman, whose office was next to mine, a few probing questions—like how big the font size should be—until she graciously offered to walk me through the process. It was quickly apparent that Linda was the kind of colleague who had my back, and I in turn helped her build relationships with clients using my protocol toolbox. We shared talents and information, and the whole company benefited. I was grateful that there was a culture of collaboration in this company.

escalating influence and violence of the drug cartel; and to refine immigration policies for fair treatment of Mexican nationals. Arizona had recently passed a law that gave state police broad authority to question anyone they suspected was in the country illegally, and made it a criminal offense if a person was not carrying his or her immigration documents at all times (which President Calderón viewed as a human rights abuse). Media cameras were trained on the podium to capture the arrival ceremony and beam it out to millions worldwide. This is the moment all visiting leaders hope for: to stand next to the president of the United States with the White House in the background. The interpreters, who serve as the voices of their leaders, were stationed at two podiums a few feet behind the main stage. President Calderón had chosen to give his opening remarks in Spanish, as most leaders deliver their public remarks in their native tongue for their country's national media.

President Calderón has a lighthearted side to him, but today he was thoughtful and serious. He knew that the relationship between these two old friends—the United States and the United Mexican States (the official name of the country)—needed an exchange of words that were a deliberate affirmation of their commitments to each other and to the world. He began his remarks with a friendly tone, even briefly greeting everyone in English, but after a few sentences his tone dropped a bit. His interpreter that day, an experienced man who was standing in for President Calderón's regular translator, started off shaky, skipping a few verbs, transposing key phrases, and leaving uncomfortably long pauses after the president spoke. Normally the interpretation happens instantly after each phrase and I noted that President Calderón was taking sips of water during the gaps, I suspect to manage the silences. I understand Spanish rather well and could immediately tell that President Calderón's remarks, meant to convey warmth and honor, were being lost in translation. At first, I figured it might be nerves—there's no bigger stage than the White House, and even veteran interpreters can succumb to the pressure.

But as he continued, it went from bumpy to train wreck. President Calderón's clear, concise words—which at this stage were centered on the sensitive topic of immigration—came out jumbled, delivering a different message and tone from the one intended. His carefully selected and eloquent remarks became a mishmash of words and ideas that failed to communicate key concepts, such as to which group of people the president was referring:

> **PRESIDENT CALDERÓN** (proper translation of Spanish): I know that we share the interest in promoting dignified, legal, and orderly living conditions to all migrant workers. Many of them, despite their significant contribution to the economy and to the society of the United States, still live in the shadows and, occasionally, as in Arizona, they even face discrimination.

> **INTERPRETER** (spoken translation): We can do so with a community that will promote a dignified life and an orderly way for both our countries, who are, some of them, still living here in the shadows with such laws as the Arizona law that is placing our people to face discrimination.

I saw the interpreter struggling, red-faced, and mopping the sweat off his brow. I then looked to President Obama's interpreter, Patricia (Patsy) Arizu, chief interpreter for the US State Department's Office of Language Services, a trusted and long-serving linguistic genius, and gave her an expression that said, "What?!" I could see that she was anxious and wanted to jump in to help, but she knows better than anyone that the voice of the president cannot be interpreted by anyone other than that country's designated interpreter. President Calderón, to his credit, continued but he was clearly upset. Because I always stood behind the US president, I could not see President Calderón's face. But upon watching the video of the remarks later, I could see him grimacing with each interpreted sentence, looking down, slightly shaking his head and shifting back and forth. His English is quite good, and he surely caught every mangled phrase.

We were all stunned. This was a man who was at the top of his profession. I caught a glimpse of Mrs. Obama, who also got that this was going brilliantly wrong. The First Lady Margarita Zavala, President Calderón's wife, was standing next to Mrs. Obama, whispering in her ear, and I can only imagine what she was saying. Immediately after the ceremony, I consulted the Mexican ambassador, Arturo Sarukhan, a well-respected diplomat and a close enough friend that I could speak frankly with him.

He too was shocked, though he suggested that perhaps the issue was a combination of opening-ceremony jitters and, most important, the fact that the interpreter hadn't had the opportunity to review the speech beforehand. (Most translators receive the text well in advance to review it. We were told later that President Calderón's aide, who hailed from academia and *not* government, and who was unaware of the processes, handed the speech directly to President Calderón upon his arrival at the White House and neglected to give a copy to the interpreter.)

This was not the moment President Calderón envisioned for himself or his country. As a visiting leader, you are on the grandest stage in the world, and you get only one shot at making the right impression, one that lives on in the historical record. The future prospects for the people of your nation are at stake. The marred interpretation began the day on the wrong note, an awkward unintentional misunderstanding that caused chaos and that had to be resolved between the leaders, the delegations, and most important, the press before we moved to the bilateral discussions.

President Obama and Secretary Clinton asked me to find out what was going on and even offered to help in any way they could. I assured them that Patsy and I and Ambassador Sarukhan were on the case, but also reminded them that this was really Mexico's issue and there was only so much we as Americans could do. Ambassador Sarukhan, who was also a close advisor of President Calderón's, recommended to the presidents that they conduct the important private bilaterals in English, assuring them that he would step in for any technical translation. The Mexican interpreter continued on for a few less important exchanges, only to create confusion every time he opened his mouth. In every instance his jumbled words introduced an unnecessary complication into an already intricate exchange.

Ultimately, it was President Calderón himself who saved the day—or the night, rather. By the time of the after-dinner entertainment (Beyoncé!), he'd had enough. He wanted his final remarks to be clearly understood. While standing next to President Obama and thanking him for the privileged visit and thanking Beyoncé for the performance, he paused with a look that said, "Here we go again," and quickly switched to English. He spoke perfectly, and finally his words were his own.

The Associated Press called the Mexican interpreter's opening re-marks "a halting and grammatically incoherent English translation," and the Mexican delegation issued a mea culpa. (Right after the open-ing statement debacle, we worked with the ambassador and the White House NSC to hold all press statements until President Calderón's were properly translated into English by the Mexican embassy before releas-ing them to the press.) And while the translation may have changed on the written page, the video and moment live on forever.

WORDS OF WISDOM

There are many effective ways to leverage your communications so that you can make as positive and persuasive an impression as possible—no inter-preters needed. When you're trying to win someone over, my first piece of advice is to say it, don't "send" it. Pick up the phone, launch the video con-ferencing software, or set up a face-to-face meeting instead of emailing or messaging. Making the case verbally—and ideally getting a visual of your colleague's face to decode expressions—gives you an edge. Face-to-face is best, but Face(time)-to-Face(time) is a close second. Having an audience, research shows, improves your verbal performance, particularly if you've already mastered what you have to say (practice!). (*Pro tip:* Behave as if it's an in-person, private meeting in *all* respects—look the part and make sure your background is appropriate. If you need to reference written material, consider placing it on the wall behind the monitor or phone so your viewer isn't looking at the top of your head as you glance down. If references are electronic, keep them as open documents on your device.)

Even a simple phone call can give you a leg up. Research shows that when job recruiters *hear* an elevator pitch about a candidate versus read-ing the same content, they will judge the person to be more thoughtful and intelligent when the pitch is spoken. "The voice conveys the quali-ties of being rational and thoughtful better than the written word," says Nicholas Epley, PhD, who has studied how people make judgments about others. (Of course, there are some legitimate reasons for using email: It's a written record of the correspondence, and with one click you can send your thoughts to dozens of recipients. But it's best reserved for business-as-usual tasks rather than decisive moments.)

IN THE OFFICE OF PROTOCOL—and within the culture of the State Department—we were well aware of the power of voice and in-person exchanges. I learned from our assistant chief of protocol for management, the incredibly experienced Rosemarie Pauli—a multidecade foreign service officer who successfully managed Richard Holbrooke as his longtime chief of staff (he was one of the most brilliant but unconventional diplomats)—to make my cases to management for additional support and personnel in person. After one meeting in which it was clear we needed to staff up, she instructed me, "Capricia, it will be received well that you, the head of the department, personally request the additions instead of sending me to make the request or sending it via written order." So I walked miles (yes, miles!) on the red line (the State Department is so huge that you have to follow color-coded hallways to the correct section of the building) that led to their department and sat in their outer office until they had five precious minutes to hear my case. Rosemarie was 100 percent right: the face-to-face allowed me to emphasize points that would be lost in an email. And I am certain that the in-person meeting underscored that I had a genuine need, and that this wasn't just a dashed-off request. My wish was granted.

Our officers also became skilled in ways to speak to diplomats that conveyed accuracy. One golden rule we always followed: *Be as specific as possible, confirm understanding, and repeat if necessary.* In diplomacy, language that is vague can cause confusion, which can lead to a disconnect and misinterpretations. Gladys Boluda, a remarkable diplomat in our office whom I turned to often for solid counsel—and whom I miss dearly since her recent passing—was one of the most intentional speakers. While observing her discussions with foreign delegations and ambassadors, at first I thought she was being repetitive due to language differences; but it was for clarity. She was also this way when training our protocol officers for what is called "duty," aka being on call for any diplomatic corps emergency involving law enforcement. In these situations, a lack of specificity could mean the difference between being detained in the country or expelled immediately: Diplomats are granted certain privileges and immunity status when they first enter the country, depending largely upon the position they will hold, and not all of them enjoy the same status. Gladys was very particular that each duty officer understood *exactly* how to respond to calls with specificity as to the level of immunity of the diplomat in question.

This degree of detail and repetition is especially important for international clientele. In some countries, accidental misinformation and misunderstandings could be interpreted as a purposeful attempt to embarrass them. Of course, we also had to carefully weigh our desire to communicate specific information against our need to keep certain details private, especially when those details were privileged or still up in the air (you never want to jump the gun and have to backpedal). There were standard phrasings and techniques we used—nothing nuanced or clever—to communicate our positions clearly and smartly. To this day, I rely on these fallbacks:

- **When you don't know the answer to a question:** I never responded to the president, secretary, or anyone for that matter with, "I don't know," which has always seemed a lazy and clumsy answer to me. "I don't know" simply states the obvious and emphasizes your ignorance without conveying any intention to track down the intel. With some hustle and a bit of time, I believe that I can always provide information to satisfy the query. So instead, I say, "Stand by, I'm attempting to gather the full information for you." For the president, of course, I went into high-octane mode, quickly leaving the room and finding someone to assist, then reporting back immediately once I had the answer. For my counterparts, depending on the situation, I might say, "This is what we know so far. As things progress I'll update you immediately."

- **When you're asking for information:** Again, precision and repetition are your friends. I am as specific as I can be when asking for details, down to the nitty-gritty. Yes, it can drive people crazy, but because so much gets lost in the broad strokes, it's worth getting micro. This is also an instance where writing out your requests helps immensely; I love a bulleted list so I can go over the written information verbally with my colleague, point by point. When you're both reviewing the same document together, there's no chance something will get overlooked or misinterpreted. I will then repeat the most important details for added emphasis. If answers are slow to come, I repeat my request but with a variance so as not to annoy but to instead send the signal of urgency. I alternate from verbal to written, and I attempt always to send my request at the top of the morning so it's the first item of their day to manage, which perhaps allows them the next few hours to resolve and respond (the benefit of being a 5 a.m. riser).

- **When you have to say *no*:** *No* one likes to hear *no*. I attempt never to utter the word. In diplomacy especially, the concept of reciprocity and equal treatment is at play, so I always weighed the results of a *no* with future consequences. But as much as I try to satisfy people's requests, it's not always possible. In my position as chief of protocol—as a bridge between the diplomatic corps and the White House and the State Department—I would often field urgent requests from ambassadors for changes to the logistics of a visit. When I knew the request would be tough to satisfy, I softened the landing: First, I eased the anxiety of an urgent ask by affirming their request—"I understand what you're asking and appreciate the gravity of your request." Then I explained the many steps I'd taken to try to facilitate their ask so they understood the process and that I was truly trying to assist. "Your Excellency, please understand that I have reached out to A, B, and even C, communicating your request with the utmost urgency." I would then attempt to provide some solution, no matter how small. If they pushed, I laid it all at the feet of (no surprise) the protocol: "I understand the urgency, but due to the process, I am unable to fulfill your ask at this time." If your *no* is a hard one, it's important to make expectations clear, not gray. Leaving an opening will only layer their current anxiety with more confusion, frustration, and ultimately anger when they are met with the actual denial.

• **When you get a *no:*** When you are negotiating on behalf of the president of the United States, you do not accept a *no* right off the bat . . . if ever. To me, almost everything is possible, especially if I've built up a relationship with someone. The first thing I say is, "Let's review." A review of the facts leading to this moment gives me an opportunity to get a read on what is truly preventing a *yes*. Then I can offer a solution they may not have thought of. ("I see, that is a challenge. What about . . .") All the while I make sure to commiserate with *their* predicament: "I understand how challenging this is for you, and I appreciate your making these efforts." This lets them know I value the relationship, and it keeps a strong bond for future interactions. Negotiations are often a long game, and many times after handling a hard *no* gracefully, I would have a special request satisfied surprisingly quickly.

There were times, of course, when I simply could not accept the "I regret to inform you." At the G20 summit in Mexico in 2012, President Obama sent word from the plenary session that he needed a room for a last-minute multilateral with several leaders of the EU. I looked at my watch and knew I had ten fleeting minutes to find an appropriate space. The standard process is to request a room through the summit organizer, but I knew that would never work this late in the game, as all spaces had already been allocated. And while we had a small room for one-on-one bilaterals on hold just in case, this was a multilateral that had to be big enough for the leaders and their plus-one (but not so big that it prevented a collaborative air). I immediately found the accomplished Ambassador Alfredo Rogerio Pérez Bravo, my friend and director general of protocol for Mexico, who regrettably said after a quick check, "I'm sorry, Capricia, nothing is available." In these moments of near desperation, I relied on determination and clarity, stating the situation plainly (without revealing the particulars) and calmly but with an edge to punctuate the urgency: "Please understand the critical nature of my request."

Because I had a good relationship with Ambassador Bravo, I added, "This is a huge favor, and . . . I need it in ten minutes." Even though I couldn't reveal to him who the meeting was with, he got the message. We raced around the conference center, playing musical meeting rooms until we landed a spot (Singapore was willing to give up a room for a meeting that was unlikely to materialize—and if it did, I had our alternative room to offer). After a few exchanges of flags, I quickly raced to the door of the plenary and guided the president and other leaders to the room without their ever knowing the anxiety of the acquisition. In the rare instance when I lost the fight, I suspected a power play was at work, and I filed it away for the future—reciprocity can be hard core in diplomacy.

- **When you have to apologize:** I follow a simple formula: I start with "I'm sorry," followed by the thing I am sorry for, followed by an explanation. "I'm sorry this didn't meet your standards. Due to security measures we had to coordinate it this way." Apologies go over much better if they're blanketed and not parsed. No one wants to hear the "but" after "I'm sorry," which leaves the impression your mea culpa is half-hearted. Sometimes, when the apology is more personal, I'll add "I understand that this doesn't change the situation, but I want you to know how sorry I am." A couple of caveats: Women tend to say "I'm sorry" for everything under the sun, perhaps not realizing that an unnecessary apology subtly conveys a lack of confidence. I am guilty of this infraction, too, and my dear friend and businesswoman extraordinaire Adrienne Arsht will often ask me, as a reminder to nix the habit, "What are you sorry for?" to which I have to admit, "Well, nothing, I guess!" On the other end of the spectrum: Don't throw someone else under the bus if the buck stops with you. In diplomacy, we were all working for Team USA, and a bad mark on any one of us reflected poorly on all of us. Plus, when you pass the buck, you imply that you are not to be trusted. I watched people at the highest levels refuse to take responsibility, and I always logged it, thinking, "I can't fully rely on that person."

In addition to the phrasings above, there are three other language "laws" that I adhere to for crystal-clear communication:

1. **Avoid slang and euphemisms.** Clarity is your North Star, and trendy language can take you off course fast. This goes double for the use of abbreviations and emojis when texting with a business contact, who may not be plugged in to the latest parlance or who has a personal pet peeve against smiley faces and the okay sign (which, as you may recall, doesn't mean okay in every culture). Using standard language is especially critical when dealing with international colleagues, who are much less likely to know jargon, let alone the meaning of cultural sayings and proverbs. Someone I've always admired in this regard is Supreme Court Justice Sonia Sotomayor. One would think that a Supreme Court judge would use language that is exclusively lofty, but her word choices are deliberately relatable and understandable to anyone. Whether she's speaking to children about the importance of books in her life, to a Senate confirmation committee, or to NPR listeners, this Bronx-born native Spanish speaker and Yale Law School graduate works to keep her language inclusive, speaking and writing clearly and slowly enough so that no one need question her meaning. (In interviews she talks about how she retaught herself how to write in college after several professors pointed out grammatical flaws in her papers.) Likewise, beware of misusing jargon or unfamiliar sayings. I've butchered millennial-speak on several occasions, as my son has informed me. For the longest time I thought that *cringe* was a compliment, in the same way that *sick* is used to say something is cool ("Wow, that car is sick!"). When I saw him wearing a shirt I liked, I'd say, "That's so cringe'!'" Until one day, when he set me straight, informing me it's really just an abbreviation for cringeworthy. I scrolled back through all the times I'd used it incorrectly and died a thousand mom deaths.

2. **Don't swear.** I've had the wonderful experience of working with many young people in my government positions across different decades, and I've noticed how trends were reflected in their manner

of speech. In the last ten years, I've regrettably watched as language has become crude and more informal; f-bombs drop with regularity. While I do not profess to being a stranger to four-letter words myself, a mouth like a sailor makes you sound vulgar, and it's jarring for the listener. I grew up with a lovely neighbor, Mr. Louis Perelman, a lawyer, who would give me a word a week to work into my vocabulary. We talked language a great deal—he explained to me that his word choices needed to be precise in his line of work. I'll never forget his advice: Don't be lazy with language. (Great advice for situations that go beyond the realm of swearing.) There is always a better word to describe a moment or feeling than swear words.

3. **Be mindful of acronyms.** The names of government agencies can be five or six words long, so many employees use acronyms as a linguistic shortcut. Abbreviations are handy when you know what they stand for, and utterly bewildering if you don't. I always waited for it . . . and there it was: the inevitable blank look on a new hire's face when they were in a meeting where acronyms peppered the entire conversation. I *know* their inner voice was screaming, "What the heck are they talking about!" I felt their pain. On my first day as First Lady Hillary Clinton's personal assistant, in 1993, I was given the exciting task of delivering her beaded-and-lace inaugural gown to the White House from the Blair House, where the president-elect and First Lady typically stay the night before the inauguration. I figured I'd just walk across the street and drop it off. I'd been told by a colleague that the way to get through the security gate was to "use waves." Ah, waves. How quaint, I thought.

I made my way to the main security gate at the White House and waved at the security guard, expecting him to open up and let me through. He ignored me. Odd, I thought. So I waved again. He continued to ignore me. I was so exhausted from all the preparations that, against all reason, I continued to wave. (The thought bubble over the agent's head surely read, "Crazy lady with a gown!! This is priceless!") This went on for several minutes until a friend I knew from the campaign, Michael "Mike" Lufrano, walked by on the inside of the gate. "Capricia, what are you doing?" he asked. "I'm waving so they will let me in," I replied. He then explained that WAVES stood for Workers and Visitors Entry System, a prescreened list of approved guests that were given automatic entry. I was mortified, as I should have been: How could I have possibly thought that White House security would give entrance to a waving stranger? Mike then spoke to the guard, who instructed him on getting my date of birth and Social Security number so I could be "WAVED IN"—per protocol—and deliver the gown in time for Hillary to wear it on that important first night. Thereafter, I would fess up when I didn't understand what people were talking about. During my first months as chief of protocol, I started meetings and conversations by explaining, "I don't speak 'state,'" as in State Department lingo. That was the person's cue to spell out the indecipherable verbal shortcuts that peppered their conversations.

OPEN TO INTERPRETATION

Clients who do business internationally often ask: How will interpretation be managed? The level and nature of the exchange—casual, one-on-one, a large gathering, a televised event with open press—determines the type of interpretation, or if any is needed at all. I am an enormous proponent of having some type of interpretation when possible. Generally, for situations that are more introductory and social in nature, a shared interpreter is fine. Once a meeting is underway, however, you don't want to rely on someone else's interpreter to be your voice. You need someone who is speaking exclusively for you and reliably conveying the meaning of the exchanges.

I learned to prioritize interpretation the moment the meeting went on the calendar. I wanted to know how (simultaneous, consecutive, whisper, headset) and who (ours, theirs, both). Early in my tenure, much to the regret of our interpreters and protocol officers—especially me—

interpretation was a last-minute thought, especially when meeting with allied nations, such as France. I recall one engagement when President Obama was scheduled to have a casual meal with President Nicolas Sarkozy of France in the United States. President Sarkozy's interpreter had worked in the Foreign Ministry for years, and she stated that she was perfectly comfortable interpreting for both leaders, a gracious offer indeed, but I knew it wasn't advisable. Unfortunately, we were all already in the elevator on the way to the meal, and when I offered to race to get our US interpreter, I was stopped by a presidential aide, informing me that President Obama was fine using the French interpreter. I had no choice but to let it go: it wasn't fair to ask President Obama to reverse course or wait, as I should have taken care of this well in advance. But from then on, I became an annoyance, raising interpretation at every one of our Situation Room meetings when planning domestic or international visits. Our interpreters so appreciated the extra attention being paid to their services, as it's not in their nature to step up and insist on being heard, in great part because they are trained not to insert their opinions in the course of their work and to recede into the background (luckily, I have no problem with that). (Interesting factoid: There is more than one room in the Situation Room, the highly secured, ground-floor area behind the West Executive Office door. Once you're buzzed in and have dropped all your electronics in a compartment—phones can operate as a mic for eavesdroppers even if they're turned off—you go to one of several rooms where your meeting is happening. The big Situation Room that's often shown in movies or the press is usually reserved for presidential meetings with lots of people from a myriad of departments.)

It's even more imperative to have your own interpreter with countries where the relationship is rocky or leaning toward adversarial. When I saw on CNN that former Secretary of State Rex Tillerson met without an interpreter with Turkey's President Recep Tayyip Erdoğan, I was surprised. The 2018 bilateral to discuss growing tensions in NATO and the conflict in Syria lasted over three hours, and Tillerson allowed Turkey's foreign minister to translate for him the entire time. Not only was it a breach in US protocol, but it was poor diplomacy, and could have tipped the scales in Turkey's favor, giving them the power pivot. Although Tillerson reportedly had established what he described as a strong working relationship with President Erdoğan, it seemed from an outside perspective that there was no way Tillerson could know whether his words were being translated accurately, and vice versa.

TONE CONTROL

I've never loved my natural speaking voice, which to me has always sounded flat and staccato; as a result I've worked hard to speak in a more serene, buttery manner. My vocal muse is a profoundly revered woman named Alexis Herman, who was secretary of labor for President Clinton and is now on various boards and CEO of New Ventures. She has this wonderfully clear and welcoming way of speaking. Her word choice is intentional and coherent in meaning, and she speaks with a smooth tone that has a slightly lower-than-normal register. I noticed that people listened to her intently, so I tried to adopt her cadence.

Modeling my voice on someone like Alexis seems like a good idea: According to a recent study by Quantified Communications (QC), a behavioral science company that works with CEOs to improve their communication skills, participants who listened and watched financial media experts were more influenced by the speaker's *tone* and demeanor than by the content of their speech. In fact, voice quality accounted for 23 percent of a listener's perception, whereas content accounted for only 11 percent (demeanor accounted for a lot, too—more on that later). Speakers whose voices were smooth and strong were rated more genuine, emotionally connected, and intelligent than those with weak, breathy voices. "People spend a lot of time preparing the content of what they will say and not enough on how they will say it," says Noah Zandan, QC's cofounder and CEO.

One trick to avoid sounding harsh and to keep your listeners tuned in: Vary your tone as you're speaking. "The human brain loves surprises, so you don't want to be monotone," says Zandan. Go louder for emphasis when you need it, then dip back down so you don't sound robotic or like you're shouting. This variance is called *vocal energy*, and the more speakers do it, the more authentic they come across. All presidents seem to develop this talent while in office. I witnessed President Clinton's voice evolve over the months and years. In the first few months, his tone was consistently low, in part due to his southern drawl. But after a few months on the job, I noticed he'd begun to vary his tone and pitch, especially when he was behind the podium for a national address, adding emphasis for those important messages of the day. You can clearly see the difference in his speech and cadence from his first, 1993, State of the Union speech to the one he delivered the following year.

In a way, we've all been primed since childhood to pay attention to vocal energy through storytelling, which naturally involves changes in cadence, tone, and pitch, as well as well-timed pauses. Even as adults, we "listen up" when vocal shifts are afoot, as they help us track the content of a story. Supreme Court Justice Sotomayor is also a master at vocal energy, captivating you with her lilting cadence, as is Fred Kempe of the Atlantic Council, a profoundly motivating leader. He uses his storytelling talent as a former journalist to build up to the point he is making with his tone and pauses, then hits a crescendo at the end, sometimes inhaling deeply like he himself is a bit surprised by the finding.

Staying within that tonal sweet spot takes effort and awareness, especially if your voice doesn't naturally go there. I recommend that women and men tape their voice and listen to it. Years ago, I was shocked to hear my tone after I watched a tape of myself giving CNN's Wolf Blitzer a tour of the White House during Christmas, showcasing the various ornaments (one of the many fun duties of my time as social secretary). I was reminded again of my tone when I watched another public address of myself speaking at the Protocol Officers Association at the State Department at the top of my tenure in protocol. At the start, my pitch was higher because I was nervous, and then it lowered as the speech went on and I became more relaxed.

One trick I would *not* recommend: Adopting a British accent in an attempt to elevate a conversation or the importance of a message, something Anglophile Americans might do wittingly or unwittingly (similarly, people may slip into a lilting southern accent to imply a certain soothing gentility). When I entered the chief of protocol position, I had unknowingly been imitating Her Majesty the Queen for a few months. I was unaware of this until my then nine-year-old son asked me, after he'd heard me introduce Secretary Clinton at a State Department event: "Mom, why were you speaking like a British person?" We were accompanying the secretary in her private elevator from the eighth to the seventh floor, and she immediately chimed in, "Yes! You do that! Finally, someone said something—thank you, Cole! We've all been having a good laugh over it. You need to see a vocal coach." Was I fascinated with the monarchy? Yes. But not enough to *fake* being British! I realized that I unconsciously adopted what sounded like a "proper" accent to assist me in defining my new position. I'd changed my hair and wardrobe—my armor—to look the part, and in my efforts to completely inhabit my new role, I'd slipped into a faux British accent. I followed up immediately on the secretary's suggestion to see a speaking coach (check out her top pieces of advice for me on page 116).

UPTALK AND VOCAL FRY

Let's talk about uptalk, the habit of ending a sentence with a higher-pitched questioning tone. Uptalk is reportedly more common among young women in the United States than young men (though both genders use it) or older folks. As much as I try not to judge, I admit I find it grating, and I'm not alone: Some research shows that those who use it are viewed as less credible, possibly because they sound as if they are questioning their own statement or give the impression that what they are saying is not serious. However, depending on the culture and context, uptalk may be viewed more positively and as a way to seem inclusive or to show deference.

Uptalk's cousin, vocal fry—dropping into the lowest end of the vocal register at the end of a sentence (think Kardashian-ese)—has also become more common in young people, particularly women, over the last decade. No one knows why it started trending, though some have posited that it began as a way to mimic male registers and assert more authority (interestingly, the lower a CEO's voice, the more he makes, according to research from Duke University's Fuqua School of Business). Unfortunately for those who speak this way, it doesn't land well: A 2014 study by researchers at Duke University found that listeners rated both male and female speakers using vocal fry as less competent, less educated, and less trustworthy—in other words, less hirable.

It's important to note there are many who defend women's right to speak however they want and think everyone should lay off the criticism, pointing out that when men use vocal fry, no one calls them out on it. In 2015, Ira Glass did a segment on it for his NPR show *This American Life* in response to email feedback complaining about the voices of a couple of female reporters on his show. He admitted that his speech has vocal fry but that no one has ever criticized him for it. It probably is sexist, and it's more noticeable in women because their voices are higher—when they drop their register, it really stands out. There is also evidence that a generational divide is at play. Research by Penny Eckert, a professor of linguistics at Stanford, shows that people over forty are bothered by vocal fry and find people who do it less authoritative, whereas people under forty pay no mind to it. So if it bothers you (like it does me), it might just mean that you're old and cranky. However, I still advise people to temper it and just be aware that it can rub some people the wrong way.

ACE THE PACE

Pacing of speech is another quality I pay close attention to, especially when speaking to someone from a different country. I'll slow my pace so they catch every word. In general, I try to stay in the middle zone of "just right." We've all been in conversation with someone who is speaking so sloooowly that you want to shake the words out of them. In fact, research finds that people who speak at a tortoise's pace are seen as less credible than verbal jack rabbits. Equally ill-advised: Using "verbal avoidance behaviors" such as awkward pauses and revising your statements over and over by saying, "That is . . ." or "I mean . . ." (Though there's nothing wrong with a pause if it's well orchestrated.) As for filler words—*like, um, uh*—everyone uses them, whether to fill a silence when we're searching for the right word, because we're nervous, or to signal to your listener that you're mid-thought and aren't finished speaking. In fact, research finds it may be better to use a filler word than to have an awkward silence. The problem occurs with overuse, which can harm your credibility and your message and cause people to tune out. Some studies, including data by Quantified Communications, find that using one filler word a minute is fine—it's relatable and can telegraph honesty, especially in informal and impromptu situations (too-perfect speech can come off as rehearsed and premeditated). But when you use too many *ums* and *uhs*—especially in formal contexts like a speech or interviews—you're in the danger zone. In addition, some findings show that the more people use them, the younger and less educated they are perceived. If you can avoid using them, do; but don't hyperventilate if a "like" leaks out of your mouth. Just keep going.

At the other extreme is the person who speaks so quickly your brain is left in the dust, trying to catch up and process the onslaught. My uber intelligent, compassionate, and supportive friend, and former chief of staff for Secretary Clinton, Cheryl Mills (who now serves as CEO of BlackIvy Group), speaks ten times faster than the average person. She's a lawyer—a damn good one—and part of her genius is that she can string together words and concepts at a fast clip. But I sometimes have to stop her midsentence and say, "Cheryl, I can't keep up, what are you saying?" She's a pal, so I can do that without fear of sounding inept or rude. But in a business or government setting, I wait for a natural break in the conversation and either repeat what I heard back in question form so they can correct or affirm it ("So you find that the result will be positive?"); or I politely ask the person if I can repeat back what I thought I heard to confirm the information (this also gives me a breather to process the information). It's *so* important to get clarity that I prefer to err on the side of asking, even if it might make me look behind the curve. The alternative—missing a key piece of information or misunderstanding something—is not an option.

After discovering I was secretly British, I sought out the guidance of a communications guru, Kiki McLean. For casual conversations, my talented friend advised me to slow down, explaining that more often than not we speed up because we think our listener is bored or not getting the point. We then inject filler words because we become anxious, trying to speed through our points. If we just hit the brakes a bit, there would be no need for fillers or anxiety. I learned to do this by practicing in front of a mirror (seriously). There was something about seeing how I would appear to others as I spoke that helped me slow down and calm down.

How to Give a Solid Speech

I've given many speeches, and I still get butterflies in my belly right before I take the stage. If I don't, I know it won't go well; the butterflies are a sign that I am pumped and ready. My friend Kiki McLean gave me these five solid tips that have never steered me wrong:

1. *Memorize the intro.* You don't have to know the entire speech by heart, but memorizing the introductory comments— thanking the host for having you and a few sentences outlining the reason you're there—allows you to speak to the audience in a natural manner, setting a comfortable and intimate tone from the get-go.

2. *Pencil in the pause.* Write on the page exactly where you want to pause—either for emphasis, to vary your pace, or to give yourself a moment to look up. Secretary Clinton often goes to a podium with *blank* pages—she has the ability to craft her thoughts into a speech while at the podium and doesn't need the written words (it's unreal). But what she does do is use the blank pages as a tool to pause and look down, varying her pace and regrouping for the next thought before she looks back up

to reconnect with the crowd. For us lesser mortals who need to read our speech (myself included), you can draw little eyes on the page (or whatever symbol works for you) for when you want to visually connect with the audience. I try to find a person or two to my right, left, and center to look at directly. We can get so engrossed in the speech that we forget we are, in essence, having a conversation with every person in that room. That emotional connection is one of the most important aspects of speaking.

3. *Perfect the page turn.* We've all seen the page flip result in a flop, causing the speaker to lose his place. Avoid this by writing the last sentence of the previous page at the top of the next page so you can smoothly keep going.

4. *Stand like you belong onstage.* Don't fidget. Own the podium by having your hands on either side of it, in a relaxed manner. (Try not to white-knuckle the podium or you'll look aggressive or exceedingly nervous.) Even better: Come out from behind the podium if you can. Walking around and owning the space, as well as turning to face different sections of the audience, helps you connect.

5. *Practice!* You don't need to rehearse to the point of memorization, just until you feel comfortable with the words, ideas, and flow. (Reading it out also helps highlight areas that aren't quite right and need a rework.) First Lady Michelle Obama would often rehearse, too, conveying a familiarity that gives her the ease and freedom to really own the words as she's saying them.

FACE VALUE

In diplomacy, the smallest of expressions can be taken out of context. You must be ultra-aware not only of what your words convey, but what your face is saying as well. The habit of raising your eyebrows, pursing your lips, or flashing a nervous smile can be inadvertent cues that confuse people or give the wrong impression. I recall watching on TV as Secretary of State Mike Pompeo met with Saudi Arabia's King Salman and Crown Prince Mohammed bin Salman in Riyadh in October 2018, a meeting that was arranged to mostly focus on the death of *Washington Post* journalist and Saudi dissident Jamal Khashoggi. Secretary Pompeo, who has worked in politics for years, surprisingly smiled during photos with the prince. The moment sent out a firestorm of social media commentary and news analysis: His expression had unintentionally sent the message that all was well and this was business as usual, when it was anything but. While it's important in diplomacy to be on cordial terms, Secretary Pompeo's countenance projected contentment when the moment should have telegraphed concern and seriousness. The outward face of diplomacy—or any negotiation—should match the goal, and the small gestures can pivot the power in your direction or away from it. Your face is a tool, as powerful as a stop sign or a green light. Someone who used the poker face to great effectiveness was General Colin Powell. Coming from a military background, he keeps a deadpan face in nearly all instances, never losing his cool and thus maintaining the upper hand in his negotiations. It was one of the many reasons he was so successful as secretary of state under President George W. Bush and as chairman of the joint chiefs of staff in the administrations of George H. W. Bush and Bill Clinton.

In the Office of Protocol, we used facial expressions as Morse code behind the scenes. Like Meryl Streep in *The Devil Wears Prada*, when she views a designer's collection and ever-so-slightly purses her lips to demonstrate dislike of a gown (the room shudders and the dress is whisked away), our facial gestures convey worlds of meaning. We became experts in covert facial cues—raised eyebrows, glances, and lip movements—as they were sometimes our only means of "talking." During key summits and events, most of us government staff had to stay quiet so we didn't intrude on the business at hand. But because we were orchestrating many of the meeting details—who was arriving and when, or where we would seat Ambassador X's surprise plus-one—we had to communicate with one another in real time. To complicate matters, sometimes the wireless network would go down. So we improvised: A raised eyebrow and a sharp glance directed at an empty seat instantly told a team member that we needed to find out where the guest was. Two raised eyebrows and an exaggerated wide-eyed expression—combined with a tap on the wrist—would mean, "Time's up, find a seat filler STAT! so the honored guest won't feel dishonored." A rolling of the fingers quickly meant to get things moving because we were behind schedule. If folks were paying attention to us, they would think we were base coaches prompting runners to steal or stay put. We became so good at reading one another's faces and gestures that the secretary commented to us after one event that our team was precise *and* stealthy—we loved hearing that!

Our team was at an advantage because we knew one another well and had the same goals in mind—always ducks on the pond, gliding smoothly while paddling furiously underneath the surface of the water. But interpreting the facial expressions of someone you don't know well—say, a planning committee chair you're having lunch with for the first time or a client you are pitching to—is a whole different ball game. It's much harder to read their face, in part because they might be trying to control what they are *really* thinking, as you are, too. If your first thought is "Really? What a ridiculous idea!" you don't allow a grimace to form across your face. Although some language experts consider subconscious *body* language a more accurate barometer of extreme feelings than facial expressions, there are some facial decoders you can use to gauge a counterpart's state of mind *and* to make a positive impression on them.

What Are They Thinking?

Aside from the basic smile or frown, there are a couple of other expressions and movements I have used to clue into another's thoughts:

- **Notice their blink rate.** You're not a scientist and you can't clock their batting eyelashes with a speed gun. But if they seem to be blinking a lot, or faster than normal, it's likely an indication they're possibly stressed or even lying. (Interesting fact: The average blink rate is about seventeen times per minute, and more when in conversation.)

- **Note eyebrow movements.** A quick up-down flash of the eyebrow may be a subconscious "I'm welcoming you" signal or "I'm interested." Primates greet each other this way, and scientists think it's a way to draw attention to the face (with the rise) and then to clear the space (the drop) for further signals of engagement.

- **Watch their eyes as they smile.** We can all tell when we're being greeted with a genuine smile or a forced one. And science backs that up: A real smile engages the muscles around your eyes, whereas a faux one involves muscles only in the lower half of the face (Botox users notwithstanding). Not surprisingly, research finds that people rate a legitimate smile as more sincere compared to a faux one. So when you flash your pearly whites, try to smile from the heart to make your counterpart trust you.

- **Go with your gut.** Most people are pretty good at masking emotions, especially during negotiations where a lot is at stake. However, if your sixth sense tells you something is off, consider this: Research finds that people exhibit micro expressions—flashes of feeling that last less than a fraction of a second—when they are trying to conceal an emotion, whether it's fear, disgust, contempt, surprise, or happiness. These split-second expressions are so quick most people don't consciously notice them, but there is evidence that you can pick up on them, mostly subconsciously (and consciously if you're really good at reading faces). So if you have a gut feeling that someone isn't being completely transparent, it may be your brain reading a micro expression.

Finally, as tempting as it is to think that we can tell when someone is lying based on their movements and expressions, there's really no Pinocchio's nose for deceit, according to experts. Part of the reason for this: Liars don't want to be caught, so they become very good at disguising their intentions.

BODY LANGUAGE

I found time and again that in diplomacy, body language is a well-known silent tell, a window into a counterpart's headspace. Researchers have found that body language such as movements, gestures, and posture are sometimes a more accurate sign of what a person is thinking and feeling than facial expressions. In one fascinating 2012 study published in *Science*, researchers asked participants to ID the emotions of people in photos who were expressing real-time extreme emotions—victory, defeat, grief, or joy. People who judged emotions based solely on the face got it right only about 50 percent of the time, whereas those who saw just the body—or the body along with the face—were more accurate. "The body communicates more information than the face, especially with intense emotions," says study author Alexander Todorov, a professor of psychology at Princeton University.

The lesson here isn't that you need to get a PhD in body language (and I've given you some clues, below, so you don't have to). The idea is that you don't want to ignore a person's body language when you're trying to get a read. Equally important, you should be aware of the silent signals *you* may be sending out, as they may not be aligned with what you want to be conveying.

- **Fidgeting.** Playing with your cuff links/tie/necklace/purse sends the signal you're nervous, uncomfortable, or bored. President George H. W. Bush did this during a 1992 presidential debate with Bill Clinton and Ross Perot. He was about to answer an audience member's question about the recession and checked his watch just before responding—probably to determine the amount of time left in the debate and to gauge his answers, or perhaps as an unconscious move—but it sent the signal he was impatient or bored. If you can't trust your hands to stay still, find what works best for you in that scenario—perhaps sit on your hands if you're at a table, or clasp them together in front of or behind you while standing, or hold a pen or coffee mug—but only if it's not the object you fidget with.

- **Sitting.** When sitting, be a middleman—or woman. You don't want to perch yourself in a stiff, ruler-straight position; research finds that people who feel threatened or who don't like the person they're speaking with will appear rigid and tense. On the other hand, you don't want to be so relaxed that it looks like you're melting into the cushions, about to fall asleep or watch Netflix. The sweet spot: Lean forward a bit so you signal that you're engaged. To prevent Secretary Clinton from appearing as if she were slumping (usually chairs are too deep for women), she would position a pillow behind herself to compensate. The more positive a person feels about a topic or a conversation partner, the more likely he is to lean in toward that person. Looking at photos of myself—and watching the elegant Christine Lagarde, former managing director of the International Monetary Fund and president of the European Central Bank—I learned that I look best when I'm sitting forward a drop, toward the edge of the chair—but not teetering!—with my legs together and angled to the side, ankles crossed to create an elegant line.

- **Standing.** Presidents seem to have a stand that says they own the space: legs slightly apart, hands at their side with assurance, and squared-off shoulders. President George H. W. Bush had this perfected. As he walked toward the podium with his square shoulders, firm spine, and deliberate gait to explain an urgent matter, you always felt the country was in good hands. I've also noticed certain women CEOs—Ginni Rometty, formerly of IBM, for one—who stand straight and tall and confident, owning their space. Stance aside, I think the hardest part for most people is figuring out what to do with their arms and hands when standing. Do you cross them? Fold them? Let them hang? The most important thing is to find an arm position that's comfortable to you but also projects confidence. Whether it's hands clasped in front of you or behind you, hands in pockets, or hands hanging loosely at your side, you need to feel at home in your body. (I'd advise against crossing arms, only because it tends to signal defiance or boredom— even if the person isn't actually feeling that way.) *Pro tip:* If you're standing and speaking, give yourself the freedom to gesticulate; it makes your listeners feel as if you're excited about what you're talking about, but control the movements so as not to distract. (As with every pro tip, practice!) "And don't rely on one single gesture over and over," says QC's Noah Zandan. In the same way that the brain likes vocal variety, a range of gestures will help keep people tuned in.

I recall a cover shoot I attended with First Lady Hillary Clinton for *Mirabella* magazine. She really could not bear photo shoots, but she understood their value as America's First Lady and was trying her best. She was wearing a pantsuit (of course she was!) with an unstructured jacket, and it was clear that she didn't know what to do with her hands and was standing awkwardly with them at her side. The photographer, who was French, was encouraging her to have some movement with her hands and, in his lovely accent, said, "Hillareee, push the sleeves up on the jacket, shove your hands deeeep into your pants pockets and look at me." She did and—click!—there was the photo. Her hand problem was solved, giving her an assured feeling and appearance . . . and a stunningly powerful cover.

THE SOCIAL NETWORK: *DIPLOMACY AT PLAY*

Prime Minister David Cameron's 2012 official visit to the United States happened to fall during March Madness, the National Collegiate Athletic Association men's basketball tournament that dominates office betting pools and TVs across the country (including in my own living room). Prime Minister Cameron had never experienced American basketball, so who better than hoops fan President Obama to share and explain this national obsession? The president has a lifelong love of basketball, having played as a youth in Hawaii, in college, and anytime he encountered a gym during his presidential campaign trips, even making Election Day pickup games a ritual. When he entered the White House, he clocked regular time on the residence's court, encouraging competitive games among his staff.

Just before the two leaders headed to Dayton, Ohio, to take in the First Four game (the first play-in game of the tournament), I greeted the prime minister in the Diplomatic Reception Room of the White House, which is just off the South Grounds, where the president's *Marine One* helicopter was waiting. Normally, these bilateral visits go according to a more traditional plan: a greet on West Executive Drive (near the Oval Office); wearing of formal business attire; and an escort to the Roosevelt Room to sign the guest book and await the signal to enter the Oval

Office to meet with the president. But today, things were less by the book, and I could sense the prime minister was feeling a bit out of his element. He was fidgety with his outfit, a charcoal polo shirt, black pull-over sweater, and dark jeans (a perfectly selected basketball outfit). Prime Minister Cameron is tall and quite handsome, but in casual clothes, he seemed to hunch a bit, shoving his hands into his pockets and looking more collegiate than world leader. There wasn't a full UK staff on hand this day, only one aide-de-camp who was normally very laid back but to-day was jumpy, asking me all sorts of questions: Was the prime minister dressed appropriately? (Yes, he was.) What would the exact schedule be? (Free flow.) President Obama then glided into the room, flashed his huge smile, and, clearly pumped, began to talk about what they were going to do. The prime minister admitted he wasn't certain about next steps or the rules of the game, and the president assured him, "It's okay, I got this" as he walked him out to *Marine One*. Once in the air, President Obama reportedly explained the ins and outs of the sport to the prime minister, including "bracketology," the process of predicting who will make it to the Final Four. The two world leaders then sat in the stands among college fans of the competing teams—Western Kentucky and Mississippi Valley State—and cheered on the players, hot dogs in hand.

Was this a budding bromance over an exciting game of competitive basketball? Absolutely. But it wasn't *just* that. It was diplomatic bridging and persuading dressed up as leisure fun. Having hoops and hot dogs on the agenda was strategic. President Obama was taking an important re-lationship outside the formal structure of state dinners and bilateral talks into a more casual setting to build a closer one-on-one partnership. Even if the two didn't talk about the fight against terrorism between slam dunks or discuss the Arab Spring at halftime, they were still advancing the partnership getting a deeper read on each other's personality. And President Obama was revealing something about himself and the coun-try's identity: "This is who I am, this is who America is, and I'd like you to know it."

That was the *bridging* element of the engagement. The *persuasion* part? By coaching Prime Minister Cameron on the rules of basketball, President Obama was establishing his authority—albeit on free-throws and fouls—and gaining a bit of a psychological edge going into the talks the following day. Showcasing expertise in a social setting sets up a subtle power dynamic that can bleed into work conversations. (To be fair, during a halftime TV interview, President Obama diplomatically mentioned that Prime Minister Cameron would be teaching him the rules of cricket in the future.)

The two legitimately liked each other, and I'd seen their warm rapport build during previous meetings. At summits they'd gravitate toward each other, hanging out in corners and chatting during breaks. At one meeting in the UK, the two had an epic Ping-Pong match at a secondary school in south London, teaming up for doubles against students. The president and the prime minister were soundly beaten by a pair of sixteen-year-olds—and the prime minister later gifted President Obama a Ping-Pong table so that he could be reminded of the visit . . . and to practice.

This basketball courtside esprit de corps deepened their connection even further and greased the wheels for the rest of the 2012 visit. Over the next two days, the leaders agreed upon a coordinated approach toward the conflict in Afghanistan; to support democratic transitions underway in the Middle East and North Africa; and to take measures to prevent Iran from developing nuclear weapons, according to a joint press statement at the end of Prime Minister Cameron's visit.

It was by design that President Obama and Prime Minister Cameron's basketball outing was arranged for the beginning of the visit. I worked with Deputy Chief of Staff Alyssa Mastromonaco, who not only was my partner in planning for many of these critical bilateral events but who also embraced me immediately as one of the team. (I'll always be grateful for her support and inclusion.) We went all out to make sure there was always a purposeful and policy-driven rhythm to the itinerary of official and state visits. Kicking off this high-stakes visit with a sporting event in Ohio, the heartland of America, was soft power at its best.

AFTER YEARS OF PLANNING both buttoned-up and relaxing events for princes, presidents, and prime ministers, I've learned that the social calendar is as important as the business calendar. Socializing with work colleagues—or people who might *become* colleagues—can trigger a relaxed state of mind that opens people up to connecting in ways that can't always happen in meetings. I've found that "work-social" events, as some people call them, function best outside office settings. Relationship building is at the heart of diplomatic and business success, and mingling away from the formality of traditional work settings helps forge alliances and tighten bonds, those fundamental human connections that make you trust and like a person. I witnessed the magic of social hour time and again, in both the Rose Garden and the beer garden. Far from being a waste of time, getting to know clients, coworkers, and even your kids' teachers in ways that extend beyond the business-as-usual relationship is a power pivot that can take your relationships to the next level.

THE RELAXATION EFFECT

The mind at rest is actually working. "Eureka!" moments happen more often when we're unwinding versus intently working, according to a 2008 study in the journal *PLOS One*. When our minds are relaxed, they are more likely to generate free-floating ideas compared to a focused mind, which often deadlocks onto a single notion. Moreover, people are likelier to solve problems and think creatively when they're in a positive mood, and you can't deny the mood-boosting effect of a party, sports game, or a weekend getaway. Even short bursts of socializing are beneficial: Research from the University of Michigan shows that simple getting-to-know-you conversations, even for ten minutes, boost your brain's executive functions, like memory and problem-solving. Socializing actually involves some mental gymnastics, calling on cognitive skills like empathy and turn-taking, according to study author Oscar Ybarra, PhD, a professor of psychology at the University of Michigan. Socializing is, in essence, a great warm-up exercise for the main event, the business negotiations that require more focus and creativity.

There are as many kinds of work-social meet-ups as there are people that attend them, but these are the four types of networking strategies I find most successful in forming and strengthening relationships.

1. Retreats and Trips

Retreats and trips—from day tripping to week-long jaunts—provide an opportunity for clients and employees to connect in unique ways. Visiting new places primes the brain to think outside the box. Trekking off for pleasure or work—particularly to foreign cultures—enhances what scientists call cognitive flexibility or neuroplasticity, including the ability to solve problems in multiple ways. Traveling with others also forms shared memories that can serve as a foundation for future partnerships.

The unexpected synergy of the foreign diplomats who participated in the Experience America trip to Alaska in June 2011 is a prime example of creating valued relationships outside of the conference room. I wanted the trip to be magical, as we were bringing thirty-five ambassadors 3,300 miles across the country, and they were personally paying for their own travel and lodging. We did not have a lot of support on the ground, and I wanted to make sure we captured the best aspects of this unique part of our country—and our largest state—in a short amount of time. Catherine Stevens, a dear friend and the widow of former Alaskan Senator Ted Stevens, offered invaluable advice and mapped out an inventive educational schedule, including a slew of briefings and site visits focused on the state's sensitive environmental issues and natural resources. She worked with me and the super-organized and ever-so-patient (with me) Sarah Nolan (who led the Diplomatic Partnerships Division) and my innovative friend Grace Garcia (a protocol senior adviser who tragically passed in 2014 after an auto accident) on every detail of the trip. Along with the entire protocol team, we curated the most ambitious and talked-about trip to date for the diplomatic corps.

It was the summer solstice, so we took advantage of the extended sunlight, starting our diplomats' activities early in the morning and going until late into the evening. On the last day of the trip, following a daylong marine and wildlife outing with local EPA officials on Resurrection Bay, we headed back to Anchorage aboard a glass-topped train with Interior Department experts to learn more about the disappearing glaciers as they floated by along the coastline. (Cocktail party fodder: Alaska has the most active glaciers—those large enough to sustain movement downhill—of any place in the inhabited world.) We brought a guitarist and bass musician on board for entertainment, and a few songs into the set, the ambassador of Chile asked Dennis Cheng, our fun-loving and multitalented deputy chief of protocol, if he could borrow a guitar. Dennis, who loves karaoke, encouraged him to go for it—which he did. Unbeknownst to me, the ambassador was an accomplished musician (so many of these diplomats have secret talents) and started playing the Rolling Stones' "Satisfaction." He was encouraging folks to chime in, and taking up his offer of the mic were the Irish, Croatian, Japanese, Ghanaian, and Peruvian ambassadors, who joined in as his backup singers—the mix of accents was wonderful. (There may have been a few bottles of red wine involved.) The train car lit up—everyone was clapping and laughing—and other ambassadors eagerly took up the mic as it was passed around (including me, as I love belting out a tune). It was a bonding moment for all of us. At the beginning of the trip, all the ambassadors had been polite but formal with one another. Now, they were wrapping their arms around each other's shoulders, laughing and having an out-of-the-norm moment, creating new ties with countries with whom they normally did not engage. Our efforts to collapse differences were extending beyond our own borders, and the lines between our country and the cultures of our guests blurred in a beautiful way. New friendships were created on that trip—the ambassadors from Peru and Japan, along with their spouses, went on a bear-sighting vacation together right afterward and remain friends—and everyone's diplomatic experience deepened, opening up possibilities for improved relations between individual ambassadors and countries.

When mapping out your own retreats, off-sites, and trips (family reunions and even getaways with friends), consider these elements to ensure the out-of-town excursion is a win:

- **Plan with specific goals in mind.** If your goal is to create bonds between employees, particularly those who don't know one another well—say you want to connect the accountants on the nineteenth floor with the marketing folks on the tenth—choose a casual setting and schedule bonding activities, such as collaborative projects like scavenger hunts that focus on learning more about the team and company. "One of the purposes of our annual off-site retreat is to introduce staff to people they wouldn't normally get to know in day-to-day office interactions," says Susan Brophy, managing director at Glover Park Group, a marketing and crisis communications company based in DC. (I met Susan in 1993 at the staff table in the White House mess, and she's been dispensing the best career advice to me ever since . . . which I follow without hesitation. She was the deputy assistant to President Clinton and deputy director of legislative affairs.) "We combine staffers vertically and horizontally, up and down the ladder and across our six different divisions, putting young and old together for scavenger hunts, skeet shooting, volunteering projects, and other activities."

  If the goal is to forge connections between people who are virtual strangers, plan ice-breaker moments that gently force people out of their comfort zone in a fun, unusual way. During other Experience America trips, like the one to New Orleans, I made sure we went to places that would encourage the ambassadors to loosen up. On the docket: Café Du Monde, the iconic coffee and beignet café, where they inhaled the delicious confections on the outside patio and took in the electricity of the jazz town. I also gave them an opportunity to join in a "second line," a freeform dance that began in African-American communities in New Orleans (which usually takes place behind the "first line," the brass band) after our introductory dinner. We really wanted the ambassadors to stand up, grab their napkins, and jump in, so Mark Walsh, the skillfully creative deputy chief of protocol, took to the floor with his white napkin in hand, encouraging Mayor Mitch Landrieu to join him. Once the diplomats saw the mayor join the line, they felt encouraged to do so, too. It was a blast, and when I watched the diplomats collapse into their seats on the bus, exhilarated and chatting about the event with other diplomats they hadn't yet gotten to know well, I knew the schedule worked.

- **Prioritize travel in your budget and get creative with funding.** Travel may seem like an area where you can trim the fat, but there is a clear link between business travel and higher profits, according to surveys by business travel groups. These planned personnel engagements matter, even when the agenda is all play and no work. Understand what you can write off, travel to off-season locations to save, and brainstorm out-of-the-box ways to pay for trips. In the protocol office, we often sought out private-public partnerships for events and trips (once vetted for conflicts). Doing so allowed us to share costs, but, more importantly, fostered relationships with participating organizations.

- **Mix it up.** If you're doing an annual business or family trip, don't revert to the same old, same old. Keep it fresh. Following are some alternative ideas to shake things up while supporting your work/play objectives.

2. Sporting Events

If you're looking to move a formal relationship into more collegial and casual territory, keep your eye on the ball. Sporting events, aside from being fun, are a natural way to grow a relationship, stripping away the formal armor we put on in the office. The atmosphere is less prim and proper, more relaxed and spontaneous. Plus, it's acceptable for fans to get emotional at a game in ways that may not be okay at a meeting.

When Vice President Biden escorted then-Vice President Xi Jinping of China to Los Angeles in 2012, a visit designed to grow their relationship (the two had been getting to know each other over the past year through a series of US-China visits), he strongly suggested to his team that Vice President Xi should take in an LA Lakers game.

We'd learned that Vice President Xi enjoyed basketball, and Biden's team, recognizing the effectiveness of sports diplomacy, agreed that it made perfect sense for an NBA game—Vice President Xi's first ever—to be the next play in our larger strategy of forging a bond between Team China and Team USA. Vice President Xi was poised to become president of China the following year, and it was critical to give him formal and informal opportunities to get to know our leadership and culture before he took the reins, something that would help avoid the introductory throat clearing that happens at the start of a new relationship. "In addition, VPs are generally less scripted than presidents, so meeting with Vice President Xi *before* he stepped into the leadership role and became more scripted was a smart getting-to-know-you move for days ahead, when we were going to have to confront some hard issues," Jeffrey Prescott, former senior deputy national security advisor for Vice President Biden and his senior Asia adviser, told me in a recent interview.

Vice President Xi arrived at the Staples Center and sat in the VIP box with Governor Jerry Brown, LA Mayor Antonio Villaraigosa, and studio executive Jeffrey Katzenberg. I was monitoring the flow and greeting folks at the door, and each time I opened it there was another surprise visitor: Magic Johnson! David Beckham! Attending this style of event was a departure from Vice President Xi's usual reserved behavior, and he was enjoying every minute of it. It allowed him to project a friendly, easygoing image to our media, leadership, and citizens. The evening became the anchor for a new intended partnership between a modern democratic superpower and an emerging communist superpower.

To have pulled all these people together in a meeting at the State Department would have been doable, but the tenor would have been completely different and likely would not have resulted in such a strong new partnership between these two powerful countries. One of the wonderful things about spectator sports is the surprising synergy between people from all walks of life. You never really know if there is going to be a connection, but at least you are creating the opportunity for something to take root.

To go one better, lace up your sneakers and show up *on* the court, field, or green. A little competition builds closer ties than sitting in the stands. The camaraderie that develops during the practices for the annual Congressional Baseball Game for Charity—Democrats versus Republicans—is legendary, and it goes beyond the field and into the Senate and the House. The media often gives President Trump a hard time for playing golf regularly, but, like many businesspeople, he may be mixing work with leisure, considering the folks he plays with: Senators Bob Corker, Rand Paul, and Lindsey Graham; Japanese Prime Minister Shinzō Abe; and business executives. Deals are developed on the green, between strokes, and in golf carts.

President Clinton was an avid golfer as president, as well, playing with counterparts and staff. During one working trip to St. Thomas— where he and Hillary graciously allowed me to bring my husband, Rob, as it was the Christmas/New Year holidays and I was on the clock—he asked us to hit a few balls with him. I was hesitant to join him because I knew the traveling press pool was always there to film the president's first swing along with whomever he was playing with. But Rob *loves* golf, and I know he wouldn't have gone on his own if I declined.

I teed up, all the while repeating in my head, "Just hit the ball, it doesn't matter where it goes, just hit the ball!" I nervously swung and, thankfully, hit it. And pretty well, too, or so I thought. But President Clinton, who loves to teach and improve people's games, walked over and proceeded to tee up another ball. "Oh no, don't make me do this again!" I thought. He instructed me—in front of all the reporters—on how to better my stance. "No, no, no, Capricia, ya gotta stand with your feet this far apart," and then started to critique my swing. "Ya gotta go back slow, slooow, like this." I wanted to crawl into a sand trap. I could see Rob in my peripheral vision, howling at the spectacle. (I actually did drive the ball straighter and longer after his lesson.)

After President Clinton finished deconstructing my terrible form, I joined him in his golf cart to go to the next hole—the press corps mercifully fading behind us—and he zipped along, holding his Diet Coke (which was splashing everywhere) with one hand and loosely steering with the other, turning to me and talking and going way too fast around the curves of the course. But I loved watching him so relaxed: Presidents (and formers) are never allowed to drive due to security issues, and one of the few times they're given that freedom is in the golf cart. President Clinton reveled in the chance to speed across the course, rocks and divots be damned.

3. The Club Scene

About a year into my consulting business, I realized that, while in government, I rarely had the opportunity to engage in the private sector. My service to our government—the president, the country, the ambassadors—always took precedence (as it should have). Working in the private sector, however, required an adaptation of my former practices. It dawned on me that my usual settings—my shared office space, home office, and sometimes Starbucks—weren't giving me enough opportunities to meet new people (and potential clients) outside of my current circle. A change of scenery works both ways, too: Others tend to associate you with the familiar contexts in which they interact with you, limiting their view of *your* potential. When I'd run into someone from a past life in a new place, they'd say, "Capricia, what are *you* doing here?" It gave me an opening to launch into a description of a venture that was not exactly in line with how they knew me. Seeing me in a different environment got them thinking differently about me.

I began to seek out alternative ways to open up avenues for networking. When my friend Jay Dunn, whose strategic communications firm I consult for, invited me for lunch to the Metropolitan Club—a Washington, DC, landmark that celebrated its sesquicentennial in 2013—I discovered a whole new environment in which to connect with the business community. Up until then, I'd dismissed these private clubs—to join one in Washington, DC, can be quite expensive, and as a government servant, could not afford the membership fee. When we entered the dining room. I encountered a bustling, mixed-gender scene of Washington's who's who from business, politics, society, media, and the arts. I recognized several prominent women from Google, the Smithsonian, and the Hill eating, talking, and clearly making connections. Relationships were being incubated across the room.

For years I'd been a member of a few professional clubs—and I have sat on the boards of such organizations—but it's always seemed a natural extension of my work and a way to pay it forward. These private clubs were something different, a new nexus of people from different sectors. The entry fees were steep, but I felt compelled to join the Economic Club of Washington, primarily because David Rubenstein, cofounder of the private equity giant The Carlyle Group, is the president and holds a number of well-attended events and discussions with a stellar lineup of guests. I knew him from my time as chief of protocol, and it was well worth the price of membership to see him in action at the Economic Club and learn through his example. (If you haven't seen or heard one of his fascinating interviews, check out his podcast, *The David Rubenstein Show*, on Bloomberg News.) Not only did I know I would learn a great deal from the careful, humorous questions he posed to his interviewees (Amazon founder and CEO Jeff Bezos, General Motors CEO Mary Barra, and Secretary of Commerce Wilbur Ross, to name a few), but I also reveled in the mix and mingle, as David is a draw for everyone from every profession.

There are equally advantageous and less costly ways to network besides private clubs. Coworking spaces are a smart go-to, especially when they're targeted to a specific profession or membership. The Wing (which I mention in chapter 3), an all-female membership community work space with multiple locations around the country, is a wonderful option for women. (Costs vary but are quite affordable, compared with traditional clubs—the DC location is $185 per month.) After decades of men's clubs' prominence I appreciated The Wing's efforts to even the gender playing field with their mission: to promote the professional and social advancement of women through community. Their members include young recent graduates, newish entrepreneurs, and powerful women who are firmly planted in their careers. Aside from providing a stylish, millennial-pink space in which to work—and a base for those traveling in and out of the city (they have showers, a place to store your suitcase and change your clothes, and even a private space for breast-pumping)—The Wing offers professional workshops (negotiating pay raises, public speaking, etc.) and crafts classes. "The crafts classes allow you to turn off your brain and help members connect," says cofounder Audrey Gelman, whom I met on Hillary Clinton's 2008 presidential campaign. "You find yourself sitting next to the only female partner at a venture fund or the editor in chief of a women's magazine or web site you're dying to get your start-up into." Gelman says dozens of start-ups have formed from connections made at The Wing.

The following are a few additional suggestions to help you access new networks:

- **Hit up see-and-be-seen restaurants.** I'm a huge proponent of networking at restaurants where you can sit in proximity to industry influencers and are only a reservation away from a chance introduction. In DC, two of my go-to restaurants for networking are the Four Seasons and Cafe Milano. A day of meet-and-greets at the Four Seasons begins at breakfast, from 7 a.m. to 9:30, with the busiest morning being Friday, when people are back from their New York City offices and briefing their DC contacts. I've gotten a lot of business done going table to table, as each grouping is a veritable mini-board from different sectors. From financial services industry wizards to creative geniuses, like my friend Luke Frazier, founder and music director of the American Pops Orchestra—who is often dining with performers from the Kennedy Center—to members of the president's cabinet and other government officials, you are bound to see A Somebody any day of the week. And once a month, DC's powerful female media/business women gather at a long table: Hilary Rosen, a partner at SKDKnickerbocker; Tammy Haddad, president and CEO of Haddad Media; and Melissa Moss, president of Moss Advisors. And so many more. In the evening the networking continues at Cafe Milano, where at the coveted corner table you will find the charming owner, Franco Nuschese, huddled in conversation with a variety of people.

If these food scenes seem too intimidating, there are less socially brazen but equally delicious ways to make acquaintances. Membership-only underground supper clubs have sprung up in cities across the country, targeting adventurous foodies in their twenties and thirties. The Tasting Collective, for example, offers chef-led eating events in Austin, Denver, Nashville, Seattle, Chicago, New York, Philadelphia, and San Francisco, among other cities. The annual fee is low and gives you access to eating events in all locations. Fork Monkey, which bills itself as the club for supper clubs, offers members access to pop-up secret supper clubs, gourmet classes, and destination dinners.

- **Use social media as a gateway to IRL meet-ups.** I haven't always been a social media person. For years I didn't have a Twitter, Facebook, or Instagram account simply because I didn't have time (I can barely keep up with email). But when I wrote this book, I joined the social-media masses, knowing that it would help me get my message out and interact with people who need my guidance. Happily, because my specialty is connecting, I know people who are at the top of their digital game, including Moj Mahdara, my friend and founder of the massively successful Beautycon, a live annual B-to-C (business to consumer) beauty summit for bloggers, companies, and fans. Her advice: "I search and follow loads of hashtags on Twitter and Instagram," says Moj, who makes it a point to include groups and hashtags that are antithetical to her POV ("I want to understand the other side"). When she finds someone she wants to connect with in the real world—"Meeting face-to-face is more important than ever, since people are so distrustful on social media and DM [direct messaging]"—she asks them to join her at an engagement or talk. "Instead of just saying, 'Let's grab coffee,' I invite them to an event, usually a small group event, which are really in right now. They're more intimate, so it's easier to talk and connect." A word of warning: Scrub your social media profiles regularly, as everyone googles everyone these days. You don't want anything up that sends the wrong message.

- **Volunteer.** While helping an organization whose mission you are passionate about, you'll naturally meet others who are like-minded. Often a conversation struck up working side by side with another volunteer can lead to new opportunities or clarity on options for your career.

- **Be a bidder.** At fundraisers, consider bidding on auction items that offer you connections in the sphere of those you want to get to know. Maybe it's dinner or drinks with an influencer, a ticket or pass to a private club or tasting event, a tour of someone's work space or estate, or a behind-the-scenes experience giving you access to a company's inner workings. (*Pro tip:* Always have a business card at the ready. I am reminded by my friend Adrienne Arsht, an incredibly successful businesswoman and founder of policy-focused centers at the Atlantic Council, to make sure I place them in all my bags: evening clutch, day purse, business bag.)

4. Curate an Event for Your Client and Goal

In international diplomacy, we thought long and hard about which types of social engagements would benefit each country's delegation, and how it would further our own goals. A social event is not just an opportunity to get to introduce delegate A to delegate B, but an indicator of what you're trying to accomplish. Did we need a one-on-one to grow the intimacy of the relationship? Should we choreograph a public event to help cement their relationship in the eyes of the world? Was there a way to make the dignitary feel extra special so they were convinced of our commitment to them?

These are some of the ways I tailored social events depending on the dignitary and policy goals, and I still use this mini-checklist for social events, both business and personal.

- **If you want to make a colleague feel special, give her a one-of-a-kind experience.** If you know a client is a big baseball fan (because you did your homework), can you get a tour of the stadium? Or during dinner, plan to have the chef come to the table to talk about the meal (my motto: You never know unless you ask). In 2012, during the NATO Summit in Chicago, Elizabeth Sherwood-Randall, who was special assistant to the president and senior director for European affairs at the National Security Council, asked me if we could serve root beer floats for one of our bilateral delegation meetings, knowing that the leader loved them. It was such a special surprise for everyone at the meeting, and I'm certain it is still a sweet, lingering memory in this leader's mind.

- **If it's a new relationship, bake some formal structure into the social engagement.** When people are just getting to know one another, there is uncertainty about how the other person will act because, naturally, you have very little to go on. Your counterpart is unpredictable (as you are to them), and mystery can breed distrust, causing participants to clam up, the exact *opposite* of what you're trying to achieve when building bridges. The solution: Create a format for the occasion so everyone knows what to expect and can start imagining how the interactions might take place.

  I did this for most social events I hosted, including the welcome lunches for newly posted ambassadors. When foreign ambassadors are first posted to our country, they don't know many people, if anyone. The president would usually credential ten to fourteen new ambassadors a few times a year, affirming them as the official representative of their country. A few days after the ceremony, I'd host a welcome lunch for them and their spouses at the Blair House and invite key people from the White House and State Department, staffers who would be officially interacting with the ambassadors. This way, they could start putting faces

to names. I designed the event to shepherd them through this
social maze. First, after being officially greeted at the door by
Randy Bumgardner, an assistant chief of protocol and manager of
the Blair House or his super-efficient deputy, Yael Belkind. The
ambassador was then met by a member of the Diplomatic Affairs
Division (either Gladys Boluda, the former assistant chief, or
Chenobia Calhoun, the deputy), who had been the ambassadors'
exemplary sherpa through the credentialing process. They were
then escorted to the Lincoln Sitting Room for their official
introduction and photo with me. I welcomed them and offered
a brief review of the officials in the luncheon and accompanied
them into the Jackson Place Dining Room, playing hostess by
casually making key introductions. When it was time to dine,
they sat down at their assigned tables. I mixed up the guests so
they were seated with people from different regions—I didn't want
them slipping into conversations in their native language and miss
connecting with new diplomats—and introduced each honored
guest to the room, enunciating their names clearly and correctly so
that others in the room had insight into the proper pronunciation.
All this gave them an immediate entrée to DC, removed some of
the uncertainty about those they would be interacting with, and
made them feel welcomed.

- **If you're already familiar with your colleague and want to deepen
the connection, consider a more informal occasion.** If you have a
foundation of trust, a more free-form activity—for example, a game
night (Escape Room, anyone?)—can help loosen up conversation
even more and take you to that next level.

How to Work a Business Cocktail Party

I learned how to navigate a cocktail party early on in my tenure at the White House. Ann Stock, who preceded me as White House social secretary, was my guru. She was elegant, cool, and DC-savvy. Because White House staffers have very limited leisure time, we had to make the most of every moment we had off grounds, using parties smartly to socialize. Cocktail parties have two different timelines: A cocktail *reception* usually lasts one-half to two hours, whereas a *dinner* cocktail generally doesn't go longer than forty-five minutes before you're asked to take your seat to eat, so you want to use the pre-dinner cocktail smartly to make the rounds. (I have a *huge* issue with cocktails lasting more than forty-five minutes before a dinner—people become tired and starving and risk being overserved.) Ann taught me how to easily move from one conversation to the next without getting locked into one for far too long:

1. ***Do pre-party recon.*** Look at the committee list and executive board of the organization hosting, as well as the PR firm handling the party, and google them all, as they will likely be at the event. Knowing titles and backgrounds gives you the lay of the land. You can also ask for the guest list. Sometimes organizations will at least outline or give you a sense of who is coming. I sometimes ask if the event is "widely attended or curated," and if they say, "Curated," I ask, "How?" If they won't share names (due to privacy concerns), the types of people (titles, industries, accomplishments) on the attendee list. I also peruse the Evite to see who has RSVPed, and if it's an annual gathering, I'll google images from past events to note who is likely to attend.

2. ***Base your route on your goals.*** Before you approach people, scan the room to see who is there and think about why you've come: Is it to expand your network? Share information? Just to have fun? Then map your route: Start with the person you're most interested in connecting with so you catch them if they

leave early, and then move on to another partygoer who will further your goal.

3. *Enter conversations smoothly.* If you're alone and don't have a natural way of sidling up to a group, start with an ice breaker like, "Excuse me, have you seen so-and-so? We were supposed to meet up here." Or ask what brought the person to the event. And I've found that you need a bit of warm-up talk before jumping into "What do you do?" or "Where do you live?" which can come off as abrupt (and in certain cultures, like British, both questions are considered rude).

4. *Gracefully move from one attendee to the next.* Once you're ready to hit eject, there are a number of ways to float through the waterways and not get moored at one dock the whole night:

   - Say you're headed to the bar and ask if you can get someone something. On the way there, stop to speak to someone else (or do so on the way back). Your excuse to move on from that conversation is that you need to get or return the drink.
   - Introduce two people and let them talk to each other before moving on.
   - Don't sit if you don't want to be anchored. Once you're down . . . you're down, so stay mobile and on your feet unless your main objective is to meet that person: then anchors aweigh!
   - *Pro tip:* I rarely use valet or coat check so that I can keep moving and not have to wait for a car that is blocked in, offering me more time in the party and less waiting alone at the curb.

7

THE POWER OF PLACE

Where you say something can be as important as what you say. While setting is important for social networking and getting-to-know-you moments, the venue for negotiations is equally, if not more, critical. The setting of a contract signing, a new client meeting, high-wire negotiations, or even a relationship milestone (a proposal or breakup) has its own messaging. A location can say, "I want us to become closer and put all our cards on the table" or "We're not quite on the same footing yet, so let's keep this purely transactional" or "This moment marks a beginning"—or an end or a transition.

In government, setting has always been one of the most powerful weapons in the arsenal of soft power tools, long before the real estate industry quipped that "location, location, location!" was at the heart of every deal. A well-chosen venue can help turn rivals into partners or persuade entire nations to get behind a war effort. No one understood the power of place better than President Franklin Delano Roosevelt. With Europe on the brink of World War II in June 1939, President Roosevelt invited Great Britain's King George VI and his wife, Queen Elizabeth, to the United States for a landmark visit. President Roosevelt knew that he walked a diplomatic tight rope. Relations between Britain and its former colony had been strained since the Revolutionary War. In fact, a reigning British monarch had never set foot on American soil. But President Roosevelt recognized the need to solidify a warmer relationship between the two countries as the threat of Hitler's next move hung over the world. Because FDR and UK Prime Minister Neville Chamberlain weren't seeing eye to eye, the president looked to the Crown to bring the two countries closer. It was crucial in FDR's mind that this visit with the King be a turning point in US-UK relations, demonstrating a united democratic front against the rise of fascism in Europe.

The first part of the visit was set in Washington, DC, and was as traditional and grand as befits an honored head of state: a celebratory arrival to the White House, followed by an elegant state dinner, and ending with a private tour of the capital city's historic highlights, including a sail down the Potomac to Mount Vernon and the tomb of George Washington. But the second half of the visit was truly transformative: Their Majesties accompanied the president and First Lady Eleanor Roosevelt to the first couple's country hilltop home in Hyde Park, New York. The visit—which included a hot-dog-and-beer picnic, dubbing it the "hot dog" summit—not only allowed the president and king to discuss Europe's complicated situation away from politically charged DC, but it demonstrated to the king, and by extension the British and American people, the connection and warmth between the two countries: The president had invited the king into his private home and treated him like a good friend.

Formality gave way to informality and acquaintance was replaced with friendship as the two ate off paper plates on the porch, along with dozens of local families. It was the neighborhood picnic that boosted George VI's stature, as public opinion was uncertain about his reign after a controversial abdication of the throne by his brother. In the American public's mind, here was a monarch willing to embrace our country's egalitarian approach to socializing by partaking of America's quintessential summer food and conversing with guests—including families of the staff at Hyde Park—who all mingled under the shade of the trees overlooking the Hudson River. This launched a budding era of stronger UK-US diplomacy and reassured Britain of America's alliance as they faced the growing darkness sweeping Europe.

Three months later, Great Britain (along with France) declared war on Germany after Hitler invaded Poland. FDR, who asked Congress to increase aid to our friends across the pond, had laid the groundwork for eventual public and congressional support with his country-cottage diplomacy.

HISTORY HAD TAUGHT ME that there were two big-picture factors to consider when doing venue reconnaissance for a state visit, an official visit, a summit, or a G20: First, how would the location itself affect the negotiations between the dignitaries; and second, how would the location affect the *perception* of the negotiations in the eyes of the media and the public. In politics, the world is always watching. From the moment I learned of a visit, I began scouting locations that would move our administration's policy ball down the field in these two ways. Venue was a *huge* element in crafting the visits, and our team devoted an immense amount of research and time to it. Would a visit to the iconic Oval Office signal to a leader and their country that they were highly esteemed in our eyes and punctuate the importance of the discussion? Or would an off-site at a more relaxed, private location convey trust to all and encourage the leaders to let their guards down and forge a deeper connection?

In addition to the policy goals, I had to consider the style of my president and his top advisers. President Obama preferred comfortable settings, nothing too ornate. He usually let me know what he liked and didn't, or I sought out the assistance of Anita Decker Breckenridge, a presidential aide (later becoming the White House deputy chief of staff for operations and currently chief of staff for President Obama), who knew more about the president than anyone else in the West Wing (a true friend, she always came through). When Secretary Clinton was part of the delegation, however, President Obama would often defer to her— "Oh, Hillary wants to do that? Okay . . . ?"—as her location IQ was high, and she cared deeply about venue. Her conviction that, as a host, you should be as gracious as possible drove her to get it right, and this inspired me to always make it a top priority. As I scouted locations, her words rang in my ear: "Setting a positive, welcoming atmosphere shows respect and that you've gone above and beyond to forge a relationship. It's especially important if you're having hard conversations."

The listings I ran through in my real estate hunt were many and varied, but I often started by considering these eight venue types before pulling the trigger. These can serve as a guide for choosing settings that will support your business or personal goals in a significant way.

1. The Oval, aka the Coveted Corner Office

In US government protocol, there's no greater location upgrade than the Oval Office. The first time I stepped into the iconic room was in 1993, the day before President Clinton's inauguration. Things were in transition and less "official," so it was possible for me as incoming social secretary to wander the hallways solo and poke my head in. There was someone from the Uniform Division of the Secret Service standing guard. And the decorators were there, still tweaking the new decor—each president makes immediate changes that distinguish him from his predecessor (couches, some artwork, photos) and then later more significant changes, such as wallpaper, drapes, and the iconic rug with the presidential seal, which is hand-woven according to each incoming president's specifications.

As I stepped into the room, my first thought was, "Huh, it really is oval!" followed by, "Wow, what an amazing space." It's refined but not overdone. The curved lines of the room are exquisite, and coupled with the high ceilings, hand-carved moldings, and doors that are built seamlessly into walls, it makes for an impressive appearance (as the daughter of a builder I really notice these things). All of these elements add to the reverence you feel when standing in the room where so many decisions of the highest order have been made. A few paintings of great significance are displayed, including an ever-present portrait of a slightly grimacing George Washington hanging over the mantel, where our country's founder somberly seems to wish his successors good luck (his smile often looked more like a smirk, since he would keep his lips together in order to hide his ill-fitting dentures—which, incidentally, were *not* made of wood). Every president chooses the art he wants displayed from the National Gallery of Art and the Smithsonian Institution's incredible gallery collections or from other fine galleries across the country. And of course all of the office's occupants bring in photos of their families. The room strikes the perfect balance between a ceremonious space and working office, and visitors feel honored but also encouraged to attend to the business at hand.

Another reason that the Oval is so effective: It's cozy. My friend Kurt Campbell, former assistant secretary of state for East Asian and Pacific affairs during the Obama administration and someone who gets the importance of venue more than any diplomat I know, attributes the Oval's power to its modest size. "When you travel abroad to other countries' government offices, such as China's Ministry of Defense and their legislative offices, the Great Hall of the People, you see they're designed to intimidate by their massive scale. They make the visitor feel small," he says. "The Oval Office, on the other hand, is designed to intimidate and impress through intimacy. I've escorted many dignitaries into the Oval and each time they are disoriented for about five minutes because they can't believe the most powerful person in the country inhabits such a small space."

———

IN THE OBAMA AND CLINTON ADMINISTRATIONS, the firepower of an Oval visit was used very discriminately with outside visitors. It was reserved for the most important meetings, such as state visits, greetings with a family after a tragedy, or other moments that telegraphed a particularly meaningful message. Who can forget the photo taken by White House chief official photographer Pete Souza of President Obama bending down for a young African American child (the son of a staff member resigning from his post) so he could touch the president's hair to see if it felt like his own? President Obama made a point to meet and take photos with the families of every departing staff member, which sent the message that he valued each person in his administration. He understood that the Oval wasn't only a place to honor and negotiate with world leaders, but also a special space for the more human, poignant moments that can shape hearts and change minds.

Attached to the Oval Office was the outer Oval reception office, a cross between a reception room and work space. The warm and gracious Ferial Govashiri, personal secretary to President Obama, was the first person you met before entering the Oval, making sure guests were greeted appropriately. She also oversaw the room's decor, working with White House florists and curators so that it mirrored the ambience of the Oval. As the room set the tone for entry to the Oval, it had to maintain the same grace and history. The small size of this space conveyed an intimacy but also a heightened sense of importance. I always felt a tingle of anxiety while I waited for my time with the president, largely due to the proximity of this room to the most important office of our country, anticipating the swing of the door when it was "go time."

Companies should designate an "Oval Office," a place that's reserved for the most meaningful conversations so that they feel more esteemed. The deluxe corner office is an obvious choice, or perhaps the room where the building's cornerstone was laid, especially if you want to emphasize the growth of a company or its history. While some companies value having a private corner office, others, like businesses whose ethos includes transparency, may do meet-and-greets in a glass conference room so the employees see the high-level engagements. Or perhaps it's the room with the company's name emblazoned on the wall or the one with the best view. Wherever it is, be sure the space reflects the company's mission and personality in addition to feeling important.

In your home, the "Oval" can be a formal sitting space or a tucked-away study that gives a sense that it's reserved for more elevated conversations. The area doesn't have to be fancy—it just has to say, "This place is special, and I think you're special by inviting you into it."

2. The Informal Space

While setting a meeting in a formal venue can be incredibly powerful, some partnerships may benefit more from an informal atmosphere. Some of the most important moments I've witnessed in diplomatic relationships happened away from the imposing and diplomatic decor of weighty gold drapery, rigidly creased flags, and grandiose historic furnishings. If what's needed is a more direct interaction, the formality of a ballroom—with hard-bottom chairs, long white linen-draped tables, and cellophane-wrapped mints—can be constricting. When the environment is relatable, comfortable, and warmer, leaders can relax and focus on the details of their differences and advancing their relationship, even de-escalating a nuclear standoff.

When President Ronald Reagan met Soviet General Secretary Mikhail Gorbachev for the first time in 1985 to launch what everyone hoped would be the beginning of the end of the Cold War, the official venue was the Fleur d'Eau, a grandiose Swiss château in Geneva. But the watershed moment, the one that began the thaw between the rivals, happened in a boathouse. On the first afternoon of the summit, the two took a stroll around the grounds, accompanied only by their interpreters (and, yes, each had his own). They eventually made their way to the estate's tiny boathouse, which President Reagan personally selected as the place where he wanted to break the ice. Because the president had come from the entertainment industry, he better than anyone understood the power of environment to influence the audience. The stage had to be set, he reasoned, to persuade General Secretary Gorbachev that they could be friends. The two sat on cushiony chairs in front of the crackling fire, looking out at Lake Geneva, and spoke for over an hour, getting to know each other and their individual cultures and—success!—agreeing to two more summits: one in Washington, one in Moscow.

Fast-forward to 2011: Prior to an official visit by German chancellor Angela Merkel—the first by a German chancellor in over fifteen years—our protocol team worked with the White House to find an intimate, unique location for her and President Obama to share a private meal before the next day's official welcoming ceremony. It was actually Secretary

Clinton (location guru that she is) who suggested the award-winning DC restaurant 1789, which is located in an American Federalist–style period house. We all agreed that a tête-á-tête—without the usual gaggle of staff—in this warm "home" would offer them a relaxed environment to advance their relationship. The name of the restaurant, 1789, also offered President Obama a great talking point and a way to share his passion for American history—it was a pivotal year in DC history for many reasons, but particularly because it was when our Constitution was adopted. (I learned that Chancellor Merkel prefers to discuss details over meals in a casual setting.) The fruits of the official visit according to the press conference afterward: finding a path forward for shared US-German issues, including financial recovery in Europe; joint support for peace negotiations in the Middle East and security in Afghanistan; and a plan to pressure Iran on nuclear weapons.

I'm also a big fan of certain hotels whose vibe is more homelike than palatial. At the top of my list: the Jefferson Hotel in DC, owned by a dear friend, Constance (Connie) Milstein, who renovated the hotel specifically to create elegant, intimate spaces. The Quill bar, with its Ralph Lauren–style decor, is a preferred spot for business meetings and after-work drinks in one of its (often-booked!) private den-like rooms. Outfitted with leather wingback chairs, bookshelves, and bar service, they're perfect for discreet discussions. There are a multitude of great hotels and other homelike venues in every city around the country and the world that strike the right balance between professional and comfortable—just be sure to visit in person first (online photos can be deceiving).

3. The Home Visit

In some countries, the start of a business relationship kicks off with a visit to a colleague's home. In the United States, however, house calls aren't quite as common as in the past, though in some communities and industries it may still be part of the business culture. Today, when a home visit is extended to a client in our country, it is meant to grow a connection that's already been established or to maintain a special bond. House calls are a lifting of the veil, a gesture that says, "I trust you." One of my final visits with President Obama abroad was to Jordan, where His Majesty King Abdullah II had invited the president to his home for a quiet dinner. (King Abdullah is one of the warmest and most down-to-earth leaders I've met. When I would greet him at Andrews Air Force Base, he had often just piloted the jet himself and would hop out, give me a quick and friendly "hello," then pop in his car and head off.) The two leaders had a special relationship—our countries are allies, with King Abdullah managing a great deal of the relationships in the region, so a home-cooked meal was a perfect next step between friends. King Abdullah and Her Majesty, Queen Rania, clearly wanted to make the US president feel special and comfortable, creating an atmosphere where the two leaders could literally kick off their shoes and just enjoy each other's company. Her Majesty greeted us warmly, wearing a typically stylish outfit (she could belt a burlap bag and look fabulous). I was invited in just past the entryway during the greetings, and all I could think is, "This is so, well, homey." It was chic, of course, but it wasn't opulent, as you might expect from a monarch. Instead, the vibe was elegantly cool, and you could tell a real family lived there. My counterpart then escorted me, Marvin Nicholson—the president's politically astute trip director—and the gifted Pete Souza to what seemed to be the staff building next door, which had been set to make us comfortable while we waited, and where we were served *kanafeh*, which my savvy and always considerate Jordanian counterpart, Amer Al Fayez, knew was my favorite dessert, making me feel right at home!

Stepping into a person's home is incredibly intimate, and it can make the host somewhat vulnerable—he or she is showing you their unvarnished side. But it can also be a power move. It's their turf and they have control over choreographing and staging the movements and mood. Kurt, who is now chairman and CEO of the Asia Group, a capital management group specializing in the Asia Pacific, has for nearly twenty-five years used his Civil War–era farm home in Rappahannock County, Virginia, as a setting for relationship building and diplomacy. Aside from delivering fresh air and a casual environment, the historic six-bedroom farmhouse with original furnishings sits in one of the hardest-fought areas of the Civil War, allowing Kurt to teach guests about US history while serving them breakfast from the antique hot pot in the kitchen. "I'm a big believer in the influence of atmosphere and leaving the office, and I've seen the effect that a casual, intimate setting has on diplomats and businesspeople. It opens new vistas of perspective to solving complex problems," he says, adding that he's in his element at the farm, allowing him to be more comfortable and confident.

Kurt, who's hosted hundreds of high-level dignitaries, recalls one visit when a senior Chinese official, upon seeing Kurt's working 1954 tractor parked in the dirt, opened up about the time he spent at a tractor factory during China's Cultural Revolution. "He actually started working on it, and immediately I perceived a change in him as he shared how difficult that time was for him, how he wasn't sure if he would ever see his family again or return to Beijing. Our professional relationship became closer after that, and that conversation would not have been possible in a typical office."

Few of us own farms or even houses with such legacies, but every home has value as an extension of those who live there. What is the right occasion to set an engagement at your place? A home visit can move the needle if:

- you are looking to deepen an already close partnership

- you want a new relationship to experience a different, more intimate side of your business ethos

- as a manager you want your team to see a different side of you and to gel quickly with one another. Hosting a holiday party or another group meet-up can create a tighter synergy between you and your staff and among team members.

4. The Secluded Retreat

It's no wonder that US presidents from FDR to Trump have used Camp David, the official presidential country retreat tucked deep in Catoctin

Mountain Park, Maryland, as a setting for both diplomacy and R&R. Its isolation provides the extreme privacy needed for high-level, sensitive discussions, and its cabins and flannel-shirt vibe trigger relaxation, so that even when discussing the most consequential of topics, like war and peace, the mind is opened up to considering alternatives that might not seem as possible when sitting in a stiff-backed chair at the gilded White House or State Department.

The camp is purposefully isolated, and the ride has you snaking through ridge gaps and winding up the passes of Catoctin Mountain for what seems like hours (though it's really just less than a two-hour drive from DC) before turning right at a blink-and-you'll-miss-it sign. (This is assuming you are not a world leader who is arriving by helicopter.) Suddenly, the gates are staring you in the face, and reality hits you: This *is* a military camp. The first sign of life: A stern yet welcoming voice asks for you to ID yourself. Once you're affirmed, the gate opens and you are subjected to various security measures. Once you've passed through all of them, you understand why FDR called it Shangri-La. (President Eisenhower later changed the name to Camp David after his grandson.) Camp David unfolds in two hundred acres of thick woods, ruggedly landscaped walking paths, and about a dozen well-hidden cabins named for different species of trees. The crisp mountain air invigorates you as you make your way to the main lodge in your golf cart (no vehicles are allowed on the camp site). Hardworking presidents for nearly eight decades have realigned their thoughts and regained some personal space with family while enjoying the tennis courts or the driving range, watching a movie in the private theater, or just unwinding by an outdoor fire.

Several commanders in chief have left their mark on the camp: President Eisenhower put in a bowling alley. A second pool was installed by President Nixon. George H. W. Bush put in a horseshoe pit. I'm not sure who built the fitness center, but I do know that President Obama and UK Prime Minister David Cameron enjoyed hitting the treadmills together during the 2012 G8 Summit. Like me, they love an early-morning workout. Luckily, the US Secret Service would give us staffers a heads-up when the two were on their way, allowing me time to race out through the back door and avoid exercising next to the prime minister, as I felt it would be odd to have him see me sweat one moment and then direct him the next. (As for the president, we'd seen each other in the hotel gym many times during our workouts while traveling.) Invited dignitaries can also horseback ride, skeet shoot, or fish, offering the president the capacity to entertain guests with a casual American style.

The camp has played host to many world leaders for official and state visits, giving delegates the opportunity to negotiate world peace in a venue that also inspires some inner peace. It's a no-tie, relax-on-the-porch, go-for-a-stroll kind of place, encouraging delegates to shed the business suits and the formality that goes along with them in favor of more comfortable attire and an approach to match. (Although the vibe is ultra-casual, the camp is cared for impeccably by the military. Being posted to Camp David is a high honor, and everyone who works there is passionate about keeping it in tip-top working order.)

The cabins and camp trails have been the setting for many pages of our history: President FDR deliberately chose Camp David to discuss the Allies' World War II defense against fascism with UK Prime Minister Winston Churchill—they reportedly planned the D-Day invasion on one of the cabin porches—and every president thereafter has followed suit, using the camp for diplomatic persuasion. President Carter—who initially wanted to close the compound to save money (until he visited and was won over by its charm)—arbitrated the landmark Camp David Accords in one of the cozy well-appointed cabins, one of which now houses memorabilia from the hard-won agreement between Israeli Prime Minister Menachem Begin and Egyptian President Anwar Sadat. The grueling thirteen-day negotiations helped defuse hostilities between the two countries in the Middle East. The discussions, which President Carter anticipated would take only three days (a negotiator can dream!), would likely have been even more challenging and lengthy had they not been set among the maple and oak trees of the Maryland mountaintops.

President Obama chose Camp David to host the 2012 G8 Summit, a gathering of global leaders and the highest number of dignitaries the camp had ever seen. The Italian, Russian, German, Canadian, British, French, and Japanese delegations all settled into the stress-free environment and spent a few nights in the woods in the name of world prosperity. At the top of the list of camp activities: discussing climate change, the eurozone crisis, food security, and transitions in North Africa and the Middle East.

From the moment the delegates arrived, they were transported into a world that was different from the usual summit experience. Each delegate's helicopter landed in front of a military cordon for a brief welcoming ceremony. I greeted every leader and accompanying delegation along with the commander of camp. Their lead military escort then directed them to their motorcade of golf carts, which immediately changed their mood from rigid to relaxed (Prime Minister Cameron jumped behind his wheel and sped off, leaving his security behind!). The looks on our visitors' faces as we drove them to their cabins told me just how magical the setting was—they were both impressed and instantly at ease.

The conversations held during the summit were official and unofficial, planned and spontaneous. "The relaxed, informal environment allowed the leaders to connect on a more personal level," explains Ali Rubin, the lead protocol officer for this G8, who witnessed firsthand how the environment primed the delegates for fruitful policy talks. "When you get to know your counterparts as people outside their official positions, you develop a deeper understanding of one another, making it easier to negotiate."

On Saturday, the leaders gathered in the Laurel Cabin, the main meal lodge, to watch the UEFA (Union of European Football Associations) Championship League final match between Germany's Bayern Munich and the UK's Chelsea. Everyone was munching on chips and salsa and scooping up handfuls of the Chicago-style, sweet-and-savory Garrett popcorn and washing it down with a beer or two. President Obama mischievously stirred the pot between Chancellor Merkel and Prime Minister Cameron, prodding one against the other with each move on the field. The chancellor sat with her eyes fixated on the screen, not to be moved by the fun-loving banter of the prime minister, and then the prime minister's team exploded with the win in a penalty shoot-out in overtime. The chancellor was a good loser and shook hands with the prime minister. It was awesome to watch these world leaders open up and express the same emotions, friendships, and good-natured rivalries playing out in stadiums and living rooms across the globe.

Staffers never had a lot of downtime, so I made it a point to take my counterparts to the Shangri-La bar (it was open almost twenty-four hours during the visit) in Hickory Lodge to talk through the next day's schedule over a beer. Shangri-La—with its Camp David–logo mugs hanging from knotty timbers and the well-worn barstools—gives you the feeling that you've just walked into a rugged bar in Wyoming or Montana. For their part, the Italians savored their free time in typically cool fashion, their cashmere sweaters wrapped stylishly around their shoulders, strolling the paths in their exquisite leather loafers and languidly taking in the afternoon sun on their porch. They seemed genetically encoded to enjoy the cabin life and to look impeccable while doing it. The Russians enjoyed the surroundings in a slightly different way. Their cabins were still rocking at midnight, with so many food and drink orders pouring in to the Camp David kitchen that the food staff waved the white flag and asked for my intervention (their chefs had to get some sleep to prep for the attendees' 5 a.m. breakfast). I had a good relationship with all of my counterparts and felt comfortable relaying to the Russian chief of protocol that the thirty-burger midnight snack would be the final order of the night. "Too much?" she asked, with a wry smile. "Yeah, too much," I said, laughing.

Incidentally, we protocol officers worked extra hard at ensuring that the decorum of the G8 wasn't diluted because of the informal setting. In fact, creating protocol for weighty discussions in a casual venue can prove more challenging than at the White House. The elegant buildings and hallowed halls of our nation's capital naturally elevate meetings, reflecting the high caliber of the discussions. Among the wooden benches and pine trees of Camp David, our team had to find creative ways to boost the sense of gravity while still hewing to the rustic ambience. For printed materials like menus and name cards, we worked with my dear friend Jeremy Bernard, the inspired and hysterically funny White House social secretary (the first man to hold the position), to create a slightly rugged-looking font that felt natural but dignified, with the delegates' names etched onto small logs—a nod to our roughhewn surroundings and a touch that showed attention to detail. (While cleaning up, we were happy to see that all the delegations had taken the logs as mementos.) And we explicitly spelled out what "casual dress" meant so the delegates would know to leave the tie and wingtips at home but not err too far in the other direction either. (For advice on dress codes, see chapter 11.)

ONE AND A HALF YEARS LATER, when we were looking for a venue for His Excellency Xi Jinping's first visit as president, Sunnylands, California, hit all the right notes. Sunnylands is the serene, private, grand estate of Walter Annenberg, former ambassador to the Court of St. James, and his wife, Leonore, who was chief of protocol the first year of the Reagan administration. For decades the Annenbergs (now deceased) invited dignitaries, C-suite executives, and celebrities to unwind at their tranquil two-hundred-acre estate. Knowing how powerful the location would be for international diplomacy, the Annenbergs established a trust in 2001 that would allow the estate to function from then on as an official venue for world leaders to discuss the critical issues facing the globe. Sunnylands, the Camp David of the West, was born.

I'd never visited Sunnylands until 2012, when I was invited by the trust's then-president, Geoffrey Cowan, to attend the grand opening of the estate's new diplomatic iteration. (I found out later that he had a precise mission with this invite: to put Sunnylands on my short-list of must-consider venues for official state and working visits.) Geoff knew well the diplomatic value of a location like Sunnylands, so he pushed me to see it in person. I was sold on its magic the minute my car began winding up the long driveway. The warm embrace of the desert air and the majesty of the grounds and elegant home won me over instantly, and I knew we had to consider it for President Obama's next big bilateral: a 2013 working visit with China's newly elected President Xi Jinping. The impending visit was billed by policy experts as the most important between a US and Chinese leader in forty years—two giants coming together to face a growing North Korean nuclear threat and to find common ground on climate change. Could this lush oasis in the desert help facilitate a fruitful, more trusting relationship between two superpowers? I strongly suspected it would.

Sunnylands is no ordinary estate. Geoff, along with Cinny Kennard, well trusted by the Annenberg family and the current executive director of the Annenberg Foundation, met me at the door and quite deliberately walked me through the atrium, pointing out Rodin's bronze Eve sculpture before escorting me into the mid-century-modern-style living room (which looked straight out of a Doris Day/Rock Hudson movie) to view the Ming dynasty artifacts encased in glass on the coffee table. I was mesmerized and could have stayed there for hours. As we walked the grounds, I marveled at the reflection pools, the Chinese pagoda, and the footpath that winds in and around the cacti, agave, and aloe plants. The utter peacefulness of it all was immediately apparent. Every view is Instagram-worthy (in fact, you can follow Sunnylands on Instagram and see its charm for yourself).

Their plan worked. When I landed back in DC, I immediately set up a meeting with Danielle Crutchfield, the president's phenomenal scheduler, and implored her to put Sunnylands at the top of our list of venue options for the China visit. She was a step ahead, understanding the importance of this selection and that the venue should set a tone that would diminish the usual formalities, encourage a personal connection, and reset the relationship. President Xi's predecessor, Hu Jintao, had a cordial working rapport with President Obama, but a chill had settled between the two countries after the United States criticized China's human rights records. Now China was approaching the States as an economic superpower, and this was a new opportunity to start the relationship off on equal and positive footing. A meeting in the Oval Office would certainly have sent the message that we respected China and were committed to working together. But President Obama had already met then–Vice President Xi at the White House a year earlier. We wanted this visit to be a fresh start and to telegraph trust.

Ultimately, it was agreed: Sunnylands checked all the boxes. The comfortable dry heat of Southern California and the estate's tranquil atmosphere would create a climate for relaxation and candor, and the optics telegraphed trust and neutrality, a venue that wasn't as politically charged as the White House or State Department. (Wallis Annenberg, the ambassador's sole surviving child and current chair of the Board of Trustees, invested a great deal of time making sure every detail of the visit was perfect so that her parents' vision was fully implemented). The June 2013 "shirtsleeves summit"—so dubbed because of the casual setting and photos of Obama with his sleeves rolled up, thanks to the warm weather (which he loves!)—was largely successful. While seated at an elegant long table in the living room, surrounded by extraordinary artwork, they found agreement on climate change and the need to rein in North Korea. They were able to deepen their relationship on long walks on the grounds, using these quieter moments to broach the most sensitive topics. It was so clear that the serenity and elegance of the grounds, surrounded by the majestic San Jacinto Mountains, helped the two achieve a comfort level and chemistry that allowed for the openness necessary to tread into high-stakes topics. (I continue to assist the current president of Sunnylands, Ambassador David Lane, with global retreats there.)

5. The Historical Venue

From the first moment I walked into Blair House, located directly across from the White House, and stepped onto the black-and-white marble of the foyer, I was taken by its treasures and historical impact. The Blair House operations fell under the chief of protocol's supervision, and attending to the day-to-day management and absorbing the history was one of the greatest joys of my job. The guesthouse is made up of the convergence of four magnificent townhouses. Eleanor Roosevelt convinced the president of the need to acquire Blair House, the oldest of the townhouses built in 1824, after watching Winston Churchill walk through the White House smoking a cigar in his nightshirt. During the Reagan administration, under the leadership of then chief of protocol, Lucky Roosevelt, the four townhouses were seamlessly merged into its elegant status today. Blair House holds within it the successes and challenges we have faced as a democratic society. Named after newspaper editor Francis Preston Blair, one of President Andrew Jackson's most trusted advisers, the residence has seen its share of historical highs and lows.

From the Lincoln Room—where our sixteenth president would often confer with cabinet members—to the Lee Dining Room (which Harry Truman used for cabinet meetings during the White House renovation) to the sumptuous library on the second floor, which houses over fifteen hundred books on American culture and history, I, like my predecessors, knew the effect the house would have on visiting leaders and foreign ambassadors: It would tell the story of our great nation and underscore any discussions within its walls. The moment a dignitary climbed the front steps—where two assassins attempted to storm the home and shoot President Truman—and walked into the room where General Robert E. Lee turned down leading the Union Army, they would feel the shadowy presence of history.

In addition to being the most exclusive B&B in all of DC and the most privileged spot to house heads of state, Blair House was one of our top venues to host events for our international engagements as a less formal alternative to the White House. There's a sense you don't have to ask permission to have a seat at Blair House, whereas the Oval feels a bit more forbidding. Scores of presidents and prime ministers were invited to spend the night in the townhouse, along with select staff members, as the home accommodates only up to fifteen members of a delegation. Randy Bumgardner, the gracious yet formidable assistant chief of protocol and manager of Blair House during my tenure (and years before), kept a watchful eye on every detail and staffer—and guarded every secret!

Events with larger delegations seemed more appropriately set at the State Department's large and ornate Diplomatic Reception Rooms on the eighth floor of the building. If you have visited our State Department, I'm sure your first impression is that it's a large block with very little attitude, elegance, or excitement. (The look is an architectural style known as Stripped Classical with some Arte Moderne elements.) But once the elevator opens and spills you onto the eighth floor, you are standing in a fabulous entryway inspired by eighteenth-century Georgian-style architecture. Enter the rooms and you can view a stunning and newly renovated terrace facing the Washington mall, from which you can see the monuments and Potomac River. It's simply breathtaking.

A tour through the extraordinary rooms—with their $125-million-plus collection of historic antiquities from America and around the world—tells the rich cultural history of our country. For many visiting leaders, their first meaningful moments in our country take place here. "The rooms were created by patriotic American citizens to welcome foreign dignitaries and friends," says Marcee Craighill, director and curator for the Diplomatic Reception Rooms, a woman whom I and many others consider to be the ultimate keeper of the spaces and artifacts. Marcee is part gracious hostess, part all-knowing historian, and part expert storyteller, and her warmth and knowledge make global leaders and diplomats feel welcomed. "The rooms set a special and formal tone for meetings, and the art, furniture, and architecture are considered masterpieces that capture the American spirit of tenacity to forge new frontiers, both in our ideas of democracy and freedom and our relationship with citizens around the world." International visitors are often surprised to find a piece in the collection that demonstrates our ties to their country.

I so enjoyed escorting visiting delegations from room to room, each defined by a specific style of architecture. One time, when I proudly exclaimed that one object was two hundred years old, the delegation snickered, as their artifacts are thousands of years old. I responded by saying, "Ah, our country may not be as old as yours, but the stories our objects tell are just as rich!" (I wanted to add, "Especially as they relate to the success of our democratic form of government, which is older than yours!" But for diplomacy's sake, I didn't.) Venues like the Blair House and the Diplomatic Reception Rooms maintain their historic and current importance due to the commitment of the Blair House Restoration Fund, the State Department's Fine Arts Committee, and the Fund for the Endowment of the Diplomatic Reception Rooms.

Researching the pasts of local restaurants, hotels, and other spaces can land you a special venue that will help shape your meeting. (*Pro tip:* Call the historical society in your area for some intel.) Doing your homework will also help you avoid any oops moments, like finding out your chosen setting has a history of racism or an unsavory claim to fame. And historic doesn't mean outdated—check out the location first to make sure it's up-to-speed technologically if you'll need Wi-Fi or other tech support.

Meetings that can benefit from a historic setting include the following:

- Those in which you want to emphasize an aspect of your business that's related to the venue's history to give clients a deeper understanding of your mission. If your product or idea was hatched in someone's kitchen or garage, it might be effective to set a meeting there. *Pro tip:* It's a great idea to preserve a "starter" location in its original glory and, if possible, set aside space in your offices to house or re-create it. The Good Housekeeping Institute, the product-testing lab of the magazine, which takes up an entire floor of the Hearst Tower in New York City, has created a replica of the original 1920s dining and living rooms of the townhouse where the magazine was launched. Some of the furniture and artifacts are original, and the space has hosted presidents, First Ladies, and celebrities.

- Those in which your company's history or product or service is tangentially related. Perhaps the location is steeped in the same time period as your product was invented, or the venue may evoke a throwback feeling that you want to emphasize in your pitch.

- Alternatively, those in which you want to *contrast* history with your modern approach. I've found that pitching an of-the-moment product or concept in a venerable venue provides a stark contrast that will make the conversation memorable.

6. Experiential Sites

Nothing makes more of an impact more than dropping someone into the middle of the action, or close to it. Treating colleagues to a walk-through of a work-in-progress space or a site visit connected to the business-at-hand creates an emotional connection much more easily than a PowerPoint presentation.

When the Diplomatic Partnerships Division team, led then by Ali Rubin, and I planned the Experience America trip to New Orleans for our foreign ambassadors, it was six years after Hurricane Katrina had devastated the city and taken the lives of nearly two thousand residents. Our goal—as with all of the Experience America excursions—was for the foreign diplomats to get to know our country in all of its beauty and power, the good and the bad, the highs and the lows. The tragedy of Katrina highlighted the vulnerability of our country to Mother Nature and the limitations of our response, but also the resilience of the residents and first responders, as well as the charity that poured in from around the United States and the world. We toured areas in the city where entire blocks had been swept away by the storm surge and, over the past decade, had been partially rebuilt, though many areas were still struggling. The tour culminated at the Superdome, where thirty thousand people had taken shelter, trapped by floodwaters. I led the diplomats and their spouses onto the turf, and we all sensed a haunting feeling in the air. The ambassadors then listened as Lieutenant General Russel Honoré—who commanded the military relief effort for Hurricane Katrina—took the stage and, in a booming voice, told the story that had happened under our feet. Sitting where such loss, heartbreak, and survival occurred made a deep impact on everyone and opened up a discussion about how their countries had faced similar natural disasters. They shared best practices for disaster relief and left shaken but feeling connected to one another and empathizing with the deep loss in our country. The Superdome did what we had hoped: conveyed the message of global aid after a national disaster and how we are so much more effective when we come together.

Setting a meeting where the action takes place—a stadium where a winning sports team trains, a factory that's producing a product related to your pitch, the stage of a hot musical or play—helps clients or staff really "get" the impact of a project or idea. And if possible, make your colleagues a part of the experience: Invite them to clip the ribbon, pull the lever, or raise the curtain.

7. Outdoor Spaces

If you can count on Mother Nature to cooperate, a meeting al fresco can infuse a gathering with a sense of possibility and relaxation. There's no better backdrop than a surf-meets-sand vista, a towering mountain range, or a sweep of green lawn (a reason doing business on the golf course is so productive). Sunlight wakes up the senses and natural views are associated with improved attention and a reduction in mental fatigue, in part because people are being physically removed from the in-your-face tech tasks that demand our attention (the computer screen! the emails piling up in our in-box! voice mails!).

Then there's the sheer expansiveness of the outdoors. The huge canvas of an open sky or vast horizon magnifies the impact of an event. When we hosted events on the South Lawn of the White House, I saw time and again how brilliantly the backdrop punctuated the moment and meaning. In 1995, after the horrible terrorist bombing of a federal building in Oklahoma City, President and First Lady Clinton held a ceremony on the South Lawn, planting a dogwood tree to serve as a living memorial for the 168 people who died in the blast, and to represent the resilience of the survivors, the city, and the country. The president and First Lady, torn by the news, shuddered as they shoveled the dirt into the hole, and then paused with drawn faces as they looked at the tree, as if to send a message to those departed. The tragedy was honorably and sensitively marked by the outdoor memorializing, as opposed to speaking to people from behind a podium in a draped room, which would not have conveyed the same reverence and emotion. When I asked her about the significance of this somber memorial, she told me, "Tree plantings may seem formulaic, but they are always so refreshing and positive. They say, 'This is what we have in common, our natural world, so let's stop the killing.'"

Secretary Clinton was a huge believer in the power of natural settings to bridge and persuade. In May 2010, she took Afghanistan President Hamid Karzai—the first democratically elected president in Afghanistan's history—to the lush and expansive gardens of the Dumbarton

Oaks estate in DC's Georgetown neighborhood, where they literally stopped to smell the roses. It was by design that she chose such a peaceful setting, one that felt special and offered plenty of distance to cover on foot. "President Karzai had been living in Kabul in a highly secured building where he couldn't roam freely. I knew he liked to walk, so we walked and talked, and he was able to relax and breathe. We then had tea at the garden's conservatory and spoke freely," she told me. Secretary Clinton found him to be more forthcoming than usual about the challenges he was facing back in his country and was able to forge a more personal connection with him, one that would prove critical in the years ahead in sustaining the legitimacy of the new democratic Afghanistan government.

To make an event feel more special, consider setting it at night, under the stars. In 1995, First Lady Hillary Clinton was hosted by the governor of Punjab at the Lahore Fort, an eleventh-century citadel fort in Pakistan. The visit was an effort to help improve US-Pakistan relations with then Prime Minister Benazir Bhutto. Hillary always thought of us and asked that her whole staff be included in this special night. The entryway was dark, but once we walked into the venue we were greeted by the light of thousands of traditional oil lamps, called *diyas*, on every wall and in every crevice. The tables, set among the red stone ruins, were elaborately draped in brightly colored silk tablecloths that reflected the light across the entire fort. There were a few dancing camels, too. The effect was magical and so much more impactful than a dinner set indoors or during the day and sent the message, "Thank you for a wonderful visit—we look forward to many more."

A well-chosen open-air setting can forge a hopeful new beginning. Upon arriving to Abu Dhabi, Secretary of State John Kerry, newly sworn in to his post, was on his first visit to the region in his official capacity. His stop in Abu Dhabi would offer him a regional prelude to the bilateral discussions he was scheduled to have with other leaders in the Middle East. We landed quite late and headed directly to our hotel. The traveling crew was exhausted and my only thought was about how quickly I could collapse in my bed. As we approached the hotel, I was advised by the secretary's traveling aide that a dinner was requested by His Highness, Sheikh Mohammed bin Zayed Al Nahyan . . . tonight. This was affirmed by the ambassador of the UAE to the United States, Yousef Al Otaiba, a long-serving diplomat, who was very supportive throughout my posting. Ambassador Al Otaiba greeted us in the lobby and escorted the secretary to a beachfront restaurant for local barbecue. With each step, the secretary seemed to become more relaxed. As we approached the site, we could hear the waves, feel the warmth of the air, and smell the local scents intermixed with the familiar beach aroma. It conveyed a friendly and welcoming vibe, perfect for creating an air of comradery between these two leaders.

8. The Utilitarian Venue

Last but not least, I always considered whether it was best to set a meeting in a place that served as a blank canvas upon which I could create whatever mood and intention I needed—particularly if what I wanted was simplicity and zero distractions (recall the Putin-Obama meeting at the G20 in Los Cabos in chapter 1). A basic, spare space gives you the freedom to style it in ways that match your goal. (I dive into the how-tos of staging and persuasion decor in chapter 8.)

THREE LOCATION HACKS

Sometimes you can't pull off a full-on location operation. When limited, consider these easy hacks that have advantages of their own.

1. The Pull-Aside

We've all been there: You're at a conference or meeting when a participant comes over to discuss a whisper-worthy topic, and there is no private room available. No problem—just drop into an alcove, a window seat, or even a recessed door space. I've seen heads of state do this at summits, taking advantage of architectural awnings or even doorjambs, manipulating their bodies into a tight space (it's intriguing to witness powerful leaders squishing together, trying to navigate space dynamics!). Not only does an impromptu withdrawal help create a barrier against listening ears, but it de-formalizes the conversation, making it more intimate.

Even when discussions don't need to be closely guarded, ducking into an alcove or taking advantage of a couple of chairs strategically placed together lends the conversation a closeness and informality without the normal schedule haggling over time and place. At a recent conference in Singapore, I consulted on a project, and I was impressed by the setup created by the talented team of Holly Lemkau Doran, head of corporate media events at Bloomberg, LP, and executive producer Victoria Summers. They staged a "leaders' lounge," a space on the patio outside the main conference space, with casual chairs dotting the area and small cocktail tables placed between them. They'd even arranged for a juice bar nearby since the weather was extremely hot. People were organically taking advantage of the setting, having off-the-cuff conversations and exchanging business cards.

2. The Walk-and-Talk

Steve Jobs did it. Senior managers, executives, and CEOs at Oracle, LinkedIn, and Google do it. Presidents do it. Walking meetings are afoot. Not only are they time-savers but they boost creativity during the walk *and* shortly afterward, finds research out of Stanford University. Those who do them report a significant boost in levels of engagement and creativity thinking, and walking side-by-side creates instant equality between the conversers. Walk-and-talks also provide privacy from those who may be listening in.

I marveled at how President Clinton and President Obama used unofficial moments during walks around the White House grounds with staff and counterparts to their subtle advantage, sharing an intimate or reflective moment outside the Oval and away from staffers who might interrupt or overhear. In the midst of intense delegation talks, President Obama would amiably suggest a stroll with a leader for a private conversation away from the buzz.

President Clinton was also known for casually draping his arm over the shoulder of his counterpart and slowly guiding them on a stroll around the White House grounds. He once asked me to go on a walk as he shared his knowledge of our surroundings—the history of the dogwoods, the children's garden, questioning why he and his wife didn't play more tennis. We ended up under the Jackson Magnolia at the farthest end of the Rose Garden, sitting in the cast-iron chairs that have been there for many administrations. Initially, my head was reeling. He had never asked me to go on a walk before, and I kept wondering what I had done wrong. But the whole time it just seemed like a lovely conversation about horticulture, leisure activities, and mainly our social events—what was on the schedule, who we had invited, and who else we *could* invite. I only realized after we had returned to the White House what the walk was *really* about. President Clinton was giving me his precious time to relay an important message: He wanted to open up the White House, and its lawns and gardens, to a more diverse group of people for all events. He felt that our invite list was limited and that we needed to reach out into the country more. "Not just Washington, DC, elite, Capricia," he said. In a sense, he was correcting my MO, but because we were on a leisurely walk, it felt like a natural sharing of information that unfolded as we ambled along. Little-known fact: President Clinton also walked around late at night while working before a trip, perhaps as a way to organize his thoughts. And he had the odd habit of rearranging figurines and mementos from trips on shelves while talking on the phone, sometimes disturbing the First Lady's carefully placed arrangements. Upon seeing this the next day, I quickly reconfigured things before she discovered the discrepancy.

Tina Flournoy, current chief of staff to President Clinton, and Jon Davidson, deputy chief of staff, affirm this habit is still in full force, rearranging his office in Harlem often. My skillful former colleagues often find themselves managing the president's global collections. *Pro tip:* In studies, free walking—aka meandering—beats out fixed path walking for creative problem-solving, so let your legs and mind wander. At

Camp David, landscape architects purposefully created curved paths as opposed to straight ones so you experience unique views—and different opportunities for reflection—with each step.

3. The Coffee Klatch

We obviously never arranged for world leaders to convene at a Starbucks. The explosive sounds of foam machines would hardly be conducive to negotiating an international trade agreement. But in the real world, convenience is often king, and there are cupfuls of benefits to café meet-ups. If you're meeting someone for the first time and want the connection to begin casually (maybe you don't want him to take it too seriously), a coffee shop has the right warmth and vibe. The hum of conversation from other tables and the barista sounds in the background take the pressure off this being an intimate or meaningful encounter, like it would be in a quiet office space, where you can practically hear the other person's heart beating. Alternatively, you may want to soften a stiff relationship or encourage a colleague to open up a bit, in which case a café can trigger a sociable vibe.

Finally, public spaces like cafés are a good choice when you need to quickly execute a transaction, such as a simple signing of a document (no three-course dinner to linger over, just in and out) or if it's a tense transaction, such as delivering bad news. The public setting of a café ensures that others may be watching and a person's behavior must stay in line with social norms.

Three Things to Consider for Every Meeting

Before you pull the trigger, think about these aspects to make sure you're gaining every location advantage to bridge and persuade.

1. *Convenience:* Unless you've given your counterpart plenty of notice and impetus to arrive at a hard-to-get-to venue—or unless

you have the upper hand and want to flex that muscle—do not require someone to traipse across town. Especially during rush hour. (Similarly, if you're hosting your investment committee or book club, you can't expect members who work downtown to make it to a suburban location by 5:30.) What they'll take away from the experience is that you didn't think to make it easier on them, and you'll have much less time to talk shop if they spend extra time commuting. *Pro tip:* Do some legwork to find out when and where they hang out so you can piggyback onto their schedule. Call their assistant to suss out favorite nearby watering holes, or ask people who know this person where they start their day or unwind after work. I used this logic for a meeting with David Rubenstein, the private equity titan. I'd been wanting to ask his opinion about a business I was thinking of launching, and before I emailed him I did some recon. I discovered from colleagues and a few well-timed visits to the Four Seasons that he went to the hotel's restaurant on Saturday mornings and sat in the same corner each week, sometimes having two breakfast meetings back to back. In my outreach, I proposed that we meet at the Four Seasons on Saturday morning, knowing this would suit his schedule and likely garner me the meeting. It did. And he implied during our breakfast that I had done my homework. I'd also observed that the meetings were usually brief, so I was prepared to drill through my main points rather quickly, before the silent alarm sounded.

If your colleague insists that it's too inconvenient to see you in person, but you know a face-to-face meeting will make a difference (it almost always does), offer to wait a few weeks until she can spare fifteen minutes and offer to come to her. Don't get talked into a phone call if the meeting is important; otherwise, you won't be able to get a gut check on body language or facial cues or make as meaningful of an impression.

2. *Familiarity vs. Novelty:* Depending on your goal, you may want to set a meeting in a spot that your counterpart is familiar with. If you're trying to convey trust or smooth over a slight—perhaps

the client is a customer who has a grievance and you need to right a wrong—it's beneficial to hold the meeting in a place the person has already visited, or at their home or office, so they don't feel off-kilter and wary.

If what you're aiming for is creative brainstorming, however, introducing colleagues to a new spot can stimulate curiosity and focus. Research on MRI scans of people's brains has found that looking at new images puts the brain into exploration mode and can enhance learning. Sharing a cool new restaurant or space with a colleague also says something about you: You're in the know. I love being taken to new places that I wouldn't otherwise know about, and it enhances my opinion of the person (she's plugged in!). *Pro tip:* If you're doing the inviting and the spot is new to you, visit it first to make sure that it's not too eclectic/dark/loud for your purposes and that the service is good.

3. *Neutrality:* In protocol our team was always extremely careful to create parity so each delegation felt *equally* respected and accommodated. While there are many elements we always had to consider—from the food we served to the number of people in the meeting—location choice was fundamental to keeping the playing field even, especially between two countries that were at odds with each other. If a US delegate met with the minister of Pakistan at, say, a five-star restaurant, we would be sure to meet with the minister of India during their next visit at a similar venue.

   Choosing a neutral location is especially critical for high-stakes situations, such as refining difficult points between partners who both have a stake in the outcome. Each party will want to make sure they are standing on firm ground and not giving advantage to the other. Neutral ground is also helpful when healing a rift between friends or relatives.

   In business, leasing a neutral conference space for big, collaborative projects that require equal pull and input from both parties is a great starting point. As I mentioned in chapter 6, coworking companies are also great options to engender a Switzerland-like atmosphere for everyone.

_____

8

RIG THE ROOM

The G20 Summit in Toronto in the summer of 2010 was supposed to be business as usual. And it started out that way, at least. In the week leading up to the summit, protesters had been peacefully demonstrating against fossil fuels, big-bank bailouts, and more. From my experience, this wasn't unusual in relatively stable countries, where demonstrators use the summit as an opportunity to shift the leaders' and media attention onto key issues. But by Saturday, the day before the G20 began, the crowd had reportedly reached ten thousand, and things took a violent turn. Several hundred black bloc rioters broke off toward the hotels and the convention center where bilaterals would be taking place, smashing store windows, looting merchandise, and torching several police cars on their way there. Twenty thousand police officers and military personnel—tasked with protecting world leaders from over twenty countries—responded by using tear gas to stop a crowd from storming the security zone of the convention center. Ultimately, nearly a thousand people were arrested (some armed with Molotov cocktails).

It was against this unexpected, ultra-tense backdrop that I was tasked with my own unforeseen challenge. At the end of Day 1 of the summit, our exhausted team had retired to the Intercontinental Hotel to wind down (or so I thought!) and eat, sleep, and repeat. We were all a bit on edge because of the rioting and extreme security measures, and I was anxious to plot out the next day's meetings and get a little shut-eye before Day 2 dawned. At 5:05 p.m. I received word from the president's scheduler that a meeting between President Obama and Turkey's prime minister Recep Tayyip Erdoğan was suddenly on the books. ETA: one hour.

My mind-set shifted from zero to one hundred in seconds. Normally, I had several days—or at least several hours—to prepare for such a game changer. I sped off to the National Security Council team to get the prized policy intel that would guide my minute-by-minute maneuvering. When we were on the road, many top secret discussions and phone calls took place in a SCIF (sensitive compartmented information facility), a small, soundproof room that Secret Service constructed in the middle of a hotel suite. Aluminum-looking sheets lined the walls, the lights were insanely bright, and there were crazy-making sound distortions humming constantly in order to scramble any voices and keep them from being detected by outside listening devices. My ears, brain, and eyes hated the SCIFs, but they were a necessity. On this day, the SCIF briefing was unusually sparse in details, probably because the meeting was a last-minute addition but also because it did not feel like "business as usual." What I did know: These two world leaders of ally nations—both NATO members—had to quickly dive into uber-sensitive topics. Such private meetings required a serious tone and a formal space with no flourishes to distract—not quite sterile, but not ornate, either.

In times like these, I was grateful for the policy of sending ahead a protocol officer to the venue along with the president's advance team. I located ace veteran protocol officer Tanya Turner, who'd been at the hotel for a week and had already made fast friends with the staff, thanks to her warm demeanor. I had a wonderful relationship with Tanya dating back to the Clinton White House, and for the next hour we tag-teamed, turbo-style. "Okay, Tanya, we need to lock in a room asap. Then chairs, tables, flags for each country, drink service, plants, rug." The tune to *Jeopardy*'s final question began playing in my head—time was ticking down. Tanya gave me a look that said, "No kidding!" and "For real?" at the same time. Under less restrictive circumstances, we would have been able to get furniture, accent items, and flags delivered from nearby stores (on loan or rental) or from our embassy within thirty minutes. But considering the extra-tight security measures, which prevented anyone from leaving or entering the area expeditiously, the course was clear: We'd have to stage the space with what lay inside the hotel.

Another hurdle: All the meeting rooms in the hotel had been booked except one: an odd, cold room with no windows and a drab color scheme—stone-gray walls highlighted with olive-green accents. Sparse pin-spot lighting, the kind that randomly hits a few places in the room, made the overall effect spooky and dim. Some random pieces of furniture were piled up in a corner. Clearly, this was the very *last* room available. As I took in the dismal scene, I quickly became grateful for two things: First, this was a closed press event, so we didn't need to think about camera angles and specialty lighting. Second, it was a one-on-one session, so other than note takers and interpreters, we needed to accommodate only the president and the prime minister, not full delegations. I looked at my watch: T minus forty minutes.

At 5:20, we swapped out the room's utilitarian, hard-bottomed chairs for several elegant black, high-backed wing chairs that we found in the corridors. (You'd be surprised how often I "shopped the hallways" at hotels, as they tend to use some of their best furniture, paintings, rugs, and plants to dress up the public areas.)

At 5:25, Tanya and I were in the hotel's events storage room, rummaging through piles and rows of boxes and furniture for side tables that were not overwhelming or too high. This was not a meeting where the leaders would be facing each other with a large table creating distance between them; instead, we wanted them sitting next to each other for direct conversation—no barriers—and the side tables were meant only as a place to set drinks. We found two perfectly sized hollow cubes that I could flip over to act as side tables. The cubes were dark Lucite with a few scratches on them, but we covered the marks and punched up the elegance by draping large black cloth hotel napkins over each at an angle.

At 5:30, Tanya found some small plants in the lobby and placed them on the tables for a desperately needed fresh burst of green. A hotel employee brought in a multicolored rug that we lay in front of the leaders' seats to help define and warm up the space.

At 5:35 an employee from the kitchen staff arrived bearing elegant glasses, cups, and trays for drink service. We placed them on a table in the back of the room.

At 5:40, my Turkish protocol counterpart arrived. We had formed a good relationship from previous visits, and I gave him a quick walk-through of the space. As a courtesy, we always tried to give our counterparts a preview with enough time to make changes, perhaps swapping out chairs or positioning seats so an interpreter could sit next to a leader's "good" ear. But today we were lucky to get in a swift once-over. He gave me a thumbs-up and left to collect his prime minister.

At 5:45, I sneaked into the bathroom for a mirror check. Because I am the face of our country as I greet the leaders, it would be horrible to have something in my teeth or a smudge of eyeliner that distracted from the diplomatic moment.

At 5:50, President Obama arrived with his staff to receive his final briefer from his policy team. I made sure everything met their expectations and got the green light.

At 5:55, I gave Tanya a high five (we did it!), and since this bilateral was at our invitation, I went to the entry of the conference area to await the Turkish prime minister. (Tanya stayed in the room for any last-minute updates.)

At 6:00, I saw Prime Minister Erdoğan walking toward me with his security and staff, who weren't crowding him. Some staff are so glued to their leader that it makes walking a challenge. (This was not the style or habit of President Obama's staff.) Erdoğan, with his penetrating, experienced eyes, is unmistakable and striking in person. Although he walks with a slight hunch, he carries himself with confidence. I greeted him, and he in turn addressed me warmly, as we'd met several times before at previous bilateral meetings. His interpreter was fantastic, and the conversation felt seamless despite the language differences. I escorted him into the room to meet the president.

This was normally where I'd pin myself against the wall, make sure all was in order, and exit. But today, there hadn't been time to round up servers who'd cleared security. Because Tanya and I *did* have top security clearance, guess who took on the role of the presidential food stewards? I'd waitressed during law school to help defray costs (in fact, it's how I met my husband), and although I chatted too much with my customers to flip tables fast enough, I'd acquired the basics and was able to reinhabit my former waitress self for the meeting—minus the talking! During these bilaterals, servers are to keep their heads down and not engage with the participants *at all*. Channeling the excellent Navy stewards—who are brilliant at being present but not seen or heard—we served the leaders their beverages and snacks and then left.

Did our whirlwind diplomacy decor do the trick? I assumed it had gone relatively well based on the body language I'd witnessed in the room and at the end of the meeting. Everything leading up to the meeting had felt heavy, and both countries' delegations waited anxiously outside the room while their leaders met. The doors opened to reveal the president and prime minister stating their farewells, looking at each other directly and with an air of profound regard for the other, their handshake lingering a bit longer than usual. It was one of the moments I recall thinking, "Diplomacy matters so very much." Though there was no formal readout of the meeting for my team, my instincts were confirmed: Press reports indicated that the leaders had covered tense topics, including the international response to Iran's nuclear program, and that it was a lengthy conversation that ultimately led to a more positive relationship. Many experts later agreed that this sideline bilateral, although heated at times, marked a needed reset in US-Turkey relations, and began a several-year period of goodwill between the countries. (In 2011, it seemed as though the president spoke more frequently with Prime Minister Erdoğan than he did with any other foreign leader except Prime Minister David Cameron.)

I breathed a huge sigh of relief, but I must admit that I thrive on a challenge. While staging at a moment's notice was certainly part of our department's portfolio, when given a longer runway for liftoff, I was able to employ a greater array of scene-setting tools. Staging a room to influence both the mood of participants and the content of discussions was one of most critical aspects of my job. (Recall in Chapter 1 the potent effect the room's setup had on the US-Russian bilateral.) I saw the shift in atmosphere and behavior when the right setup was in place, and noticed its effects (or lack thereof) when traveling abroad, experiencing how a room setup or a piece of furniture or artwork selected by my counterparts helped moved the needle in one direction or the other.

FROM CENTERPIECE TO WORLD PEACE

A smart centerpiece can drive conversation, educate, and underscore your goal. During my tenure as social secretary, I'd experimented with unique table decor and centerpieces, using artifacts, art, and plants to take the engagement to the next level. Stilted conversations between delegates would light up when their attention was directed to a historical object or unusual sculpture on the table, an indigenous plant that told the story of a locale, or an archived gift from a previous leader to one of our presidents, telegraphing years of friendship. Discussions about a country's history and identity became more impassioned when accompanied by a physical artifact or another representation of their culture. In turn, when a visiting leader saw something from their culture showcased by the host country, the appreciation was palpable and the walls came down. Relationships blossomed when the conversation identified commonalities between their countries.

I knew it was critical to formalize these relationship builders so they could become a key part of every diplomatic engagement, so the protocol team and I developed Edu-Cor, a protocol strategy combining "*edu*cate" and "de*cor*" that became one of our pre-meeting processes when preparing for an engagement. The goal of an Edu-Cor element—whether it was a centerpiece, a menu, or an agenda—was to engage participants, encourage collaboration, and drive home the goals of the meeting. During event planning sessions, the protocol team came to understand that every detail we could preordain *before* the parties came together for that precious hour or two was important, and that Edu-Cor was rich with opportunity to spark and guide the flow of conversation and ideas. Before our Experience America trip to the New Orleans Superdome, where Hurricane Katrina's victims had evacuated to (described in the previous chapter), we knew we needed to reinforce the concept of global charity and how the disaster had connected Americans with citizens around the world. Ali Rubin, leading the DPD team in New Orleans, illuminated our goal and created a foldout that had the menu and event agenda on one side and, on the other side, a map of the globe marking the dozens of countries that had donated funds or resources to help New Orleans recover. When I escorted the ambassadors into the stadium and seated them at their tables, I was taken by how intensely they studied the maps, which primed them to discuss how one country's suffering unites the world. Similarly, for the event launch of the Patrons of Diplomacy program, an initiative to help fund restoration and preservation of the State Department's antiquities collection and Reception Rooms, we took objects from the collection and placed them at the center of each table, along with cards explaining the objects' provenance and historical significance. Viewing the incredible pieces close up—silver tableware made by Paul Revere (a teapot, a sugar basket), skippets (small metal boxes that protected the pendant wax seal to secure official documents), and more—drove home the importance of the effort.

Edu-Cor also played a logistical role, helping to elaborate on the reasons for the meeting. We've all attended events whose purpose or mission was unclear. To help fill that information gap, our team would dream up creative ways to incorporate details connected to the engagement onto table cards, agendas, and menus. This way, participants had visual cues that underscored the objectives. When we invited the ambassadors to a Washington Redskins–New England Patriots football game—a spectator sport that is uniquely American and an integral part of our identity—our team created a football-shaped menu with the rules of the game on the back, along with the stated goal that this outing was meant to broaden the diplomats' understanding of our culture's national pastime, so different from other countries' "football," aka our soccer.

At a women's diplomat mentoring event in DC—where we curated a guest list of high-achieving professional women from all sectors and who brought young mentees as their plus-one—we created an agenda of the gathering on one side of the program and on the other side, listed quotes from famous women throughout history to spark discussions that stayed centered on women's issues. All the Edu-Cor pieces were designed and executed in house. It was fortunate that the State Department had a calligrapher as talented as Jennifer Nicholson, who took on every challenge we presented to create remarkable pieces that perfectly messaged our goals for the event.

Sometimes the menus themselves became the Edu-Cor: Instead of simply listing the courses, we informed our guests as to why the dishes were deliberately chosen—perhaps an appetizer was a new twist on the recipe served fifty years ago at the first state luncheon between two countries. At the 2012 state luncheon honoring Vice President Xi, we had the menus laser cut to emulate the Chinese art of paper cutting and provided a description and history of the technique inside the menu.

There was another, more pragmatic reason we depended upon Edu-Cor: the bottom line. Items were often free or on loan from museums and info could be printed economically on table cards or menus. Our office had a very finite budget to work with for all aspects of protocol, so I had to be creative in areas where I had leeway. Decorating tables with indigenous pottery furnished by a museum or Americana artifacts from the State Department, instead of floral arrangements, helped our budget. I was grateful as social secretary to have had access to the flower shop in the White House. But the State Department did not have a similar service. Still, depending on the engagement, we sometimes opted to spend a bit more on bouquets, as there is diplomatic power in flowers. We sometimes featured specific flowers and colors meant to pay homage to a country: For engagements with delegates from Colombia, we'd appoint tables with vases of roses—the country is the world's number two exporter of flowers, with the rose being one of their top crops; when hosting events related to Israel, whose flag colors are blue and white, we'd blend bouquets of white and blue hydrangeas.

LET HISTORY REPEAT ITSELF

Confession: I'm a card-carrying history nerd, but for those who already have their finger on the corner of the page to skip ahead (perhaps you're having flashbacks to your mind-numbing American history class in high school), consider this before you fast-forward: When connecting with a counterpart—whether it's a new client, a manager you've had for some time, or the resuscitation of a relationship that went cold—the history that *preceded* this moment is important and a reminder of what came before. An Edu-Cor item that speaks to the history—a copy of a former speech, a long-ago contract, posters depicting a timeline of your company's development and history—may be exactly what you need to pivot the power for what is to come *next*. People can become so consumed by the details of the present, that a prior relationship or commonality—one that can rescue or enhance the goal at hand—may get lost. "Knowing your history and telling it is important," Secretary Clinton reminded the State Department staff regularly, impressing upon us that you want to extend the present moment backward into history and forward for younger generations.

I've often found that people with a stage or television background are brilliant at using history in a dramatic and visually memorable way to tell the story that will draw the audience in and make the current moment count. Take the gifted producers Robert Pullen and Ricky Kirshner, who have staged extraordinary events at the Kennedy Center, one of our nation's most celebrated theaters, home to the Kennedy Center Honors, the Mark Twain Prize for American Humor, the "9/11—Ten Years Later" Memorial Concert, and more. These powerhouse producers know how to use history to enrich the experience, for example, by composing the set in a way that steeps the current honorees with past recipients, so that the impact of the now moment is heightened by those who've graced the stage *before*. It's clear to the audience and television viewers worldwide watching the Kennedy Center Honors—via placards, banners, and photographs—that Lin-Manuel Miranda, LL Cool J, and Gloria Estefan are today's Frank Sinatras and Ella Fitzgeralds. In business, the origins and the continuum to the present matter as well. You can't expect investors to buy into a rebranding or a new program if they don't have an understanding of how the organization has successfully served past needs and pushed boundaries over time. Whether you hit this critical note with props or in spoken remarks, the historic through line is a power pivot.

Secretary Clinton found historical objects and discussions helpful in pacing conversations and priming relationships. "Too many Americans jump straight into business, whereas memorabilia can help you connect and form that relationship first," she remarked to me on more than one occasion. Before certain meetings with foreign dignitaries in the State Department, we would work with the curators to bring in related objects—paintings, sculptures, furniture—relevant to the history of the relationship or subject matter being discussed.

For all these reasons, when appointing meeting spaces in DC, I borrowed artifacts and pieces of furniture from the unparalleled museum-caliber collection on the seventh and eighth floors of the State Department, home to the Diplomatic Reception Rooms, where many official State Department meetings and events take place. As I share in chapter 7, the rooms—renovated and decorated over three decades through the sheer willpower of Clement "Clem" Conger, their chief curator—house and display our country's artifacts and spiritual past. Clem, known in DC as the Grand Acquisitor, used ingenuity and good old-fashioned legwork to build the $100 million collection, tracking down high-quality pieces and then visiting homes and antique dealers to encourage owners and sellers to donate them, appealing to their patriotism. When I tour diplomats through the rooms or discuss a piece from the collection at an engagement, telling people about his efforts—and the continued unparalleled work of the director and current chief curator, Marcee Craighill—I get a bit choked up.

In 2011, we honored the fiftieth anniversary of the opening of the Diplomatic Reception Rooms with an evening of diplomacy and endowment for the collection that still ranks as one of my favorite engagements ever. I hardly needed to stage the space, as it already had the effect I desired: elegant and historically alive. However, working with our outstanding ceremonials team, led by the visionary Jessica Zielke, deputy assistant chief, we enhanced every element—from the guest list to the menu to the program—to reinforce the importance of the artifacts and the rooms.

Our guests of honor were the former secretaries of state themselves, including Secretary Henry Kissinger, General Colin Powell, and Secretary Madeleine Albright as well as former chiefs of protocol, and the family of Clem Conger (he passed away in 2004 at age ninety-one). I wanted the evening to feel historic, impactful, and fun. I suggested we find actors to play the roles of Benjamin Franklin, Martha Washington, and Thomas Jefferson, who all stayed in character throughout the night and made authentically historic small talk with guests. Jessica enthusiastically agreed and found the most amazing performers. We invited America's famous opera soprano Jessye Norman to sing "America the Beautiful," sending a warm shiver up everyone's spines and elevating the magnitude of the evening with each note. Attendees then dined on the all-American feast, executed in collaboration with one of my favorite people, chef extraordinaire José Andrés. We discussed with him the significance of the event and what we hoped to achieve through the menu. An admirer of American history, he got it right away and researched ways to incorporate history and meaning into every delicious dish. While guests dined, they studied the Edu-Cor-inspired menu, which explained how each dish was tied to a specific diplomatic moment in history: celeriac soup, which was served at the signing of the Treaty of Paris; the entrée, a thirty-six-hour braised beef, had a more modern reference, inspired by the dish served for a dinner hosted by Secretary Dean Rusk (JFK and LBJ's secretary of state) for Chinese diplomats in 1961; pecan pie represented the nuts most loved by both George Washington and Thomas Jefferson; and everyone drank Albemarle Pippin cider (a favorite apple grown by the two aforementioned presidents) and cabernet sauvignon from the Brotherhood winery, America's oldest. The secretaries' head table was set with dishes, flatware, vases, and candelabra from the antique vermeil collection from the family of John Jay, a signatory of the Treaty of Paris and first chief justice of the Supreme Court. It was a history-making, history-preserving night.

WELL SEATED

In February 2019, President Trump met with the Chinese Vice Premier Liu He in the Oval Office for a round of economic talks centered on trade. Nothing about the meeting setup departed from usual format except for the seating arrangement: President Trump sat behind the Resolute Desk and fanned out in a semicircle in front of him sat the five members of the Chinese delegation along with several US delegates. The message was clear: I, President Trump, hold the position of power. By contrast, when President Obama met with Vice Premier Wang Yang for a round of economic talks in the Oval Office in 2013, he seated the vice premier next to him in one of the leather side-by-side chairs in front of the fireplace, with the Chinese and US delegates on respective couches. The message: We are discussing this as partners. Each seating plan was purposeful in its intended message.

Seat positioning is a subtle but powerful way to reinforce how you want your counterpart to feel and behave during discussions, as well as how you want people to perceive you. From the moment we enter elementary school we are influenced by seating dynamics: The all-powerful teacher sits in a larger desk at the front, kids in rows or table stations. Judges sit on a high bench behind a huge desk, with attorneys in front of them at regular tables and the audience in seating behind them. In work settings we fall under seating's spell as well: The chairman of the board sits at the head of the table; certain lunch tables in work cafeterias and restaurants are reserved for VIPs only. Where we're positioned in social and work situations hugely affects our psychology and interactions and can tilt the playing field. In a twenty-year study of US senators, researchers from the University of Toronto found that junior, less-influential senators relied upon those who were seated next to them (ostensibly more influential senators) to garner support for bills they introduced, whereas more influential senators garnered substantial support no matter where they sat. Seating truly matters to the newer, less experienced senators . . . and to the constituents of those states.

Being a big believer in social engineering and seat psychology, I arranged my office in the State Department to help achieve my big-picture goals: collaboration and creativity. When you entered my office, there was a small open space that served as an entryway to receive guests. Then you'd see a seating area to the right, with a sofa and club chairs. To the left of this area was a conference table, where I held smaller staff meetings to draft seating plans for events, review models of conference centers, and more. Both of these spaces immediately telegraphed "group think" and connection, but in different ways. I wanted the seating area to feel inviting yet formal, since it was where I often met with ambassadors and other dignitaries. I swapped out the low-set, seafoam-green sofa, with a higher, more formal-looking sofa from another office that had a relaxing palette of beige and pastel tones. In the far-left corner was a credenza where I rotated gifts from dignitaries around the world (Edu-Cor at work) and displayed artwork from the State Department's incredible art bank supplied by the Smithsonian.

Set in the back-left corner facing the entrance was my desk, which had a venerable history of previous "owners," including Secretaries of State Henry Kissinger, Alexander Haig, and George Shultz. It's now rumored to be in a very senior government official's ceremonial office—the tales that desk could tell! The eighteenth-century oak-and-pine beauty had just been restored and was sitting in storage awaiting a taker when I entered the job. Aside from its lineage of occupants who executed critical foreign policy decisions while sitting at it (a fact that reminded me daily of the gravitas of my job), it was ideal because it was a double-sided partner's desk; whomever I was brainstorming with had enough space to spread out his or her materials and computer, so one-on-one work meetings felt collegial. The desk also provided an excellent conversation point, warming up the interaction with newcomers and steeping us in the past for a few minutes before time-traveling back to our present topics.

For high-level, official work meetings, I moved staff and visitors to our official conference room or other venues, and I use a prescribed seating plan and specific strategies, which anyone can adopt to make the meeting matter:

Meeting Seating 101

1. **Center the Number Ones at appropriate sides of the table.** The most senior people should be seated in the center of the long side of the table (not at the heads, which is more appropriate for social dinners). This way, they are embedded in the conversation. The host of the meeting should be seated facing the door for several reasons: It's the best place to see and welcome a newcomer. It's also the best vantage point to get a nod or look from an assistant poking their head in to let you know that time is up (your invitee will not see this, as their back is to the door). Finally, if there are beverages being brought in, you can acknowledge servers and provide directions. Another consideration for bilaterals: Security protocols in most countries require that leaders have their back to a hard wall if possible (it's one less place to secure) and that they face the door so they can immediately see signals from their security.

2. **Situate everyone else by precedence.** I seat the Number Two to the right of the Number One, and the Number Three to the left of the Number One, and so on. In business meetings, this allows the next two highest in staff to provide information to the leader, exchange silent notes, and remind her or him of talking points. For government meetings, especially between two countries, this seating arrangement also respects the all-important hierarchy of titles. Precedent dictates just about everything in diplomacy.

   For social functions, or when seating a head table (a table facing the audience), I position the guest of honor to the right of the host so the two can form a relationship during the event.

   A note about head tables: I think they're underutilized. Some may find them to be too regal, but they're an excellent way to seat participants during panel discussions or meetings with a large audience so that everyone can see who's who via name placards. Even for staff-only meetings, some employees won't have met

C-suite execs in person, so it's an easy way to see the faces of the corporate leadership and feel as if you're having a direct engagement with them.

3. **Check out the chairs and the view beforehand.** I try to have all the chairs at the table be the same, which conveys that all shall be treated equally. (I also make sure everyone has identical memo pads, pens, and water glasses, and at times I even use a ruler to measure placement so nothing looks haphazard—presentation matters!) If we had to accommodate a VIP who required a larger chair to sit comfortably, I would find two chairs that were similar (or more if needed) so the counterpart was similarly seated and the VIP wouldn't feel singled out.

   Then I test drive the seating: I sit myself in the principal's chair and ask staffers who are both shorter and taller than me to sit directly opposite so we can make sure no centerpieces are blocking sight lines. I also make note of what else is in the sight line of the principals on both sides. Their views should not be hindered and should take in as much of the room as possible. I also tried to give the guest of honor the best view—a landscape, an incredible piece of art hanging on the wall, or the clearest sight line of PowerPoint presentations on a screen.

4. **Consider a meeting's length and phases and accommodate the shifts.** Bilateral meetings would often run in phases, requiring adding or subtracting participants for different portions of the agenda. Meetings might start out with the full delegation—plus media if they were open to the press—then dial back to a few key members for more targeted conversations. It was critical to have a setup that could grow and shrink accordingly. What you *don't* want: a large group crammed together at a too-small table or a small group sitting at a gigantic table, which can make participants feel diminished. If the table itself wasn't adjustable, I'd connect several tables together and cover them all with a

white tablecloth, a color which never fights with other colors in the room (though sometimes at the State Department they'd use "State Department blue," a sky-blue hue that instantly reads as government official). The tablecloth would create an *almost* seamless look that I perfected by placing a memo pad or flower arrangement over the edges. When the group shrank, I'd remove the end tables, grab the excess cloth hanging over the edge from the center, bunch it, then wrap a rubber band around it and then pull it apart to create a rosette, which raises the hemline and prevents it from puddling onto the carpet.

5. **Don't always assume you'll need a big table.** "Fireside chat" meetings—with two chairs angled toward each other and a small side table in between—is a good alternative setup, depending on factors such as room size for creating intimacy and conveying the sense that "there are no barriers in this conversation." I find that leaders conducting one-on-one meetings, depending on the intentions of the discussions, are more comfortable with this style than having a table between them, and the body language during a meeting tells the tale: They often lean in or will even reach out and affirm a point with a clasp on the arm. This setup works well, unless there are presentations to be reviewed, papers to sign, or a particular need to create a barrier between each other or between the speakers and the audience or press.

6. **For work-social dinner or lunch events, mix it up.** I've seated more large-scale meal events—fundraisers, anniversaries, honorary dinners—than I can count. And I will tell you that old-school seating boards, with moveable Velcro tables and tabs, work just as well if not better than new software seating charts. So if you're not digitally adept, feel free to visit the 1990s with me. Tools aside, here are my social seating commandments:

DO break up couples. If couples are seated together, they are less likely to talk to their tablemates. Depending on the couple or the event, however, I make exceptions. If a couple seems to be in need of each other, which may be the case with elderly spouses, or if it's a Valentine's Day dinner, I keep pairs together.

DON'T seat all the spouses/couples at one table. I don't relegate the "other" partner to a table filled with a bunch of "others"—instead, I mix up couples and singles from different sectors. I have found that many spouses and accompanying guests are often the more interesting attendees.

DON'T seat people alternating by gender. This archaic seating plan is so outdated. I believe, but do not know for certain, that this seating style was created because it was assumed that a woman had less to talk about and her more knowledgeable male partner could "guide" the conversation. Instead, I research connections between people—similar interests, region or hometown, careers (thank you, Google!)—and seat folks with like-minded tablemates.

DON'T get free-form and tell people to sit wherever they'd like. While this may sound egalitarian and modern, it actually makes people uncomfortable (this is true for high-level meetings as well). When given a choice, I've noticed that there's always that moment where people freeze, not knowing where to sit. It's the rare bird who confidently sits down first. Put everyone at ease and give them an assigned spot in advance or stand by the table inviting people to specific places. *Pro tip:* The people who host the annual luncheon of my international neighborhood club (an organization that promotes international peace through the development of personal relationships) let everyone pull a name out of a fishbowl so there's no stress about who sits where—it's a fun surprise for guests and takes the pressure off the hostess to figure out where to seat everyone.

WORKING THE ROOM

Over 70 percent of a chief executive's workday is spent in meetings, according to a 2018 study by Michael E. Porter and Nitin Nohria of Harvard Business School—and that figure is 35 percent for middle managers, suggests other research. So it makes sense to pay attention to where you and your colleagues station yourselves for hours each week and to learn how the room can affect the flow of conversation and buttress your goals. A study from Australian researchers Mark Pearson and Helen Wilson that looked at how the decor in counselor offices affected clients discovered that people were more emotionally open in spaces that had natural lighting, large windows, plants, and views of greenery. The same was found to be true for carpeting, soft-cushioned furniture, warm lighting, and wall art. Soft lines and cushy furniture in particular can keep the vibe friendly: MRI research done by neuroscientists Moshe Bar and Maital Neta finds that simply looking at sharp edges and objects can stimulate the fear portion of the brain, and that people prefer looking at soft, round objects. In one study from Brandeis University, people actually felt physically changed, depending on the decor, reporting headaches and fatigue in rooms they considered "ugly," as well as sensing hostility and boredom. Retail marketers know these decor hacks well: Soft lighting leads people to experience a store as a pleasant space, causing them to linger and upping the chance they'll purchase something. Stores with long, narrow aisles can make customers feel it might be difficult to find something (sending them out the door prematurely), so some stores, such as CVS, have opted for shorter shelves to create the appearance of an efficient experience. Wine stores sell more expensive wine when they play classical music than when they play Top 40. All these cues are being absorbed by our senses and creating impressions of which we're not consciously aware.

Inviting settings are particularly important if you want your participants to stay in the room until you seal the deal: If you have a tough-as-nails negotiation, your counterpart is more likely to stay at the table if he likes his surroundings and feels physically comfortable. And in meetings with many phases that stretch on for hours, you don't want participants leaving early because their backside is going numb or the color scheme is driving them to dark places.

Alternatively, you may *not* want your counterpart to feel comfortable sticking around for a long time, or you might not want her to misinterpret the engagement as an intimate bonding session. Perhaps you want to execute business quickly, then move her up and out, asap. Or maybe you want to push a colleague into a quick decision. In these cases, I suggest opting for not-so-comfy chairs and a hard-floored room with no windows.

When I was given a long lead time and some wiggle room, I brought everything to bear in creating an ace space. I paid especially close attention to these proven influencers: size, lighting, view, and decor. Knowing how these elements dial the intimacy and warmth factor up or down can put you in the driver's seat.

BE WISE ABOUT SIZE

A too-small room can feel claustrophobic, so unless you want your counterparts to feel as if they're in an escape room competition, avoid cramped spaces. On the other hand, too much space can make people feel insecure, so don't book a big conference room for a one-on-one. In addition to choosing a table that could handle a changing number of participants, I would also make sure that the room size could accommodate meetings with the potential to expand or diminish. And if the meetings threatened to go through mealtime, I factored in the extra space needed for food service. We often had screens and curtains—"pipe-and-drape" in industry lingo—to section off smaller areas or create privacy for delegations in a huge room or convention space.

If your goal is creative brainstorming, consider setting the meeting in a room with a high ceiling. A study from marketing researcher Joan Meyers-Levy found that in rooms with ten-foot ceilings, participants who were given word puzzles were more likely to create words related to freedom and openness, compared to those in rooms with eight-foot ceilings, who were more likely to create words dealing with confinement. Alternatively, when you need folks to focus on concrete details, a shallower ceiling will prime people to think more literally and narrowly, as I noted in chapter 1.

LIGHT IT UP

Because bilateral perimeters had to meet strict security measures, I often didn't get the chance to set meetings in a sunlit space, which is shown to boost mood and wake up the senses. The only person who could override security rules and let the sun shine in was the president himself, as I discovered during one bilateral in Jerusalem. President Obama and Prime Minister Benjamin Netanyahu were meeting in a hotel suite on a high floor overlooking the city. The view and natural light were spectacular, but just prior to the meeting, the security teams went in and closed the drapes, per their practice, creating a cave-like feel. When I went in to check on the progress of the meeting, the drapes were open, and the security detail—who were watching through the slightly opened door— signaled to me to close them again. As I approached the drapes, the leaders saw what I was about to do and directed me to leave the curtains open. The prime minister noted that they were on a high floor, it was a beautiful day, and they were tired of being the in dark. I informed security that I'd been overridden, and they relented, I suspect, due to how high a floor we were on, and the fact that there were no other buildings in the line of sight, which minimized the safety risk.

If natural light is in short supply, try to go with warm artificial lighting such as halogen, or LED over harsh CFLs (compact fluorescent lights). While CFLs are environmentally smart, some of the brighter gradients can cause headaches and eye fatigue in some people, as well as trigger a hormonal stress response and an increase in blood pressure (luckily, there are now CFLs on the market in varying hues and warmer, softer shades). We've all sat under an old-school flickering fluorescent light, shielding our eyes, about to go mad; it's no wonder, as it turns out the flickering fluorescent light is actually hard for your eyes and brain to process and can cause fatigue.

LET NATURE NURTURE

It's well known that looking at green spaces ushers in a sense of calm, but newer research is showing that "blue spaces"—bodies of water or a fountain—are equally effective at triggering that "ahhh" feeling. When you can't have that meeting on the patio near the lake or lawn, bring the outdoors in: Plants reduce stress and are amazing air filters as well; indoor Zen water gardens can channel nature's calm. When I was on the road, I found it was easiest to get ahold of green plants (mostly from lobbies and hallways) versus flowers. But when I had the option to order flowers, I steered clear of scented flowers, especially lilies, whose pungent scent can trigger an allergy attack and whose pollen-covered stamens can stain furniture and clothing. Some of my go-tos: orchids (for a light and airy feel), hydrangeas, peonies, and cherry blossom branches, when in season. Cherry blossom branches are particularly wonderful for a DC springtime event, as the fluffy pink flowers bloom in late March/ early April. The roughly three thousand cherry trees—gifted to us by Japan in 1912—line our monuments along the Tidal Basin and feel part and parcel of DC itself. We often used them at the sides of podiums to give the staging a beautiful freshness and an optimistic message, as the blossoms symbolize renewal in Japan. Again, when using flowers on tables, be sure they don't block sight lines: you've spent hours planning a space and seating the right mix of participants—the last thing you want is for a huge spray of petals and leaves to interrupt the flow of conversation across the table, or for a beautiful centerpiece to be moved onto the floor or under the table.

RIG THE HOTEL ROOM

At the State Department, certain high-level personnel (like the president and cabinet members) had dedicated advance travel staff called Remain Over Night persons, or RONs. These travel genies knew every trick in the book for creating the best ambience for jetlagged dignitaries who had to be at the top of their game. The RON team members had a challenging job. When our delegation arrived at a hotel, we were bone-tired, but we still had a few hours of prep for the next day and had to manage the needs of our principals. A great RON rose above and was prepared for the onslaught of late-night requests and needs. Two of my favorite RONs, Bonnie Berry and Connie Coopersmith, were clever, and I studied them for smarter ways to stage rooms. To wit: They traveled with special lightbulbs to create soft lighting in hotel rooms, scented candles (lavender or gardenia are crowd-pleasers) to cover up bad odors, and soft robes and slippers in case the hotel didn't provide them. Presidents and First Ladies are on a harried schedule; often their personal mind-set and needs are put aside, with focus only on the minute-by-minute schedule. Connie and Bonnie always found a way to bring harmony to the madness.

Connie's mantras—"Don't be mediocre" and "Make everyone feel special"—guided her genius. Here are some of her room hacks to go above and beyond for your boss and clients or your friends and family:

- **Create a "rest zone" in the middle of the insanity.** Breakneck-pace conferences, large-scale speaking events—certain engagements have a frenetic quality that begs for a place to get away and decompress. In the political world, it was often impossible to move the principals out of a convention center or speaking venue to a quiet space because of security concerns or a tightly timed schedule. When Connie couldn't take our principals to a Zen locale, she brought the Zen to the principal. "I made it a point, especially for President Clinton and the First Lady, to have a space separate from the chaos that was an oasis, even if it was small." On a 1994 trip to Seattle during the First Lady's rollout of her health-care campaign, supporter rallies and protesters got very heated. "I knew she needed a place to re-center, so I transformed a nine-by-nine coat closet in the convention space into a little mini–green room for her, bringing in some local Native American blankets and art that reflected the region's Native American influence and candles. It was a place where she could go and not have to worry about photos being taken, a space that only she could access." Connie would also arrange pop-up boutique shops selling local crafts and collectibles (that's another one of her mantras: go local) in a private space at the hotel for a late-night shopping spree for principals who couldn't get out to vendors and markets during the day or night because of security concerns (it's nearly impossible to seal off every threat in a mall or a marketplace, which is why you almost never see high-ranking delegates and world leaders and their families milling about at the corner market or street festivals).

- **Turn a holding space into a fun place.** Spaces where people often congregate to wait or shift gears, like lobbies and holding rooms, don't have to feel or look like a doctor's office waiting room. People won't mind the wait as much if there's music, drinks, and entertainment. Connie would bring in a live pianist and set up a champagne bar to amuse staff and guests who were stuck waiting for hours due to schedule changes and last-minute venue changes. Mark Gearan, president of Harvard's Institute of Politics and former director of the Peace Corps under President Clinton, would often play the piano for the campaign crew after a long day on the road, lifting our moods instantly.

- **Use art to shift the room's mood for gatherings that are challenging or emotional.** Oftentimes the meetings that politicians and government officials attend are rooted in tragedies—families who are victims of crime, military families, and people who have lost loved ones to disease. In these instances, it's helpful to make the meeting space comfortable and positive, within reason, of course. Many of these trips were, regrettably, to meet the parents of children who'd died of gun violence. Connie created some warmth and intimacy for those meetings. If the windows had to be blacked out for security reasons, she'd get murals painted by local schoolchildren to hang over them, or she'd bring in colorful art from a local gallery.

- **Do recon and put up signage.** There isn't a hotel or event space that an excellent RON didn't get to know intimately. Before anyone else arrived, they'd have trekked over the entire space, mapping out where the bathrooms were, meeting all the hotel service staff, figuring out which areas would be open to the press and which were private, and whether the "smoke-free" room really was (back in the nineties, smoking indoors was still a thing). Connie was especially good at taking it a step further with her famous signage to alert people: Bathrooms to the right. On camera after this point. Stage time at 3 p.m. As she likes to put it, "The idea is to idiot-proof everything so there's no confusion."

DECORATORS IN CHIEF:
THE DECOR OF THE OVAL OFFICE

No other room in our country evokes as much awe or invites as much scrutiny as the Oval Office. President Roosevelt made the current Oval Office the official executive office in 1934 to take advantage of the light from the Rose Garden, which lies just outside, and to give him easier access to the residence. (Pre-renovation, the "Oval" Office was in the center of the West Wing, which is now known as the Roosevelt Room.) The room is a study in contrasts: it's the seat of executive power, but it also looks like someone's really nice living room; its oval shape is unusual, but its size, aside from the high ceilings, is quite conventional. At first glance, the furniture arrangement may seem unremarkable—a couple of nice sofas here, a few chairs there, a big desk, a painting above the fireplace. But there's nothing haphazard about the placement or choice of furniture and decor at the highest levels of government, particularly in our nation's corner office.

If you've watched *House of Cards*, *Scandal*, or *The West Wing*—TV shows that have painstakingly re-created the Oval Office—or if you've spent any time watching CNN or Fox, you know that the presidential desk sits in a position of prominence in front of the windows. Most presidents—including FDR, Reagan, Clinton, George W. Bush,

Obama, and Trump—have used the Resolute Desk, which is crafted from oak timbers of the HMS *Resolute*, an abandoned British ship discovered by an American crew and returned to the Queen of England as a token of friendship. It was then gifted to President Rutherford B. Hayes by Queen Victoria of England in 1880 in a similar gesture of goodwill. Various leaders have made adjustments to the desk, in a sort of presidential "I was here" gesture: FDR built a hinged modesty panel into the front to hide his leg braces; Truman added a carved eagle relief on the panel; Reagan requested it be raised with a two-inch base to accommodate his height (he was six feet one inch), which also benefited successive commanders in chief who were even taller (Clinton is six feet two inches and Trump is reportedly six feet three inches).

The configuration of couches, chairs, and tables has stayed relatively the same since President John F. Kennedy, and their placement is quite deliberate. Having the two sofas face each other accommodates two separate delegations during a bilateral or a political debate, allowing for a soft division between them with the low cocktail table. The armchairs, as I mentioned earlier, almost always host the principals—the chairs are equal in size and clearly flanking the fireplace to indicate the position of importance. (Only President Carter moved one sofa to face his desk and used the other facing the fireplace.)

What has changed: Nearly all presidents have tweaked or overhauled the decor, making changes in varying degrees that reflect personality, comfort, and even political leanings (again, Carter was the renegade, choosing to use Ford's decor out of frugality, though it was assumed that if he'd won a second term he would have made some changes). I've had a front-row seat to the Oval Office makeovers of two presidents, and I watched as their political and personal identities shaped the iconic room into their own, broadcasting how they wanted to conduct business and the effect they wanted it to have on the people who met them there.

The Clinton Oval: Bold and Presiding

I watched the Oval Office undergo its transformation from President George H. W. Bush's sedate and traditional style to the lively and modern elegance of our forty-second president during my first days working for President Clinton. Little Rock–based interior designer Kaki Hockersmith had also designed the Clintons' governor's mansion, so she knew her client was not afraid of color (he wore pink, yellow, and purple ties, after all). In came the cherry-red-striped couches, a royal blue rug, and golden curtains. The room felt punchy and patriotic, cheery and strong, just like its new occupant. "The drastic change from the previous decor—President George H. W. Bush's soft palette and colonial style furniture—was a shock to the system, but once you got used to it, you couldn't remember that it wasn't always this way," says designer extraordinaire Michael Smith, who made over President Obama's Oval Office and has studied the Oval face-lifts that came before. Further personalizing the space: President Clinton's four-hundred-plus coin collection—coins from every military unit in the US armed forces he'd visited—as well as gifts received from around the world.

The contemporary vibe was balanced with the small historic busts of four presidents, cut from unpolished sapphire: Abraham Lincoln, Thomas Jefferson, Franklin Delano Roosevelt, and John F. Kennedy. The artwork paid tribute to the past as well. Hanging close to the desk—an easy place for a president to rest his eyes while pondering the most consequential of challenges—was Childe Hassam's 1917 impressionist oil painting *The Avenue in the Rain*, a gauzy view of New York City's Fifth Avenue draped in American flags. The muted colors reflected the room's hues, and the subject matter is simultaneously somber and inspiring. On the opposite wall hung Norman Rockwell's painting *Working on the Statue of Liberty*, a scene of workers hoisted and tethered with ropes cleaning the torch's amber glass, gifted to the White House by Steven Spielberg and Kate Capshaw. And, resting on a table, a framed Union general's letter about the bravery and goodness of African American soldiers who fought with him in the Civil War.

For the coffee table centerpiece, President Clinton chose to display a rock from the moon, lent to the White House by NASA and Neil Armstrong. The president sometimes used it to put things in perspective when conversations got tense. "When people are sitting here and getting agitated and angry about something, I just tell them, "Wait a minute, let's call a halt to this. See this rock? It's 3.6 billion years old. We're all just passing through, so calm down. We'll be fine."

Surrounded by symbols of democracy and freedom, and bathed in patriotic hues, the Clinton Oval inspired its occupant and visitors to think, create, and execute boldly, following the slogan on the president's desk: It can be done.

The Obama Oval: Composed and Commanding

President Obama's "get to work" mentality and his studious, calm, deliberate traits were reflected in his office face-lift, which he entrusted to preeminent Chicago designer Michael Smith, a close friend of the Obamas. "President Obama's intention was for the Oval to be a true working office," Smith told me. "But he also wanted to retain a continuity with those who came before him and to acknowledge the iconic nature of the office, so he brought in elements of President Lincoln, whose understated style matched his." The striped wall, the textiles such as leather, and the earth tones all channeled Lincoln, as did a portrait of our sixteenth president by George Henry Story. The brown leather chairs (inherited from President George W. Bush and economically reupholstered) were comfortable and functional—you weren't afraid of spilling something on them. And the soft-caramel, velvet couches (which had red, white, and blue thread woven into the fabric), telegraphed a relaxed, unfussy vibe that said, "Let's get comfortable, but let's also get down to business."

One benefit of an understated color theme: It doesn't compete with the other design elements in the room. The architecture, artwork, and historical pieces popped against the neutral backdrop. President Obama retained the Lincoln bust from President Bush, but he swapped out the Winston Churchill bust (which he sent to the Treaty Room) for one of

Martin Luther King Jr. Our first African American president held such a reverence for the civil rights work of Martin Luther King Jr. that he embedded the leader all around the Oval: On the wall was a framed program from King's "I have a dream" march. And one of King's inspirational quotes was spun into the border of the rug, along with quotes from four presidents (Lincoln, Teddy Roosevelt, FDR, and Kennedy).

The sleek, modern mica cocktail table displayed a functional, health-minded centerpiece: apples. "I began getting options for flowers from the White House florist, but I also suggested filling a bowl with apples, instead.' The president loved that idea," says Smith. And yes, he ate at least one a day from the bowl.

All these accents in total had the intended effect on visitors: welcoming yet elevated. During the ambassadors' credentialing process, I loved watching their reactions when the door swung open . . . and there was President Obama with an outstretched hand on the other side welcoming them to a space not open to the public, his private office. The ambassadors and their family members stood frozen for a split second, almost surprised that he was there greeting them, then the president would graciously coax them into the room to begin a ceremony that was the crowning achievement of their careers. I noted how the ambassadors' spouses looked at the artwork and photographs and took it all in while their husband or wife was talking to the president and while the children, well, acted like children. I recall one credentialing ceremony where the ambassador's children—much to his and his wife's horror—raced over to the apples and began to roll them across the Oval rug! The president just laughed at their antics while the ambassador raced after them. All the diplomats were so moved by the experience, and they all always commented on the many doorways it had (four) and how small it was in their humble opinion.

During bilaterals I attended in the Oval, I would stand with the delegation to the side of the desk while the press briefing took place. I always felt the sedate patterns and colors allowed the importance of the meeting to stand out and never overshadowed the principals. Again, I noted how foreign delegations looked at the personal photographs on the desk and review the bookcases to see which books were there. The manner in which President Obama had appointed his office—calm, studious, and steeped in history—reflected his approach to diplomacy and the monumental tasks at hand. I strongly suspect that he also drew inspiration from his surroundings, using the symbolism, configuration, and artifacts to remind him of the gravity and power of the office to unite the country and the world.

9

HUNGER GAMES

When most people think of Middle East peace talks, they probably imagine high-level discussions of a two-state solution. I think of hummus. In September 2009, just after entering my post, I organized the protocols for the first trilateral meeting of the administration between President Obama, Israel's Prime Minister Benjamin Netanyahu, and President Mahmoud Abbas of the Palestinian Authority. The trilateral, which would immediately follow bilaterals with each country, was monumental for so many reasons, especially as this was the first step for President Obama in continuing the ongoing challenge tended to by his predecessors.

The protocol team was ultra-fixated on the elements we knew could tilt the playing field in favor of a successful negotiation. We triple-checked every detail, from seating arrangements and table types to flags, pens, and the leaders' routes with the US Secret Service. We rehearsed how we would swiftly guide dignitaries through the labyrinthine corridors of the old Waldorf Astoria in New York, where the trilateral—as well as countless other meetings during the UN General Assembly convenings—was being held that day.

At around 11 a.m., after putting out a few fires for other meetings, my adrenaline was racing in anticipation of the trilateral. I escorted

President Abbas from the thirty-fifth floor down to a holding room on the third, where the engagement was about to take place. It was my first time interacting with him, and I was happy to find that he lived up to his reputation as a soft-spoken leader with a wise-man quality and a kind nature—he generously accepted my suggestion to ride in the service elevator since the regular elevators were taking too long. His staff called him by his nickname, Abu Mazen, an honorific that means "father of Mazen" (his oldest son, who passed away in 2002), but I addressed him with the formal "President Abbas." I then popped over to Prime Minister Netanyahu's holding room to check that everything was in order. I'd met the Israeli PM before and found him to be gracious and perpetually inquisitive, always ready with a string of personal questions that I happily answered. But as I approached, I noticed he was looking about the space with a bewildered expression, and I could sense something was off.

"How is everything, Mr. Prime Minister?" I asked, hoping I was misreading his countenance. With that famous accented baritone, he replied, "Capricia, we have been here for many hours, could I get a cup of coffee and maybe a . . . a cookie?"

I suddenly realized that these leaders were starving. I had forgotten to feed them. Not even a cookie. I was mortified. Immediately, I contacted the hotel chef, a talented man whom I had gotten to know extremely well in the days leading up to the meetings, along with many of the Waldorf's superb service staff. "I need food on three . . . fast!" He knew from my tone I was desperate. Within minutes, platters of food were sent to each leader. I made sure that both delegations received the exact same platters of hummus, vegetables, cheese, crackers, and pastries. On this day, more so than on others, our usual treatment of parity was being closely watched by each delegation.

I still cringe at the memory. I had obsessed over covering the basic protocols but had inadvertently set a land mine by failing to provide food and coffee. This was not merely an oversight of hospitality and respect. Hunger can cause people to experience impatience and to be more risk-averse: Researchers from the University of Dundee in Scotland have found that when people are hungry, it can impact their ability to make decisions, making them more impatient and more likely to settle for a small, short-term reward versus a larger reward that they must wait longer for.

What impact might hunger have had on these delicate negotiations between these Middle Eastern nations? What effect on risk taking and focus? On an already tense day, I had compromised the climate necessary for success and created a needless slight. I felt that I had failed the president. After that no one went hungry again.

THE "HANGRY" DIPLOMAT

Meeting the basic needs of a diplomat or any guest is the most fundamental rule of protocol. Not much can be accomplished when people are hungry or thirsty. It's well known that skipping meals slows thinking and productivity. The brain uses a surprising number of calories to think, and when our brain is low on fuel, reaction time and memory suffer. But hunger has other effects, too: For one, it makes people focus more on their own needs than on the needs of others. When we start hankering for a club sandwich, our state of mind shifts to "What can I do to make myself feel better?" This self-centered thinking, even if it's subconscious, can handicap a negotiation. Research from Cornell University and Dartmouth finds that when people enter a negotiation on an empty stomach, they feel they are more entitled and deserving of a positive outcome than their colleagues. You may wonder: Shouldn't we all feel deserving of positive results? Yes, but believing you are *more* deserving than your counterpart makes it harder to see the other person's perspective. On the flip side, a full belly likely ushers in a state of body and mind that encourages outreach and social connection: You've handled your own needs, now you can focus on connecting with others.

Hunger can also make people aggressive and snappish. I've seen presidents become snippy when a craving strikes; fortunately, they always have a chef waiting in the wings to whip up whatever they'd like, whether they're in the White House, on *Air Force One*, or on foreign soil. And President Obama's personal aides always had a bag full of high-protein energy bars. I'll admit to getting a bit hangry myself, issuing a sharper-than-necessary comment if I've skipped a meal. I've tried to avoid this by always having a pocketful of almonds on hand—I was nicknamed "the squirrel" by the staff. You can blame biology for hunger-induced outbursts: It's harder to exert self-control when our brain is low on glucose, our brain's preferred form of fuel. Perhaps regularly timed platters of food at summits really could broker world peace.

NOURISH YOUR NEGOTIATIONS

As crucial as food is to the brain and the body, the ancient tradition of breaking bread is also an important cultural tool and a potential source of power in interactions. "Food diplomacy was really the first kind of diplomacy," says Secretary of State Hillary Clinton. "It was about reciprocity—if I share what I have with you now, you'll return the favor to me if I get lost in the desert."

I knew its influence from my White House days, when I witnessed food bringing people together during social events and resulting in serendipitous, game-changing conversations. At the White House state dinner in 1994 for Russia's President Boris Yeltsin, the confluence of Steven Spielberg, David Geffen, and Jeffrey Katzenberg at a table launched a discussion that hatched one of the most successful collaborations of all time. Over rack of lamb in an apricot chutney and fine wine, the three began forming the concept for DreamWorks, the motion picture studio responsible for producing films such as *Shrek* and *Kung Fu Panda*.

But it wasn't until a certain chicken luncheon that I understood that a carefully planned menu could play a pivotal role in work settings. Early in my term as chief of protocol, Secretary Clinton was hosting an important bilateral meeting at the State Department. We were in the James Monroe Reception Room, a Wedgwood-blue-and-white salon named for our fifth president. (The secretary loved the room's soft colors and held many lunch and dinner meetings there.) On that day, I was doing what I often do at functions: standing discreetly in the corner, surveying to make sure all was going according to the careful plan. (I've always wished that the chief of protocol could be issued an invisibility cloak, as in *Harry Potter*.) I watched as the main course was placed in front of Secretary Clinton: a simple meal of baked chicken, steamed rice, and vegetables. I noticed her pause and take it in, and then she turned and looked directly at me. Apparently, I was not invisible, after all. From years of service, I knew immediately what her expression meant: We could do better. It wasn't that the meal was poorly prepared, but we had missed an opportunity to showcase our country's culinary traditions and introduce our guests to another aspect of who we, as Americans, are. A light went off in my head: Here is another opportunity for our team to engage in smart power. Food would become an important tool of our diplomacy, a creative and delicious way to share the best of our nation and to advance any engagement.

The next morning, I huddled with the team, in particular the wonderful State Department chefs Jason Larkin and Chris James, who until then hadn't been asked to fully unleash their creativity, and told them we had a new mission: to make food a key ingredient of smart diplomacy. Natalie Jones, who was then assistant chief of ceremonials, the point person in the office on all social events at the State Department, used her genius to help me develop this new initiative. Together we cooked up the Diplomatic Culinary Partnership (DCP), an innovative program— created in partnership with the James Beard Foundation—that used food as a strategic tool to strengthen our relationships with other countries' dignitaries, whether it was through a carefully selected State luncheon menu, or teaching foreign diplomats' children and American schoolchildren how to cook a meal together. Within the DCP I assembled the American Chef Corps, a group of talented chefs from every corner of our country who volunteered to be called at a moment's notice to serve as culinary advisors or prepare food tailored to a policy goal for the president and secretary of state and their foreign counterparts. "To me, food is one of the most powerful tools of diplomacy there is," José Andrés, the Spanish-American chef extraordinaire and humanitarian, has told me. "The soft power of a thoughtfully prepared meal goes a long way to bridge any divide, large or small. I've cooked for heads of state and for people in need after disaster, and I can tell you—every person on earth, no matter their situation, is made more human when sharing a meal with a neighbor." The American Chef Corps also blogged and tweeted about events here and abroad, as other bureaus used them as traveling speakers about American culture, since food tells a rich story that goes beyond the contents of the plate. The program was so successful that I brought on Lauren Bernstein, who, with her coordination talents and can-do attitude, helped us grow the program to around eighty participating chefs. (Unfortunately, the DCP program and American Chef Corps ended under the Trump administration.)

Thus, culinary diplomacy was born in our US State Department—officially, that is. Food has always brought people together in government, strengthened bonds at state dinners, and persuaded tablemates to see things a little bit more from your side of the plate. But this was next-level food politics. "A thoughtful, elevated menu says, 'We respect you. We may have differences, but we can sit down and break bread together,'" says Secretary Clinton, who championed the soft power of cuisine from the moment she became First Lady, hiring a White House executive chef who was born and trained in the United States, the talented Walter Scheib. The First Lady believed that the White House cuisine served to dignitaries should reflect who we are as a country, and Scheib impressed her with an all-American menu during his audition.

What does top-shelf culinary diplomacy in action look like? In February 2012, Vice President Biden and Secretary Clinton hosted a state luncheon for China's Xi Jinping, who was vice president at the time but was expected to assume the presidency the following year. The visit, including a high-level luncheon, was a prelude to his becoming the next leader of an economic superpower that was quickly achieving parity with the United States. I knew that this visit was an opportunity to showcase just how vital a tool food could be and that a "business as usual" luncheon wouldn't be acceptable. This meal needed to serve as an element of the launch for a new era of US-China relations.

We began thinking about which member of our developing American Chef Corps could create a tempting feast that would represent the best of our culture and keep these countries at the table for years to come. Incidentally, I knew better than to serve Vice President Xi a meal that was 100 percent Chinese; I never fed high-level dignitaries their own culture's food, as they can *always* do it better, and it wastes the opportunity to share our culture. (It was always a disappointment when we traveled overseas and were served steak and potatoes at an event, when my taste buds were hoping for a bite of their country's delicacies.) But I also held true to the practice I learned from Chef Scheib during my time in the White House that a nod to a visitor's culture was important, and best done within the components of the meal. This could be achieved by incorporating a design element related to the counterpart's country or by using traditional spices in a dish or two. For the 1994 President Nelson Mandela state visit, for example, Chef Scheib (in consultation with African American guest chef Patrick Clark) cooked a healthy, traditional American meal for the South African president, but infused traditional South African flavors of lemongrass and red curry into a vegetable dish as a salute to his country's cuisine.

Natalie and I reached out to the "kitchen cabinet" of volunteer advisors, and their unanimous recommendation was chef Ming Tsai. I knew we'd hit the jackpot with the talented and outgoing Chinese American chef, who had founded two highly lauded restaurants, the Blue Ginger in Wellesley, Massachusetts, and the Blue Dragon in Boston, which specialized in delicious East-West fusion. What better way to share who we are—a country made up of many ethnicities—and to signal a desire for collaboration than with cuisine that literally blends several cultures? After months of planning and tastings and collaboration with the vice president's team, led by Dr. Biden's chief of staff, Catherine Russell, a dear friend and an accomplished diplomat, the perfect menu emerged: soy-marinated Alaskan butterfish (or sablefish, depending on which fishmonger you ask), roasted sweet potato soup with crispy duck confit roulade, gingered swiss chard, eight treasured rice packet (traditional Chinese recipes often feature eight "luxury" ingredients, as eight is a lucky number in China), and flourless bittersweet chocolate cake with cardamom ice cream. Mouthwatering, memorable, and unifying.

I was also over the moon that Ming spoke Mandarin. When Vice President Xi arrived for the formal greetings held in the Monroe Room, it was language that broke the ice. First meetings are always a bit awkward for leaders. They are cordial, but there is often a slight strain in the air. After my formal introduction of Vice President Xi to Vice President Biden and Secretary Clinton, she introduced Ming, hitting all the right points, including the fact that he'd flown in from Boston for the honor of cooking just for him. Vice President Xi's eyes lit up. The two men—the son of Chinese immigrants and the powerful world leader-to-be—began talking in rapid-fire Mandarin, laughing and sharing stories. When we turned to our interpreter, eager for the translation, he held up one finger for us to wait because it was all happening at such a fast pace. Ming turned with a huge smile, thankful for this once-in-a-lifetime opportunity, and told us how proud his parents would be that he had spoken to the next leader of China about them and his passion for food. Vice President Xi also smiled upon hearing these words translated. It was a complete change in tone, from diplomatic formality to pure intimacy and warmth. The Chinese vice president could see that we had designed a special welcome for him, and the food spoke of the fusion between our cultures and the value we saw in our relationship.

And the meal? It was one of the most divine I've ever had—I can still taste the melt-in-your-mouth fish. I'd like to think that the goodwill sparked over that afternoon feast helped set the stage (and the table) for the leader's official state visit as the president of China the following year, when he and President Obama met at California's Sunnylands. As I mentioned in chapter 7, the Camp David of the West proved the perfect setting for the June 2013 historic "shirtsleeves" summit. President Xi had just been elected, leading a country of 1.3 billion people. Although important topics were being raised, the meeting's umbrella goal was to give these two world leaders an opportunity to get to know each other and grow a warmer relationship away from the formality and hustle and bustle of the White House. Food became a big piece of this effort. It started with the selection of a chef, an American master whose participation would convey how important this relationship was to the United States. We shot for the (food) stars and landed the unparalleled Bobby Flay, restaurateur extraordinaire and *Iron Chef* alum. Flay was flattered by the opportunity and dived into the planning. Next up, the menu: Unlike the blended fusion dishes of the luncheon a year earlier, we wanted the courses to be all-American, telling the vast and earthy story of our nation, from the rugged midwestern plains to the flourishing West Coast vineyards to the rocky Atlantic coast to the spicy Southwest and savory South, regions that had inspired Flay's signature dishes for decades. The menu was also a lineup of some of our most down-home and traditional foods, a relaxed and hearty breaking of bread with friends.

The magnificent menu revealed our identity, course by course: New Mexico lobster tamales with corn and green chiles (paired with Iron Horse 2004 cuvée commemorating the Chinese "Year of the Snake," 2013, as a tip of the hat to President Xi), porterhouse American steaks and individual California cherry pies topped with Kentucky bourbon, vanilla, and mint ice cream. In a reciprocal and friendly gesture, President Xi brought Maotai—a brand of baijiu, a very fragrant and deceptively strong distilled Chinese liquor made from red sorghum—to share a toast with the table. Between bites of tender beef and sweet, melty dessert, and sips of Maotai, the world leaders and their advisors laughed, bonded, and broached sensitive topics that were made more palatable by the scrumptious food. President Xi was also incredibly impressed with meeting Flay, who had a global reputation.

The Friday-night meal set the tone for the next day's talks, which, as press statements afterward indicated, resulted in some consensus on greenhouse gas emissions and how to respond to an increasingly threatening North Korea. Ultimately, the two nations sat at the literal and proverbial table, coming together to solve some of the globe's most pressing challenges.

WINNER DINNERS FOR CONNECTING AND IMPRESSING

All of us wish we had Bobby Flay on speed-dial, but there are plenty of other ways to elevate an executive lunch or dinner party—or a family gathering—and create the just-right conditions for your event.

1. **Consider the time limit and scope of the discussion.** Are you aiming to cover a number of intricate issues? You may need to introduce a fourth or fifth course to match the dining pace to the conversation. Or do you have a short window and need to deliver the meal equivalent of an elevator pitch? If so, arrange for a meal that's already plated so that you can dig in right away, and serve or order an uncomplicated entrée so that you're not waiting for courses to come and go. Bento boxes are great for quick business lunches (the contents don't have to be Asian), and they're a wonderful way to present the food. One caveat: Allow for ten minutes of starter conversation at the outset so that you're not trying to talk through chews of Cobb salad. Alternatively, lay out a timeline that lets everyone eat first with the understanding that after fifteen minutes you'll segue into a hard data discussion: "Let's first enjoy our meal, then we can get down to business." If the lunch is formal and you'll have more than a couple of attendees, you may want to place an agenda next to everyone's plate so that timing and topic expectations are defined.

2. **Let your goal set the tone.** You're going to a lot of trouble to come up with a menu and an enjoyable experience, so you want your choices to support what you're trying to achieve. Is the event a celebration? Include festive elements in the mix such as a party-worthy appetizer, a signature cocktail, and a wow desert. Is this meal bringing people together for a funeral or memorial? Comfort foods such as a lasagna, chicken pot pie, or meat loaf are best. If it is the sendoff for someone who is moving on, serve never-forget-us foods reminiscent of the city your colleague is leaving (Philly cheesesteak or Dallas barbecue). If it's a retirement lunch, you can have fun with the presentations in a way that honors the milestone—a cake decorated like the face of a watch or a beach and golf tees adorning your platters.

3. **Express yourself.** Use the opportunity to reflect your values, history, and passions. Serving an all-organic, locally sourced menu says you

care about the environment; ethnic or indigenous selections can speak to your travels or your heritage.

4. **Use the menu to drive the conversation.** A carefully selected course lineup and descriptions of the dishes can open the door to topics you want to broach. Identifying meat as "locally raised" can hint at your business's local ties. If you want to discuss the history of your company, have some heirloom tomatoes or ancient grains on the menu—it may sound corny (no pun!), but the menu elements can subtly underscore your goals. If you are floating the idea of a partnership, describe the menu in terms of "pairings," perhaps a wine and a dish that go together well, or two ingredients that balance each other.

TABLE MANNERS

Helping people feel comfortable at the table with the age-old rules of etiquette is one of my passions. Eating, drinking, and behaving in the manner that our ancestors did is a beautiful way to stay connected to older generations—although thank goodness we've moved beyond using pieces of stale bread as plates, as they did in eleventh-century England. In the past, table manners were a way to reinforce social distinctions—royalty and the "well-bred" ate one way, the peasant classes another. That newfangled eating instrument, the fork, became popular with the upper classes in pasta-loving Italy during the eleventh century and eventually filtered down to the middle and lower classes.

There are some who may find the many dining dos and don'ts onerous and unnecessary. But the fact remains that table manners define polite society, and in most cases there are legitimate reasons as to why they endure. They were not simply invented to annoy your curmudgeon of an uncle or surly teen. Playing by mealtime rules also signals a willingness to participate in the social norms of a culture, and no one wants to be that person at the table who gets it wrong. I was recently in Singapore on business and was surprised to see an American tablemate stabbing the food with chopsticks, a faux pas equivalent to someone piercing and eating pieces of food with a knife in the United States. My tablemate, a Singaporean, who clearly also noticed the offense, dashed a look at me with a faint shake of the head.

Here's how to avoid common mealtime mistakes and create an experience that everyone will remember for the right reasons. (I include a detailed list of table dos and don'ts in the Appendix.)

- **Which fork first? Think: Outside in.** Utensils are set in the order of use beginning with those on the outside. So salad forks are set to the left of dinner forks on the left side of the plate; butter knives are set to the right of steak knives on the right side of the plate (or on the bread plate, handle to the right, with the blade facing in). The surest sign that a diner knows cutlery etiquette: Just after the main course is removed, slide the dessert spoon placed at the top of your plate down to the right, and the dessert fork down to the left to prepare for dessert.

- **Table your napkin.** Don't leave a crumpled napkin on your chair when you get up for a restroom break—it's a huge no-no. I recently explained this to a friend who begged to differ, stating she learned you always leave your napkin on your seat. I asked her, "Why would you put the cloth that you bring to your mouth in the same place you park your seat?" (I saw her have an "aha" moment.) Instead, place it on the table to the right of your plate, folded neatly. (Several etiquette experts do advise that placing your napkin on the seat is proper. I do not. Even at fine restaurants, a waiter will never leave a folded napkin on your seat.)

- **Pass to the right, hold for the serve.** When I'm hosting, I bring out the serving platters, staggering them one by one for flow, and hand it to a person while saying, "Sally, will you begin and pass around to your right?" (I like setting expectations as much as I like setting tables.) Always offer to hold the dish for the person to your right while they serve themselves . . . and ask the same of your tablemate to your left. Pretty soon everyone catches on.

- **Tines and spoons face down.** Before you pass the serving dish, place the serving fork tines or the serving spoon facedown so that utensils stay put and you don't flop sauce on your tablemate.

- **If you're hosting a large group, consider ways to direct the conversation so that everyone is included.** We've all been at dinners where we talk to only the two or three people seated near us, and it feels as if we've missed out on the party at the other end of the table. There are several ways to get everyone involved:
  - *At the start of the meal, casually direct everyone to stick to a single conversation.* I find it's easiest to do this by listening in on some starter chatter between seatmates, picking one of those convos, and bringing others into it. My dear friends Lee Satterfield, executive VP of Meridian International Center, and Patrick Steel, CEO of Politico, normally try to maintain a one-conversation table, partly because they can't stand missing out on what's being discussed at the other end of the table. Patrick is brilliant at asking a guest to explain a topic specialty or angle to the table, and he is always prepared to chime in with interesting news if there is a lull. If you want people to avoid politics, be clear at the outset (though also be prepared for people to bring it up anyway.)
  - *Use a tool.* My friend Adrienne Arsht has a collection of unique antique silver napkin rings. After cocktails she asks guests to pick one and, at the dinner table, explain why they chose the one they did, whether because the design invokes a memory, reflects a current news topic, or they just like its imagery. I've learned the most interesting details about people's family or recent events in their lives thanks to her napkin-ring ritual.
  - *Swap seats.* This is trickier to maneuver, but you can plan ahead to exchange seats with someone at another table or at the other

end of the table for the appetizer or dessert course. This allows all the guests to have time with the host.

- **Consider hiring help for business dinners you host at home.** A friend recently asked me whether she should hire a server for her dinner party of ten. I told her, if the function is business-related, absolutely. Anything that keeps you at the table is a smart choice—you don't want to miss a business opportunity, nor do you want to interrupt the flow of conversation by having to get up multiple times during the meal. If it's a social dinner, it's not necessary to hire help, but do plant yourself in a spot that makes it easy to go from the table to the kitchen, so that you're not squeezing past guests every time someone needs a condiment. I've also found it helpful to have a person who's not on the guest list (so guests can fully relax) to help with things such as coats, drinks, refills, and clearing the table. College students who are looking for pickup jobs are a nice fit (thank you to all my son's friends and to Craigslist).

- **Take care of tipsy guests.** If someone has drunk too much to keep his composure, it's time to help him wrap up the evening. The best thing to do is enlist the person he came with to help out. A walk outside for some fresh air during which you discuss how he'll get home usually does the trick (or offer up your guest room).

  At a few events I've had to rescind the invitation of an out-of-control guest. I'd learned during my time at the White House that rescinding invitations mid-event was possible and occasionally necessary and very effective at calming the situation.

  To avoid enabling overindulgence, be careful of how much alcohol you're serving your guests. Instruct waiters at a catered event to ask before collaring (topping off) a person's drink. It's difficult to keep track if someone keeps filling up your glass.

- **Eat what's on your plate.** Mom was right! Unless you have an allergy, you should find a way to eat at least some of what you're served. This is especially true if you are in another country. Secretary Clinton, who holds food diplomacy in high regard, is a diplomat who practices what she preaches. Once, when traveling in Mongolia when she was First Lady, she was offered mare's milk from a nomad family. "It was all they had and they offered it to me ceremoniously, so I drank it," she told me later. This may sound like no big deal, but the traveling White House doctor, upon discovering she'd drunk unpasteurized horse's milk, told her she'd have a good chance of getting brucellosis, a bacterial disease contracted from infected cattle, sheep, or horses that can cause serious symptoms in humans. (Thankfully, she didn't.)

- **Refill? Accept the first offer, refuse the second.** I eat and drink by this rule when I'm traveling. The host will continue to offer unless you cut it off, so this guideline ensures you appear neither greedy nor ungrateful.

TOASTS

If you deliver a top-shelf toast, your host will take note and it can shift things in your favor. Or it can have the opposite effect if you bungle it. In 2011, during a state visit to the UK, there was an oops moment during President Obama's toast to Her Majesty. And I accepted complete responsibility. The toast protocol at a state dinner at Her Majesty's table is *very* specific. I confirmed all the details with the Royal Household, then conveyed them directly to the president, both through a briefing and in person immediately before the dinner. "I got this, Capricia," he assured me. I stood with all other attendees at the elegant long table and watched the president begin his toast. It started out perfectly—his glass was held outward and high but not directed at the Queen, per protocol. President Obama then said the fateful words midway through his toast, ". . . and to Her Majesty, the Queen." Ouch. In the UK, when you utter the words, ". . . and to Her Majesty, the Queen," it cues the royal band to begin playing "God Save the Queen." Those words should come only at the tail end of the speech—and nowhere else. The band heard the first phrase and began to play over his speech. Clearly, the band could not stop playing and he, appropriately, could not stop his toast to Her Majesty. It was a train wreck that I could not stop, either. Both continued for what seemed like an eternity. I saw the annoyance on Her Majesty's face as she glanced upward to the band, and I caught the discomfort of President Obama as he shifted his stance and slightly paused. The protocol faux pas was targeted by a few press outlets with one headline that acutely hurt: "Burnt Toast." I felt terrible. I'd been so focused on the multiple elements of the evening, especially reminding him not to clink glasses—British royals approach the glass but don't touch—that I'd neglected to read the speech, and always asked for an advance copy thereafter. (Incidentally, President Trump did inappropriately clink glasses with Her Majesty during a June 2019 state visit to the UK.)

So why do we toast? And why in the world is it called a toast when there's no crispy bread involved? Drinking to your tablemates' health and prosperity goes back as far as alcohol consumption, but the term *toast* likely stems from the fact that an actual piece of toast would be floated in the large vessel (a "loving cup" from which everyone at the table would drink) in order to improve the taste of the wine.

Here are some pointers to make your toast the most. (See the list of countries on page 385 to drink up more advice.)

- **Always stand.** Never toast from your seat, it will come off as dismissive.

- **Don't raise your glass if *you're* being toasted.** In many countries, this can make it seem as if you are toasting yourself (though in some countries it's appropriate to stand—check with your host).

- **Say no to H$_2$O.** Toasting with water is a no-go in most countries, even for teetotalers (juice is fine). Some cultures may believe a water toast to be bad luck or associated with death, since water can signify "a watery grave." You should let your host know in advance that you don't indulge so they can have a non-alcoholic beverage on hand.

- **Know whether to empty your glass before setting it down.** Different countries have different customs, and the type of alcohol can play a role, too. During President Clinton's first visit to China in 1998, I was invited to the state dinner. At my table, a very thin colleague was downing a very hefty glass of wine after each toast, having been told by the protocol office that this was the custom in China. Naturally, the effects of the alcohol hit her immediately, prompting the Chinese diplomat next to me to remark: "Is your friend all right?" I was worried too. I have since learned that in China, the classic "cheers" is *gan bei*, which means "dry cup," and the practice of downing it in one gulp stems from the tradition of doing shots of the fiery Chinese liquor *baijiu*. In traditional China of yore, people drank *baijiu* (no wine or beer) and drank only when there were toasts. In more modern times—with increased consumption of many types of alcohol—there may be a disconnect. It is not expected that one down an entire glass of wine or beer after a toast, though if you were poured a shot glass of *baijiu*, it would be appropriate to "dry your cup." My poor colleague had the right intention, wrong alcohol (and wrong-sized glass).

- **Master clinks.** In nearly every country it's considered rude not to make eye contact during a clink or toast. As for clinks, it varies. Americans do; Hungarians do unless they're drinking beer; and as I've already noted, British royals never do. The night after President Obama's royal toast hiccup, he and the First Lady hosted Her Majesty and Prince Philip at the US ambassador's residence in London. All the guests had a quick cocktail and then made their way to the dining room. As we were walking, President Obama leaned in and asked me, "Are there any special notes for tonight's toast?" That stung a bit—he didn't mean for it to, as he was sincere in his request—but it reminded me of the previous evening's misstep. "Like clinking?" he asked. At the US ambassador's residence, we were technically in the "United States," so the etiquette was on his terms, and I replied, "Sir, we are on American soil, clink away!" And he did.

How to Give a Proper Toast

In 2009, I had my own "burnt toast" moment. I was invited to a luncheon in my honor as the newly minted chief of protocol at the home of Jo Carole Lauder, a member of the Estée Lauder family and one of the kindest and most generous people I know. I realized at the very last minute that I should toast the hostess. It was the first toast of my office . . . and the last one I ever tried to wing. I stood up and delivered the most jumbled, ill-prepared string of sentences imaginable. I sat down and wished I could melt into my chair. Bari Lurie, an accomplished woman who'd been my truth-teller intern when I served as social secretary—and who is now an experienced business executive and chief of staff to Chelsea Clinton—turned to me. "Capricia, I thought you would have this down by now," she gently chastised (I'm so grateful for my posse of straight shooters). She later reminded me of advice I had shared years earlier with the office: Pick just three things to cover. It makes sense—anyone can remember three things. Plus, your audience, who are often waiting to eat, don't want to hear a long toast, either. I've honed my "three things" over the years and find that this approach works in most countries and circumstances, taking some of the terror out of toasting:

1. Thank the host and state why the event is important. ("Thank you, Ann and John, for hosting us this evening. Your support for the arts and the annual event is exemplary.")

2. Identify the audience (note any special guests and briefly express appreciation for their presence) and connect them to the event. "Ann has brought together some of the city's most influential arts and culture decision makers, and we are especially pleased to have Sally Smith with us this evening, a

contemporary art expert. It's wonderful to be able to share best practices with each other." If the event is a personal one, acknowledge how gratifying it is to see everyone (family, friends, etc.) gathered together.

3. This third point can be your wild card, which fluctuates depending on the event. You can mention a future engagement: "I look forward to reaching out to you all to discuss your involvement in our art internship program." Or drop a bit of juicy news at the end of the toast to make people feel in-the-know. "I want to let everyone know—and mum's the word, since this is not being released until Monday—that we just exceeded our goal with the incredible support of Ann!" Or for personal gatherings, I might share a short anecdote about the guest of honor. Then bookend it with another reference to the honoree(s), "To Ann and John."

10.

SECRETS OF A GIFT WHISPERER

Gifts are a language. When you learn to "gift" fluently, you can take every relationship to a higher level. Presents have the potential to transmit a world of concrete ideas and goals, packets of information encoded in a single object. Just as important: They can pull at the heartstrings and communicate emotional sentiments in a manner that is subtler than stating your feelings and risking an awkward moment. In protocol, we used the gift exchange to forge and reinforce relationships between individual dignitaries and nations. The gift exchange is a long-held tradition of goodwill and a powerful way to forge or cement a connection. It speaks volumes about the current relationship between the countries and the direction you want things to go in, and it can invoke sensitivity and intimacy in a natural and easy way, no words needed. When it went right (which it almost always did), it was brilliant diplomacy. And when it didn't, we made sure the misstep was never repeated.

When President Obama was invited for a UK state visit in 2011 to meet with Queen Elizabeth II, our gifts team went into hyperdrive. For this particular visit, we needed a selection that would reflect the special friendship between President Obama and Her Majesty, as well as the bond between our countries. We also needed the perfect present that would erase from the press's memory an oops-of-a-gift given by the president to Her Majesty in 2009 (just before my arrival as chief of protocol), an iPod loaded with video footage of her visit to the United States in 2007 as well as some of her favorite songs. The offering was so well intentioned, but it was considered too familiar for the first meeting between these heads of state. (Plus, Her Majesty already had an iPod). This story is noteworthy mainly in that the gaffe had diverted the attention away from the intended focus of the visit, a getting-to-know-you session between leaders whose countries have long shared a special relationship. Understandably, the UK press corps were now on high alert to report on the president's gift—what would those Americans bring? Recognizing the high stakes, I was unrelenting with the gift staff for months. David Solomon, a career protocol officer who had an innate understanding of the importance of symbolism in diplomacy, and whose dedication I so appreciated, was tasked with this visit. After a few rounds of not-quite-right ideas, we went into major team collaboration (David worked night and day researching), dreaming up what we hoped would be a collection of stellar choices, and presented our best-of-the-best options for the entire Royal Family to the president in an official Gift Memo, from which President Obama made his selections. My gut told me that every gift on the list was a winner, but I wouldn't know for sure until the unveiling.

As we entered a grand room at Buckingham Palace where the exchange was to take place, I took a breath and gazed above me—every elegant arch and crystal chandelier was steeped in British history. I snapped out of my daydream when I saw the long tables in front of us, bare except for their white tablecloths. It was Game Time. Katie Jack, *the* gift wizard—she is emblematic of a true protocol officer, possessing the most gracious demeanor—showed me exactly how to arrange our gifts artistically on the tables. The UK staff placed theirs next to ours. We had not shared with our British counterparts what our gifts were, nor they with us (as was always the case), so there was a lot of peeking over shoulders as we laid them out.

Suddenly, the enormous pocket doors slid open. In walked Her Majesty, leading the president. She pointed to her wristwatch—I found she liked to stay on schedule—and told him it was time for the gift exchange.

Her Majesty first presented her gifts (she is her own chief of protocol—who knows protocol better than the Queen, after all?) to the president and Mrs. Obama: a lovely portfolio filled with original letters from past presidents and an antique gold-and-coral brooch. President and Mrs. Obama were so genuinely touched. Then it was our turn. I stood near the president, close enough to assist if there were any questions (though he didn't need assistance). As he presented the gift meant for Her Majesty, I felt a tingle of anticipation and hope that she would receive our gift with the intended emotional ties. Her Majesty had a deep love for her father, King George VI, so the president ultimately decided upon a special album commemorating his and his wife's visit (the Queen Mother) to the United States in 1939, the first time a ruling British monarch had visited the States (the visit I describe in chapter 7). My inspired and treasured friend and colleague, the infinitely resourceful Tracy Bernstein (who brought her invaluable retail expertise to the job) had tracked down rare, archival mementos of the trip, and we'd compiled it all in a handmade leather-bound album. When the Queen turned to the first page and I watched her expression, I knew we had a winner. She was visibly moved, sighing heavily as she read each invitation and note we discovered for her. She then looked at the president with such emotion and appreciation that I almost started tearing up myself. (The album also happened to dovetail perfectly with the personal tour she gave President and Mrs. Obama later that day of her private collection, which contained a great deal of memorabilia about her father.) President and Mrs. Obama additionally gave Her Majesty an exquisite American-made vintage moss agate floral brooch (she affectionately wore the brooch the following evening at a reciprocal dinner hosted by President and Mrs. Obama at Winfield House, the US ambassador's residence, and at the state visit of President and Mrs. Trump to the United Kingdom in 2019).

Her Majesty then called to her husband, Prince Philip, to see what we had brought for his ponies. He made his way to the table and lifted the gift, Fell Pony bits and shanks—hand-crafted by artisans from Colorado and Ohio and with the presidential seal soldered on—for the carriage ponies he loved to race. He gave a slight "Hmph?" I was immediately concerned. Did he like them or not? Her Majesty wanted to affirm for him that these were high quality and called over a staff member who must have been an equestrian expert to review the gift. He lifted the bits and shanks and gave them a good once-over, assuring Her Majesty that they were excellent quality. Her Majesty gave her husband a "Ha, see?!" look, then asked, "Who are the bushes for?" For Prince Charles, a champion of the environment and sustainability causes, and Lady Camilla, the Duchess of Cornwall, we had created a hand-crafted wooden crate made out of a fallen magnolia tree from the White House South Grounds, which we'd recovered after a 2010 winter storm—our team was always on the hunt and ready for a rescue! (We used the wood from fallen trees collected from the White House grounds often in creating one-of-a-kind presents, as well as materials from renovated historic monuments. Recipients cherished these types of gifts, and the adaptive reuse ensured that historical pieces would not end up in the dumpster or compost pile.) We then filled the container with saplings and seeds from the White House, Monticello (Thomas Jefferson's home), and Mount Vernon (George Washington's home and a site her father had visited), along with honey from Mrs. Obama's beehive on the South Grounds.

The staff was dismissed back to our hold space (an exquisite room on a lower level), where I nervously awaited the press reaction, periodically pinging Katie, who was at our hotel watching the BBC to see if there was any news. About fifteen to twenty minutes later, she called to say that the British press was reporting that the Americans had gotten it right! "Obama scores with better gifts for the Queen" read one memorable headline. The media also reported the history and importance of each gift, sharing details that honored every hour of work our team had put into these historic selections. I was beyond elated and immediately called the team in the States to thank them. We'd made the right move, but you never know until it's played out if the gift you spent months creating will bump the relationship to higher ground or turn into an international incident.

A poorly chosen gift is never good, but it can really go south when you have no gift at all. I learned an important lesson—never go against your instincts and always have something at the ready—in the midst of a nuclear arms deal. In 2010, Russian President Dmitri Medvedev and

President Obama convened in Prague to sign the New START agreement, which set lower limits on the numbers of Russian and American nuclear warheads. While the leaders and their teams spent the previous months negotiating the life-and-death consequences of the agreement, our protocol teams had been negotiating the gift exchange.

During high-level bilaterals, leaders either exchange gifts through their protocol team or personally—a leader-to-leader ritual that sometimes happens in front of the press to broadcast the relationship. On this occasion, because the presidents would be consumed with the details of the arms deal, and because we wanted to keep the focus on the signing, it was decided that the exchange would be carried out privately between the US and Russian protocol staff.

As we rolled up to the palace where the meet-and-greet and signing would take place, I debated whether or not to leave the gift in the car. I have a great gut, and I usually pay heed. But on this day, I argued against my instincts to bring the gift along. I told myself that getting the gift through would take up too much time. Plus, we already secured and triple-confirmed the details of the exchange, so I wouldn't need it until later in the day. But as the initial meeting was drawing to a close, I saw that President Medvedev had a small gift bag, which he gave to President Obama. I was surprised, and I hate being surprised. I looked over at my Russian counterpart, the elegant and cool Marina Entaltseva with a wide-eyed "Really?!" expression. I hadn't yet met Marina in person— this was our first engagement together. She returned my gaze with a shrug.

After graciously receiving the present, President Obama—who was genuinely touched—turned to me with an expectant look. I knew what was coming, the dreaded moment where I would disappoint my president. "Capricia?" It would have been undiplomatic to try to explain that this wasn't what we'd agreed upon and thus I had not brought our gift with us. So instead of creating unnecessary tension, I offered, "It looks like ours was held up, sir. I am trying to retrieve it."

After the meeting, I sidled up to Marina and formally introduced myself. Then I asked, "Why the side gift? As you know we agreed no leader-to-leader exchange." "What can I do?" she said. "He had it with him; he wanted to give the gift, I cannot tell my president not to give the gift." She was right. And I knew it wasn't meant to throw us off-balance. President Medvedev seemed to really like President Obama. Over the past year, the two had built a respectful rapport. He'd felt the spirit move him and he acted on it in the most natural of ways: offering something meaningful, a bonus gift of sorts, to a leader he was beginning to see as a partner.

Although the gaffe didn't affect the outcome of the visit, I'd put my president in an awkward situation. Later that day, in the briefing room, I apologized to President Obama and explained the circumstances. "It looks like we got out-gifted, huh, Capricia?" he said. I knew he was making light of it to spare me some embarrassment, but he was also pointedly making note of it. I apologized and promised always to be prepared in the future.

Filing the incident away, I vowed never again to go against my instincts or be unprepared for the unknown. Thereafter, we always had a well-selected gift for the president to present *just in case*, especially for President Medvedev, who'd proved himself an impromptu gift giver. The two leaders met again the following year at the G20 in France. This time, the gift exchange particulars were not defined by either side in advance, as is often the case at large summits (a slew of back-to-back meetings tightens the itinerary). Marina and I had developed a trusting relationship by this point, but I was now forever overprepared and brought along a wonderful present I'd had in my back pocket for some time: Tracy and the gifts team had researched President Medvedev's pastimes and discovered he was a huge fan of American jazz and collected vinyl records from the jazz greats. So we went to a vintage collector in DC that Medvedev's staff was known to frequent and curated a selection of original jazz albums. We knew this sentimental gift would hit the right note: the leaders' relationship was moving in a more positive direction, and a personal gift would emphasize that.

Just before the meeting, I reminded the president of the gift, and we agreed I'd place it on a table at the far end of the room, leaving it to him to determine whether or not to make use of it. The meeting seemed to have gone very well, and as it wrapped, the president turned and, in his easy manner, said to President Medvedev, "Ah, Dmitri, I have a little something for you." Marina and I hustled over to the gift table and I quickly displayed the albums. When President Medvedev saw them, he looked at us with an expression of deep appreciation. Marina turned to me and said, "Nice, Capricia. Touché."

The president was clearly giving this gift as a symbol of friendship and to move the needle toward affinity (for me, I can't deny, it was also a bit of friendly one-upmanship). Historically, gift giving between countries and delegations has contained (and sometimes still does) an element of competition: If you bring me a bucket of silver, I'll bring you a chest of gold. In some ancient cultures, such as the Islamic and Byzantine empires, elaborate gift giving was meant to signify how God had generously bestowed the nation with riches. In our case, this "chest of gold" had an intended message: "Our nations' relationship is growing, and this personal gift of American music you have a passion for is symbolic of this developing bond." Personal gifts also open the door to a different kind of interaction. The two had just discussed the hard-core issues of international relations; now they were relating to each other as jazz lovers, as President Obama was also a fan. Moreover, I hoped the gift would leave a lasting impression. Long after the joint press statements and airport departures, when President Medvedev was back on Russian soil, the vinyl records would be a reminder of the meeting and the moment, one more snapshot about the giver and the meaning of the engagement.

ANATOMY OF A SELECTION

When I first arrived in the chief of protocol position, I reviewed every element of what we did to enhance our bilateral relationships and knew that bettering our gift giving would make a difference. By investing more effort through our own creative process (we had strict financial limits) and enlisting a national army of talented artists who volunteered their time, we were able to create game-changing moments and de facto diplomacy. I worked hard with the team to realize the far-reaching potential of strategic gift giving, including tying an object to the bigger-picture policy discussions and influencing the personal relationship of the leaders or countries.

In diplomacy, a gift has to be carefully chosen for the occasion and the context. The moment we learned of an upcoming visit, the entire protocol office was activated, including the Gifts Division—a staff of three—which operated within the Visits Department. The talented gift whisperers hewed to my mantra: Each gift should be one of a kind, something that could only have been given by *us* to *them* and that symbolized the special bond between the principals and the countries. Avoid cookie-cutter items that would fade from memory or send a "whatever" message. In addition, we made sure that the gift was grounded within the element or environment of the moment and the significance of what was happening right then. We also considered the giver's style, the recipient's interests, and cultural norms.

In diplomacy, the occasions for a gift are clearly delineated: any high-ranking visit, a first-occasion meeting of significance, diplomatic social occasions (such as a dinner in someone's honor or celebration of a national day), and most personal celebrations like birthdays and anniversaries. Similarly, in business there are engagements and milestones when a gift is expected and appropriate. When someone leaves or retires, is getting married, has a baby, or (obviously) celebrates a birthday, it's customary to give a group gift, especially if the person is a manager with a lot of direct reports—a group gift takes the onus off one person and allows for a more splurge-worthy surprise. Other occasions that are present-worthy: When an employee has wrapped up a big project or has gone above and beyond.

Regarding office hierarchy, the rule is: gift down, not up. Employees are not expected to give to their managers, although if you can't help yourself, an inexpensive token of appreciation or a small personal gift (your homemade holiday sugar cookies, for example) is always appreciated. The reason for this, besides the fact that your income may be tight, is that you never want to invite the appearance of currying favor. For this reason (among others), federal employees' gift giving is regulated; they may not give, or solicit a contribution for, a gift to an official superior;

and they may not accept a gift from an employee receiving less pay if the employee is a subordinate.

With clients, there aren't hard-and-fast rules, although you should be mindful of whether your company has a limitation on the value of gifts so they could never be construed as a bribe. Be wary of the comparative, again. All it takes is one Instagram posting for another client to see they were thought less of. The winter holidays, New Year's gifts, first-time meetings, and important follow-ups are all occasions that might warrant a gift, depending on the relationship and status of the work project. (*Pro tip:* If you're on the receiving end of a gift that is over-the-top and could be misinterpreted as pay-to-play, either report it to your HR department and hand it over or turn it down graciously, as it may have too many strings attached.)

In your personal life, there are occasions other than the obvious—birthdays, anniversaries, birth announcements—to make someone feel special. A thoughtful gift can soothe the sting of a serious medical diagnosis, divorce, or job loss and convey heart-felt condolences when someone has lost a loved one. A present can also mend fences, reinforcing an apology or ending a feud.

Now that you have a sense of whom to gift and when, here are recommendations on what to give and how. What follows is an abbreviated version of my "gift guide" and the questions I asked the team to steer the selections.

Phase 1: Gather Information. Lots of It.

No detail was too tiny when it came to gift recon. We always asked:

- **What is the goal of the visit?** In the same way one might consider the purpose of a gift for a friend, boss, or family member (to show moral support? to celebrate a milestone?), we started with this essential question: What are we trying to achieve with this country? To learn the top-line policy goals, I met with President

Obama's National Security Advisor, Tom Donilon, or Vice President Biden's National Security Advisor, Tony Blinken, and fed pertinent background to the protocol visits officer and gifts officer. If a visit was designed to reset a relationship that had grown tense or distant, we considered gifts that would emphasize a shared history of fellowship to signal the intention of a unified future. When President Xi Jinping visited President Obama at Sunnylands, California, for his first official visit as the newly elected Chinese leader—a meeting designed to create an intimacy between these two young presidents representing the next generation—we chose a simple and hopeful symbol of a path forward: a wooden bench where two men could sit and talk together as equals—and perhaps as friends—looking out at a common future. Our gifts team, led for this visit by Sarah Henning, who enjoyed the adventure of finding the right symbol of a relationship between leaders, succeeded brilliantly with this gift. We commissioned the bench from a California company that carved it from redwoods, a tree indigenous to China and the United States (a token of the bond between the countries) and styled it to look like the famous benches at Sunnylands, a reminder of this valuable visit. Sarah oversaw the personalization of the bench with the Sunnylands logo and the Mandarin inscription. We also paid homage to the Chinese culture by constructing it using eight planks—as we saw in the previous chapter, eight is an auspicious number in China. The bench was placed outside for President Obama to present it to President Xi on a walk around the grounds after their one-on-one discussion. Following a lengthy, impromptu tête-à-tête the two leaders had sitting on chaise lounges, President Obama led President Xi to the bench, where they sat, smiling and at ease, like two friends plotting their next adventure. The gift would always remind the Chinese leader of his time at this serene locale and of the productive conversations had there with President Obama.

- **Who is the recipient?** Often, gifts were meant to grow or solidify the personal relationship of the leaders rather than (or in addition to) addressing larger policy goals. In these instances, we relied heavily on our ambassadors and counterparts in other countries, asking about the recipients' interests and how past gifts had gone over—and of course we never wanted to repeat a gift! (*Pro tip:* Keep a record of all gifts you give people over the years so you don't end up gifting your niece several jewelry boxes, as I accidentally did.) One of my favorite gifts was built around a man's passion for a strategy board game. We had learned that President Hu Jintao was an avid player of Go, the ancient Chinese board game that uses playing pieces known as stones. So in preparation for President Obama's first state visit to China, I commissioned a board made from Hawaiian koa tree wood, a nod to the president's home state. Deputy Chief of Protocol Dennis Cheng suggested reaching out to Feng Yun, the Chinese American Go champion living in the United States, to ensure we were designing the board correctly, and she generously donated her winning jade playing pieces. President Obama presented the gift to President Hu, who was visibly moved by the gesture. My counterparts were uncharacteristically effusive with admiration at the gift. I was so thrilled that they had embraced this gift as a positive next move in the game of diplomacy.

President Obama's favorite pastimes—golf and basketball— inspired gifts from world leaders. Canadian Prime Minister Stephen Harper presented the president with a basketball signed by the 2010–2011 team roster of the Toronto Raptors. Chancellor Merkel gifted the president a stainless-steel putter set from the prestigious German golf equipment company Kramski. Leisure gifts weren't simply a way to say, "Hey, go have fun, Mr. President!" They also conveyed an intimacy, a knowledge of a person's private life, and how he or she liked to unwind from the pressures of running a country, something only another world leader could truly understand.

- **What does the gift say about the giver?** No one wants to hand over a generic gift that's indistinguishable from other presents and will easily be forgotten, particularly at the highest levels of government, which was why personalization was a key part of every gift. Often a gift from a high-level dignitary would bear the mark of their office, either the seal and/or the occupant's signature. In addition, each principal had a style he or she wanted to express, and I met multiple times with the chiefs of staff to incorporate their preferences. Our Gifts Division went one further, and suggested that First Lady Michelle Obama have a signature symbol, a bee, primarily because she was the first to install a beehive at the White House, but also because the symbol connected so well with issues she cared about: gardening, healthy eating, and getting outdoors to move. We created a collection of gifts that either bore a bee (a scarf, stationery, jewelry) or involved honey or bee's wax (honeypots, tea sets with honey, candles) and presented examples of gift ideas to Mrs. Obama's deputy chief of staff, Melissa Winter, whose keen judgment the First Lady relied upon (we all did). Melissa meticulously considered whether each choice would reflect the First Lady's missions and passions. (Incidentally, not all First Ladies have symbols, and we were thrilled that Michelle embraced this idea.) The First Lady also loved American-made crafts such as blankets, baskets, and jewelry. One of the office's favorite designers (and mine) was Joan Hornig, whose gorgeous golden leaf-bark-and-bee arm cuffs were gifted to the spouses of all the leaders at the Camp David G8 in 2012 (bonus: all profits from the sale are donated to charity). We suggested to Vice President Biden that he, too, choose a signature emblem: the anchor, a symbol of the United States Naval Observatory, which also houses the VP residence in DC. We often gifted bookends bearing the anchor and personalized them for each recipient. Vice President and Dr. Jill Biden also loved their German shepherd, Champ, and we worked with American manufacturers to create plush "Champs" as gifts.

- **What does the gift say about us as a nation?** All of our principals wanted to present made-in-America objects, as well as items that represented our diverse cultural identities, ideals, and history of great craftsmanship. One of the First Lady's beloved go-tos was a quilt made by a collective in Gee's Bend, Alabama. Most of the women in this rural town are descendants of slaves and have been making quilts for over a century from recycled clothes, feed sacks, and fabric remnants. (You can view the stunning pieces and read about the artists at SoulsGrownDeep.org.) The quilts acknowledge our country's legacy of slavery and triumph over it, as well as the artistic tradition and community bonds carried on through generations of resilient women. (The quilts affected the First Lady so much that they influenced her official portrait: Her dress is a virtual quilt reminiscent of the designs of the Gee's Bend quilt makers.)

The state visit gift—which is presented publicly to every leader during a state visit (in addition to a personalized gift) and which is the same for each leader—is one of the most symbolic gifts we gave. At the top of my tenure we brainstormed ideas for a new standard state visit gift and pondered the question of our own national identity. Katie, who took the task to heart, announced that the White House carpenter's shop (where the residence's discarded beams and the like are housed) had recently given her some reclaimed scraps of wood from the Truman White House renovation, as well as some felled magnolia wood from the White House grounds. We immediately recognized that this historic wood would be ideal for crafting a gift that would be representative of our country, and I knew just the artist to do it: Zachary "Zack" Oxman, a supremely talented American sculptor (and one of the kindest, most life-affirming humans on the planet) whom I'd met during my years as social secretary, when he'd designed a fantastical bronze menorah—buoyant dancing men, women, and children—for the Clinton White House's menorah lighting ceremony.

Our team had been tossing around ideas for symbols that would represent our country's ideals of unity and friendship—doves? clasped hands?—but when Zack suggested a laurel branch, an ancient symbol of peace, we agreed it was perfect and gave him the green light. Made of stainless steel sculpted in his masterful baroque style (he'd studied in Florence) and capped with the wood from the president's home, the People's House, the beautiful and inspiring branch came to life, heralding a hopeful future.

- **What is our history with this country and leader?** Similar to how relationships with family and friends span decades of ups and downs, no gift in diplomacy is presented in a historical vacuum, and we paid special care to the countries' current and past relationship. When President Obama met Taoiseach Enda Kenny (*Taoiseach* is Irish for prime minister) in 2013, we wanted his gift to speak to the centuries of shared values and the ancestral ties between our countries—10 percent of the US population claims Irish ancestry (though that percentage suspiciously jumps to 100 percent on St. Patrick's Day). The countries also enjoyed a robust economic partnership, and wouldn't you know, both President Obama (on his mother's side) and Vice President Biden (on both sides) claim Irish ancestry. To cover the personal, political, and historical waterfront, we landed on an exquisite gift: a pair of cuff links for the prime minister and a brooch for his spouse, Fionnuala Kenny, made from elements of Ellis Island that were discarded during its renovation. They were created in the spirit of the first immigrant to arrive to the United States and pass through Ellis Island, an Irishwoman named Ann "Annie" Moore. Ellis Island—so meaningful to the Irish immigrants who came to our country in the nineteenth century, escaping famine—and the personal nature of the accessories spoke to the camaraderie. All credit for these poignant mementos goes to Katie and Liza Ballantine, who diligently oversaw the gifts department early in my tenure. During one of their hunts, they'd discovered a jeweler who'd been given materials from the Ellis Island renovation. The prime minister and first lady were incredibly moved by the gifts and spoke to me during the visit about the significance of the Irish diaspora, one of the largest communities in the United States.

  Sometimes the gift reflects the personal history between leaders or delegates. I've been gifted so many wonderful presents over the years that have mirrored the connections I've made with my counterparts.

One of my favorite gifts, a framed hand-crafted basket, was given to me by the ambassador of Botswana, Her Excellency Dr. Tebelelo Mazile Seretse, to honor my departure from my protocol post. Scarves given to me from leaders in Mexico and Croatia have also meant a great deal, and I so enjoyed wearing them upon a return visit to their countries. The Chinese government gives some of the most exquisite and meaningful gifts, and their talent in this diplomatic effort is unmatched. They intrinsically know how to create impact with the gift exchange, from the region of the country that may match a sister city where the recipient was from to the history of the gift's origin or the materials—it was all very intentional.

Phase 2: The Gifts Memo

Armed with information and options, we culled the choices for the principal-to-principal gifts (that is, anything given personally from the president, First Lady, vice president, Dr. Biden, or the secretary of state to their counterpart) and presented to each a Gifts Memo with three options. We ranked the one we thought best as number one, and President Obama usually went with it. But on occasion, either he or his team disagreed with our top choice. In these rare instances, I visited the White House to deliver the hard sell and explain why I thought the first option was ideal. This turned out to be the case in 2013, when I recommended that President Obama's gift to Israeli President Shimon Peres be a magnolia tree from the White House for planting at the presidential palace in Jerusalem. President Obama was on board, but his team was concerned, knowing how difficult it would be to jump through the hoops of their Agricultural Department (trees carry disease, and most countries, including ours, have strict limits concerning what can cross borders). I insisted it *could* be done—I would see to it myself—and that it would be worth the effort: The Israeli president's residence, the Beit HaNassi, has a peace garden where world leaders were invited by President Peres to plant trees. The pope had planted an olive tree in 2009, beginning the tradition, and I believed it would be important for the United States to have a living, growing presence there, representing the strong roots between our countries over generations. After much back and forth and faxes, phone calls, and forms, a small magnolia tree sprouted from the seeds of the oldest tree on the White House lawn was flown over on *Air Force One*. President Obama shoveled dirt onto the tree in the garden and later at a joint press conference spoke about its significance, stating it was for a man who'd planted "the seeds of progress, the seeds of security, the seeds of peace—all the seeds that have helped not only Israel grow but also the relationship between our two nations grow." It is now installed in the garden, for every Israeli president and prime minister to witness its growth and contemplate its symbolism.

Phase 3: The Romance Card

The card that accompanied a principal's personal gift—fittingly called a romance card by us protocol officers—contained a message and gift description that got nearly as much attention as the gift itself. We were telling a story with the gift, and the card framed that story, articulating the intention and meaning. The crafting of the message was as challenging as drafting a note to celebrate a grandparent's centennial birthday or to express how much a person meant after their passing. Jennifer Paolino, a diligent protocol officer, crafted the most poignant romance cards. I know with every visit she felt the pressure to script the perfect note, as we carefully had to weave messages that related to the visit and often reflected on the policy and relationship. She was especially moving in her description of the gift President Obama gave former President Nelson Mandela, presented during his last visit, shortly before the South African leader's death. The note lovingly described the charitable donation of blankets to hospitals in President Mandela's hometown, drawing a poignant connection between the ailing leader—whom all of South Africa (and the world!) wanted to wrap up and cherish—and the blankets that would go to warm the sick and needy that the president loved and had sacrificed so much for.

Sometimes the message would be lighthearted, particularly if the relationship was close and if the gift was fun and referential. This was the case for the custom-made BBQ grill we gifted British Prime Minister Cameron after discovering his team had to borrow one for a picnic honoring UK-US veterans at 10 Downing Street (famously dubbed "Obama-cue" by the prime minister's daughter, as the prime minister and the president flipped burgers and served the servicemen and servicewomen themselves). We tracked down a wonderful American grill designer, Engelbrecht Grills and Cookers, which was no easy feat, as we often learned that so many formerly American-made items are now made outside the country. The craftsman stamped the UK-US friendship flag into the metal, making it a one-of-a-kind gift.

Other times the note would be poignant or elevated. When President Obama met with President Medvedev in Seoul, South Korea, at the Nuclear Security Summit—their last meeting before Putin resumed the presidency in May—we selected a poignant gift for the leader-to-leader exchange, one to remind the Russians of their participation in America's early exploration: a chain link from the original fence of the first Russian settlement in North America, California's Fort Ross, established in 1812. It was an actual and metaphorical link symbolizing how our countries were, and continue to be, connected. I stood next to Marina and opened the gold and red-velvet box, watching President Medvedev take in the beautifully framed gift and read the meticulously engineered message. He expressed deep gratitude, and they spoke about how this place in California is important in Russia. Below is the actual text of the romance card, painstakingly written so that each word contributed an important and intentional element to the message, a snapshot of the past, present, and hoped-for future:

Fort Ross is a unique symbol of Russian participation in America's early exploration. This historic framed link is a testament to the long-established ties between Russia and the United States and our enduring commitment to international stability and economic cooperation. From the New START Treaty and the fight against terrorism in Afghanistan, to the World Trade Organization, we have laid the foundation for a better tomorrow.

(For guidelines on writing notes, turn to page 387.)

Gift Tips

The just-right gift is a workhorse, multitasking in ways that can affect the present moment, the path forward, or even a rethink of the past, casting it in a more positive light. In business, as in personal relationships, even a small offering (they don't all have to be as extravagant as a handmade BBQ grill) serves as a way to bridge and influence. These are elements I always consider when selecting a gift for anyone—friend, family member, business client—to avoid a gift miss and to allow for the best experience to be unwrapped.

- **Consider the culture**. When traveling abroad—and even within the United States—pay attention to religious or cultural norms. The last thing you want is to offend someone when you're trying to impress them. We had a close call in 2011 just before a last-minute trip to the Middle East for Secretary Clinton. We had a prepacked trunk of our standard gifts for the secretary's trips for foreign ministers and other dignitaries. Just before we loaded the gift trunk, I double-checked the gift list in my binder to confirm that all was in order, and discovered that the prepacked items bore human images—crystal sculptures with Thomas Jefferson's bust lasered into the center. Jefferson is an international icon of diplomacy, and the busts were always well received, but for a visit to a Muslim country, presenting these could have been a real problem, as some practitioners of Islam consider the image of a human face in art as false worship of an idol. (The team and I hustled to the gift vault and quickly packed in my personal bag several of our contingency items that did not risk running afoul of this belief.)

Other cultural dos and don'ts:

- **Know your numbers.** The number four is bad luck in China—it essentially holds the same place in their cultural imagination as the number thirteen does in ours, and some buildings and hotels don't mark a fourth floor. The reason: When spoken aloud, *four* sounds similar to the word for *death*, so unless you're wishing an imminent end for your recipient, steer clear. You should also avoid giving someone four of any one object: If you're gifting pairs, go with two or six. The number six, like eight, is considered good luck.

- **Know your objects.** In Chinese, the phrase *give a clock* sounds like *attend a funeral*, so don't gift a watch or a clock. And leather gifts are an offense in India: Cows are revered as sacred in Hinduism, which is practiced by around 80 percent of the Indian population.

- **Learn the gifting rituals.** In India and African and Muslim countries, give and accept with the right hand, as the left is considered unclean. (For an extensive list of global gift tips, turn to page 388.)

- **Consider raw materials as elements of the gift.** The materials that make up the gift itself, as well as the person crafting the gift, can layer in meaning and emotion. On one of her many international visits, First Lady Hillary Clinton and I were honored to meet with Bosnian mothers who'd lost children in the horrific Bosnian war in the early 1990s. Hillary invited the women to sit in a circle, something she often did in countries where women were experiencing troubles, as it made everyone feel included and on equal footing. The women then spoke, one by one through an interpreter, about losing their children in the war. The mothers gave us each a small sculpture they'd made out of bronze spent artillery shells, with intricate design work on the sides pounded into the metal. To this day Hillary and I count these sculptures as among the most moving gifts we've received, exquisite in design and sorrowful in meaning. The women's grief and unimaginable pain seemed welded into the metal that had extinguished the lives of their children. As I contemplated my sculpture, it forced me to consider: Am I doing enough to help? What more can I do to prevent this in the future? For me, as a Croat, it provoked so many emotions, and I imagined what my own father had gone through as a child when war ravaged his land, remembering his descriptions of warplanes overhead and hiding under trees so as not to attract bullets from above.

Because I've experienced the impact of such a significant gift, I advise people to hold on to raw materials that are meaningful—broken ceramic pieces of an antique teacup or plate, single heirloom earrings missing a match—and gift them in a reimagined, creative manner, perhaps as a mosaic or in a shadow box or keepsake display case.

Zack Oxman relied on the significance and integrity of the raw material for his most challenging gift creation: a sculpture for President Obama to give to the pope in 2015. Zack was supplied with a portion of the Statue of Liberty, a three-foot-long iron bar from the original armature, and told to have at it. He now laughs at the unlikely probability of a Jewish artist crafting a gift for the most famous Catholic on the planet. "Then there was the fact that this was the least materialistic pope in history, so the gift had to be special but not too grand. No pressure, right? They told me I could melt it down, but I wanted to preserve the shape and the patina. It looked like a bird taking flight, and I thought about the birds that fly around the Vatican. I knew I wanted to nestle a dove into the bar." The result was a stunning stainless-steel-and-iron winged sculpture that now sits in the Vatican. (I was thrilled that my successor, Pete Selfridge, had continued the department's relationship with the talented Zack Oxman.)

- **Connect it to the business at hand.** For key meetings, fundraisers, or red-letter family celebrations, consider items that will help attendees remember the gathering and the reason for it. The gift can influence the negotiation if it punctuates the goal. It can also serve as a reminder of the talking points long after the meeting has ended. What businesses miss out on when they hand over a standard company gift—a pen or mug bearing the business's logo, which is more marketing than gift giving, really—is the opportunity to reinforce a message and relationship (and frankly, those traditional items often end up in the trash or on the company's giveaway table). The gift doesn't need to be expensive; it simply needs to speak to the connection and the goal. For example, presenting seeds of a plant indigenous to your and the recipient's location. The effort you've gone to personalize it also becomes part of the gift, further proof that you value the relationship. When we held the fiftieth anniversary for the Diplomatic Reception Rooms at the State Department, each invitee received a silk scarf (for women) or a tie (for men) with a design inspired by the blue and white Thomas Jefferson Room. The mementos would remind recipients of the importance of the event—preserving our nation's artifacts and diplomatic traditions—every time they wore the item. When I left the Office of Protocol, the team gifted me a beautiful cloth evening bag that incorporated the discarded trim from drapes at Blair House that were being replaced. I cherish the bag and every time I use it, I recall the phenomenal men and women of this department and the dedication to our country. (I was also pleased they'd heard my many complaints about women's evening bags being too small for phones, keys, lipstick, and a slim wallet—they made it just the right size for all the essentials!)

- **Make it personal or from scratch.** A gift you bake, stitch, carve, paint, or otherwise personalize (engraving a memento or framing family heirlooms) ratchets up the special factor—it clearly took time and there isn't another one like it on the shelves. I love to gift homemade food. I adore baking and am relatively good (thank you, Mom), and I find it instantly warms up the relationship. One year, having maxed out on banana bread, I turned to baking the perfect apple pie by determining just the right amount of lemon, sweetness, and flakiness for the crust. Many folks on my gift list received one, and I even delivered holiday pies to the Navy mess stewards since they were always so nice to me. A senior steward kindly gave me some constructive feedback. "This is fantastic, but let me tell you a secret," he confided. "If you want less juice in the pie, use quarter-inch-cut apple pieces." Before the gift, our relationship had been purely logistical, but the Art of Pie discussion moved us into the friendship zone.

Businesses will especially benefit from a more personal approach to gifts. Make your company's signature gift memorable by using artisans and materials that are local or speak to the history of your product or industry. If your town is known for its whiskey/lemons/chocolate, bake cupcakes or cookies using these flavors and ingredients (and perhaps fashion your company's logo into the frosting). These unique gifts are infinitely more Instagrammable, too, for those who have a social media presence. Our protocol team gifted a most personal gift to President Susilo Bambang Yudhoyono, President of the Republic of Indonesia, and Mrs. Yudhoyono on the occasion of the state visit in Indonesia: a piece of batik fabric from President Obama's mother's collection, personally selected by his sister, Maya Soetoro-Ng.

- **Never refuse a gift.** It's a huge offense in any country to decline a gift or leave one behind, even when the logistics of transport seem nearly impossible. I give you exhibit A: President Obama's 2013 trip to Tanzania. From start to finish it was off-the-charts amazing, including one of the most culturally vibrant arrival ceremonies ever, with cheering crowds—wearing shirts bearing President Obama's face—flanking a boulevard temporarily named Obama Drive. Their enthusiasm extended to their gifts. When the US delegation arrived at President Jakaya Kikwete's palace, we were shown into a room filled with gifts for the president. I noted a seven-foot wooden *Ujamaa*, or Tree of Life carving, in the corner, thinking it was there for decor. But then President Kikwete presented all the gifts, including the Tree of Life, to President Obama. President Obama, of course, graciously accepted it all on the spot. A Tree of Life carving is an intricate work of art made by Tanzania's Makonde people depicting interlocking human figures, symbolizing unity and community. This gift spoke to the interconnected relationship between our two countries, so it was truly an honor to receive it. But the piece was taller than everyone in the traveling delegation, and I wasn't confident we could ship it back to the United States. As the two presidents conversed, I looked to Sarah and saw her shooting me the "We need to talk asap!" look. She was as worried as I was, and I knew we'd need to rely on her charm to negotiate an extrication plan. Next to her was our globally respected protocol officer Asel Roberts, who knows an urgent issue when she sees one.

After the gift exchange, Sarah and Asel confirmed my fear: They'd spoken to our embassy about pouching it (a delivery method that embassies perform for diplomats) and were told it was a no-go—due to its size, they could not assure that the piece would arrive in its current condition. So off we went to our pals on *Air Force One*. Was there enough room in the cargo hold? They refused. Security concerns always dictate what goes in and out of the belly of the plane (for obvious security reasons); plus, it's often packed to the gills. As this was the third country on our multiple-nation tour, we'd hit the limit. Our last resort: the car plane. The president's limo, the Beast, travels with him to every country in its own plane, and we hoped there might be room for this artwork to tag along. They gave us a hard no, saying that there would be no way to strap it down. What to do? We went back to the *Air Force One* team, desperate. I knew we could not leave Tanzania without the gift. The entire visit to Africa had such special meaning: These countries—Tanzania, Senegal, and South Africa—were tied together to celebrate the continent's democracies and to strengthen economic partnerships. When times get tough, we often go with the charm offensive. Summoning as much charm as we could, we asked one more time: "Is there any way you can help us?" Secret Service gave us a glimmer of hope: The carving could travel topside with the staff, but with a caveat: "You have to get it to the plane by 7 a.m. tomorrow morning." Sarah and Asel miraculously got hold of a bus, and at 6 a.m., the three of us drove to the palace, talked the guards into letting us in, carefully hauled the sculpture into the vehicle, and drove out. The Tree of Life traveled in the conference room of *Air Force One*, strapped down so it didn't get damaged or knock anyone unconscious during turbulence.

- **Consider whether to make the exchange public or private.** In diplomacy, exchanging gifts in public is a diplomatic tool. Doing so broadcasts the importance of the relationship, relays our appreciation of the receiving culture, and reflects pride in our own. Not all gifts are meant for public consumption, however. When I receive a gift, especially at a business or social function, I always ask: Should I open it now? Some people prefer not to have you open it in front of everyone and risk judgment, whereas others want to witness that wow moment. (Hint: *Always* be wowed.) As a giver, I encourage my recipient to open it with me right then and there, as it makes for a shared experience and a quick explanation if needed.

- **Know when to give the gift.** Although gifts can be exchanged at any point during a visit, in diplomacy they are usually presented after the main meeting, which is quite deliberate: Two powerful individuals have just made decisions of huge importance for their countries and the world. The just-right gift at this juncture can positively punctuate those talks. Similarly, for business meetings, I recommend that clients make the gift presentation at the end of the meeting to underscore what was just discussed (and if the gift is fabulous, they are also left with a great taste, like the perfect dessert to wrap up a memorable meal). If you make a gift presentation in the middle of the exchange—even if it's connected to a topic that's currently being discussed—it can cut off the flow of a good discussion. The one exception: If your host makes a presentation at the top of the meeting—which they often do in the Middle East—you should reciprocate at that time. For social meetings, I advise against perfunctorily giving the gift at the outset, which can set an awkward tone, especially when you're meeting for the first time.

- **Be a wrap star.** In many cultures, such as Japan, the wrapping is almost as important as the gift itself. Packaging can also dress up a gift that is simple and add to the significance. My close friend Lalie Tongour always adds a twig of lavender from her garden within the ribbon. The attention to detail takes extra time, but the lovely scent makes it worth it. I also try to package gifts in ways that will be easy to transport, especially if the client is traveling on a plane. Liza was always on the hunt for the best box makers within our budget. She found several in New York, but depended upon Book Arts in DC, a bookbinding and invitations specialty store that ensured that our presentations were up to presidential standards and under budget. Cellophane wrap is better than paper, since it doesn't tear. In protocol, we all learned how to craft a DIY handle out of ribbon or string (you can google it) so our counterpart didn't have trouble carrying larger items.

- **Choose charitable gifts.** Not all the gifts in diplomacy reflected a personal relationship or a policy goal. Some were simply about filling basic needs in countries we were visiting. During most trips the president and First Lady would stop at schools, churches, hospitals, and community centers. We would reach out in advance to learn their needs, then ask US companies for donations. We worked with Scholastic to provide books to schools; with Johnson & Johnson for infant formula, diapers, and bottles to nurseries; and with Nike for shoes and soccer balls to schools and community centers. Businesses can find out the charity passions of would-be clients and partners before meetings and present a donation as a gift. (It also shows you took the time to learn what they care about.)

- **Play up the display.** Giving gifts that have a built-in display element encourages your recipient to present them for viewing. Framing or mounting the object makes it easy for the recipient to find it a home where others can appreciate it, too. I dedicate areas in my office and home for displaying gifts. If I had enough lead time, I would display gifts from the country of the ambassador who was visiting, or that had a special significance.

Presidential Gifts Over the Years

Most gifts given to US presidents must go straight to the National Archives (or to the park services or a zoo if it's a live animal), since nothing over $390 (an amount reevaluated every three years) can be kept unless the recipient pays the appraised value themselves. The State Department sets a $2,000 gift limit for gifts given to foreign leaders by the president. Many other countries have no gift limits, which accounts for the million-dollar value of some gifts now sitting in our archives. Here, some of the greatest hits.

- *Queen Victoria to President Hayes in 1880:* the Resolute Desk that now sits in the Oval Office.
- *The King of Siam to President Lincoln:* a "supply of elephants" to populate American forests. Lincoln politely declined. (Nowadays, it's rare to gift live animals, as it's understood it might endanger the creatures.)
- *The President of Indonesia to President George H. W. Bush:* a real Komodo dragon. It's now at the Cincinnati Zoo (and has sired thirty-plus baby dragons since its arrival).
- *The President of the Russian Federation to President Clinton:* a hand-sewn reproduction of an American flag similar to the flag given by the US to Russia in the 1860s as a symbol of gratitude for their intervention on behalf of the Union during the American Civil War.
- *The government of Argentina to President George W. Bush:* three hundred pounds of raw lamb.
- *The government of Australia to President Obama:* crocodile insurance for his family during a visit to a croc hot spot in 2011. The coverage: $50,000 in the event of an attack.
- *Pope Francis to President Trump:* an encyclical, a papal document urging the government to address climate change.

11.

_____

KEEPING UP APPEARANCES

Personal presentation is your outward calling card, telling a great deal about who you are—your beliefs, culture, mind-set, and goals—within seconds. A woman's sari—how it's draped, the type of fabric—may reflect her geographic and religious roots or social standing. A man's turban and beard signify an adherence to the religious tenets of Sikhism. Wearing a cross, mandala, or yarmulke lets people know that your spiritual beliefs are an essential part of who you are. Clothing also communicates a professional identity, whether it's military fatigues, a fireman's uniform, or culinary apparel. We may not think of them as such, but dress and appearance guidelines are a form of protocol, rules people utilize and follow to telegraph meaning. These choices have potent consequences, which can differ drastically depending on the context and the beliefs of the people you're interacting with. The reality is that our choices about appearance aren't simply an outward extension of _our_ identities; they cross-pollinate with the preconceptions of those who are viewing us. Meaning is in the mind of the wearer _and_ the eye of the beholder. As viewers, we should consider the significance of another person's choice with tolerance and an appreciation for cultural significance. And as wearers, we should remember there's always a visual conversation with others that is occurring.

Even when your choices are not consciously meaningful—perhaps you selected what you're wearing today simply because it was clean or comfortable—your appearance is still speaking for you, and doing so at a rapid-fire pace: In chapter 4 I discuss the psychological process of thin-slicing—our all-too-human inclination for sizing people up within seconds of meeting them, based on many things, including visual signals. These split-second judgments may be inaccurate, but they'll take up real estate in our brains until we're cued to think otherwise. A crumpled shirt may telegraph a harried mind-set (even if you're mentally on point), whereas a smooth, well-fitted shirt says "I'm prepared." The power of appearance especially holds true in diplomacy and international engagements, where one's choices convey an intention and tone and where a visual misstep can shift attention away from the important work at hand. Bottom line: Appearance is a potent tool that sends intended and unintended signals, and the more awareness you bring to how your looks affect perceptions, the more in control you will be in an interaction.

Both the Clintons and Obamas welcomed—even encouraged—the critiques and assistance, which gave me the confidence to take charge with many a world leader. Staff are often intimidated by the idea of advising their bosses of something they don't want to hear or that might be seen as frivolous, as appearance is often erroneously thought of. While it may be hard for a staffer to tell her boss when she has arugula in her teeth, it's the kind of help that's essential for leaders who are consumed with the minutiae of a meeting rather than the details of their reflection. Hillary has always had a posse of candid, straightforward staff around her to provide guidance on a variety of issues, and for her, as a high-profile woman, attire was one of those issues. From her early days in the White House as First Lady, she had Kelly Craighead—her extremely skillful trip director (who became my kindred spirit)—and me (of course) to tell her when her outfit was dated or ill fitting, to suggest that she add more blush, or that perhaps it was time to retire the headbands (Hillary loved her headbands—and they're finally back in fashion!). We were frank and honest and I know always appreciated. Huma Abedin, a longtime aide of Hillary's and a colleague, travel mate, and friend of mine, is comfortable and creative with fashion and has always been able to guide Secretary

Clinton so that her clothing was representative of the positions she held. For all of us women who traveled with the secretary at the State Department, Huma dispensed great counsel on how to dress in ways that were stylish and professional, and that appropriately acknowledged the culture of the country we were visiting.

Despite a cadre of fashion-savvy staffers and truth-tellers, extra appearance assistance was sometimes needed, and no one escaped my obsessive stare or my Mary Poppins bag—so called because I could magically pull almost anything out of it—not even President Obama, though he rarely needed more than a last-minute "Sir, you have a little something just . . . right . . . there." I'd decided early on in my career that I'd rather risk offending someone with my input (they could always say no, though they rarely did) than allow them to make a bad impression. I'd taken it upon myself (after asking his permission—always ask for permission!), to dust off and straighten Prime Minister Cameron's jacket, and suggesting he swipe it across his hair to tame the flyaways just before he walked out onto the global stage with President Obama for a press conference. When I lined up leaders for the traditional "family photo" at summits, I was their last-minute mirror (we did not allow them to bring their staff into the prep area, as it was usually a tight squeeze). I went from leader to leader making sure that collars were down, ties were straight, jackets buttoned, hair was not randomly sticking up or out, and that there was nothing unusual on their faces or shoulders.

If leaders were meeting the president for the first time, I made extra certain they were ready for their close-up. This was the case during the annual September United Nations General Assembly (UNGA) in New York City, when I watched yet another leader emerge from the elevator on the thirty-fourth floor of the Waldorf Astoria looking how most of us felt . . . exhausted. Nearly everyone is in back-to-back bilaterals, racing from hotel to hotel and then back to the UN, and this leader—like many people of her position—was singularly focused on the immediate work and not necessarily on appearance. It was also clear that this sophisticated, politically savvy leader was without assistance from a "body person," as we call them in government. As I escorted her to the holding room suite, I surmised that no one in her all-male delegation would suggest a quick comb of her windblown hair. We had about ten minutes before the meeting, and knowing this photo would set an impression that would live on forever, I offered: "Your Excellency, would you mind joining me in the other room?" She quizzically agreed. I pulled out some essentials from my Mary Poppins bag—a bit of hair spray, a lint brush, and a few other items—and within minutes she was ready for her global moment. She looked at me with gratitude and appeared confident as she shook President Obama's hand for the official photo. It was perfect.

I was well aware that the errant tuft of hair, the too-short skirt, or the sweaty brow could even alter history. It's well accepted among historians that then-candidate Richard Nixon lost the 1960 presidential election to JFK due to their first televised debate, which took place a couple months before the election. Nixon's appearance—pale, underweight, and sweaty, due to a recent hospitalization—gave viewers the impression that he was nervous and not up for the job. JFK, on the other hand, appeared vibrant, relaxed, and confident, the picture of health. Going into the debate, Nixon was slightly ahead in the polls. Those who listened to the debate on the radio thought he had done better. But those who viewed it—an audience of 70 million—chose Kennedy as the clear winner. So did the voters come November.

Not only does looking the part lead others to see you in a better light, it makes *you* feel more confident and comfortable. This merging of appearance and thinking is known as "enclothed cognition" in the scientific world, and its effect is quite potent. One study from Northwestern University found that when wearing a doctor's white lab coat (which almost everyone associates with attentiveness and intelligence), people performed better on attention-related tasks. Other research has shown that dressing in formal clothing makes the wearer feel more powerful, which in turn affects how you act and how others see you.

And everyone can benefit from this kind of assistance. I may be a pro at running appearance interference for others, but I've needed and accepted assistance too. Thank you, Ali Rubin, for the high-hair signals when I back-combed just a bit too much. And I'm so grateful to the Secret Service "intel" on an errant zipper that needed to be attended to just before a meeting with the president. I often stood in the hallway outside the Oval to await the start of a meeting. The area is always staffed by Secret Service agents, who are straight-faced and rigid. One of the agents kindly and discreetly asked Paul Hegarty, assistant chief of visits—who has the calmest demeanor and was clearly reticent to deliver the message—to inform me of "the breach." (I once saw President Obama tell Hillary that she had a seed in between her teeth at a bilateral meeting—we all had each other's backs.)

FASHION DIPLOMACY

For centuries dignitaries have been dressing to impress counterparts, sway the public, and telegraph intentions to international delegates and their citizens. Choices of color, style, and vibe (casual and relaxed? formal and serious?) all move the needle of an interaction by transmitting respect and solidarity and conveying something positive about yourself. President Jimmy Carter wore cardigans, probably to signal that he was still a man of the people and hadn't veered far from his peanut-farmer roots. The president of El Salvador, Nayib Bukele, a young leader who is taking his country in a new direction, never wears a tie, an omission that conveys a modern outlook. Wearing a country's national color, even as an accent item—a coat, tie, or purse—is also an easy way to instantly connect and let your counterparts know you did your research. It can also help support the agenda, and I used this tool regularly in my job as chief of protocol.

The 2011 state visit from China's President Hu Jintao gave me a unique opportunity to employ fashion diplomacy. Vice President Biden and I were greeting President Hu on the tarmac at Andrews Air Force Base—a special honor reserved for certain leaders—where gusts blew freely across the open space, especially in November. The official arrival ceremony would also take place outdoors on the South Lawn of the White House if the weather held—delegates loved the backdrop for photos, so we always tried to give them the option of an outdoor reception. I knew I would require a very warm coat that would also help me look official and pay homage to the Chinese. We needed every bit of luck and persuasion to ensure this visit went smoothly. An official Chinese visit during a previous administration hadn't gone according to plan (there were several major protocol and ceremonial breaches, which I describe in detail in the next chapter), and we had a great deal to make up for in order to pave a productive path forward. From a policy standpoint, we were striving for economic parity—our country was pulling out of a recession and China's influence had mushroomed since their last state visit. We needed to appear confident while at the same time signaling respect and honor. Red signifies good luck and vitality in China, so I went to a local Goodwill—I'm a bargain hunter at heart—and found the perfect red coat with red crystal buttons. Wearing the bright color was a way to connect with our visitors and show them that I respected their traditions. My flame-colored coat also served a functional purpose: it helped me stand out in a sea of black coats so the president, secretary, and protocol staff could easily find me.

Perhaps one of the best examples of fashion diplomacy: Secretary Madeleine Albright's pin collection, which is so famous it got its own nine-year traveling exhibit. Her collection of three-hundred-plus pins (mostly costume jewelry) was more than decorative: each specially chosen piece signaled her foreign policy goals, fortitude, and sharp sense of humor. Albright's jewelry-box diplomacy got its start in the mid-1990s when she was the UN ambassador and a frequent and forceful critic of Iraq's infamous dictator Saddam Hussein. She famously tells the story of being called an "unparalleled serpent" by the Iraqi media, and shortly thereafter showed up to a meeting with the Iraqi officials wearing a golden snake pin as a way to say "I am not slinking away." She loved the symbolism so much that she went out and bought and borrowed a number of pins to provide subtext to her diplomatic interactions. On days when negotiations were going frustratingly slow, a turtle or crab pin would grace her lapel. On days when her mood was upbeat, positive symbols—a butterfly, a sunflower, a sun—decorated her left shoulder. (The pins also gave her or her counterpart a way to break the ice if things got awkward.) In some cases, she used them as a way to disarm her critics, in other instances to honor counterparts.

Fashion diplomacy isn't always a serious business; it can also be a way to have fun and build camaraderie. One of the most enduring clothing traditions in international diplomacy is the wearing of the APEC (Asia Pacific Economic Cooperation) garments at the annual summit. The custom was started by Bill Clinton in 1993 when he hosted the summit at Washington State's Blake Island. He brought fighter pilot bomber jackets, made in the United States by Golden Bear, for each Pacific Rim member, and nearly every year since the host country has selected an item that all the invitees are encouraged to wear, one that reflects the national culture. The custom can be fun, campy, practical, or reverent: colorful batik shirts in Indonesia, raincoats in Australia, traditional ponchos in Peru—but the purpose is ultimately to bring the group together, to emphasize the intimate and friendly nature of the gathering, and sometimes to symbolize APEC goals of free and global trade.

I advise clients to be careful about wearing another country or ethnicity's traditional attire when visiting a country or meeting with international clients stateside—you don't ever want to come across as if you're playing dress up with garments that are rife with cultural and historical meaning. This is why minor nods to a culture are often a safer bet than a head-to-toe makeover. Politicians and First Ladies have been doing this seamlessly for decades. The most notable First Lady to use fashion as a diplomatic tool was the effortlessly elegant Jacqueline Bouvier Kennedy. During a 1961 visit to Paris with her husband to meet President Charles de Gaulle, she made the savvy choice of wearing a gown by Givenchy, then one of the top French designers. Jackie, a true Francophile (she spoke French fluently and had French ancestry) made such a notably positive impression on the media—and on President de Gaulle himself—that during one appearance, President Kennedy introduced himself as "the man who accompanied Jacqueline Kennedy to Paris." Nearly every First Lady thereafter has followed suit in the style department. When Hillary was First Lady, she asked the extraordinary Chinese American designer Vera Wang to design a gown for the visit President Clinton was hosting for Chinese President Jiang Zemin. (Wang was honored by the request.) First Lady Michelle Obama wore a gown by Indian American designer Naeem Khan on a state visit to India in 2009, a dress by Korean American designer Doo-Ri Chung for South Korea's state dinner at the

White House in 2011, and a fiery-red Alexander McQueen for China's state visit in 2011, a color that signaled cultural knowledge and respect.

First Lady Michelle Obama used her wardrobe choices to connect with the women of America who didn't wake up every day and reach for a designer dress or high-end shoe: She wore J. Crew, Ann Taylor, Talbots, and Target brands alongside a huge and varied roster of both well-known and lesser-known labels. Being First Lady during the meteoric rise of social media meant millions of eyes were following her every move and wardrobe change in real time. The First Lady understood the power of clothing and social media, and leveraged both brilliantly, bringing a diversity of price points and designers to the office. While most First Ladies wore a few signature designers, Michelle democratized dressing by "playing the field," giving many styles and labels a shot on the world stage. She also moved markets: In 2010, David Yermack of the Stern School of Business at New York University studied the stock prices of twenty-nine brands the First Lady wore at public appearances for one year and found an abnormal increase in returns on investment for all of the brands. Translation: The increase in profits in the days and weeks after she wore an item couldn't be attributed to normal market variations.

The exception to not dressing in full traditional attire: when an invitation suggests it. For a dinner in Pakistan in 1995, the First Lady Hillary Clinton and her staff (including me) wore the *shalwar kameez*, tapered silk pants and a tunic that is traditional in many South Asian countries. The First Lady, who was on a cultural diplomatic mission through the region, was gifted a red *shalwar kameez* by Pakistan's Prime Minister, Her Excellency Benazir Bhutto, and Hillary honored the prime minister by wearing it to this elegant evening event, exhibiting camaraderie and an acceptance of the culture.

Even within the United States it's smart to do some research on the city you're visiting before you pack. While there are geographical generalities (the South tends to stand a bit more on ceremony than the West Coast, for example), regional differences are extremely varied and depend on the personality of the city and the vibe of the industry. Wearing a pair of vibrantly hued shoes or a bright tie and shirt relay an appreciation for Miami's Latin influence and colorful vibe. A southwestern-print shirt or dress with a touch of denim plays well in Dallas or Albuquerque. And the uber-curated "I really don't care how I look" look—dark-wash slim jeans paired with stylish sneakers—will have you blending right in in Silicon Valley.

It's also smart in certain instances to dress in your *own* country's style when traveling. World leaders, particularly from Middle Eastern, African, and Asian nations, where religious and historic customs dictate clothing codes, don't often dress in Western styles when they visit the United States—they arrive as proud representatives of their cultures draped in national attire. I loved seeing all the vibrant and diverse styles and fabrics when hosting foreign dignitaries. I'll never forget the brilliant satin green robe draped with orange- and sienna-colored kente cloth worn by President Jerry John Rawlings of Ghana at the US-Ghanaian state dinner in 1999. He practically floated down the grand foyer and took everyone's breath away (as did his wife, Nana Konadu Agyeman-Rawlings, who wore a matching traditional dress). It added such an element of global appeal and elegance to the evening.

But I must admit I have a bit of a stress response to robes and capes, due to a harrowing incident during the 2012 NATO summit in Chicago. I was escorting Afghanistan's leader Hamid Karzai from a high-security area (a tightly controlled sector reserved for countries who may receive threats) down a very long, steep escalator to the leader's lounge. If you've ever seen images of the elegantly dressed former President Karzai, you've likely noted his purple-and-green cape, or *chapan* robe, which is reminiscent of the Uzbeks' traditional garb in northern Afghanistan. It's fabulous and chic—his signature look (he has dozens of them)—and he rarely removes it in public. We stepped onto the escalator, with one security agent in front of him and one behind him. About halfway down, he suddenly jerked backward—his robe had become caught in the escalator! The agent behind him very quickly yanked it loose, but my protective instinct was already in full swing. I flung my arm out in front of him to keep him from tumbling down the escalator, whacking him in the chest (as if the adult leader of Afghanistan were my ten-year-old son). "We're not gonna lose a leader on my watch!" my inner voice screamed as I went into protection mode. President Karzai looked at me in horror, as did his agents, who moved to stand closer to him. But after a few beats of tension, the president's look turned to relief, and he smiled, saying, "Thank you, these things happen at times." We all laughed and agreed that would have made quite the entrance, and the incident felt like a bonding moment. All I could think the rest of the way down was how ironic it was that with all the security arrangements we'd made, the real threat turned out to be his outfit.

PANTSUITS AND POWER DRESSES:
THE BENEFITS OF A SIGNATURE LOOK

Steve Jobs had the black turtleneck. Anna Wintour has her chic bob and dark sunglasses. Hillary has her pantsuit, which launched a 3.8-million-member secret Facebook group. A personal "uniform" can set you apart (or help you blend in if that's what you're after). A signature look can serve as a visual shorthand for what you value—modernism, precision, pragmatism—and codify an attitude, whether it's confidence, power, sophistication, or relaxation. Presidents have developed signature looks, though it's much easier for them to make their mark with casual wear than summit wear (there's only so much leeway you have with a suit and tie). President Reagan and President George H. W. Bush both wore denim during off-hours, and wore it well, hailing back to their rancher roots in the same way President Carter used the sweater.

Hillary's iconic pantsuit was born out of functionality: for ease of movement in and out of cars and alighting stages. It also put her on par with all the suited men in the room, as she was oftentimes the only woman at the table. A suit allowed her to don a uniform, as men do—the well-cut suits created by her favorite designer (and mine), Oscar de la Renta, were feminine and figure flattering—and to keep the conversation focused on what she was saying, not what she was wearing. (As Hillary wrote in her recent book: "Some people like what you wear; some don't. You can't please everyone, so you might as well wear what works for you.") Although she was the *first* First Lady implicitly to give women permission to wear pants in the White House, she is quick to give credit to another trail-blazing politician for changing the landscape. "I was not the first woman in the Senate to wear pants," she says. "It was Senator Barbara Mikulski from Maryland, who, in 1993, wore pants in the Senate to protest the rule that women must wear a skirt or dress on the floor of the senate." (Yes, this ridiculous rule was in effect until the early 1990s.) As much as Hillary often tried to keep the conversation off her clothing choices, on occasion she used her wardrobe to make potent statements. As the Democratic nominee for president, she knew all eyes would be watching the night she took the stage to accept the nomination, so she chose a color that would symbolize the possibilities for women around the world: a white suit. It was not only stunning (a made-for-her Ralph Lauren original) but powerfully emblematic as the color worn by suffragettes during their struggle for the right to vote years ago.

Hillary shares a love of pantsuits with Germany's Chancellor Angela Merkel, who also favors an array of solid-colored suits. The two are so often photographed in their pantsuit uniforms that Merkel used the twinning look as inspiration for a gift to Hillary at a state luncheon in 2011. She presented the secretary of state with a framed page from a German newspaper with side-by-side photos of the women, headless, in suits, and asked Hillary to guess which woman was Merkel and which was her. Hillary laughed loud and hard. It was such a funny and warm moment—two of the world's most powerful women bonding over their sartorial passion.

For me, being dressed in a "uniform" always made me feel more effective and confident, the armor that telegraphed to my colleagues—and to myself—that it was go time. It helped define me in my role and let others know what I was about: no fuss, no frills. I figured out pretty quickly that I was a dress person—zip it up and you're done—and, an A-line dress person at that, as they're more forgiving than some other styles. And I also understood why Hillary liked pantsuits—they were so easy. When I did suit up, I made them dressier by pairing them with a crisp white shirt or drapey silk blouse with a V-neck (it opens up the neckline, especially if you have an oval face like mine).

I wanted the "helmet" of the uniform—my hair—to be a non-distracting and classic style. When I was nominated for the chief of protocol position, my stylist, Michael Awad, convinced me to go short for the ease factor. I had long hair at the time and he mercifully weaned me over a few sessions (long hair can be an addiction), first to a bob, then to my current shorter length. I fought him at first and then thanked him for the effortless ten-minute prep style and for giving me a simple, unfussy look. Before landing in a new country, after eight-plus hours on a plane, I had a few minutes in a small restroom to change from loungewear to chief-of-protocol wear. The shorter hair was a blessing—several Velcro rollers set for a few minutes and I was ready to greet moments later.

Why go to all that trouble? Because although appearance matters for everyone, it matters significantly more for women. Hillary calculated the amount of time she had spent getting her hair and makeup done during the presidential campaign: six hundred hours, the equivalent of nearly a month in the stylist's chair. A 2016 study coauthored by Jaclyn Wong at the University of Chicago, which looked at gender and attractiveness in the workplace, found that women's attractiveness was based much more on grooming (hair, makeup, clothing) than for men, who could be deemed attractive even if they were not well groomed. (Incidentally, salaries were also significantly more correlated with grooming for women than for men—women who were well groomed earned more than those who were less well groomed, regardless of how naturally attractive they were judged to be.) For women, if anything is out of place (too much blush, toothpaste on the front of the blouse, a loose hem), the press will often needlessly work it into the copy. Additionally, media comments on a female political candidate's appearance—whether commentary is positive, negative, or neutral—directly correlate to voters' negative impressions and lower their likelihood to vote for the candidate, according to the 2013 survey "Name It, Change It" by the Women's Media Center and She Should Run.

As secretary of state, Hillary's hair—which almost always looks fabulous—seemed to get interpreted as a code for her mood. I'm not sure where the rumor started, but people in government actually sent official cables about her hair. When asked to recount some of her most bizarre interactions with leaders, Hillary often tells this story: "Once, when I flew to Bulgaria as secretary of state, the former Bulgarian prime minister greeted me in the conference room and was looking at me strangely, and said, 'I was told when you had your hair pulled back, you must be in a bad mood.' I said, 'No, I'm just having a bad hair day!'" She used to joke with us that if she wanted to change the news cycle all she had to do was change her hairstyle.

WORKPLACE DRESS CODES

In the Office of Protocol, which is an incredibly outward-facing job, there is a very particular expectation of appearance for the staff. We were representatives of our government engaging with representatives of other governments, so it was critical to look as if we worked for the president of the United States. Myrna Farmer, one of the most seasoned protocol officers, who understood implicitly the diplomatic pitfalls of a fashion faux pas, was the office go-to advisor when staff were unsure about a certain style or clothing choice (every office should have a Myrna). In addition, at any given moment, we might be called to attend an impromptu meeting at the White House or State Department (to this day I keep a pair of heels and a scarf in the office for anyone to borrow for an important meeting, as well as a drawer filled with jewelry to dress an outfit up and an extra outfit hanging on the back of the door for emergency spills).

Beyond the Beltway, office dress codes can run the gamut from the three-piece suit with a full Windsor knot tie (bankers) to stilettos and avant-garde dresses (fashion industry) to cardigans and loafers (teachers). The most important thing for anyone entering a new work space, as an employee or visitor, is to figure out what the norm is and hew to it, within reason, of course. If you can't get a read before the meeting, err on the side of formal (you can always take off a tie and jacket when you're there), and once you have the first or second meeting with them, dress for future engagements within their office style.

THE LOOK BOOK

Saving leaders from death-by-wardrobe and providing hair styling and dress suggestions were a part of my portfolio as soon as I started in government. I often thought it would be handy to have a book fashioned after the *The Official Preppy Handbook*, the one I used as a teen to be more in sync with the times, but instead for heads of state. I walked leaders and delegates through many elements of what to wear and what not to wear, and over the years I have culled together some golden rules to dress and primp by. These rules also apply to video-conferencing, by the way, as you are being judged on your appearance as much as if you were in the room:

- **Color:** Gone are the days where men's suits were only black, navy, or gray. Nowadays even employees in traditional industries can branch out into tan and pale blue, especially in warmer seasons and depending on the occasion. Women have more leeway with color, but steer away from red if you're going to be on camera (TV, Skype, or FaceTime)—it bleeds.

- **Patterns and materials:** In general, I warn against loud patterns, since they can come off as busy and distracting. Patterns tend to vibrate on television or video, especially diagonals and graphic prints. Take note of the stylings of television anchors like Savannah Guthrie, Katie Couric, Gayle King, or Norah O'Donnell, all of whom I admire very much. They know well what will capture attention in a good way and what will distract. For men a seersucker suit is a wonderful stylish warm-weather choice, as evidenced by the beloved *Today Show* host Al Roker, who rocks them all summer long. Flag pins and cuff links are appropriate accents, but it's best not to wear your or another country's flag as actual clothing. Depending on the crowd and country, offense may be taken, so don't risk it.

- **Accessories:** Jewelry can be symbolically potent, culturally informative, and as communicative as a word or gesture. Wearing a visiting country's national color, flower, or animal shows honor and gratitude, whereas donning your own nation's or religion's symbols identifies you and communicates your values. I highly recommend wearing friendship pins—the flag of the host country connected to the visiting country's flag—as a way to signal affinity. While traveling, I was fascinated by the different protective amulets and expressions of faith and status that jewelry conveyed. The interconnected plaiting of the East African Maasai people's beaded engagement necklaces (representing the intertwining of two people) and the elaborate marriage collars containing a map of the entire village impressed me greatly.

- **Shoes:** Two words: polish and resole. This is especially important when you're sitting on a stage and your feet are at eye level with the audience—they can see the top and underside of the shoe.

- **Socks:** Sock fashion is a thing now, even in government, and men are even wearing their pants a tad shorter to show off a little ankle personality—pastels, paisleys, tartan. My sock muses: the fabulously tailored protocol officer Nick Schmit and his husband, Jonathan Capehart, who have perfected sock creativity without it being diverting.

- **Ties:** They offer men the opportunity to make a statement with their attire. Whether you're a conservative tie guy (solid, neutral colors or light patterns like stripes) or a more avant-garde tie guy (skinny, colorful, unique patterns or a hipster bow tie, which is at once reverent and modern), the tie can make a great difference. But beware those with commentary or hidden messaging in the designs, as they may confuse or distract.

- **General advice:** Invest in a good tailor. Again, you don't have to get a suit that's made to fit, but I advise having at least two suits that have been adjusted for you. Or you can hire me: My finest tailoring moment occurred aboard *Air Force One* during a flight to Europe with Secretary Clinton and Phil Gordon, who was the assistant secretary of state for European affairs. When we boarded the plane, I noticed the hem on one of his pant legs had come undone (many men in government rotate only a few suits, and they all get a lot of wear on the road). I pointed it out immediately and Caroline Adler, the secretary's savvy, trusted press aide (who became Michelle Obama's press secretary), and my seatmate on the plane, said, "Capricia, please, you're embarrassing Phil." I replied, "No, what's embarrassing for him and for his country is for him to be seen with a muddy, fraying hem!" I whipped out my ever-present sewing kit, found the needle and thread that matched his dark suit, propped his leg up on my knee, and stitched it back into place in minutes. Phil smiled appreciatively while we disembarked for our next adventure.

(For more appearance advice, including travel and packing tips, turn to page 392.)

12

THE MIND-SET OF DIPLOMACY

Confidence. Decisiveness. Fearlessness. Most discussions stand a higher chance of success when the negotiator possesses these attributes. But these traits alone aren't going to steal the show. Just off stage right, waiting patiently to step into the spotlight, are the quieter but equally potent traits of empathy, humility, and collaboration. Time and again I've seen and experienced the incredible soft power of these mind-set tools, the peaceful giants of diplomacy. I've marveled at their ability to blunt sharp edges and move discussions beyond seemingly impassable obstacles. And not in a mere kumbaya way, but in a goal-oriented, strategic manner. The Gandhis of the world have just as much power as the Genghis Khans. Perhaps more so.

EMPATHY:
THE HEART OF DIPLOMACY

Empathy is literally putting yourself in another person's shoes—understanding what your counterpart is thinking and feeling—and then making a decision by integrating that information into your own outlook. We often do this automatically, even if we're not aware of it: noticing the tired look on someone's face and offering him a seat, or seeing someone tense up and asking if she's okay. In fact, our brains are wired for empathy. Neuroscientists have pinpointed an "empathy network" in our brain that activates when we witness certain facial expressions.

Far from being just a touchy-feely reflex, empathy and emotional intelligence (the ability to decode your own and others' emotions and apply that understanding to decision-making) involves higher-level thinking and is linked to a number of concrete benefits in the workplace. Managers who show more empathy toward their direct reports are viewed as better performers by their own bosses, according to a 2007 study by the global Center for Creative Leadership. About 20 percent of US employers now offer empathy training to managers.

At its most basic level, empathy helps close the gulf between ourselves and others, serving as a key tool for connection. It creates trust and strengthens relationships, and you cannot have cooperation and social interactions without it. In fact, many of our social rules and government protocols have been baked with empathy. We treat one another in a respectful manner, because how would we feel if we didn't greet someone cordially upon meeting them, thank someone for their gift, or acknowledge someone's cultural customs? In protocol, we relied heavily on empathy to achieve parity between nations, leaders, and delegations. Parity reigns in diplomacy—each party must feel they are being treated the same as the other—and in order to create an even playing field, the protocol team had to constantly put ourselves in the other person's shoes.

During the signing of the New START agreement in 2010, when President Medvedev and President Obama met in Prague, our team knew that the optics for this landmark nuclear arms deal needed to telegraph the importance of these two great nations collaborating for the betterment of their countries and the world. Asel Roberts, the lead US protocol officer for this visit, had been working on the details for a few weeks. Once I arrived, we worked directly with my Russian counterpart, Marina Entaltseva, to ensure that both of our leaders had equal presence and stature during the signing. All seemed to be in order, but as Asel and I conducted a last-minute check of the signing table and chairs, asking stand-ins to sit in each seat to assess camera angles and comfort, we realized that, when seated, President Medvedev—who is just shy of five feet five inches—would appear dwarfed by our six-foot-one-inch leader. We called in Marina and her team to discuss the issue, agreeing that the chair needed to be adjusted. Some may wonder, "Why not let your leader look more powerful, isn't that a bonus for the United States?" The answer is: Often we would, but certainly not here. Consider, empathically, the downstream effects: The photo of this historic signing appears around the world, Obama sitting a foot over Medvedev. The photo capturing this moment, which is supposed to be a win-win for both countries, would contradict this equality, signaling, "One of you is more powerful than the other." Memes would ensue, dignitaries may feel embarrassed, and President Medvedev would return to his country with the pride of accomplishment muted. The hard-won treaty negotiations would be eclipsed by the symbolic inequity of the photo, a lose-lose for both countries.

To avoid this potential calamity, Medvedev's chair was slightly raised by extending the legs (using blocks cut from the legs of an identical chair and nailed in place) so he appeared the same height as Obama when they were seated at the signing table. Not only did this do the trick (google the image and you'll note the slightly elongated legs of President Medvedev's chair), but it built a foundation of trust between Marina and me. She saw that we were thinking about her leader and it started us on solid footing for future interactions.

NEXT-LEVEL EMPATHY

When you take this mind-set tool and apply it strategically to an interaction or negotiation, you begin to open up new channels of communicating and understanding that would not have been available had you not asked yourself: What is my counterpart feeling and thinking right now, and how will that affect my behavior, the process, and the outcome? The ability to see through another's eyes is especially important when interacting on the international level, given the vast differences in life experience and cultural norms (a concept I cover in depth in chapter 4).

In some cultures, such as Asian countries, empathy is an incredibly valued asset. This is likely because the harmony of the group is paramount (people are primed to think of others first to maintain group cohesion), as is saving face: Public embarrassment is one of the worst things you can suffer in Asian countries, and people go out of their way to ensure no one is shamed in a group setting. In a heated negotiation discussion, employing empathy allows you to save the dignity of your opponent and ultimately the deal.

I relied heavily upon my empathy instincts during President Obama's state visit to Indonesia in 2010. The level of anxiety and preparation on the part of the Indonesian government was sky-high: this visit marked the return of someone whom they revered. The boy who had spent four years of his childhood in their country was now the leader of the free world, and they wanted to honor him with nothing less than perfection. The state dinner was to take place on the perfectly landscaped gardens of Merdeka Palace in Jakarta, the official residence of President Susilo Bambang Yudhoyono. The gardens' exotic flowers, which emitted the most exquisite aroma, would have made a heavenly backdrop, but the weather that day was not cooperating—hard rains were coming in—and they had to fall back to plan B: an indoor event. Everyone scrambled to shift gears, and although we were all exhausted, I agreed to partake in new logistics walk-throughs to affirm that President Obama would be fine with the changes. As they led me through the entry point to the state dinner, the elegance and beauty of the setting, and how quickly they'd managed to arrange it given the tight turnaround, took my breath away. Though there were a few minor tweaks I would have made, I didn't remark on any of them—in the larger scheme, they did not matter. My empathy kicked in, and I recognized how very important this visit was to each and every one of them. Minutes earlier, just before my walk-through, I saw from afar President Yudhoyono himself inspecting the new arrangements. Normally, leaders don't preview logistics, but this visit was so important he wanted to be the final set of eyes. I knew that requesting a change after he'd given a green light would be distressing for everyone. I also put myself in President Obama's shoes, recognizing he would never want any embarrassment for the Indonesians, a people that he knew valued saving face, and with whom he had a personal history. "Everything looks wonderful; this will be perfect," I said. I saw the immediate relief on their faces—they could report back that President Obama, their most esteemed visitor, was pleased with the current state of affairs.

Because I was constantly interacting with other cultures (as well as with other political parties, organizations, and people who maintained a very different perspective from mine), I constantly asked myself the most basic of questions in my government roles as social secretary and chief of protocol: *What is the other person feeling right now and how will my decisions affect him or her?* The answers drove my operating procedure. Hosting the NATO fiftieth anniversary dinner at the White House as social secretary required that I put myself in the shoes of forty-four different leaders (and cultures!) as I made decisions about how to greet and seat dignitaries, the order of announcements of leaders to the press corps, and the order of the motorcades, which (thank goodness) NATO has a protocol for (sometimes it's A to Z, sometimes Z to A). As often as I could, I worked within international protocols, as they are inherently objective: No one would feel like undue preference has been given to one country when everyone is following preset rules that have been created with parity in mind. The premise of NATO is that all member nations are equal and together form a collective, egalitarian coalition. I couldn't allow anyone to get higher billing.

Empathy also helped me grasp the importance for the first-time visitors to the White House, that pinch-me moment they feel as they are entering arguably the most iconic residence in the world. I needed to understand those moments (and recall my own marvel from my very first day) to help me guide these individuals in putting their best foot forward. We—the global protocol team—succeeded collectively if we were in unison in presenting the best of every leader. Ultimately, I had to prepare their leaders in the same way I was preparing my own.

During the Clinton administration, when hosting White House events for Congress, our social office team went to great lengths to make sure each invitee, whether Democrat, Republican, or Independent, felt welcomed. Our social office ethos was founded on the president and

First Lady's requirement that every guest be treated with honor and dignity. It was a bit tricky, considering the philosophical divisions, but we made sure the White House operated with a respect for divergent beliefs and that no one felt slighted due to party affiliation. (Looking back, we thought we had experienced the height of divisiveness and disparity, though today's interactions make those days look like the golden years!) I developed criteria the social office implemented to help ensure every invitee felt taken care of:

- Provide a full briefing of the events well in advance so no one felt in the dark about the expectations.

- Treat their staff with respect, offering our services (printing of documents, providing food for lengthy meetings, giving support staff access to their principals when needed) to assist them in the performance of their duties.

- Seek out their feedback on the plan and allow for last-minute requests (I couldn't always grant them, but the mere consideration was appreciated, as was a full explanation if it couldn't happen).

- Make sure there were no wait times or security hiccups at the White House gates for their entry (there's nothing like being sidelined and asked to wait for verification while streams of your colleagues walk right on through, noting you've been targeted).

What made my job easier: President Clinton always set an empathic and respectful tone, something I believe came naturally to him because he genuinely likes people and is curious about every person's perspective. During bipartisan convenings, he would pay particular attention to Republican Party members, pausing for their input, commenting positively on their opinions, and considerately acknowledging those with opposing viewpoints.

I was lucky to have shadowed First Lady Hillary Clinton for years and witnessed her powers of empathy, especially in connecting with those whose life experience was very different from hers. In 1995, when she was First Lady and I was special assistant, we visited Gujarat, India. There, she and fifteen-year-old Chelsea met with women who were deemed "untouchables" because of their lower-caste Hindu status. The women were treated as second-class citizens and had banded together—socially and economically through a microloan program—to try to rise above the position their society had allotted them. Later in the trip we visited the village of Moishahati in Bangladesh, where she and Chelsea again listened to a group of women who were living in extreme poverty. Hillary entered the thatched bamboo and tin-roof hut and sat with them in a circle. They sat upon thin mats laid on the dirt ground—many villagers were nursing children and cradling several others in their laps. It was a hot, dry day—no breeze whatsoever—and I watched from the side as she began to answer their questions about work, having children, and cows (a sign of wealth in Bangladesh) with a sensitivity that allowed her to bridge the gap. I knew she was drawing on her own family background to empathize with these women. Hillary's mother, Dorothy Rodham, left home to fend for herself at age fourteen, having had enough of a childhood where she suffered neglect and abuse. The women sensed Hillary's intense focus as she listened, nodding and "mmm-hmmming" as outward signs of empathy (something I believe she does unconsciously, which makes the listener aware of her effort to connect).

I was, frankly, distracted away from the conversation to an area where the women had displayed their handcrafted goods for sale. As I and Melanne Verveer, deputy chief of staff to the First Lady who expertly organized and managed the First Lady's international engagements and is a world-class shopper, marveled at the beading and glassware, we noticed a sudden pin-drop silence, and turned to see what had happened. All the women—even the many children on their laps and huddled around them—were intently listening to each and every word Hillary spoke, so as not to miss a single syllable. I could see they were desperately hoping that she was going to help set them on a path for a new life. They sensed her desire and investment—emotional and political—to change their lives for the better, with her own daughter by her side as proof of her compassion. Despite the huge cultural, economic, and social barriers, Hillary had found an emotional thread that allowed her—the wife of the US president—to connect with these resilient Bangladeshi women who were relegated to a place in their communities that severely limits employment, social opportunities, and basic dignity. The commonality: They were mothers and wives, women who wanted the best for their families. The visit itself was an act of empathy, as it legitimized these women in the eyes of the male-dominated government of their country, and in the eyes of the world.

All this talk of empathy might seem like a no-brainer to those who come to it naturally, but believe me, it is not always the norm, especially when competitive juices are flowing and stakes are high. People often erroneously think that in these situations they must drive full speed down the "my way or the highway" route. Being egocentric is human, and it can serve us well in certain situations (the "put your own mask on first, then help your child" analogy applies), but socially, diplomatically, and in business, an ego-driven mind-set can be divisive and misleading. It can also make your counterpart feel diminished.

A lack of empathy can also lead to a standoff between two parties with divergent viewpoints. You could even argue that most wars can be traced back to a lack of empathy on the part of one or both sides. But when empathy is applied in critical diplomatic moments, it can usher in peace. In 1978, when President Carter invited Israeli Prime Minister Menachem Begin and Egyptian President Anwar Sadat to the sedate and woodsy Camp David for peace talks—an attempt to end thirty years of conflict in the Middle East—he spent thirteen arduous days trying to broker a deal between the leaders, each entrenched in his own corner. Toward the end, all seemed lost. As Carter recalled in a 2014 CNBC interview, "We were in our thirteenth day at Camp David and I decided that it was over because Prime Minister Begin was so adamant about not removing his Israeli settlements from Egyptian territory." Just before leaving, Prime Minister Begin asked President Carter to sign photographs of the three leaders for his eight grandchildren. President Carter's secretary got the names of each grandchild and, instead of simply writing a generic "Best wishes," he wrote their names out with individual messages. He delivered the photographs personally to Prime Minister Begin, who was quite angry with Carter by that point, and turned his back on him.

Carter writes in his book *Keeping Faith*: "He looked at each photograph individually, repeating the name of the grandchild I had written on it. His lips trembled and tears welled up in his eyes. He told me a little about each child . . . we were both emotional as we talked quietly for a few minutes about grandchildren and about war." The two discussed what the consequences of war or peace would mean to their respective grandchildren, and what it would mean to be able to say, "Your grandfather chose peace." And then . . . the watershed moment. "Begin said, 'Why don't we try one more time?' And we tried one more time. And we were successful," he told CNBC. Later that day, the accords were signed, with the official treaty signing taking place six months later on the White House lawn. At this defining juncture, when failure seemed all but imminent, the two leaders were able to break the tension and the impasse with empathy for future generations. This compassion reconnected them and moved them into a mind-set of trust, sensing that the other possessed the will and potential to see beyond the hurdles. Today, relations between Israel and Egypt remain peaceful.

WALKING THE LINE

Not everyone is a fan of applying unbridled empathy in government or business. A debate ensued in 2009 when President Obama listed "empathy" as one of the many qualities he looked for when selecting a Supreme Court justice nominee. During the confirmation hearing for the president's selection, Justice Sonia Sotomayor, his opponents asked the justice whether a judge should rely on what is in his or her heart. Justice Sotomayor said she did not agree. "It's not the heart," she said, "that compels conclusions in cases. It's the law. The judge applies the law to the facts before that judge." But—and here's the rub—she also stated that "the process of judging is a process of keeping an open mind." That is, in effect, what empathy helps you do: It does not push you toward a subjective decision; on the contrary, it guides you to a more *objective* decision because you are opening up your mind to another person's experience instead of solely relying on your own. Unfortunately, our culture often misaligns empathy with a bleeding-heart, overly emotional, and irrational mentality, when in truth it's a sign of a healthy mind-set. (Interestingly, a total lack of empathy is one criterion for being a psychopath.) President Obama clearly knew what he was doing!

Some experts caution that empathy should be tempered, and that getting caught up in the suffering and feelings of others can cause you to act impulsively. It's certainly true that if empathy is the *only* thing that informs your decisions, it can invite biases and create tunnel vision. But to dismiss it wholesale is shortsighted. Information you perceive through empathy is one more important piece of the puzzle. People may also worry that by imagining their counterpart's experience and taking it into consideration, they might be weakening their own position or placing themselves in a vulnerable mind-set. No one wants to be exploited, of course. But when you couple empathy with specific strategies that protect you from being taken advantage of, you needn't worry about falling off this cliff. To avoid this, I always identified the overlapping goals between negotiation partners—they almost always exist (otherwise, you would not be meeting in the first place), and reminded myself that everyone wants a good outcome. The best way to find that merging of goals is to sense your colleague's position. To grasp why they are so adamant about their perspective you must understand it, and when you do, that understanding strengthens your ability to find the common ground and achieve the common goal. Their endgame might be slightly different than yours, but empathy allows you to see how they got there and how to build a bridge between you.

This was my MO during the APEC 2010 conference in Japan. On the calendar was an important bilateral with the Chinese, and my team and our Chinese counterparts had been ironing out many points for days. There were so many policy initiatives at odds that the negotiations seemed endless. And yet, there remained a few details that lingered without resolution, and we each had orders from our superiors to secure certain logistics. My counterpart and I met on the lower level of the hotel where the summit was being held for what we hoped would be the final arbitration. When I looked at him, he appeared worn out and sleep deprived. I know he saw the same when he looked at me. We recognized that the policy objectives were going to be tough for our delegations, so getting them in the right frame of mind by achieving parity would be essential. We both understood that what would work best would be complete honesty, a cards-on-the-table approach that would allow empathy to flow and for negotiations to happen smoothly. Empathy, I'd learned, is best facilitated by an honest approach. In order to "feel" the other person's perspective, there needs to be a clear and true understanding of the hurdles the other person is facing, and that can happen only if you each reveal what you need. If you begin negotiating based on half-truths and misperceptions, you are taking a long and winding detour away from your objectives rather than the most direct route. Thankfully, to assist us in this approach, we already had in our tool belt another critical aid: trust. We had worked together closely throughout our diplomatic engagements, never blindsiding the other.

Hungry, overcaffeinated, bone-weary me was so grateful my counterpart understood this essential starting point. He'd come alone—no other staffers, which is not the usual process—ready for a just-the-two-of-us conversation. I gleaned by his opening there would be no throat-clearing. "I have a 'must do' objective," he said calmly. We were huddled in a private space away from distractions or interruptions. He laid out his request forthrightly, I laid out ours—no made-up narratives (people can sniff out inauthenticity and it sets up an immediate cautionary roadblock). With every open reveal and request, we each felt more confidence in the other, facilitating a greater ability to empathize with the other's perspective. I was given the directive to have the meeting closer to the president's suite. His directive was to add more delegates to the bilateral table. Within five minutes we were both able to go back to our respective delegations with our win intact, which made it easier to explain the alternative need of our counterpart. This is not spin—it was important for the delegations to enter the negotiations feeling strong and confident, setting our teams in a good place for success and enabling them to employ empathy in their own negotiations.

BUILDING EMPATHY

Some people are naturally more empathic—whether it's through nature or nurture. Thanks to our brain's plasticity, we can develop empathy like any skill if we practice it, even in adulthood. To raise your empathy quotient, experts suggest mindfulness training and compassion meditation (yes, as New Agey as that sounds, there's a huge body of research showing it can grow empathy) and volunteerism. Or you can just follow the playbook of one of the most empathic people I know, President Bill Clinton. I'd seen him express empathy for years. But it wasn't until I watched his reaction to my own dear father's White House gaffe that I felt deeply how truly compassionate he is. My father, upon his first visit to the White House to meet the president, arrived in the Diplomatic Reception Room bearing two handmade gifts: blue-and-beige raw wool socks his mother had knit for the president and a bottle of red wine that he had fermented in his basement (he and my uncle, Ivan, competed each year to see who could concoct the better blend). He proudly handed President Clinton the socks. "Oh, Frank, these are beautiful, I'm gonna wear these, tell your mother 'thank you'!" the president exclaimed, genuinely happy to have them. Then, to properly present the wine, my father fervently placed the bottle on a nearby table to showcase the label saying, "This is from my own bottling, Mr. President, all for you." But the table had a hinged leaf that wasn't locked and the moment he let go of the bottle, the leaf gave way. The bottle smashed to the ground, sending glass shards and red wine everywhere, including on the exquisite Diplomatic Reception Room carpet. We all froze, except for the president. Without missing a beat, he said, "Don't you worry about that, Frank, we have good people who can clean this up. You don't think this hasn't happened before? Of course it's happened." My father was mortified—his big moment meeting the president had been soaked. But the president's gracious response made a terrible situation a lot less terrible. "You just gotta send me another bottle, Frank, I need to try that wine!" The president managed the moment beautifully. And I managed the moment by darting out to get the curators immediately to ensure that Frank Penavic's wine, which was offered to make a lasting positive impression, didn't also leave a lasting impression on the carpet (which it fortunately did not).

HUMILITY:
EMPATHY'S QUIET COUSIN

Humility is a superpower, but it's often misunderstood in the business realm. Some erroneously equate the trait with having low self-esteem or being a pushover—cue the stereotype of the humble assistant who sits silently in the corner. But nothing could be further from reality. Humility—the ability to appreciate others' strengths and differences while keeping your own skills and talents in perspective—is critical for connecting and finding unique pathways to success. Research shows that people who are viewed as humble are assessed as being more cooperative and committed, especially when those people are from a different country, where there's a need to bridge a wide cultural gap. I've seen displays of humility between leaders and dignitaries set the stage for collaboration, and a lack of humility end what should have been an easy win. The trait promotes a "we"-ness versus a "me"-ness—a humble ego doesn't feel threatened in the face of another person's contributions. In a sense, it's the opposite of narcissism.

Why is humility such an effective tool? When you understand your own limitations and value others' input, you are stepping into a flexible mind-set and opening up possibilities for collaboration. In diplomacy and business, especially with other countries, it's important to exercise humility and resist the inclination to always impose an American way of doing things. The moment we adopt a "better than" mind-set, we are closing off a channel of communication, believing we have nothing to learn and giving the impression of arrogance, which creates distance. (I've always found it surprising when Americans think of other countries as being archaic when it comes to women's rights . . . behold the full-force #MeToo movement that unfurled in 2017, shining a much-needed light on our country's glaring misogyny.) Going in with preconceived notions also closes us off to an objective experience.

Humility also allows you to dial down feelings of competition and seek diverse feedback from others. It's shown to strengthen social bonds, especially when there is conflict involved or in situations where differences threaten the health of the relationship. In this way, it buffers the wear-and-tear in competitive relationships, similar to how oil in a car can keep an engine from overheating. In fact, the trait is linked to more successful leadership. A 2001 study of CEOs by business researcher Jim Collins, author of *Good to Great*, found that the most successful executives (what he calls a Level 5 leader) have a rare combination of both fierce resolve and humility. Expanding on Collins's findings, researchers Don Davis and Joshua Hook note that while performance was the driving factor in being selected, being *too* competitive can spell trouble. Humility mitigates that negative effect, allowing competition without breaking down relationships. Fundamentally, a humble mind-set begets equality—i.e., no one is better or worse—thus creating a foundation for successful alliances and relationships. In diplomacy, humility is at the core of many protocols: You show respect to an emperor with a nod of the head. You exhibit deference to a sovereign by not touching her, turning your back on her, or walking ahead of her.

Humility is a quality that both President Clinton and President Obama had in spades, and I believe it's one reason they connected so strongly with voters and dignitaries. They were able to appreciate others' strengths—without fearing that shifting the spotlight away from their own accomplishments would diminish them—and as a result people felt heard and taken seriously. President Clinton's ability to admire others and get to their essence made him a popular speaker at eulogies. (No one wanted to follow him, as he never left a dry eye in the house.) His humility helped boost others and galvanize the country. At the 2012 Democratic National Convention, he spoke just before President Obama took the stage. I was watching the convention with Secretary Clinton in Timor-Leste (East Timor), where she was visiting the prime minister. We huddled in the ambassador's bedroom, of all places, where the multi-talented duo of Philippe Reines, the secretary's gifted senior adviser, and Nick Merrill, her clever communications officer, were able to jerry-rig a way for us to watch a recording of the just-delivered speech. The speech was stirring and energizing, plainspoken but inspiring, and focused on the hard-won accomplishments of President Obama's administration (hardly a word about the home runs of the Clinton years) and the cooperation and inclusion of the Democratic Party, which drove many of its economic and social successes. It was Clinton at his finest. As he finished up and President Obama walked out, President Clinton did something fascinating: He bowed to President Obama—a deep, at-the-waist bow. The gesture said, "You are the leader, and I cede you the stage." This is humility, one former president showing such deference to another in front of the whole world. You could see in President Obama's body language—and the huge hug he gave President Clinton—that while he may have felt it was unnecessary, he was also grateful. It was gratifying to witness such humility and shared admiration on the political stage by our country's leaders (one I still get a bit verklempt about watching on YouTube). Through all of this, I had been observing Hillary—I loved watching her watching him, her hands clenched, worrying whether all would go well for her husband on this national stage. When he bowed, she broke out in a big smile and laughed warmly. She knew what he was doing, using a gesture of quiet grace and humility to punctuate the point. He called her that night. I answered the call and handed her the phone, hearing him ask, "Did you see it?" in an almost childlike tone. "Yes," she said. "You were perfect!" The connection was quickly lost, but that was all that needed to be said.

Humility is also a tool that is incorporated into the ethos of some businesses, allowing great ideas to flow from every employee, regardless of their title or job description. Creative Artists Agency (CAA) in LA has taken the idea that talent is an equalizer to heart by soliciting screenplay pitches from every level of the organization. A mailroom assistant famously jumped up several rungs on the career ladder after pitching a comedy to mega-producer Brian Grazer, and the idea for *My Best Friend's Wedding* (starring Cameron Diaz and Julia Roberts) apparently came from a lunchtime pitch meeting with CAA assistants. Michael Kives, former CAA agent and current CEO of K5, a media and financial services advisory firm, affirms that, telling me, "While rising through the ranks of CAA, I was encouraged in my early years there to collaborate both up and down the chain of authority; all creative ideas that advanced our business objectives were welcomed. As CEO of my own company, I find fostering an open-door environment for creativity leads to greater business opportunities." W. L. Gore & Associates, known mostly for innovating Gore-Tex, the breathable, waterproof fabric, is also known for its remarkable "lattice" structure of organization. The company has no traditional supervisors, relying instead on people who show an ability to attract followers, shifting them into leadership positions for various projects. Its unique, flat approach has brought several successful products to market (including Elixir acoustic guitar strings, whose coating protects against debris which can distort tone) that were hatched by associates during spitballing sessions.

The trait of humility served me well when I entered the Office of Protocol. From Day 1, I adopted an attitude of "beginner's mind," an openness and belief that one can learn anything from anyone and should consider all possibilities before jumping to any conclusion. In psychology circles, "beginner's mind" (which is derived from Zen Buddhism) is thought to expand awareness and possibilities, whereas "expert's mind" uses prior experience to narrow awareness (which is sometimes necessary, like when a surgeon is performing a bypass or a president is negotiating an arms deal). Having a beginner's mind allowed me to forge relationships with everyone, including the interns (who happen to know an awful lot), clerical assistants (keepers of so many shortcuts and processes), and White House butlers (they see everything, and are so skilled at human interaction—I found they had some of the best intel). The protocol front office team of Rayda Nadal, career foreign service officer extraordinaire, and Rachel Salerno, an exceptional honors graduate from the School of Advanced International Studies, prepared my mind-set with their collective intel on each visit. While I was rushing through the front office on my way to a greet or an event, with their signature smiles they would quickly mention that the leader I was about to greet had just suffered a loss in the family or the assigned protocol officer had just been promoted, which immediately factored into my approach and conduct. (Rayda tragically died as the result of a gas explosion in her last posting in Moscow.)

I also came in asking, "What is already working?" so I wouldn't upset the applecart. Entering with, "How can I immediately change things and make my mark?" would have been a bad idea. The State Department is full of lifers—people who work for decades through multiple administrations—and we political appointees were affectionately referred to as the "Christmas Help" because we rotated with each administration and were only there for a few years. I had to respect that. I'd witnessed the negative results of a know-it-all, let's-change-everything attitude. On a few occasions, when a new State Department senior-level manager arrived (usually from the business world), they'd fire the old guard in order to bring in their own fresh hires, which sometimes backfired— they were met with fierce opposition during their tenure as a result. So often, the "new" ideas they brought to the table had been tried before . . . and had failed. Had they simply taken the time to ask questions of those who had been there for years, they may have needed only to tweak a few things to improve a process.

Interestingly, beginner's mind is taught in some med schools and physician groups as a way to open the mind to *all* possibilities for improved diagnoses and treatment, as well as to enhance the doctor-patient relationship. Beginner's mind helps people avoid labeling and stereotypes. For example, instead of seeing a patient or colleague as difficult because they have a lot of demands and questions, a beginner's mind recasts them as interesting, someone who is giving you a different experience of interacting.

COLLABORATION:
A MORE PERFECT UNION

Once empathy and humility are activated, they feed into the mother of diplomatic attitudinal tools: collaboration, an essential element to diplomacy and democracy. Finding common goals—while respecting differences—rests at the heart of a successful negotiation and nation. A mind-set of collaboration—where each party is bringing their talents to the table in order to meet agreed-upon goals—ultimately strengthens both of your positions and the whole endeavor. The most successful collaborations find the overlap in objectives, a Venn diagram of shared goals. The effort may seesaw, of course—in one instance you may do more heavy lifting; in another instance your counterpart takes on more weight—but the sum total is a win-win. Like humility and empathy, collaboration requires a flexibility and an openness to consider things from a slightly different vantage point. Ultimately, it raises the chance of forward movement for both parties.

While certain organizations, industries, and personalities may have to work a little harder at adopting a collaborative MO, it's actually something that comes naturally to us humans. Our ability to collaborate is one of the things that evolutionary biologists say has kept our species alive for thousands of years. We are, at the end of the day, ultra-social creatures—it's one reason our cortexes are larger than other mammals, as our brains are primed for interacting with others. Collective action, aimed at mutually beneficial goals, can achieve so much more than individual paths that can lead to isolated destinations. When you boil it down, collaboration is essentially what fuels successful international political alliances. Alliances or coalitions—groups with some shared values—are the basis of capitalism and modern democracies, in great part because of the assumption of shared risk and shared benefits.

In international diplomacy, particularly for large gatherings such as G20 and G7 summits and NATO and APEC meetings, the protocols of the events were developed with collaboration (with its shared risks and responsibilities) as the ultimate goal. Protocols incorporating parity for equal respect (no one feels slighted and less motivated to participate), an adherence to tradition (the expectations are set and well practiced), and organization (chaos and confusion can easily undermine partnerships) ensure that leaders can plow through enormous agendas in a short time frame to achieve a collaborative result.

One of the greatest examples of individual collaboration I witnessed was the relationship between President Obama and Secretary Clinton, though they weren't always on the same page. During the 2008 presidential campaign, the two staked out distinctive political real estate, particularly on Iraq. Then-candidate Obama opposed the decision to invade Iraq and he sharply criticized then-candidate Clinton for her vote to authorize President Bush to go to war. Clinton defended her position, claiming that her opponent conveniently had no skin in the game (he was not a US senator at the time of the vote) and that she'd made a reasoned judgment based on information she had at the time. But after President Obama won, he wanted to surround himself with a Lincoln-esque "team of rivals" who would challenge his thinking and sought out Secretary Clinton as one of those sounding boards. (The president also—in a collaborative fashion—kept as his Secretary of Defense Republican Robert Gates, who was appointed by President George W. Bush, making Gates the first secretary of defense asked to remain in that office by a newly elected president of a different party.) President Obama and Secretary Clinton respected each other's perspectives and quickly found a rapport that served the administration's policy goals (it also helped that they were both policy wonks). There was no one-upmanship, and they were always deferential to the other. To watch their diplomatic interactions at the bilateral table was like watching a beautifully choreographed dance, whereby each sometimes had a solo, and then they rhythmically swirl back in unison.

To wit: There was a defining moment early in his first term, during the 2009 Climate Summit in Copenhagen, where dozens of heads of state had convened. President Obama arrived on the last day of the summit and joined Secretary Clinton, who'd been there for two days already. That morning, they learned that the Chinese, Indian, Brazilian, and South African leadership were meeting without the Americans to come up with an alternative plan, and they decided together to head this off. As a team they were aligned to get the talks back on track and convinced the other principals to agree to the Copenhagen Accord, which set the table for the Paris Climate Accord three years later. Director of policy and planning at the State Department, Jake Sullivan, who has witnessed multiple engagements of our senior leadership at critical junctures, observed that it was an early bonding moment in their tenure, an outward signal that they were united, and an amazing display of teamwork.

Their tough, joint stance enabled the Obama administration to successfully negotiate nuclear weapons reduction with Russia with the 2010 New START agreement (the only Russia-US nuclear arms treaty still in existence as of the writing of this book); setting the table for negotiations with Iran on a nuclear deal (completed and signed under Secretary Kerry); and arbitrating a cease-fire between Israel and Hamas in 2012. Secretary Clinton also aligned with the president on the "go" decision with the high-stakes US Navy SEALS raid on the Osama bin Laden compound, killing the world's most wanted terrorist. Their professional respect eventually deepened into a strong friendship. I'll never forget President Obama's response when I thanked him for calling to check on the secretary when she was in the hospital. She'd injured herself and was unable to host the State Department Diplomatic Corps holiday event, and he'd stepped in to represent her. He stopped me in my tracks, looked pointedly into my eyes, and said, "She is my friend, and I love her."

This loyalty and collaborative spirit may sound de rigueur, but it isn't always, and when it's missing, it can have negative fallout. The relationship between President George W. Bush's secretary of state, Colin Powell, and the president's other top advisers—Defense Secretary Donald Rumsfeld, Vice President Cheney, and Deputy Secretary of Defense Paul Wolfowitz—was described as strained. It was reported that they often found Powell's diplomatic approach in opposition to their unilateral stance and hard power preference. Similarly, President Carter's two foreign policy advisers, Secretary of State Cyrus Vance and the more hawkish National Security Advisor Zbigniew Brzezinski, came to an impasse over how to deal with Soviet Russia, China, Africa, arms control, and the Iran hostage crisis.

In addition to individual collaboration, cooperation between agencies and divisions is critical for the success of government and business goals. All it takes is for one group or person to deviate from the overall goal to compromise a leader's efforts as he threads the needle of a high-stakes negotiation. I (and the world) witnessed a collaborative breakdown in 2011 during Chinese President Hu Jintao's state visit. For months prior to his arrival, every single part of the US diplomatic apparatus—from the Secret Service to protocol to the interpretation team—had been pre-paring to execute this all-important visit with perfection, and not simply because it was the Chinese, our economic rival and key trade partner. We were also determined not to repeat the ill-fated Chinese visit in 2006, when several major errors had marred President Hu's visit.

In my department, we worked overtime for weeks going over every detail. I pushed everyone to the limits (and I was so grateful to have my deputy Lee's friendship, gently reminding me when it was time to ease up on the weary staff). I was on edge in part because I had been strongly advised by a Chinese official in the Foreign Ministry on a recent trip to Beijing. What I thought was a friendly courtesy visit that all US diplo-mats performed turned out to be an intense protocol tête-à-tête. When I entered the reception room and sat down in the elegant chairs, he began by saying, "I would like to discuss the upcoming state visit." He then proceeded to go over several key requests in no uncertain terms. "First, I want to affirm that this will be called a state visit." (Check! The status of the visit had already been agreed upon.) Regrettably, in 2006 there was considerable confusion and conflating over the name and style of the visit. There was ultimately an arrival ceremony, but no state dinner—and it was simply called "a visit." "Second, please confirm that our national anthem will be announced as that of the *People's Republic of China*, not the *Republic of China*." (Check! It had gotten mixed up as well in 2006.) I was beginning to feel a tad uncomfortable as I was now the face of the country that had embarrassed President Hu five years earlier and real-ized that it was on me to ensure it wouldn't happen again. Next: "Can you ensure we will not have protesters at the arrival ceremony?" (Check! A heckler from the Falun Gong spiritual sect had interrupted the Chi-nese president's remarks on the previous visit.) There were a few more points and requests made as well. I left his office knowing that with the help and collaboration of every arm of government I would have to de-liver the visit that both the Chinese and the United States hoped for and expected. I had to empathize with them: They had felt very slighted on their last trip, and while it wasn't intentional, none of it helped with the visit, which yielded no new diplomatic agreements between the coun-tries.

When I returned to the States, I met immediately with the senior director of the NSC, the assistant secretary of state, and the Chinese ambassador posted to the United States, and, once he arrived, the US ambassador posted to China to relay my Beijing conversation. We determined that the four of us would collaborate on every single term of this engagement, affirming nothing to anyone unless we all agreed on it first. We recognized that the 2006 visit had, in part, gone sideways because of a lack of communication and collaboration between agencies and individuals, so we created protocols that would result only in unison and agreement among us and the Chinese. Our small group negotiated every element, in addition to China's five all-important requests. I'm happy to report that everything went in accordance with our and the Chinese expectations . . . save the regrettable moment when the interpretation protocol went fantastically awry. Our team had negotiated for the press conference to be conducted with *simultaneous interpretation*, where each interpreter is in a soundproof booth off to the side translating into each principal's earpiece in real time, a process that results in fluid conversation, and which is always the case for a US president when we are hosting. In contrast, *consecutive interpretation* requires that one wait for the interpreter to translate each phrase after it's spoken, resulting in a more halting and much slower delivery, losing precious time allotted for the interaction. (Consecutive interpretation, which the Chinese negotiate for when we visit them, gives more time for absorbing the question and crafting the response—each leader has his or her own preference.)

The press briefing took place in the East Room of the White House, but I watched it on the screen in the Usher's Office nearby—I always like to see how the event looks on television, since, at this point, all should be rolling as expected. The opening statements took place as they always do: we heard President Obama's remarks live directly from him in English, while, simultaneously, they were being interpreted into President Hu's earpiece in Chinese by the American interpreter. Then, during President Hu's remarks, his interpreter's voice could be heard over the sound of President Hu's Chinese for the English-speaking television audience, as well as for those in the live audience on their headsets. (The White

House distributes headsets to the audience, who can listen in their language of choice—in this instance it was either English, channel 1, or Chinese, channel 2).

Next, the Q&A portion began. The first question was asked by a reporter, in English, to both presidents. Assuming the agreed-upon simultaneous interpretation was still in place, President Obama spoke in full, lengthy paragraphs. Moments after he stopped speaking, chaos ensued. Suddenly, President Obama's interpreter's voice boomed into the room, translating his answer all at once in Chinese for President Hu. Apparently, nothing President Obama had just said had been interpreted simultaneously in real time for President Hu, who was shifting uncomfortably from side to side. President Hu pointed to his earpiece that there was something wrong and called over a staffer, who seemed to explain that the Q&A would be consecutive. President Obama's eyes darted about as he reached for his earpiece and fiddled with it—yes, something was clearly wrong.

I dashed back to the East Room to determine what was happening. As I entered the room, I noticed the audience seemed very confused, looking about while consecutive interpretation continued being heard in the room, as opposed to an interpreter's voice coming through their headsets. I headed to the interpreters' booths, which were now empty— the interpreters had raced up to the one mic near the dais to provide consecutive translation for their leaders.

I asked a nearby staffer in the room what had happened. Did we have a technical failure? No. Did one of the interpreters get ill? No. Did the president send a signal to change the mode of interpretation? No. "It just changed," I was told. Well, interpretation changes don't "just" happen. We were on live television, discussing important global policies—even one missed detail or skipped word can shift the meaning and impact. I noted the three other core decision-makers were seated in the audience and also looked bewildered, so they clearly did not approve the change.

By this point, President Obama had become visibly unhappy, and announced from the podium to the audience that he assumed we had simultaneous interpretation and was forced to apologize to his interpreter for not pausing in between thoughts to allow him to translate properly.

He tugged the earpiece out and tossed it to the side, as it was now useless. He remained composed throughout the rest of the Q&A, but there were high costs: First, he had been poised for a certain kind of experience and was forced to recalibrate and take the hit, with a global trading partner on the world stage, no less, because someone (someone who *clearly* did not have the authority to make such a critical call) had changed the process. Second, because of the confusion, his response was too long to be properly translated by his interpreter (as the official White House transcript later revealed). Third, due to the faulty translation, President Hu, our honored guest, was put in an awkward position on the sensitive issue of human rights: He did not initially answer the first question on human rights, as it wasn't translated for him, which he noted emphatically when the question was asked again in a manner that implied he had avoided answering it. He assured the audience he was not ignoring the question and subsequently responded. Lastly, because consecutive interpretation takes double the time, the press conference went on far too long and became disruptive to the rest of the schedule of the state visit.

The perfectly knitted collaboration had broken down. While the Q&A continued, I frantically questioned a few more people and discovered that just before the press conference, a US staffer had agreed with a Chinese communications staffer, unilaterally, to change the methodology. I suppressed the urge to scream. This one concession had undone weeks of purposeful and positive collaboration. I understood that our staffer likely believed he was trying to be helpful, and I later discovered he was beside himself once he realized the damage caused to both presidents.

Immediately after the conference wrapped, I escorted the presidents to the North Portico to bid President Hu farewell until the dinner that evening. He left, and my president then stopped and paused. My colleagues and I were now gathered in the grand foyer, waiting for what we knew was coming. I looked around for a sympathetic face, and landed upon Ben Rhodes, deputy national security advisor for strategic communications, who offered a consoling smile (we were frequent seatmates aboard *Air Force One*, and you get to know someone well when you log many hours together on long flights). I realized that not only had this infraction embarrassed the president but also mangled the hard work of so many people, like Ben. The president looked around and asked, "What happened, people?" He was calm—never raised his voice—but he was clearly displeased, as he had every right to be. We explained that, regrettably, someone had changed the plan. He gave us a "no kidding" look, then said he wanted us to affirm that all other engagements would be simultaneous translation, as agreed to. We assured him we would. And they were.

I know the protocol team would never have made such a unilateral decision. We prided ourselves on being in lockstep with one another and followed a strict process for everything. The ethos of the protocol team during my tenure was founded upon sharing of information (no hoarding of sources or details) and a nonhierarchical atmosphere. I relished our brainstorming sessions encouraging the team to contribute ideas. I firmly believe in the benefit of collaboration, trusting that we can all come at an issue with a unique perspective, one that enlightens everyone in the circle. These gatherings embraced a spirit of openness so no one would be afraid to ask me or other officers questions.

Another important fringe benefit of a collaborative mind-set: you build a wolf pack of supporters who will have your back because you invited them to be a part of the process. Assembling a deep bench is helpful in all aspects of life, but it is essential in business and in government, especially in DC, where landscapes can shift suddenly, and a strong foundation of colleagues who can vouch for your ability to cooperate will come in handy when the deck chairs get shuffled. When I left government, the incomparable Lloyd Hand—the most trusted of aides to President Johnson and one of the most revered people in Washington, DC—and I began a tradition for the former chiefs of protocol to pass our knowledge on to the incoming chief, a tradition I'd been initiated into when I became social secretary in the 1990s. Social secretaries dating back to Truman and Eisenhower had been convening for years to pass along invaluable wisdom and resources to their successors, providing a blanket of nonpartisan support. I was treated to a luncheon aboard the *Sequoia*, the former presidential yacht (now privately owned) and received endless amounts of support from several formers, including my elegant predecessor, the impeccable Ann Stock, who became a trusted friend, and the iconic "doyenne of decorum," Tish Baldrige, JFK's social secretary. I wanted to build this same network for the Office of the Chief of Protocol, so together we arranged a luncheon to download all things protocol to my successor, Pete Selfridge, a perfect selection, a courteous and experienced public servant who already knew the president's style well. When President Trump appointed his chief of protocol, Sean Lawler, a former military officer and National Security Council aide, the tradition continued. In many circles in DC, particularly in the State Department, there is a strong heritage of passing collective wisdom down to incoming employees, regardless of party. It's wise to adopt this mind-set in business as well. Hoarding intel never ends well for anyone and puts the whole organization at risk. I've always found it irritating when people cradle information, waiting to one-up a colleague with coveted details that they should have shared earlier, and which, if they had, would have benefited the end goal for all. And it usually backfires on the hoarder: That person comes off as scatterbrained (Why didn't you say so earlier?), ungenerous (Are you with us or against us?), and insecure (Is coveted information the only thing you think makes you valuable?). You always get better results for the overall goal when you loop in your colleagues and are seen as a trusted team player.

Many successful companies know this and have built collaboration into their organizational structure. I've had the great benefit in the private sector of working with smart, collaborative teams at the Atlantic Council, where each center has a very different objective but the ultimate goal is the same: to work with our partners and allies to shape the future. The organization's ethos is evident through their approach to staff interactions. On the first Monday of every month is a town hall–style discussion led by Executive Vice President Damon Wilson, where staff are encouraged to offer opinions on the council's operations, knowing there will never be any retaliation. The annual staff retreats and monthly director meetings are also designed to encourage a collaborative spirit by seating people from different centers together and having those diverse groups offer solutions to issues facing the council. Equally, I am amazed at how a behemoth like Bloomberg encourages collaboration. From the London office to the Indonesian branch to the New York City headquarters, they loop in everyone globally when there's an issue or endeavor. It is immensely clear that there is no true hierarchy (try to get them to tell you their titles—it's impossible—you only get their job descriptions) and infamously their leader requests that all employees refer to him as "Mike" (a hard one at first for me to do—I kept calling him "Mr. Mayor").

Google is also well known for its team-based approach. Recruiters screen candidates to determine how "Googley" they are (can they work in a collegial, flexible manner?)—and assess managers for their ability to listen and invest in their charges' career development, qualities the company recognized were helping with retention rates.

The most compelling illustration of collaboration is the convening of our country's founders, whose opposing views did not prevent their effort to create "the perfect union," to work as one unit and sign one document to express this unity: our Constitution. This document, our country's rules of governance, has allowed our nation to thrive since its debut in 1789. That spirit of alliance continues through those who pledge to protect and defend our nation and commit to working together no matter their differences. I'll never forget the moment when I recognized the weight of the Constitution and how it symbolizes the American collaborative spirit. It was January 20, 2001, at around 10:30 a.m., and I was standing in the foyer of the White House, witnessing the changing of the guard between President Bill Clinton and the soon-to-be-sworn-in president-elect, George W. Bush.

As social secretary, I was on hand to help smooth the transition. The logistics of inauguration day are complicated enough under normal circumstances, but on this day, everything was extra heavy. The 2000 election had been brutal: President Bush received the most electoral votes, despite Vice President Al Gore's having won the popular vote. Ultimately, the decision had come down to Florida, where Bush's winning margin had been close enough to require a recount. The country's fate hung in the balance for thirty-six days post-election while ballots were recounted and Florida's Supreme Court and ultimately the US Supreme Court deliberated the constitutionality of recount deadlines. In the end, Bush prevailed.

Just before the Bushes arrived, President Clinton grabbed Hillary's hand and they went from room to room, recalling the wonderful memories they'd had in the iconic residence. He then went into the Grand Foyer and asked Charlie Corrado—the White House's fabulous piano player in the President's Own Marine Corps Band—to play "It Had to Be You," one of their favorite songs. President Clinton swung the First Lady around, dipping her as she flipped her head back. Vice President and Mrs. Gore arrived to join in on the moment (though he was a bit less social—this was a day he had hoped would have been his).

Regrettably, I had to break up the fun to let everyone know that the PIC (presidential inaugural committee) motorcade was arriving with the Bushes and the Cheneys, kicking off the long-standing protocol of this day: The outgoing president receives the incoming president and his vice president and spouses by hosting a coffee. The North Portico door swung open and we all felt a moment of anticipation. What was about to happen was the living embodiment of our Constitution. This peaceful passing of the democratic torch is what our forefathers fought for and what our men and women in the military protect for us on the battlefield.

The Bushes and Cheneys entered, and everyone was escorted to the Blue Room (so named for its blue drapes and carpet), where coffee was served. The air was thick with so many emotions and awkward moments, but "glass half-full" President Clinton broke the tension in his usual manner with funny stories recalling events from past years that took place in that room. President-elect Bush, always affable, followed suit, chatting with staff members he already knew from when his father, George H. W. Bush, was president.

After twenty minutes, it was time to load up the motorcade for the ride to the inauguration ceremony on Capitol Hill. I escorted the First and Second Ladies to their cars, then Vice President Gore and Dick Cheney. Back inside, I watched as President Clinton walked over to President-elect Bush and looked him in the eye. Although there was no *official* protocol for this moment, we all instinctively stood at attention, sensing the historic significance of these last seconds, of one president stepping into the leadership and one stepping out. President Clinton reached up to straighten President-elect Bush's jacket with both hands—a move that seemed almost paternal—then patted him on the back and said, "Let's do this." I saw President-elect Bush affirm the gesture by returning a look that said, "Don't worry, I won't let you down, I got this." Just like that, punctuated by a physical expression of camaraderie, the history page turned from one administration to another. I had just witnessed the peaceful transfer of power. No one ever thought that this element of our Constitution would be tested, but the 2020 election proved otherwise. Perhaps our democracy is more fragile than we thought.

In an ideal world, collaborations deliver the goods for all parties. But we know that's not always the case. When opposing political parties cannot see beyond their partisan demands or when partnerships break down, despite both parties' employing empathy and humility, the disconnect may be due to a lack of meticulous planning (foreseeing where things might go off road so you can put appropriate guardrails in place) or the inability to pivot in the moment. These two additional protocol tools, which I cover in the following chapters, can help keep engagements on track—and rescue ones that are on the verge of collapse.

13

THE ULTIMATE CHECKLIST:
EXTREME PREPARATION

I f you fail to plan, you plan to fail. You've heard this before, of course, but what you may not know is that failing to plan means you also miss out on the many hidden benefits of preparation itself. Beneath the to-do lists and the careful forecasting lies a world of untapped treasures that are tightly tethered to preparation: Influence, stability, confidence, and the ability to be spontaneous—reacting smartly to a surprise opportunity (or an unforeseen roadblock) is much easier if your ducks are already in a row. In the Office of Protocol, we knew that to skip a prep step was to jeopardize an advantageous place at the negotiation table, and that the run-up to an engagement was a precious window of opportunity to head off mishaps, direct the flow, and exert leverage. Our gospel: Extreme planning is the foundation of any successful interaction. I preached it—and I practiced it.

On June 24, 2009, I faced the Senate Committee on Foreign Relations as they held the confirmation hearings for my chief of protocol nomination. My husband, Rob, who has supported and encouraged me to do what he believed I was best at—serving my country—sat patiently behind me with my concerned, proud parents and assured them that their daughter would pass this most monumental of tests. I was nervous but not overly so. I'd been prepping for this day for weeks (though, frankly, I felt as if I had been preparing for it my entire life). I'd painstakingly read testimonies from previous confirmation hearings and reviewed (and reviewed . . . and reviewed some more) the official protocol guidelines for global interactions. But the most important step I'd taken: I'd submitted to a brutal process called "murder boards." Used by the military, government, academia, and business, the aptly named murder boards prepare a "victim" for any question that may be thrown their way, killing the possibility that an opponent's "gotcha!" questioning will inflict significant damage. Cheryl Mills, counselor to the secretary, worked with Denis McDonough, deputy national security advisor, on each nomination, requiring nominees to go through the process. The process can be daunting, so they advised me to seek out the guidance of the respected foreign service officer Patrick Kennedy, the undersecretary for management, for an overview. He encouraged me to put myself into the hands of my future colleagues. I did . . . and I was subjected to four grueling murder boards of three to four hours each by the protocol team.

I was blessed to have a brilliant crew to ready me for the inquisition—protocol veterans, colleagues, and friends who cared deeply about preparing me completely (not every nominee does). Ali Rubin was my murder board "manager in chief"—as someone who highly values extreme preparation, she researched prior chiefs' testimonies and spent a few hours every day grilling me. Along with the acting chief, Laura Wills, they brought in a stellar lineup of staff from every department to dream up the most damning and esoteric topics that might get thrown at me during my hearing.

The murder boards are meant to be worse than the actual confirmation—the idea is that you mess up and humiliate yourself in the process so that you don't choke during the live hearings. The procedure was incredibly humbling, and full transparency is necessary in order for it to work. You must lay everything bare—your finances, any suspicious gaps on your CV, or questions raised on your background check. Knowledge is a weapon, and for weeks I'd been studying at my desk, with additional hours clocked on my elliptical, sweating and memorizing so I could fight back (exercise improves the memory, after all). On the day of my first murder board, I did not anticipate that I would have butterflies in my stomach, these were my future colleagues, but they were there in full flight. I walked into a large, bare conference room in the State Department—no decor or warmth to make you feel at home—and sat at one of four long tables configured in a classroom-style square. Moments later about fifteen stony-faced inquisitors walked in and sat fanned across the three other tables. They played their parts perfectly, extending no greetings or smiles, and immediately began to fire question after question at me: If the police call you at 3 a.m. and say the child of the ambassador of X country has been caught drinking underage, what is their diplomatic immunity? Are same-sex spouses of an ambassador recognized? What is the gift limit of the president when accepting gifts from foreign dignitaries? After I answered, they reviewed my responses, offering blunt criticism.

One of my murder board sessions was entirely devoted to a single topic: my taxes. Nominees' taxes were examined—as they should be—for payment and submission. Many people were halted in the process due to irregularities, usually non-payment. But my issue was unique: I'd overpaid significantly but forgotten to file. We strongly suspected it would come up. Professional inquisitors and friends who had expertise in this area convened with me in a small room and asked the same essential question—"Why didn't you file your taxes?" Over and over they lobbed, but in subtly distinct ways that required that I hone my answer and authentically deliver a response, regardless of any tricky nuances in the phrasing of the question.

Having to articulate my answers out loud in the face of aggressive scrutiny and the occasional mean questioner forced me to get it right. Two of my inquisitors were longtime friends, Philippe Reines, senior advisor to Hillary Clinton and a strategic communications expert, and Richard Verma, assistant secretary of state for legislative affairs and renowned for his congressional insights. They had my best interests at heart, and as such they grilled me for hours. (I'm deeply grateful to them both). I realized that the way I'd answered the tough questions in my head didn't always translate when I opened my mouth (*Pro tip 1:* Roleplay with someone before a big interview—I guarantee your carefully crafted answers won't roll off your tongue the way you think they will. *Pro tip 2:* If a question stumps you, be forthright and say you're not fully prepared to answer the question and that you'd like some time to consider it. This is preferable to responding in the moment and getting it wrong.)

The day of the confirmation hearings I held my breath, hoping that only a smattering of committee members would show up. Oftentimes senators do not attend due to other more pressing matters. But on this day, I wasn't the only nominee in play; so was Dan Rooney, the beloved owner of the Pittsburgh Steelers, who'd been nominated as the US ambassador to Ireland. He was revered in the Senate—respected by both parties—so the place was packed. As we sat together in the hearing room just before the action started, he turned to me and jokingly asked if I wanted to wear one of his gold Steelers' pins, knowing I was from Cleveland and the rivalry our football cities have. The wonderful Senator Sherrod Brown of Ohio, who had joined me at the hearing to sponsor my nomination, overheard. We looked at each other and laughed hard. I responded like any good Cleveland Browns fan would: "Not today, sir, and frankly, not ever, but thank you anyway!" Soon-to-be ambassador Rooney laughed as well (that day marked the beginning of a deep friendship with him and his son Jim and I've missed the ambassador since his recent passing).

As I glanced toward the back of the room, I stopped laughing. The late republican Senator Richard Lugar had walked in with a serious expression on his face, which signaled my tax issue would be addressed, as he had sent me written questions prior to the hearing asking about my taxes. I relaxed a bit when I saw my friends and committee members New Hampshire Senator Jeanne Shaheen and Wyoming Senator John Barrasso (whom I knew through my dear friends Rob Wallace and Mike Tongour and our time in Wyoming). About eight senators in total (out of about twenty) were there for the hearing. Everyone asked insightful questions, which I answered succinctly and easily. Immunities? Check! Gifts? Got it. I hit my stride and was feeling good. And then the tax question came. The room, already hushed, seemed to go utterly silent. As my murder board mentors advised, I stated it succinctly and directly, no blame or excuses. I took complete responsibility for not filing, stated that my taxes were fully paid, and assured the committee that it was unintentional and wouldn't ever happen again. The senator seemed satisfied and moved on. During the murder board process, I learned that by offering up details that I believed would make me look better (i.e., accounting errors and mailing snafus), I would only come off as equivocating or scapegoating. Although it's hard to say "I was wrong," doing so shows that you're trustworthy. People can sniff out inauthenticity, and being evasive only makes them want to know what you're hiding.

All the prep paid off. I was confirmed at the end of July, and I was elated. Not only could I dive into my dream job, but I hadn't let down the people who'd put so much effort into my hearing. Most important, I hadn't disappointed President Obama or Secretary Clinton: I learned later that my nomination was the subject of much contention behind closed doors, and that it was President Obama—against the advice of some staff—who gave the green light for my nomination, trusting Secretary Clinton's strong recommendation. (Once I was on staff, there were no issues, and the topic was never raised again.)

I shudder to think what would have happened had I not practiced "extreme preparation" (for one, you might not be reading this book). I have known people to give short shrift to the murder board process—to their detriment. CEOs are often the most skeptical of the hearing process, believing that because they have successfully built and run their own companies that they can wing it. But like any critical interview or client pitch (or even a challenging personal conversation), the hearings aren't simply about past accomplishments or your capacity to think on your feet (though that helps). These types of interviews reveal your ability to walk into a high-stakes situation and handle it, previewing how well you would execute the job: Have you done the homework to demonstrate full knowledge of the position or the project you're being considered for? Have you anticipated the right questions, and formulated accurate, concrete answers that reveal who you are? Interviews are clearly about your qualifications, but additionally they are the first face-to-face (or FaceTime-to-FaceTime) opportunity for a would-be client or employer to get a read on you. They're wondering: Can I trust your judgment? Are you adept at speaking, particularly when this job may require you to speak publicly? All these underlying judgments are taking place throughout the targeted questioning, and the interviewee is sending either affirmative or negative signals back. On paper you may be perfect, but when asked a round of questions you didn't prep for, you can come off as the wrong choice.

WHAT LIES BENEATH

If planning is so integral to success, why do so many smart people neglect to do it? Overconfidence, for one, especially at the top of the food chain. Senior-level folks may adopt a "been-there-done-that" attitude that lulls them into a false sense of security. Others tend to *under*estimate what could go sideways or assume that fail-safes will keep things on track. For those just starting out, inexperience can lead them to walk into situations unarmed—rookies simply don't know what they don't know. But in my experience, one of the biggest reasons for the Preparation Gap is an incomplete understanding of planning's power and benefits. Plotting things out is more than mere type A behavior. Planning carries potent advantages. When I launch into preparation mode for any project, I do so knowing these four unsung benefits are materializing with every prep step I take:

1. **Planning is influencing.** When you pay attention to the details well before the interaction—as I've demonstrated in previous chapters— you can strategize in ways that give you, your principal, or your team an edge. History had taught me well that the act of prepping can win the day in a big way. Consider a story I once read, credited to Thomas Jefferson biographer Dumas Malone, of how our third president laid the groundwork for the building and organization of the University of Virginia in the early nineteenth century. He wanted to plant his vision quickly, before others had an opportunity to hatch their plans. So he arrived at the first planning meeting—

and subsequent early meetings—with nearly every aspect drafted, including richly detailed architectural drawings and budgets for construction and operation. He even suggested a curriculum with faculty he'd become acquainted with on his travels to Europe. Because the other meeting attendants weren't nearly as prepared, Jefferson's vision—so well thought out—was the obvious one with which to move forward, and the university was eventually founded in accordance with his plans.

Planning need not be so elaborate to be influential. At summits, I always took advantage of pre-event walk-throughs in order to game a space for my president. (If these opportunities weren't offered, I'd arrive early and lean on my trusted relationships for a sneak peek.) During my recon, I'd scope out the best spot in a leader's lounge for President Obama to do his pull-asides, as he depended on these impromptu discussions in addition to the more formal bilateral. The pull-asides gave him an edge, as their purpose was to address his specific issue, as opposed to the more formal setting that called for a longer agenda serving both leaders. The tactic was a savvy one but called for us to be on guard and well prepared to pop these up (with the appropriate chairs and table) at a moment's notice. Where could he best have a semiprivate tête-à-tête with Mexico or a huddle with Germany? On the day of, the team would enter the leader's lounge and make a beeline for the preordained space and start putting our belongings out on the tables and chairs to "save" them (you think it's tough trying to hold seats at the movie theater, try competing with international delegations for coveted spots like generous corners and private nooks behind screens).

2. **Planning is intrinsically optimistic.** When you lay out a blueprint for how you envision things will flow, you are concretely investing in your goal and upping the chances you'll achieve it. Some psychologists call our mind's planning process "anticipatory thinking" and point out it's quite different from making predictions. Anticipatory thinking isn't guessing the future; it's informed thinking, identifying things that might go wrong and putting in place practices to avoid threats to

success. While this might seem like pessimism—a "choose your own adventure" that leads only to bad outcomes—imagining the worst *with the intention to avoid it* is really the definition of an optimist. An optimist scans the horizon for possible pitfalls and plots routes that avoid those obstacles (a true pessimist likely wouldn't go on the trip to begin with or would just accept the worst as inevitable). This is one of my favorite parts of the planning process: Solving for the "what ifs" makes me feel a bit like a sleuth, seeking out where I can be tripped up and making sure there's a fix for it.

3. **Planning facilitates spontaneity.** Why take a detour on a whim if you've mapped out your journey? Because with everything in place, you buy yourself a bit of wiggle room for life's surprises, both good and bad. The moment I wake up, I review the hard-and-fast "must-dos" in my phone's digital calendar, then I write another plan for the day on paper: a list of "want-tos." Drawing a line down the middle, one side of the paper is what I would like to accomplish and the other side is a timeline, placing the wish list within the "must dos" from my hard schedule. If an opportunity arises last minute to meet an exciting new acquaintance or attend an impromptu concert/panel/dinner, having everything else locked down makes it so much easier to shift a few things and accommodate those wonderful (or stressful) bombshells. I discuss the importance of a flexible, yoga-like mentality in the next chapter, but I like to remind people who are anti-planners—those who eschew to-do lists and like to live and work on the fly—that a preparatory mind-set is not the enemy of creativity and improvisation. It pairs perfectly with it.

4. **Preparation quells anxiety and provides emotional stability.** Doing your homework delivers a sense of calm that can take the edge off a nerve-racking event. The larger occasions in life such as funerals and weddings can be daunting, even paralyzing. How do you manage it all in the midst of a roller coaster of emotions? Gratefully, there are years of protocols set to assist with the planning and execution of milestone rituals. Not only do preset protocols give you a template

for planning, but they offer you and attendees a way to absorb the varied emotions coming at you during the event. Additionally, revealing some of those particulars to guests helps spread the calm. When you reassure others that all is in order—and when you share planned details—they, too, will feel more confident in what is to come.

This is true for the smaller events and interactions, as well. Our brains are always predicting and playing out different scenarios—it's the price we pay for being able to reason (and one of the things researchers say has kept our species alive). Anxiety worsens when you don't know what to expect—you start forecasting every which way, anticipating a lot of different scenarios "just in case." But once someone says, "Here is your conference schedule with a layout of the building and your meeting rooms," your brain can dial down the "what-if" scenarios. Harnessing information is the best strategy to avoid being overwhelmed by anxiety and emotion.

I relied heavily on planning and protocol to help manage extreme distress during the most somber event of my tenure: Assisting with the Dignified Transfer of Remains at Andrews Air Force Base after two extraordinary diplomats, Ambassador Chris Stevens and Information Management Officer Sean Smith, and two brave Navy SEALs and CIA contractors—Glen Doherty and Tyrone Woods—were killed in a September 11, 2012, terrorist attack at the American consulate in Benghazi, Libya. The unparalleled importance of this tradition—returning the remains of these four patriots to their home country and transferring them to their families to lay them to rest—was monumental for our country and the families and friends of the fallen.

Shortly after the attack, our office was asked to help prepare the event for the Dignified Transfer of Remains. Every nuance of this military tradition has great meaning, as it is intended to commemorate American heroes in the honorable manner they deserve and give the families a process from which to start healing. I sat with a small core of the protocol team, the military at Joint Base Andrews (JBA), and Phil Fowler, director of ceremonies and special events directorate with the Military District of Washington (MDW)—one of the major commands of the US Army whose mission includes ceremonial tasks—as military protocol would take precedence. Firstly, we had to learn the proper terminology: It was a *movement* (not a *ceremony*, though many well-meaning people still refer to it as a ceremony) to acknowledge *the return of the remains*; and the vessels were *cases* not *coffins* (a coffin should only be referenced for the personal funeral). I had to reinforce these terms and lessons repeatedly with everyone I interacted with throughout our preparation. Other critical planned details included the musical selections, which had to be painstakingly reviewed to affirm they were in alignment with the tone of the event and that there weren't lyrics or associations that would be considered offensive to the families.

When the families arrived at their hotel the night before, I met with each one separately to outline the plan and to discuss any issues they may have so as to address them quickly. I am sure this was all disorienting, and I tried to be a steady force for them, relaying assuredness and support. I quietly explained what they would be experiencing, minute by minute. I wanted the families to be armed with knowledge, and I saw that they were immensely grateful for the information. I was struck by how the process of planning—discussing the details and learning about the significance of each step—helps to fill the void during moments of grief. Not only were they likely in shock and exhausted, but now they had to navigate the surreal experience of grieving at Andrews Air Force Base with the president of the United States while the world watched. There were so many unknowns facing them, but I could at least help them plan for the next twenty-four hours. The single, most firm request from the families was to avoid the media. I let them know that there were specific press protocols in place to protect their privacy, introduced them to State Department communications aide Nick Merrill, who would help manage media logistics, and assured them that they'd be escorted into the venue before the press entered and that they would be seated with their backs to the press corps. (Reporting on the return of the remains is considered to be an important message to the nation about the human cost of war and its effect on civilians, on soldiers, and on the conscience of the country.) Then I returned to my office to continue my preparations for the next day, staying late into the night. I'd made myself a diagram of where everyone would be at various points during the ceremony, and I went over the movements dozens of times. I wrote and rewrote the brief for the principals. Any deviation would be interpreted as a slight to the families and would fail to honor the deceased in the manner they deserved.

I arrived at Andrews Air Force Base early the next morning to prepare for everyone's arrival. At about 2 p.m. I saw the cars approaching with the families. The day was unseasonably warm, with a strong wind on the open tarmac. I welcomed each family at the front door, then guided them to different areas of the VIP lounge (where we had food and drinks) so they each had private space to sit and talk. Then the principals arrived—Vice President Biden, Secretary Clinton, Ambassador Susan Rice, and Defense Secretary Leon Panetta—who paid their respects to each family. Along with Gary Davis, deputy of ceremonies for MDW, and the Joint Base Andrews commander, I met President Obama at the foot of his helicopter and began my brief with him as we walked across the tarmac so he was fully prepared before walking into the guest lounge. I introduced him to the families, then gathered the heads of our government into one space to brief them with more focus and authority than I'd ever summoned before or since. I ran through each and every detail so there were zero information gaps about the venerable military tradition and so they could move through the event with surety. Everyone had to be in lockstep in order to do justice to the families, who were experiencing this on a personal and emotional level that the rest of us could not fathom.

The group was then transported to the airplane hangar where the Dignified Transfer of Remains would take place. As promised, we protected the families from unnecessary press coverage by having them seated before the press corps entered. I led the president and the other dignitaries directly to their seats so there was no confusion—I wanted the first moments to set the tone of solemnity and precision. The protocol of the movements became the force that carried us all through it. When it was over, and after the families had been driven off the field, I stood behind the curtained space that the Secret Service had put up to provide the president some privacy. Standing behind the secretary, vice president, and president, I held hands with a couple of protocol team members and exhaled for the first time in twenty-four hours. I, too, found relief in the protocol, the framework for honoring these men and their families. I hope it delivered some comfort to the families, though surely it was the last place they wanted to be that day.

PROTOCOL FOR THE PROTOCOL

In the Office of Protocol, we were a close-knit team of anticipatory thinkers, optimists, influencers, and emotional managers: Anything is possible with the right plan in place. Still, I layered on prep steps over existing protocol—protocol for the protocol—to ensure that things would unfold exactly as intended. When you are managing presidents, prime ministers, and royals—all of whom are making life-changing decisions for their countries and the globe—there is no room for error.

- **The tick-tock:** What is on paper steers the event. The tick-tock, as we called it (other industries may refer to it as "event run of show" or "minute by minute"), was our script and guiding document. Every move goes into the original version—all cues, staff assignments, escorts, press issues, possible red flags—so that all information every department created or gathered was in one convenient place for all to access. The versions I like best have the countdown from three to four days out with setup and arrivals, because the event "starts" in the planning process, well before the time of kickoff. Once the tick-tock felt built out, we would have a group read-through, almost like a table reading of a movie. It was an opportunity to offer alternatives or tighten up the plan. As we got closer to the event, more streamlined and tailored versions were created for distribution to key offices—the secretary's copy would have notes that pertained only to her or his movements, for example. If we were distributing one to our foreign counterparts, we made sure that it referred only to the basics (we did not need to share how the sausage was made). I still use the tick-tock in my consulting business. All too often, only the CEO's schedule will drive an event and setup plan, leaving out important elements from related departments that will affect the outcome. A tick-tock gives you a full perspective—a satellite overview, if you will—as opposed to a single snapshot.

- **Six eyes on everything.** From flag protocol to motorcade precedence, every element and movement was meticulously reviewed by at least three people. The protocol officer assigned to manage an event was responsible for ensuring this rule was adhered to. We moved at such a high pace (not to mention on very little sleep) that triple-checking had to be the norm, period. Lead officers (every event was assigned a point person in charge of the event or visit) sometimes become so laser-focused on priority logistics that little details (with big consequences) could have been overlooked. In addition, protocols from, say, US Secret Service might have changed since the last time we implemented them and needed an update.

  Another reason to bring in several sets of eyes: One person's focus may naturally trend toward something others have missed. We all operate with different levels of awareness depending on our mood, mind-set, and experience level. Each person's brain is constantly determining what is most important to bring into sharp focus and what to blur, depending on many factors. In addition, we all on occasion experience what psychologists call "inattentional blindness"—not seeing what is right in front you, especially when we're focused on one thing in particular (i.e., looking for our keys and walking straight into the coffee table in front of us). Everyone is susceptible regardless of his or her level of expertise. Having several people studying a seating plan, a flower arrangement, or an invitation template gives you a better shot at catching any big or small aberration. On the very rare occasions when we inadvertently skipped this protocol, we regretted it (I refer you back to chapter 1, when the Philippine flag was hung wrong and mistakenly signaled that the country was at war).

- **Do a dry run of the meeting.** I loved working with my protocol
  colleagues because we all had high expectations for an event—I was
  in my element with other type A's who cared as much as I did. After
  running through the logistics on paper, we'd do a comprehensive
  physical walk-through, a dress rehearsal of the meeting from start to
  finish. We tested everything as if we were the principals, including
  the entry and exit path (were there carpet edges to trip on? if so
  we'd tape them down) and steps leading to a dais, assessing whether
  anyone attending might need a handrail or assistance from an aide.
  We sat in the principals' chairs to determine whether they were the
  right depth (would we need to add a pillow for those with shorter
  legs so they could sit higher and straighter?) and stable enough
  (no wobbly wheels or legs). If stools were offered for women, we'd
  swap them out for traditional chairs: it's nearly impossible for a
  woman to sit on a stool and look and feel comfortable, especially
  if she's wearing a skirt (even in pants a woman appears inelegant
  if she sits, knees splayed, as men do). If the chairs didn't match, I
  didn't care—it was much more important that my people looked
  confident and comfortable. (If it seems as if I'm chair-obsessed, it's
  because seating caused me more concern over the years than nearly
  anything else.) We tested anything technical—ideally with the
  technician—including connections for satellite feeds and rolling
  Twitter responses on a screen for any live feeds. We'd also set the
  temperature for the day of the event and periodically note whether
  the sun's changing position through windows caused the room to
  get warmer or cooler. I learned to monitor temperature and test the
  heating/cooling systems after the G20 in Pittsburgh, when, during
  the roundtable discussion, Italian Prime Minister Silvio Berlusconi
  called me over to let me know he was shivering. He asked for the
  temperature to be made warmer in the room and needed an espresso
  to get the chill out of his body. The problem was that the president
  of the European Commission had just told one of the staff that it
  was too warm, hence we were cooling the location down. Most
  thermostats in older venues are really finicky and the pendulum
  can swing too far, even when calibrating up or down by just a few

degrees; by experimenting in advance, you avoid the discomfort and agitation of your guests.

A few weeks before the event, I would lead a formal walk-through with our US attendees (or aides of attendees), going over many of the same elements in an abbreviated way. If an attendee would be utilizing technology, we ensured she knew how to operate it. We ascertained in advance whether any attendees would need special accommodations. If someone had a disability, for example, we mapped out where the access ramps and elevators were; if he was a great distance from the meeting room, we advised the guest to arrive a bit early to allow for the extra travel time.

In addition, I always gave the advance teams of foreign dignitaries the courtesy of a walk-through whenever convenient for them, usually about two weeks before their arrival—this was critical for them to communicate important elements about logistics and the space to their leaders, and gave us an opportunity to accommodate special requests early on, avoiding a last-minute surprise. During one walk-through, we learned of one leader's health condition, which required he take medications at specific times. This meant we had to escort him to hold rooms and build in time for breaks throughout the visit so he could comply with doctor's orders.

We'd do a final walk-through the day of, checking every detail again with six eyes. On the day of the event, we also confirmed whether a participant's schedule had changed abruptly, requiring her to leave early. If so, I positioned that person close to the exit, as nothing drives me crazier than having a person on the far side of the room get up midspeech to leave (every eye in the room is on her and not the speaker).

When we were on another country's soil, we did not have as much control. I was almost always offered a walk-through, which allowed me to check the details, such as the spelling of my president's name on table tents and place cards (they often forgot the *c* in "Barack"). We generally turned down any last-minute unnecessary add-ons simply because we did not have the time to review the implications.

- **Share the details smartly**. Once we had the logistics cemented, we communicated every detail to the meeting attendants. This began with querying how they liked to receive their briefings: memos, emails, phone calls, or in-person? Regardless, I always sent a written briefing well in advance (this provided a record that they'd been given the information and also allowed it to be shared with invested staffers for their input); and just before the event, I gave everyone a verbal walk-through—I found that some people absorb information better when it's spoken, and it was an opportunity for them to ask any last-minute questions. Even if they insisted that they were all set, I'd continue with the briefing, assuming that there was always an important detail they might otherwise miss if it wasn't communicated in person. (*Pro tip:* Set arrival times to account for the time you will need to give people a verbal briefing; otherwise, they'll be tempted to dismiss it for fear of running late.) I also communicated directly with the individual operators (venue management, camera and lighting crew, technical specialists) and had their contact information for texting. You do not want to have to crawl across the room or wave madly at them if there is an issue during the event. And don't forget the lighting: I'd ask camera and lighting folks where the lights would be set or whether they were aiming for a straight-on or angled press shot. The answers guided me in how I arranged the space. For instance, if they wanted a full-body shot as opposed to just a headshot, I knew to figure out a way to avoid showing all the wiring and distracting scenery.

CONSIDER YOUR SOURCES

Being truly ready starts with mining the right source material. If you get your information from the wrong person or department, you are not only ill prepared but you could be introducing errors into the process (you never want to be the person who steers the herd off the cliff). Whenever possible, I went straight to the source. Like in the childhood game of telephone, when information is passed through several people, what you receive probably isn't in its unadulterated form. While administrative staff are wonderful and know an awful lot, they sometimes don't have complete intel. I always made a call to the point person of an engagement to check my facts.

I'd also learned that those who'd served through multiple administrations had vast institutional knowledge and were some of the smartest people in the room. They'd honed their skills over time and not only knew the answer to your question but would provide information you didn't even know to ask. In the early days, as personal assistant to the First Lady, I'd purposefully arrive early at the White House and hang out in a small back pantry where the huge coffee urns were located. There, I'd get to talk to butlers, caterers, and assistants as they doctored their morning coffee, learning everything from how President Bush enjoyed comfort food to how President Clinton reacted to dairy (he loved it but should avoid it). They discussed who preferred the temperature of a room to be cool (the presidents) and who wanted it warmer (the First Ladies). The butlers were savvy, always maintaining the line in favor of the First Ladies. George Hannie, one of the most beloved White House butlers, who was promoted into the esteemed position of maître d' of the butlers (aka head butler), became a dear friend and advisor. As one of the five top-slot butlers, he interfaced between the staff and the first family in their personal residence on the second and third floors. They all had a keen eye, and each was often the first person the family would see in the morning as he served breakfast or left interesting articles on the counter that the president or First Lady might enjoy reading.

The White House butlers are considered to be among the most sacred keepers of invaluable information and advice, and they all—George, Buddy Carter (beloved by so many presidents and still working at the White House), Ricardo "Sam" Sanvictores, James "Jim" Selmon, Smile Saint-Aubin (though everyone just knew him as Smiley), and James Ramsey—shared their wisdom generously with me. What they taught me first and foremost is to listen. As special assistant during the first term, I was sometimes asked to step in and keep the president on schedule when he was in the residence, as I spent a great deal of time there and had a good rapport with the residence staff. Finding the right spot to hear but not be seen was key: I would wait silently around the curved wall or behind a doorjamb. The vibe of the discussions—were they heightened or slowing down?—determined whether I would pop my head in and remind the president of his next appointment or to stand by while a tense moment resolved . . . or to offer coffee to help things progress after they'd hit a lull. Occasionally, it was clear I would need to offer to bring someone in who could assist with the conversation. I wasn't listening to the actual words of the discussion; it was more about filtering cues and hearing the nuances of conversation between the president and his guests. The flustered sounds, tenor of the discussion, and snippets of conversation clued me in. The butlers all taught one another this talent, and it became almost instinctual. But not to a newcomer like myself. I would ask them, "How do you know it's time to interrupt? Did the president look at you or say something?" They would reply, "I heard his tone and watched his body language. When he is done, he pushes his chair back and looks away." Their insights—like anthropologists studying a leader in his natural habitat—were critical shortcuts that would have taken me years to discern on my own. "Sometimes the president himself isn't sure when he's done," one of them told me once. A man of many fascinating tales and insights, President Clinton was known to have the gift of gab. "When it's time, you gotta step in and stop him and say, 'Sir.' They depend on you to do that, and you have to listen for those clues."

Then there were the moments when I would purposefully step in firmly to be seen. The president or another principal would often "blame" me for dragging him away. I frequently stepped in when I was chief of protocol, as did other protocol officers. "Oh, here come those protocol people, I guess we need to wrap!" We knew it was a bit for show. The president wants to make sure that the guest sees you—evidence that it is indeed time to wind down. Sometimes I'd enter holding a note on paper as a fail-safe—everyone would see me give it to the president (oftentimes it would simply say "time to wrap up") and then respond to it either with a nod . . . or out loud if they really want to move things along. (I imagine many an executive assistant reading this is nodding in agreement.)

My intel didn't just come from inside the residence but from outside it as well: specifically, sitting in traffic, talking to the wonderful Sterling Watts, a protocol officer who has served several chiefs of protocol in his primary duty of driving us to official events (he also has a security clearance for confidential materials). Our car rides were filled with his wisdom—Sterling-isms, I called them—and important logistical insights. Having observed multiple chiefs and countless arrivals over the years, he would offer pointers about whether a certain greeting might work better outside the door or inside, for example. He would often drop a pearl of wisdom about the person I was meeting right before my visit so I could use it to our advantage. And he knows every expedited route: I now can navigate every alley and side street to save precious minutes in DC traffic, though I am still occasionally a teeny bit late. "Time is what time is, Capricia, you can't test time," he'd tell me when I would insist that we could shave off five minutes here and there and hit all four embassy events in one evening. (Sterling, with his vast knowledge, somehow made it happen.)

TRAVEL PREP 101

Planning takes on an extra importance when you're on the road or in the air. You don't have access to your usual support services—doctors, pharmacists, stores—and you may not have time to search them out or get to them (in some far-flung locales you won't find a convenience store within miles). I clocked millions of miles on planes, ships, vans, and buses, and got pre-trip checklists down to a science. In addition to my essential pack lists on Page 398, here are five pre-trip tasks everyone should do well before ordering a car for the airport.

1. **Create a Mary Poppins bag.** Having ready access to anything needed to make my delegates look and feel their best was a game changer. The bag got its start when I was Hillary's traveling aide during her husband's first presidential campaign. It began as a

jewelry roll-up, then it grew bigger as we added items, becoming a briefcase (think Gary's satchel on *Veep*) and then a full-on duffel. The more Hillary did—stump speeches in different states, local appearances at county fairs and schools—the more I put in the bag to keep her on point for her marathon fourteen-hour days: an extra pair of pantyhose in neutral and black, nuts for a quick protein hit, several bottles of hot sauce because Hillary loved to put it on literally everything, hair spray for breezy days on the tarmac, a virtual pharmacy to treat any number of afflictions. You don't need to stuff your own Mary Poppins bag with Tabasco and Aqua Net, but I recommend some basics on page 396, including a sewing kit (*Pro tip:* pre-thread the needles so you can start stitching, stat) and a battery-powered alarm clock: if your phone battery runs down, the electricity goes out, or your wake-up call doesn't come through, you won't oversleep, which is exactly what happened on a trip to South Africa with the First Lady for Nelson Mandela's inauguration—we barely made the ceremony, and I never traveled without a clock again!

2. **Register with the consulate *before* you travel.** For international travel it's a must to register your itinerary with the State Department so they have a record of your movements and can send you in-country travel alerts. (Go to step.state.gov/step for registration.) Next, send an email to the American consulate of the country (or countries) you're visiting so they will know where you'll be staying and how to reach you in an emergency. (They will also ask for a copy of your passport, which is great insurance in case you lose yours.) The consulate is there specifically to help you in times of need, and they want to be of service. I did this for my son when he was studying in the Yunnan Province of China, and it paid off. He broke his collarbone, and when I learned he was admitted to the hospital, I called the State Department. Because he was registered with the consulate, they knew exactly where he was and got to him pretty quickly. A representative of the consulate visited him in the hospital and updated me on his condition, sharing information from the doctor that my son hadn't told me (like the fact that he

also had a concussion, which he held back because he didn't want to send me into a panic).

3. **Duplicate your passport and keep it locked up.** Make a copy of your passport, either on paper or electronically, in case your original is lost. I'm old school and pack my copy in the lining of my suitcase so it's not visible for the taking. Some travel agents also recommend scanning your passport onto your phone as a PDF—just make sure your phone is password protected. At your hotel, place the original *and* the copy in the safe and carry only a driver's license for ID. If the hotel does not have a safe, then carry your passport in a radio-frequency identification device (RFID) that will protect your personal information.

4. **Prep your tech.** It's no longer just okay to make sure you have the right electrical plug adapter; you also need to think about cyber security and connectivity.

VPN: At the State Department they handled all of our technical details for us (when they think your electronics might have been compromised, they will wipe them clean and reinstate them), but when I went into the private sector, I had to figure out cybersecurity for myself. My dear friend Kim Cubine, president of Chapman Cubine and Hussey, manages a great number of political clients, and cyber protection is a key part of her business. She introduced me to her cyber guru, Blake Cooper of Pioneering Network Solutions, who explained in plain English what I needed to be secure, from how to use a VPN (virtual private network) to completely securing my motherboard, aka encrypting it so that if my laptop is broken into, whatever is downloaded will be scrambled. VPNs allow you to join a private network when using a public connection, making it much harder for cyber spying. And it scrambles your location so hackers won't know where you are, physically, and allows you access to sites that may be blocked in certain countries. You do need to join a VPN subscription service to get the benefits (I use NordVPN and Astril VPN, depending upon the country).

5. **Share your itinerary.** I have had the benefit of working with
   the most organized schedulers in the world. They taught me the
   advantages of creating an itinerary that details every movement
   of the trip, with exact contact information for every stop. Lona
   Valmoro, the secretary's skillful scheduler for over a decade and
   a great friend, had the process down to a science. She strongly
   believed in distributing the same itinerary to affirm that all were on
   the same page. I now share my itinerary with coworkers, the client,
   and my family so that there will be no information gaps, and in case
   there is ever an emergency, they will know exactly where I am.

PERSONAL HOTSPOT. As an alternative to a VPN, you can travel
with a personal hotspot (Mi-Fi) through a wireless carrier (check
with your carrier for rates). It not only secures your connection, but
it also enables you to have Wi-Fi no matter where you are. Using
a hotspot saves your phone and laptop battery for other tasks, and
many hotspots double as phone and laptop chargers as well. (In a
pinch, you can also use your mobile phone as a personal hotspot.)

EASY, FREE, SECURE TEXTING. WhatsApp is easy to download,
everyone around the world uses it, and it's encrypted. It's available
pretty much everywhere there's an Internet connection. Some
people prefer Signal, since it's not owned by a social media giant.
(WhatsApp is owned by Facebook, which may give some people
pause.) Signal can also be installed on your laptop, and messages
disappear two minutes after they're read, so if your phone is stolen,
those messages are gone. WeChat is preferred in China and offers
limited encryption.

meeting between the two young leaders as presidents of the world's strongest economies was as high stakes as it got, with press reporting that powder-keg topics like cyber security and North Korea were on the agenda. Sunnylands' reputation as an exclusive and historical venue—which I describe in chapter 7—was not lost on the Chinese. They were just as thrilled as I was to be planning the visit at a locale that reflected the supreme importance of a renewed relationship between our countries. Together we spent months excitedly plotting out each aspect and movement—all seemed in lockstep to provide an in-sync experience for our presidents. So imagine my and the Chinese protocol staff's astonishment (judging by the bewildered looks on their faces) when President Obama took an unplanned hard left on Day 1.

The two leaders began the morning by walking across the golf course, giving the press an opportunity to photograph them minus their translators or delegations. The plan was that they would then return to the estate's formal living room to begin official talks. Instead, President Obama stopped when he hit a cluster of chaise lounges and umbrellas just off the footpath. He indicated to President Xi to take a seat. Jackets off, knee to knee, leaning their elbows on their legs, shirtsleeves rolled up due to the one-hundred-degree heat and less formal ambience (hence the moniker "shirtsleeves summit," which the two administrations had coined), they began speaking intimately and intensely. The interpreters, who are trained to stick by their leaders come rain, sleet, hail, or, in this case, sizzling sun, sat with them. The Chinese chief of protocol nervously asked me about the abrupt change in course. I understood his concern—this most monumental of meetings had been mapped out to account for every minute. I assured him all was fine, but that we had a new plan and needed to heed President Obama's lead. I had faith in the president and trusted that he was following his instincts and had felt they needed a private moment out of the well-choreographed plan. I also suspected he perhaps wanted to broach some of the most sensitive topics before the interactions became "business as usual" back inside. I realized both the Chinese delegation as well as the Sunnylands staff, who were experiencing their first presidential visit ever, were taken aback by the sudden change and were feeling uneasy. I sent word that all was well but that beverages should be sent immediately, along with an umbrella to cover the Chinese interpreter, who was wilting in the hot sun. Daniel "Danny" Russel, the NSC senior director for Asian affairs and a well-respected foreign service officer, was the policy lead on this engagement. Usually he was unfazed by changes, but he approached me with a quizzical look. I let him know that it seemed the leaders would be outside for a while and then updated him and the Chinese delegation every fifteen minutes on their status so that all invested parties felt informed during this deviation. Additionally, we needed to keep the press informed, which we managed through our media-savvy protocol officer, Jason Rahlan, who was on site to provide guidance. This visit was being tracked moment by moment, and we produced a readout for the press about the activities taking place on the patio. (Freedom of the press is one of our country's prized values, and even small detours of an official agenda are shared to keep citizens informed.) Everyone seemed surprised that this spontaneous side talk occurred, let alone that it lasted nearly an hour. My Chinese counterpart and I stood nearby to attend to any further changes and then to resume the plan once they had concluded their outdoor talk. When the presidents finished, they rejoined their delegations and resumed the prearranged schedule. I later learned from Danny that this improvised chat gave the presidents an opportunity to discuss planned topics in an unscripted manner—away from their policy handlers—opening up the dialogue and building trust.

Toward the end of the next day, I, too, employed some diplomatic yoga, taking an impromptu opportunity during a free moment to approach the presidents, along with President Xi's spouse, First Lady Peng Liyuan, with a letter and gift from Mrs. Obama, who had been unable to attend. I listened as they spoke to each other about their children and family matters in the warmest of ways, their interpreters talking rapidly to keep up with the easy flow. I noted there had been a shift in their relationship since the day before, with much less formulaic diplo-speak. The ice that had been broken during their intimate one-on-one had now completely melted. Their new rapport served as a strong foundation for the successful two-day visit: both sides described the meeting in the press as historic and positive, finding solid common ground on many issues and pledging to continue discussions in areas where they diverged.

WHEN AND HOW TO BEND

Like any skill, flexibility should be implemented with some measure and control. Bursts of spontaneity are wonderful. Unbridled spontaneity can be chaotic. Julian Birkinshaw, a professor at the London Business School and coauthor of the management tome *Fast/Forward*, has written about the necessity in organizations for *ambidexterity*, a skill he defines as the right balance of adaptability (flexibility) and alignment (firmness). The most successful companies, his research finds, master this at both the organizational and the employee level. Staff who are allowed a certain amount of discretion and personal judgment are able to react instantly to fluid market conditions, yet within a structure of existing models and protocols that keeps long-term company goals in play. This same ability to respond on the fly within a framework is key to diplomacy and most negotiations, personal or professional.

So how do you know when it's okay to take that detour and how far to go? I've had so many moments in my career where I had to determine when that pivotal moment was. My guiding factor is always this: Is the current plan still serving the overall goal, and will an adjustment help my president or principal? Secondarily, I would consider whether the change will cause unmitigated confusion if others cannot adjust, or whether the pivot will cause embarrassment to any of the participants, as it might if the event is going to be televised or the plan has been pre-released to the public.

Sometimes the decision is easy and painfully obvious. Early on the first day of the 2011 state visit of South Korean President Lee Myung-bak, we held our routine 5 a.m. call between security, protocol, the White House social office, and other departments to review any concerns. That morning, the foremost issue was the weather. The forecast called for rain, which always presents a conundrum. Should we have the ceremony outdoors and hope for a light rain? Or move it indoors if we think the heavens might open up? We tried to have most arrival ceremonies outside—as I've noted, every country wants that visual of standing next to the president of the United States with the White House as a backdrop. Moreover, a move indoors shortens the ceremony by skipping some venerable customs (the inspection of the troops, during which the visitor reviews the host's military, as well as the military march to "Yankee Doodle," which is quite the spectacle). Every leader wants the full ceremony in order to show he or she is being treated with as high an honor as any predecessor or rival nation (again, parity is supreme). And, perhaps most disappointing, an indoor ceremony means that the general public is sent away, since they cannot be accommodated inside. On this day, hundreds of Korean Americans had already come from all over the country to personally witness these two presidents continue their forward progress. (They had a promising start in 2009 when President Obama visited Seoul, and this trip was meant to further strengthen the bond between the countries, particularly since North Korea had become an increasingly threatening presence in the region.)

On the early-morning call, the group decided to recommend an outside ceremony, and President Obama agreed, as long as President Lee was in favor. He was, so outside we went. Notifications were sent to all invested parties immediately to prepare for "outside wear." The Military District of Washington took on umbrella duty, providing coverage for the senior members of the delegation, including two very large umbrellas to be held over each leader by a member of the military. Two young military aides, who'd been selected by the Military District just moments before the ceremony, stood on the dais behind each leader, ruler-straight arms stretched out, handles gripped tight, umbrellas canopying over the principals. When President Obama stepped up to the podium for his opening remarks, his umbrella, I noted, did not move with him. President Obama shifted his speech pages and, noticing the rain falling onto them, turned around and motioned for the military aide to move up. He turned back to the crowd, then realized he was *still* getting rained on. He turned around once more and saw the aide hadn't budged. President Obama then asked the aide in a low, urgent voice to "please move up." The poor young man was frozen with fear—I'm sure he had never been on the world stage before. Someone had to do something, and I realized that someone had to be me. I ran up the few steps to the platform. Feeling a bit reticent in touching a military aide, I gently placed my hands on his hips and gave him a nice nudge forward until the umbrella was covering the whole of the president and the podium, and raced back in place next to my Korean counterpart. I felt for the man. These military members are young and nervous and excited about the responsibility of sheltering the leader of the free world, and they are trained to stand absolutely still. At least he hadn't fainted, something I'd seen happen many a time when military aides have to stand straight-legged for long periods during official ceremonies. And it's not just nerves that contribute to passing out—standing for that long causes blood to pool around the lower extremities, which slows its path back up to the heart and can trigger a fainting spell (according to my cardiologist husband). On extremely hot days, the aides drop easily (heat, stress, and dehydration up the risk), and you have to constantly remind them to bend their knees to keep blood circulating. Luckily the remainder of the state visit went according to plan, with a stunning state dinner that evening (held indoors, I might add).

I'd learned early on in my government service that these spontaneous moments and yogic responses—having to stretch beyond the norm of what's been planned or expected—may involve a bit of luck and ingenuity. During President Clinton's first term, I traveled with him, the First Lady, and thirteen-year-old Chelsea to Moscow. Chelsea has the finest qualities of both of her parents, sharing in particular their intellectual curiosity. From the time she was a toddler, her parents wanted her to be exposed to her father's work so that she understood it and the occasional tough issues associated with his job. Chelsea was always quite mature for her age (probably in part the result of being an only child), and therefore putting her in adult situations was easy. On our final day in Moscow, I stayed back at the Kremlin (the official presidential residence) with Chelsea while the president and First Lady were attending an event before heading to the airport. With us was a US Secret Service agent we were all particularly close with, his Russian counterpart, and the president's valet, Lito Bautista, a charming man who always traveled with the president. We were told to wait at one particular door where the motorcade was due to pick us all up on the way to the airport for our flight back home. The motorcade approached . . . and just kept going. It was a huge motorcade of at least fifty cars and we waved wildly at each passing one to get someone's attention—to no avail.

To complicate matters, for some reason Chelsea's security agents had no communication with anyone in the motorcade (perhaps because we were at the Kremlin and communications were limited). I went into contingency mode and started to brainstorm, as everyone was turning to me to fix the situation. I looked about and saw a laundry truck parked about fifty feet away. "Let's take that," I suggested. The agents protested, but Chelsea was with me. "Yes, let's go!" she concurred. We approached it with Chelsea's Russian agent, who explained to the driver that we needed to use his vehicle to get to the airport, that this was the child of the US president. He agreed to drive us and we loaded the luggage and took off. Navigating the security check points was a challenge, but the agents somehow finessed these moments. Finally, we arrived planeside, and Chelsea walked straight up to her parents and said, "Did you forget something?" It was frankly an awesome moment. Her parents looked at me, and I said, smiling, "Oh no, this is all on you all." (I later learned that the president's team assumed we would go directly to the airport.)

Sometimes these diversions and decisions happen instantly and your response is almost instinctive. In other situations, you have a bit more time to consider your options—can I zig and zag within the existing protocol? If an adjustment was necessary, my preference was not to invent a new format but to tweak things within existing procedures (which people are already familiar with) or fashion hybrids, especially when time and resources were finite. This was the case during the 2010 nuclear security summit the United States hosted in Washington, DC. The summit was complicated due to the number of countries—about fifty in all—as well as the tight schedule. On the first day, the president's agenda was packed, every minute accounted for. And yet, as we greeted the many foreign ministers and ambassadors who arrived, we continued to get a stream of requests for President Obama to meet with their leaders. I felt for these countries who repeatedly asked and hoped for time with our president. But even if a twenty-minute mini-bilateral could be squeezed in, there was virtually no place to do it: Every space at the convention center had been booked weeks in advance. And if I managed to secure a room, there was no time to travel there and back. That morning, as I was preparing with the team in the large plenary room, I noted that the space between the chairs and walls was relatively wide—just wide enough for a couple of flags and seats for two leaders. An idea began brewing: What if we arranged a series of quick bilaterals back-to-back right here? At ten minutes apiece, it would be just enough time for a handshake and a photo (every country wanted this iconic moment with President Obama preserved on film) and a quick discussion of the most critical policy topics. I went to the NSC with my idea, they liked it, and our team was able to set up several stations for the countries deemed a priority.

ANTICIPATING CHANGE

In addition to reacting efficiently in the moment, you can learn to identify situations in advance that may call for yogic maneuverings. Due to years of experience, I've honed the gift of anticipation, often realizing the need for a change before it arises. Things that tip me off that change may be afoot: delays in schedules (people want to rush or skip steps), agitated moods (unhappy folks are more likely to dismiss or adjust a standing element), and previous experiences with an individual or country where modifications happened. From the day I entered the Clintons' world, I'd discovered that they loved to entertain and that guest lists often swelled for dinners, picnics, and more. I always anticipated that the number of invitees would need adjusting and approached it as a moving target. Still, I was caught off guard by the rapid, exponential guest-list growth of a certain luncheon during my tenure as social secretary. It was a sweltering July in 1999 (I remember the weather clearly because I was four months pregnant at the time but still trying to keep it under wraps) and Ehud Barak had recently been elected prime minister of Israel. I received a call from Sandy Berger, who was then national security advisor, dedicated public servant, and invaluable advisor, alerting me that the president had invited the new prime minister to the White House. President Clinton was hopeful that this new leader would serve as a strong partner who could help broker peace in the Middle East. "Capricia," Sandy said in his low, even voice. "I'm sitting here with the president, and he'd like to put together a nice luncheon for Prime Minister Barak for the eighteenth." It was the thirteenth, which gave us five days. "Of course, no problem, sir. How many are we thinking?" He paused and said, "We're probably thinking a big one, like twenty or thirty people." Significant, but nothing the team couldn't handle. I hung up the phone and gathered the staff. Ten minutes later the phone rang again. I wasn't certain, but I had a sneaking suspicion the number of folks on the guest list was about to increase. "Hi, Capricia, it's Sandy again. Well, the president is thinking the luncheon might be more along the lines of one hundred people, can you do that?" I did not hesitate. "Absolutely, sir, not a problem." I put the phone down, unsurprised, and thought, "Okay, this is more challenging, but doable." I told the team we had to get the guest list together asap. Then about ten minutes later the phone rang again. "This is the White House operator; the president would like to speak to you." Alarm bells started ringing in my head—he rarely called me directly. (In retrospect, I thought it was incredibly generous of him to do so, knowing how much work would go into the planning.) "Hello, Mr. President," I said. "Capricia," President Clinton began, "I know you can do this luncheon, but I think it would be perfect to do a dinner." I waited a beat. "Yes sir, of course, we've already started the guest list." But he wasn't finished. "Listen, I'm thinking a dinner for about five hundred so they can bring who they need and we can have the Americans we need to invite . . . do you think we can do that? Do you think we can get that together?" I give myself credit for not choking, and immediately responded in the affirmative. As a tree who could bend, I embraced the change instantly. In my head, in marquee lights, flashed the government official's mantra: *I serve at the pleasure of the president.* I hung up the phone, paused, took a deep breath, and told the team, "Okay, change of plans!" and outlined what our leader had just asked. I imagine we all had a little voice inside our head saying, "Can we actually do this?" Yes, I told myself, but only with a number of really, *really* late nights and a lot of hard work by every single staffer, working with every caterer, butler, and State Department and NSC counterpart. In truth, I knew that this crew could do it. The talent and extraordinary flexibility of the Social Office team and the dedicated career public servants in the Usher's Office (the reception and management office of the residence) could pull off just about anything. I also held tight to the certainty that a confident leader can inspire the impossible, so when I addressed the troops I shared my certainty that they—that *we*—were up to the task, as well as emphasizing the level of commitment needed so that people understood what was being asked of them.

This was to be an official working visit, not a state visit, so the usual pomp and circumstance didn't apply, relieving us, thankfully, of the need for an arrival ceremony. But working outside the usual frame and improvising on the edges only added to the angst. The amount of planning and executing we did over the next few days was immense and required incredible flexibility and creativity. The preparations for flowers, music, menu, tents, and invitations usually take six to eight weeks to plan, and several more to implement. But we did it, despite learning that week that John F. Kennedy Jr.; his wife, Carolyn Bessette; and her older sister, Lauren, were lost at sea and then pronounced dead. It was as if the president's own son had passed. People who had worked in the White House during the Kennedy administration and who knew John were devastated. The Clintons were close to the Kennedys and were deeply saddened by the news. Everyone who knew him—and even those who did not—were beyond consolation. I recall sitting on the floor of my office trying to keep it together as I managed the seating arrangements for heads of state. Eric Hothem, my special assistant who was with me late that day, noticed that my heart was heavy and encouraged me to take a break. I listened, knowing I needed to process it for myself and that I had to show resilience for the team, who took their cues from me. I walked the South Grounds, reflecting on John, his family, and what they had all done for our country. I returned with a clearer head in order to push everyone forward. A motto from a friend rang true that week:

You and your collective team are only as good as your ability to pivot. And despite—or perhaps because of—the veil of sadness hanging over everyone who was working to pull the dinner together and reinforce this important friendship between our two countries, it was one of the best we had ever executed.

COMMUNICATING CHANGE

Small hiccups can often be managed solo, but big changes require immediate communication, first to your team so everyone is operating with the same information and goal, and—once you have command of the situation—to your principals. All too often, however, significant changes are made by the principals themselves, and then the challenge becomes confirming that everyone on the team—as well as the other principals—has the same information, especially when there are over forty countries and dozens of languages involved! During the NATO fiftieth anniversary celebration in 1999 at the White House—the largest grouping of heads of states I'd ever managed as social secretary—I was thrown a last-minute curveball that could have toppled weeks of meticulous planning. As I mentioned in chapter 12, I worked hard to create parity between all the countries attending this NATO event, not just with the nineteen members, but also with the countries who wanted entry (today there are twenty-nine members). Every movement was timed to the exact second to assure that there was parity, as we knew any deviation would be seen as a slight to that country. Communication was a huge part of this effort. Each delegation was assigned a liaison officer to keep them in the loop on every aspect. I did not want any country's leader to end up in the wrong place at the wrong time due to a transmission oversight or misunderstanding, which would have left them feeling disappointed and diminished, particularly the nonmember countries that were expecting to be treated with equal stature and honor on this global stage by the United States president. So when the First Lady decided a mere ten minutes before the arrival of the first guest that the receiving line placement at the top of the mansion's grand staircase would create a logjam and should be moved to the Yellow Oval Room, I immediately stopped everything to think.

I understood her reason for the change—she knew the president would be speaking longer than the usual allotted amount of time with certain leaders, and the Yellow Oval offered a private area for him to talk without all eyes watching. This anniversary was taking place during the Kosovo War, and NATO, an intergovernmental military alliance, had forces committed to the engagement, so the president needed more than a minute to discuss key issues with attending NATO nations. But the last-minute switch presented several serious potential problems: First, all the teams—from the Social Office to the military to the protocol staff—had rehearsed the movements of the receiving line at the top of the grand staircase with precision. Furthermore, we had explicitly communicated to each delegation—and all forty-four heads of state—that this was to be the plan. I suddenly had a terrible vision of one of the newest entrants to NATO, Poland, arriving at the top of the staircase and finding . . . no one—no US president to greet the leader, no receiving line of principals—and wondering, "What is happening? This is not what *I* was instructed." This left-at-the-altar scenario kicked me into gear. I immediately called upon calm, cool Kim Widdess, who was the deputy social secretary and lead, and told her that we had to inform about fifty point people about the change in mere minutes. She nodded. "Mmm-hmm, okay, let's deal with it," and dashed off to begin the communications process. I then turned to Emily Feingold, whose phenomenal judgment surpassed that of many twice her age, to radio Laura Schwartz, my hyper-effective logistics director, to join us on the second floor so that a small group of us could confab in person (this was not something we wanted to discuss over the radios, as it had to be contained and dealt with privately). Our team possessed astounding poise in the face of calamity—their tranquillity has always inspired confidence in me—and this day was no different. We quickly divvied up all points of contact, determining who would reach out to which liaison, taking into account language barriers and methods of communication (we were working with a motley mix of beepers, phones, and radios, depending on which device a liaison was using). I've never been so proud to see the team come together at a time when minutes counted. It mostly worked out seamlessly, save a couple hiccups that—in the bigger picture—were small compared with what would have been a giant bottleneck at the tip-top of a staircase or a delegation being left stranded, alone, on the landing.

MAINTAIN FOCUS, GET BACK ON TRACK

Once you veer onto a sidetrack, it's best to find a route back to the mainline as soon as possible. There are two surefire ways, I've found, that help you course correct. The first, humor, helps dial down the tension in a stressful situation so you can refocus quickly. Psychologists actually view humor as an effective form of emotional regulation, since it allows you to shift your perspective from distress to amusement. I've often found that humor can help you get back on your feet after an unexpected mishap. Sometimes literally.

My most famous slipup as chief of protocol happened during the 2010 Mexico state visit on the North Portico stairs in front of two world leaders, two national delegations, and a multitude of cameras beaming everything out to the globe. As usual, I was walking just ahead of President Obama and the First Lady, en route to greet the Mexican president, His Excellency Felipe Calderón, and his lovely wife, Mrs. Zavala, who were entering the North Gate in their motorcade for the start of the state dinner. As I descended the marble steps in my long pink Oscar de la Renta gown and strappy, extremely high-heeled Manolo Blahniks, I felt the importance of this special moment. Here I was, representing protocol and all that comes with it—those Emily Post associations of manners and elegance—welcoming the Mexican government, which held a special significance for my family and me. I knew all my relatives of Mexican descent (especially my mother and Aunt Rose) were gathered around the television in Cleveland Heights, Ohio, watching C-SPAN live with pride and anticipation. Suddenly, my heel caught in a divot and in a flash, everything changed. Luckily, as I started to fall forward I was able to jump slightly to the next step before dropping onto my bottom. As I landed, I swear I could hear all of Cleveland scream in horror. Thankfully, I did not fall forward, nor did anything become undone in my attire. But I was mortified. I remember the president reaching for me to help (it was too late, alas) and then shouting to the press, "Don't take that picture!" echoed by Mrs. Obama. The media did not pay heed, and I was blinded by the number of camera flashes. Somehow—miraculously—I quickly pulled myself up to standing (thank you, P90X core exercises), regained my balance, and gave everyone a thumbs-up—a knee-jerk gesture that signaled to onlookers, and to myself, that I was taking it all, er, in stride. I looked up at Kamyl Bazbaz, protocol's sage communications director—mashed between the masses of the international press—who offered a reassuring look and okay sign (maybe it wasn't that bad after all?).

It is amazing how many thoughts zing through your head in that split second. "What just happened?" "Am I okay?" "Now what?" That is the critical juncture: Now what? Having a yogic mind-set prepares you to simply continue on with the duty at hand, instead of being so flustered you lose sight of the objective. I approached the remaining steps with an abundance of caution and greeted the Mexican president—a bit sheepishly. For my part, I so hoped this would not co-opt the news cycle and interfere with the diplomatic goals of the presidents. So the next morning when asked about it by the press, I strategically employed humor by telling the *Washington Post*: "As a proud Mexican American, this historic day at the White House moved me in ways I never anticipated." I was not the only one with a sense of humor about it: Upon our next state visit, when we approached the stairs, President Obama whispered in my ear, "Will she stay up, or will she go down?" And Mrs. Obama, overhearing, said, "Oh, Barack, leave Capricia alone!" The episode has also provided hours of entertainment for my son, who loves the many YouTube remixes available.

The second highly effective way to resume your original course: Fall back on the meticulous planning that should have preceded the event. (If you skipped chapter 13: "The Ultimate Checklist," I suggest you flip back a few pages and peruse it.) My in-depth preparations during the 2011 Asia-Pacific Economic Cooperation (APEC) conference in Honolulu,

Hawaii—along with some quick thinking and a tiny bit of fabrication—averted what would have been a twenty-one-country pileup. The protocol team and I had planned and reviewed every detail, including seating, for the high-level luncheons and dinners and the cultural entertainment portion (which I actually cannot recall, as the horror show that preceded it clouds my memory forever). In addition to ensuring there was impartial and protocol-based reasoning for each leader's positioning at the tables, whether it was alphabetical order or by the date of the leader's inauguration, we'd made sure to seat particular delegations strategically so as not to create friction between them in case there were any conflicts. I'd gone over the placements so many times that I'd unwittingly committed them to memory.

Shortly after the dinner, just before the cultural performance, I was sitting at the edge of the leaders' dinner venue with a few of my chief counterparts grabbing a quick bite to eat. Suddenly, as if in choreographed unison, I noticed that each country's staff were approaching their chiefs—whispers abounded, phones started going off, and deliberate looks were being shot my way. I then saw our staff rushing toward me, and the first to reach me whispered in my ear, "We're having a serious seating issue in the entertainment venue!" I couldn't believe it. How was this possible after so much groundwork and scrutiny? I raced over to the open atrium—normally a four-minute walk that I shaved down to two (in my platform heels, no less)—to get there ahead of the other chiefs. I arrived at the atrium, where an area had been cordoned off for the principals' private seating with rows of chairs and tables. I looked at the seating cards and discovered that what we had outlined so carefully and distributed to all the other chiefs several days earlier had been changed. One of the protocol officers rushed over to explain that a certain US delegation staffer had inserted himself in the eleventh hour—he'd taken advantage of our absence from the site during the gala dinner and flipped the cards for his own agenda. I knew we couldn't allow this—these arrangements had been shared with the countries well in advance so the leaders would be able to prepare critical policy side conversations with their seat mates, discussing prearranged talking points. These "social" conversations were nearly as important as a formal bilateral, as they allowed for yet another opportunity to broach specific topics (often more easily done in a casual setting), fine-tune details, and lay the groundwork for the next day's summit talks. If the planned seating shifted, it took a critical prepared discussion out of the equation. Now, not surprisingly, each chief was approaching me to demand an explanation. Each had their own urgent reasons for how the new seating arrangement did not serve their leader well—one country was even threatening to leave because of the musical chairs.

This called for senior leadership. I immediately phoned National Security Advisor Tom Donilon, who was wrapping up a dinner with his counterparts. As the NSC always drove the mission we implemented, any further changes would have to be in lockstep with them. He'd just received word from certain delegations that we had a serious protocol problem. "Please fix it," he said with urgency.

I looked at my watch—we had about three minutes before the first leader would arrive—and I turned to the protocol seating team. "Pick up all name cards, asap," I said. I first had to remove all the misplaced markers. But there was no time to reposition them properly. With my counterparts anxiously waiting, "I explained that the wind had come along and blown the cards around. I apologized for the confusion, and assured them not to worry, we will guide your delegations to their planned seats. (Thankfully, there *was* a bit of a breeze that balmy evening.) They looked at me as if I had gone mad, but they nodded in agreement. I'd worked hard at cementing a trusting relationship with many of them over the months and years, and those bonds held tight now. My right-hand officer and I worked in unison to get it all straight. Moments later, I greeted President Obama, who was the first to arrive. He knew there was an issue just by looking at my face. "You got this?" he asked quizzically. I nodded and guided him to his seat. We did the same for every one of the twenty-one delegations until each person was positioned exactly where he or she should be. As the entertainment began, I saw the staffer who'd made the change and gave him my best withering look. I still, to this day, don't know why he did what he did, and I didn't have the time or interest that evening to understand, as there was so much more work to do. I simply moved on to my next task, with all guests happily in attendance and no one the wiser.

ACCEPT HELP

On occasion, regardless of how limber you are or how many seating charts you've memorized, you simply cannot find your way back. In instances when you are so far from plan A that you're looking at the end of the alphabet—due to circumstances completely out of your control (such as the weather or illness)—raise a hand. When the event veers off the well-planned highway and you no longer maintain command, allow others to step in and help with their talent and optimism. When all seems lost, trust that someone else can lead you out.

My marriage to Dr. Robert James Marshall has been utterly blissful for twenty-nine years (and counting), but the wedding logistics were a bit of a disaster. Still, it remains the happiest day of my life, thanks to some last-minute moves by my creative parents and amazing friends and family. The planning began in true Capricia fashion: I, the protocol expert in the making, sent out a thirty-page memo introducing every member of the wedding party, with bios of each person involved. I was my own wedding coordinator, and I thought I could control everything, down to sketching out a family tree that I included in my document. There were, needless to say, many, many rehearsals.

Yet, on the day of, everything that could go wrong did go wrong. If this had been a movie script, the producers would have said it was too unrealistic for so many things to go awry. But as many will confirm, this is a true story: The morning of our wedding was sunshine and bird chirping. But a huge limo bus (hired to transport our wedding party of twenty-two people to the church) did not show up to my parents' house, leaving the bridesmaids stranded. My dad, always a fixer in these situations (I get my yogic sensibility from him) went with my maid of honor, my California-cool college bestie Lisa Battaglia—whose easygoing attitude and stunning smile are irresistible—to ask the uninvited neighbors to drive us all to the church. (They agreed.) I took my dress off so it wouldn't get crushed, put it in the trunk of the bridal limo, and crammed into the back with as many people as would fit. I arrived at the church in shorts and a T-shirt . . . late . . . in a downpour. My cousins Heather, Monique, and Kim kept my beautiful hairdo from getting wet by tenting it with my dress (which my mom had smartly encased in plastic she found in the garage). We raced to the sanctuary, where I began to change, and the unbelievable happened: Father Jim (think Richard Chamberlain in *The Thorn Birds*) flung open the door to invite us to begin the ceremony to behold me wearing only what Rob should see later that evening. We were both horrified, and I let out an all-too-audible "OMG!" that the entire church heard. My ever-composed law school pals Mara Cushwa and Ann Marie Intili Gardner looked me in the eye and told me to shake it off while buttoning my dress. I listened to them and refocused, rechanneling the excitement of a bride on her special day. My father walked me down the aisle beaming, only to see poor Father Jim red-faced and Rob wondering *What is going on?*

Ah, but there's more. . . . The entire wedding party stopped by the hospital to visit my maternal grandmother, with whom I had a very close relationship and who was very ill. My aunts sobbed, and my grandma, Nonny, thought I was an angel in heaven, making her distraught. My mother assured Nonny that the angel had come to cure her—it worked, and she smiled and fell asleep. We left for the reception, but once we arrived, we were greeted by the venue manager, who was unkind (to put it kindly) about our late timing, so we rushed through the cocktails to the main course. We sat down for the meal and waited for the food to be served. And waited. And waited. I then watched my dad, brother, and my always helpful brother-in-law, Ken, stomp off into the woods with waders on to see what the problem was. They discovered that the earlier rain had affected the electricity, so the kitchen could not cook the food. (The outage also backed up the toilets—seriously.) The fun just kept going. The nineteen-piece band we selected could not play without electricity, and then proceeded to get drunk, as the bar was in full swing. A candle in one of the centerpieces fell over, setting fire to the dress of one of the guests, the mother of Rob's best friend Dan Tierney. (Dan was quick to act and doused her with water.) To top it off, many wedding guests joined in playing with a Ouija board!

What did my dad and mom do? They ordered out for pizza and started to dance without music. It was chaos. Apparently, memorable chaos, as so many guests to this day say it was the best wedding they ever attended! (My husband agrees, claiming it to be the happiest day of his life. How blessed am I to have him?) Every single person that day stepped in to tackle the issues that repeatedly popped up like a game of whack-a-mole. I took from that day, especially from my mother, father, and husband, that with a little ingenuity and flexibility, there can be great success even when *most* things do not go according to plan. (*Pro tip:* Curate your guest lists well, as your attendees may be the most important element of any event.)

NEGOTIATING WHILE FEMALE

The tools of protocol and diplomacy are as potent in gender politics as they are in international diplomacy. The same soft power resources that leaders leverage to arbitrate an arms treaty or a bilateral trade deal can be wielded to level the gender playing field at work and in everyday life. Women are almost constantly in a state of negotiation for equality, whether courting an international client, negotiating a pay raise, or simply fighting to be taken seriously by their banker or mechanic. You may not be mediating with a government counterpart in a semi-hostile foreign country (though some work environments may feel that way), but the stakes can be just as high: Not being hired for a job you're qualified for—and that gets handed to a less-experienced male colleague—can result in serious financial hardship; being taken off an account with a big male client because of the stereotype that women aren't "closers" can lead to career derailment, and being turned down for a loan because of conscious or unconscious gender bias can spell bankruptcy. These are extreme scenarios, but they are all too common (how many of you are thinking of yourselves or someone you know?) and underscore the profound need for women to arm themselves with every possible advantage when it comes to bridging and influencing in a male-dominated world.

GLOBAL SNAPSHOT:
HOW ARE WOMEN DOING?

Depending on the country, the gender equality gap can be chasm or a sliver. For many countries, it's a dismal picture, writ large. The average global gender parity gap is about 31 percent, meaning that women are afforded around 69 percent of the economic opportunity, education, and political empowerment of men, according to a 2020 Global Gender Gap report of 153 countries by the World Economic Forum (WEF). This divide is the result of many inequities, including barriers to education, lack of childcare (women are expected to raise children and therefore can't go to school or work), and the restrictions on owning land or homes (some countries allow sons to inherit a larger percentage of assets, such as land, compared with daughters). And because women are less likely to be in positions of power to make or model changes, closing the gap will take decades—99.5 years, to be exact, if current trends hold. As of June 2019, only eleven countries had women as elected heads of state, with an additional twelve serving as heads of government. The WEF report found that women hold just 36 percent of senior managerial positions in the private sector. While there are bright spots—Iceland has reached 88 percent gender parity; and Norway, Finland, and Sweden are closing in on 85 percent gender parity, with Nicaragua, New Zealand, Ireland, Spain, Rwanda, and Germany close behind—the reality is that women around the world are disadvantaged well before they get to the boardroom, and certainly once they're in it.

As a woman who has seen gender dynamics play out at the highest levels of foreign policy, I know that conscious and unconscious biases affect women at every level and stage. But I've also witnessed the long arc of progress bending slowly toward equality. I've stood shoulder to shoulder with formidable female heads of state—Chancellor Angela Merkel of Germany, former President Michelle Bachelet of Chile, and former Prime Minister Benazir Bhutto of Pakistan—who have shown that an effective leader knows no gender boundaries. I've worked with female C-suite executives who are thriving in male-populated industries. I've traveled to countries whose political systems and cultural protocols enable equality, and I've met and worked with extraordinary women and men (women need male allies!) who have stepped up to mentor the next generation of women. Forward-thinking leaders know that bringing in women benefits the bottom line: Companies in the top quartile for gender diversity on executive teams are 21 percent more likely to outperform on profitability, according to the 2018 McKinsey & Company's report "Delivering through Diversity." The Bloomberg Gender-Equality Index (BGEI), which compiles and analyzes data from companies around the world who are investing in women in the workplace, is quickly becoming a badge of honor, and its transparency encourages competition, inspiration, and sharing of best practices. When compared to the standard MSCI (Morgan Stanley Capital Index) the BGEI clearly demonstrates that those companies in developed markets who invest in women outperform those that do not. Dee Dee Myers, executive VP of worldwide communications and public affairs at Warner Bros., and one of my closest confidantes, has experienced the disparities at the highest levels in government and the private sector. She, like the McKinsey and Bloomberg findings, affirms that "by now, the evidence is overwhelming: diverse groups of decision-makers make better decisions. And they make them faster. In virtually any organization, more gender and ethnic diversity among leaders helps avoid the kind of groupthink that can stifle innovation and honest conversation. And it leads to better results—in politics, business, diplomacy, science, medicine, education, you name it. Women need to understand and internalize this important data, whether they're building organizations, leading them, or working as part of the team. Their presence in the room isn't a nice-to-have, it's a need-to-have. It will improve the outcomes for everyone, full stop." Dee Dee has been an illuminating example, to me and many other women, of success through hard work in a male-dominated, highly competitive profession.

IT'S REGRETTABLE that a GENDER equity index and gender diversity reports are needed at all. But until we are living and working in a utopia, women must negotiate smarter in order to close the gender gap. What follows is a seven-point targeted approach using the tools of diplomacy and protocol to help achieve workplace gender equality.

1. RAISE YOUR CULTURAL GENDER IQ

When men travel across borders, they experience something women do not: a privileged status quo. Businessmen are generally treated the same whether they're in China or Chile. They can often wear the same suits they do in their native country, greet counterparts with a standard handshake, and speak up in meetings without fear of offending or overstepping. Women, on the other hand, must carefully calibrate their behavior, dress, and strategy according to each country's gender codes, which can be vastly different culture to culture. Men rarely have to thread the needle in this manner, alleviating them of one less challenge. A woman's defense against a constantly changing negotiating environment and a core premise of this book: knowledge of the culture. As I've demonstrated in previous chapters, knowing these cultural codes is like having the secret password to the clubhouse. It gains you entry. When women are culture-savvy, their adherence signals: "See? I belong, so let's get on with the business at hand."

In countries where gender equality is well on its way, cultural expectations are minimized, and as a global businesswoman you aren't as hindered by biases or burdens. If you're lucky enough to do business in the Nordic countries, you'll experience a boot camp of sorts for how true gender equality operates. Much of the parity in these nations is the result of policies that provide generous paid parental leave and subsidized child care, allowing women the opportunity to fully pursue career and family goals simultaneously.

But in many cultures, women are still required to look and behave differently in business situations. A myriad of factors—religion, cultural stereotypes, laws governing gender equality—play into how a woman is treated in each nation. There are over 100 countries that have at least one law on the books limiting a woman's economic opportunities, and eighteen countries where husbands dictate whether their wives work at all, according to a 2018 World Bank study. And sometimes the laws don't accurately reflect how women are treated in reality. Take Egypt, a country that recently reformed its constitution, committing to equality between men and women. I recently met the minister of tourism of Egypt, Rania Al-Mashat, a highly impressive economist who speaks out on gender equality in her country and who, hopefully, heralds the future of Egyptian leadership. But while the new constitution is a commendable change—and women like Minister Al-Mashat are shining role models—the written reforms are not really enforced: According to the WEF report, only 7 percent of managerial roles are filled by women in the country. The unwritten rule: You're basically operating in a country where women hold a tiny percent of managerial positions and wield very little power or respect.

Some countries have made strides in women's equality, thanks in part to quotas. In Latin America, the vast majority of countries have legislative quotas requiring a certain percentage of women be named as candidates in elections or nominated for ruling party positions, increasing female political participation. While quotas alone will not transform a society, they are an important piece of the puzzle. Women traveling to Latin America on business can expect a more egalitarian reception than is typically assigned machismo cultures, although they may still encounter a glass ceiling, according to an Atlantic Council report which I spearheaded called "Women's Leadership in Latin America, the Key to Growth and Sustainable Development."

I advise women to enlist a guide or peer in the country they're traveling in to advise them on precise cultural norms. If you don't have inroads, contact your country's embassy in the nation you're traveling to for a jumping-off point. In addition, here are three top-line rules to keep in mind for any international business travel:

1. **Be sensitive to physical contact.** Some conservative Muslim sects prohibit men from touching women to whom they are not related and will usually place their arms across their chest as a signal and only nod in greeting (which a businesswoman should return). This is a hard-and-fast rule to which even First Ladies are held. In 2010,

during a state visit President Obama and the First Lady made to Jakarta, Indonesia, every eye was watching. The first couple were making their way down the receiving line of dignitaries, shaking hands with each Indonesian official, all while the cameras were rolling. Indonesia's information minister, a member of a conservative sect, was in the line and when the First Lady reached him, they shook, clasping both hands together in a brief, enthusiastic shake. The media firestorm began almost instantly, given that the minister is known to avoid contact with women not related to him. Facebook posts and tweets from Indonesians scolded the minister for touching her and condemned him for a lack of commitment to his faith. To make matters worse, the minister took to Twitter that night, saying that *she* had forced the contact and he had tried to avoid touching her. "Mrs. Michelle held her hands too far toward me (so) we touched." The First Lady's experienced, calm-under-pressure deputy chief of staff, Melissa Winter, sought my assistance to resolve the issue. I immediately went to my counterpart for clarity on the claim. As I stood next to her, I knew what had transpired and dashed off to find the proof. The First Lady and her team were extremely aware of the importance of cultural interaction—she always pored over our cultural memos, taking the time to meet with me personally before every international engagement—and I suspected she had been following *his* cue, which Melissa confirmed. In murky matters of international intrigue, we always went to the videotape. The slow-roll replay revealed that he had extended his hand first, and she was simply responding, which was the right thing to do. I returned to my counterpart with verification that the First Lady managed this appropriately.

Other countries, however, are more tactile with both genders. In Brazil, you can expect some patting on the back or touching of shoulders or arms in business settings, and for people to stand closer to you than in the United States. That said, it's important to keep it professional, and as unfair as it may seem, in each situation the onus is often on the woman not to send the wrong signal; women who do business in Brazil, for example, have told me they make a point not to touch the arm of an older male colleague.

2. **Dress accordingly.** Do your groundwork. In Saudi Arabia, for example, women visitors are often advised to wear pants or long skirts so they don't reveal any skin. (I always packed a couple of maxi dresses for my visits there.) For most other countries, I recommend an elegant business pantsuit or a tailored dress that covers upper legs and knees, as well as the upper chest to avoid showing any cleavage. If the country code is "no bare skin," wear opaque tights or a long dress or pants (avoid nude or seminude stockings, which are considered the same as bare legs). There's more leeway with footwear, even in conservative countries, where women can wear open-toe shoes and get as glamorous and tall (five-inch heels!) as they desire. But do not make assumptions that all countries in the same region require the same dress code: In the United Arab Emirates, for example, which I have had the pleasure of visiting on several occasions, a female visitor/businesswoman can wear styles she normally dresses in (caveat: avoid miniskirts) and is not expected to cover her head or shoulders.

3. **Transmit authority carefully.** If you're in a senior or decision-making position, you must ascertain how to signal authority in a manner that does not violate cultural norms. In Nordic countries, you're on firm meritocratic ground and will be taken seriously in any role or position by both men and women. But in the Middle East and Africa—and in some Asian countries where hierarchy matters—you may need to use subtle but clear cues to gently communicate that you belong at the table. Don't assume duties of someone of lower status, such as passing out memos. Ask any colleagues you're traveling with or trusted counterparts to help set the tone by deferring to you in the presence of others. If you are the principal, sit in the middle of the table and take the center position for group photos. Open the discussion or, if you're speaking at a

gathering, be the keynote at the microphone. Even women doing business in countries that are fairly progressive, such as the United States, can benefit by shoring up clout. Cultural stereotypes die hard, and "she's just a woman" can be the subconscious default no matter how many degrees or positions a woman has. And even the most self-professed "woke" men often assume that a female counterpart from an external organization joining a conference call or a meeting with her male colleagues is their junior.

Even in a woman's home country she will encounter work cultures that require she employ some cultural IQ. There are plenty of employment sectors where testosterone drives the MO—finance, agriculture, utilities, transportation, engineering, politics, and tech—calling for savvy strategies to bridge the female-male cultural divide. All the techniques I discuss in chapter 4 for how to suss out an office culture apply to women entering male-dominated fields and offices. Figure out the dress code (formal or casual?), the meeting style (tightly run or free-flowing?), and the after-work bonding rituals and join in. Your goal is to be successful in *that* environment, so the more you understand the accepted rules of engagement, the easier it will be to achieve your goal.

Being a savvy reader of the work culture is one of the strategies women of previous generations used to make strides. Kay Belfance, the mother of my cherished friend Eve from law school, is one of my personal heroines and a role model for how to assimilate *just* enough to be accepted while still moving the needle, climbing her way to the top of the bankruptcy law field at a time when very few women were even in the field let alone excelling at it. She advised Eve and me early in our careers that to manage a workplace culture that is acutely male, you must be authentically yourself. "By being clear about your own identity it means you are conscious of unloading the social paradigms that are being thrust upon you, allowing you to reject the archetype of who you are supposed to be." Eve, the law director for the city of Akron, Ohio, adds that keeping her mother's struggle and advice in mind allowed her to strategize for success in every male-dominated environment from her undergraduate studies to prominent positions in law and government.

2. APPLY THE YOGA OF PROTOCOL TO SUBVERT TOKENISM

Let's talk tokenism, the practice of placing a woman or a person of color in a visible position of inclusion or authority in order to achieve a superficial end: "Look, we love women/African Americans/Latinos/Asians, here's one on our panel/board/conference schedule/hiring committee." It's a nice image, and it's great to see institutions normalizing images of underrepresented groups, whether in publicity materials like social media posts or in actuality; it shows young people that this could—and should—be the new normal. But members of those groups know that it's not the whole. There may be a minority or female board member on the annual report cover, but she's going to quarterly meetings with a dozen or so white men.

In 2012, I witnessed an example of nearly comical gender tokenism. I escorted Secretary Clinton to a meeting with a male foreign minister and military general, where she seated herself at one side of an elaborate table with several staff members from the State Department. Seated on the other side of the table, near the foreign minister, were two women. After greetings were exchanged, the minister gestured to what we assumed were his female aides. "I heard you like women at the table," he remarked plainly, not bothering to introduce them. As the meeting proceeded, it became clear to Secretary Clinton and her staff that he probably did not even know their names. She tried to engage them, but to no avail. No one on our side ever learned the exact roles of these women. They may have held important career posts in their government, but in that moment, we assumed their roles were for show only.

Tokenism is a glaring symptom of inequality, a subterfuge to hide the fact that a group or company is not really diverse after all. (To be clear, tokenism is not the same as a quota system, though quotas can slip into token territory when women are placed only in middle- or lower-tier positions and not taken seriously in their roles.) And female tokenism is by no means something you'll only encounter in "other countries." In the United States, companies, universities, law firms, and the like are guilty of it as well.

Have you been a page from a *binder of women* or propped up to give a false impression of a commitment to diversity? If so, be flexible and maximize it. I truly believe that you can still make progress even when the path you're being shown isn't the one you'd choose. If you're asked to participate in a meeting, panel, or media spot or to serve on a board at the last minute because they need a woman in the mix, use it to your advantage. This make-hay-while-the-sun-shines strategy is one embraced by a person reinventing the global economy, and who happens to be a woman: Christine Lagarde, president of the European Central Bank and former managing director of the International Monetary Fund, who is ranked twenty-second on the 2018 *Forbes* list of the world's most powerful people. Christine's talents range from reducing global poverty to mastering an aria, and she has profoundly affected my life through her example. She recently told me, "Being a woman in a room full of men is a challenge, but also an opportunity. What I have managed to do in my career is turn that discriminatory attitude into an advantage through hard work, being extraordinarily well prepared, and having confidence. Your voice can stand out." It doesn't matter how you got in the room or on the stage—you now have the opportunity to shatter the notion of tokenism by proving yourself valuable. Here are ways to bend biased rules and traditions in your favor:

- **Fight the "manel."** I hear a great deal these days about the "manel," a panel made up of only men. There is a raging battle against them, so call them out and then get into the ring. Circulate your name in the office or industry as a qualified speaker, and lift up your female colleagues and contacts by putting their names forward as well.

- **Don't shun being the moderator.** Some women bristle at being "only" the moderator. Why? You control the conversation and how long each person gets to speak. I find that position most pivotal and not at all a toss away.

- **Embrace female celebration events.** I know—if only we didn't need days/months/events dedicated to establishing equality and respect for half of our planet. But cynicism and nonparticipation won't move the needle. I have found that most foreign embassies in Washington are so eager to lift up and highlight the extraordinary women that work for their country, hosting events and introducing them to the DC community. Their enthusiasm and creativity is inspiring and catching.

- **Network with women leaders who have seemingly benefited from tokenism.** In foreign governments, women of great substance are often sent to the United States as the highest representative of their country or to lead international multilateral organizations. Perhaps some aspect of their placement was the result of tokenism or a quota system, but in all cases they more than deserved the position. I sought out ways to highlight the ambassadors and deputies at events in an effort to raise their profiles in the DC community. During my time at the State Department, we had the highest number of female ambassadors to date. It seemed there was a belief that while Hillary Clinton was secretary of state, women ambassadors would be more effective. Not so, but this mentality netted us more female ambassadors than we've ever had.

3. SOCIALIZING WHILE FEMALE:
NETWORK BETTER

Because women tend to be pigeonholed, they need to work extra hard to find new avenues out of the cul-de-sac and onto the highway. You must connect with people who can build your brand and introduce you to the next opportunity. One caveat: As much as I'm a fan of joining clubs and attending conferences, I warn women neither to create nor to attend a "women's convening" that is light on substance. Women do not have a need to gather simply to gather. We need to be fed well with substantive information that will give us an advantage in our careers. I have attended a great number of female-tailored conferences, and I've become adept at sniffing out and avoiding ones that are ineffective. Before you buy in and commit two or three days of your busy existence to the conference life, do your homework to ensure you're getting something worthwhile out of it: Do recon on the speakers and sponsors or investors to determine whether they will expand your horizons in the direction you want. Attend conferences where men are invited to speak—the idea isn't to cut men out of the equation, which is an enormous disservice; you want to be exposed to diverse perspectives, including those of men. As my friend Adrienne Arsht advises, "Excluding anybody and creating barriers of entry is ultimately self-limiting."

For women building their international networks, a surefire way to meet the most influential people is to be invited to a consulate, embassy, or university foreign language department event. Getting on a consulate or embassy invitation list is key. Better yet: offer to volunteer or speak at an event. Global women convenings and events are occurring with more frequency at embassies and consulates, as their home countries are increasingly emphasizing the relevance of women. In DC, the social secretary network of the diplomatic corps is vast and their guest lists are top tier, but they are always looking to enhance them. Visit the embassy websites and send an email to the social secretary (it will be a general embassy email, but your request will eventually make it to the proper person for consideration). Each embassy has the most extraordinary people serving as bridges between their country and ours.

4. DO YOUR HOMEWORK:
KNOW YOUR WORTH

When you enter any negotiation, you must have all the data at your fingertips. This is true for anyone, but much more so for women: The moment a female speaker gets a stat wrong or forgets a figure, the thought running through the minds of many men in the room is likely to be, "Ah, *she's* just not cut out for this." I'm generalizing, and there are some evolved men who look past gender, but even those who think they support equal opportunity may suffer from unconscious gender bias. This is not something only women take note of: A 2015 global gender parity survey by Ernst & Young of four hundred managers found that men listed unconscious bias as the top barrier they witnessed to women's career progression. "Women have to work three times as hard as everyone else, even in the digital space where younger CEOs tend to have a more progressive outlook than traditional companies, and where the shift to a meritocracy is degrees better," says Moj Mahdara, founder and CEO of BeautyCon. "As a woman there is no BS-ing, no fudging numbers, no cutting corners, no getting lucky."

One obvious area where having the facts is critical: salary negotiations. It's sometimes tough to get data on what a man at your level and title is making, but those industry or company numbers are often the best leverage you have for being paid your worth. (*Pro tip:* Direct conversations with your HR Department, recruiting companies, and sites like GlassDoor and Salary.com are methods to determine a base salary. And 990 forms for not-for-profit organizations are publicly available, listing salaries and job titles for officers and directors, as well as the five highest-compensated employees who earn over $100,000.) I know from my experience that a woman—particularly a *young* woman—will be expected to take less. In 1997, when I was hired as deputy assistant to the president and social secretary, I discovered from a *Washington Post* article that comparative deputy assistants to the president were receiving salaries that were higher than mine. I realized that I was younger than my predecessor and others at my level—I was the second youngest social secretary in history (by seven months—the lovely Bess Abell edged me out)—but I was doing the same job. I immediately went to the chief of staff, John Podesta, who was unaware of the disparity and argued my case. The facts I brought to his attention in addition to the salary disparity: I worked twenty-four/seven and was expected to perform to the level of senior staff, including all management duties. John worked diligently in the Clinton administration on issues of parity, and he corrected the error on the spot and granted me both the salary and title of those in similar positions. The lesson: You have to ask and come armed with facts. While institutional gender bias does exist, it's not the only reason women don't make as much as their male counterparts: Women don't negotiate for a higher salary as often as men. Linda Babcock, coauthor of *Women Don't Ask*, found that 57 percent of male MBA graduates attempted to negotiate for a higher starting salary compared to just 7 percent of women MBA grads, which may partly account for the 7.6 percent difference in salary between them. Executive recruiter and coach Kristin Mannion, founder of Aura Leadership and Development—and a cherished friend who has counseled me and many women at all levels in their careers—says women need to experience a seismic mind-set shift in order to fight for themselves. "Culturally women are taught to be caretakers. While we can promote others easily, we often need to learn to better ask for ourselves, and to tell our own stories of strength and capabilities." Use the data to tell *your* story.

5. ADOPT AN EQUALIZING MIND-SET: CONFIDENCE

Earlier in the book I discussed empathy and humility as critical mind-set tools for connecting and persuading. At the risk of stereotyping, I'm adding a caveat, as I think many women already employ quite enough empathy and humility in the workplace, whether it's because our society nurtures these qualities more in women or because we've learned to excel in them as a matter of survival. The often-missing mind-set I believe women need to adopt as a counterbalance to an overdeveloped sense of deference is this: certainty in your value and a don't-back-down confidence.

This knowingness and belief in self is something you naturally develop throughout your career, becoming more assured with each move up the ladder. But it's not always a given for women, who are often overlooked in meetings or mansplained to—even older office floorplans can feel demeaning, as many are designed for men, with the women's restroom situated in some far-flung corner or even in another building. I've seen women at the top of their game defer to men who are equals simply as a knee-jerk reaction (and not as an actual strategy, which is a whole other discussion). Research shows that women systematically have lower expectations than men when negotiating for salaries. I, too, have occasionally behaved in rote ways that undervalued my worth and contributions. When I launched my consulting business, I was so thrilled to get my first client that I did not account for my time and experience appropriately. It took a bad contract and some industry recon (I discovered that people with less experience were charging more) to recognize I was underestimating my market worth. I'm certain a man would have charged market rate (or more) right out the gate. Confidence is a muscle we have to flex to feel more comfortable with it. And when we do this for ourselves, we do it for all women, modeling the change we'd like to see in the world.

While finding my footing in the private sector took some time, I was usually on solid ground in the government sector (having been under the tutelage of a certain confident First Lady), and I had no problem asserting myself. During my first month as chief of protocol, I was invited to a meeting at the State Department about the planning of a new initiative. When I arrived, the group of six or so men, led by a long-serving male diplomat, seemed surprised to see me. He was kind in his greeting but then quickly stated that someone at my "level" was not needed. As first I believed he was flattering me, but then I quickly realized he wanted the only gal at the table out of the room so they could manage the preparations themselves. To emphasize my outsider status, he stated, "This is how it is always done" (a common refrain sometimes intended to make people feel out of the loop). I was being dismissed. At this point in my career, I was accustomed to working with men who valued my input as an equal and had the confidence and experience to know I could and should stand my ground. After a few long pauses—an indication that he was waiting for me to go—I assured him, calmly and in an upbeat manner, that I would be staying. After what seemed like an eternity, he finally started to outline the plan for the engagement. I injected my thoughts throughout the meeting, and he would just furrow his brow and stare hard at me. I felt for the other participants, who were clearly uncomfortable. But I knew that this was going to be a long road with this particular public servant and that I had to remain unyielding, demonstrating early on for him and any others that bumping me, the woman, out of the room was not going to happen. Sometimes these moments will be uncomfortable because you are trying to change an attitude that a person—or an entire office or culture—has held for years, and change does not happen easily. But when you do it with aplomb, you can move the needle.

My friend and international businesswoman savant Deborah Lehr, CEO of Basilinna DC and vice chairperson of the Paulson Institute, advises that in situations where you take a position in opposition to the male status quo, two things can help you achieve success: One, be authentic *and* professional. "It is okay to stick to your principles, to push back, to disagree, as long as it is professional and not personal, keeping the focus on the issue and not the behavior of the person. And most people appreciate candor." The second tip: Pick your battle. "While you may not always achieve what you want, often you can come close if you focus on what is truly important, fight for it, and be willing to compromise on those issues that may not be essential for your success." In my case, the core issue was to stay in the room, not necessarily to score points throughout the meeting. Although I certainly offered my professional suggestions, I also kept an open mind and showed a willingness to negotiate ideas and goals.

And yes, it is incredibly frustrating that in addition to chipping away at cultural and workplace gender bias—which takes an awful lot of mental energy—women must also think about how to manage men's responses to our attempts for equality. Furthermore, the double standard for success persists despite the progress women are making: High-achieving women are routinely seen as more selfish and less likable—by both men *and* women—especially when a woman is successful in a field that is traditionally male, finds research by Madeline Heilman, PhD, a professor of psychology at New York University, who studies sex bias in work settings. When you violate a cultural norm, there will be pushback. But history has taught us that progress, while glacial, is made by those who stay in the game.

6. CALIBRATE YOUR VOICE—LITERALLY.

While you're working on finding your voice, consider how you might sound while expressing it. It's a hard reality that hitting the right tone and volume is a fine line to walk for women, who are judged more harshly than men in the vocal department. On the one hand, women are advised to speak loudly enough to be heard and to appear confident, but not so loudly they come across as harsh. Being on the campaign trail with Secretary Clinton, I saw this double standard over and over. When she was at the podium speaking to large crowds, she would naturally amplify her voice to be heard above the din. Invariably, someone in the press or behind the scenes would describe her as shrill (a term that is never used to describe a man, mind you). The irony is that Secretary Clinton's voice has an average pitch and volume for someone of her age and gender. How do I know? A speech researcher at Cleveland State University analyzed her voice for a piece in *The Atlantic* called "The Science Behind Hating Hillary's Voice." The mic amplifies a voice, making it sound shrill—and many people, Secretary Clinton included, tend to speak loudly into a mic, especially at rallies. But she is also the victim of a society that allows far more vocal latitude to men than women. Unfortunately, the general public is not trained to hear the tone of authority from women—especially from the podium—so they either tune it out or have a negative response to it. We need more women in positions of authority so that we can become accustomed to their tones and messaging.

7. OFFER A HAND, NOT A HEEL:
COLLABORATE AND ELEVATE

If working for Hillary Clinton for twenty-five-plus years taught me anything about getting ahead, it was the value of women helping women. Well before she became the first lady of Arkansas, she recognized she was in a position to help shape and buoy everyone in her employ, especially the women. Politics was and is still frustratingly a man's world, and Hillary knew her influence was needed all the more. In my earliest days with her on the campaign trail during her husband's first presidential run, she solidified the lesson that all women, as we climbed the career ladder, should be giving each other a hand, not a heel. During one of our first staff meetings she explicitly told us, "I want a team of people who watch each other's back, and when you don't, you'll be asked to leave." She knew that camaraderie was critical for making our way forward. We all embraced it, and I believe it's one reason that people stayed on her staff longer than on other principals' teams. The friendships we all developed allowed us to read each other's signs for SOS and respond in kind. The traveling team consisted of Kelly Craighead, her trip director (currently president and CEO of Cruise Line International Association), Lisa Caputo, Hillary's press secretary, who brought her years of Hill experience and analytical thinking to the group (she is currently executive VP and chief marketing and communications officer for Travelers Companies, Inc.), and me. We developed our own sign language on the campaign trail. Lisa's crossed arms and head tilt always signaled to Kelly and me, even from across a big ballroom, that there was a problem, ladies, we need to fix it. I will forever want these women in my foxhole during troubled times.

We learned a great deal working toward a goal for an administration, led by a woman with tough standards and great vision. The following Tools of Female Collaboration are ones we used and developed while in the White House and during our travels around the world, and I've shared these with many a woman in my workplace and social life:

The Echo Chamber

The "echo chamber" is a technique born out of an experience that probably sounds annoyingly familiar to most women: offering advice on a specific issue without anyone seemingly hearing us, and then having our idea repeated by a man in the room to sudden and great acclaim. We would sit and wonder, "Did I speak too softly? Did I not accurately communicate my thoughts?" At one of our White House weekly scheduling meetings where we discussed this phenomenon, First Lady Hillary Clinton suggested that when two or more of us were in meetings together we should echo each other's comments. Thereafter, when a colleague made a suggestion, I would quickly jump into the discussion before it was hijacked, saying how much I liked it and asking her to repeat it. My colleague would repeat the idea with emphasis . . . and suddenly she was heard! It worked every time.

Workplace Support Systems

Hillary helped the women on her staff adjust their schedules so they could work throughout their pregnancies and new-mom days, doing the same for me when I became pregnant with my son, Cole. While mom-friendly offices and schedules are becoming more prevalent (though still not common enough), it was fairly groundbreaking in the 1990s, especially in DC with its always-on status. I wasn't sure I'd be able to juggle being pregnant and fulfill my official duties—I was the first social secretary to be pregnant during the post—and when I decided to stay in the job, Hillary did everything to help me make it work. She sent broccoli to my office to make sure I was eating enough folate and ordered me home when my feet swelled. She also encouraged me to delegate—something women rarely like to do, as it may make them seem impotent in their duties.

But the office spirit of support erased that concern for me, as did the track record of women on her staff who had babies and resumed their duties postpartum. Patti Solis Doyle, her scheduler, had a beautiful baby girl (Lee, my dazzling goddaughter), and once Patti was back full-time, she stepped in to offer me support, along with work maternity clothes and awesome advice. Lissa Muscatine, Hillary's speechwriter, demonstrated how we could make the work-mommy balance happen, with office operations changes (that Hillary adopted) such as a work-from-home option, which seems simple now but was rather rare then. When work-from-home wasn't practical, the office transformed into a virtual on-site day care. At one point, there was a baby boom on Hillary's staff, and cribs nestled in every nook and cranny of the White House. My son slept in Chelsea's old crib when my mother brought him to the White House, and I was blessed to have him there. Patti, Lissa, and I were also fortunate to have senior women on staff to support our new life-styles. For example, Stephanie Streett, the president's scheduler and the greatest multitasker I know (she's currently raising three amazing young women and serves as executive director of the Clinton Foundation), held scheduling meetings at times that accommodated our mommy commit-ments.

Nowadays, more companies and organizations are structuring their environments to suit the needs of their employees, and this includes breastfeeding rooms and, in some places, nurseries. When on the job hunt, know what your personal needs will be to support your growth in the workplace. If you are a new mom and are weighing the job that allows you more maternity leave versus the one with the corner office, go for the perk that will relieve you of some of the worries of new moth-erhood. Extended paid maternity and paternity leaves are one of the big reasons why gender equality in Europe and the Nordic countries is way ahead of other countries, including the United States, which doesn't even rank: Sadly, we do not guarantee any paid maternity leave at all (it's down to individual employers to decide how much to offer), and we are the least generous member of the OECD (Organisation for Economic Co-operation and Development), a group of thirty-six industrialized na-tions that works to create policies that foster well-being. Hillary took this issue on as First Lady, senator, and even secretary of state, appoint-ing Shirley Sagawa and Jennifer Klein, two titans in the field of gender equality policy, to attack the status quo and push for family and medical leave. Melanne Verveer was appointed by Secretary Clinton the first-ever US ambassador-at-large for Global Women's Issues to confront parity is-sues for women around the world. Secretary Kerry continued elevating the importance of this role with the appointment of Catherine Russell.

Raise Each Other Up

Women often neglect to see the value in themselves that their friends and colleagues see so clearly. For all my puffery, I am a self-doubter. (Confession: I was never sure I would ever write this book.) At certain junctures in my career I had to be persuaded of my value by other women (and men, especially my awesome husband), and I advise all women to keep friends in your circle who motivate you to move to higher ground. I owe my ascendancy into the position of social secretary to two colleagues who convinced me I could take up the heavy mantle of the position and fill the shoes of the legendary Ann Stock. When Hillary offered me the role, I told her how appreciative I was and that I'd have to think about it. My mind was racing—mostly with reasons why I shouldn't accept—when my phone rang. It was the incomparable duo of Maggie Williams, Hillary's brilliant and measured chief of staff, and Evelyn Lieberman, the candid and all-knowing White House deputy chief of staff (sadly, Evelyn passed away in 2015). They already knew—in fact, they had recommended me for the job. "I just don't know if this is the right move, so I said I'd consider it," I told them. It was the doubt talking, and they were having none of it. They convinced me that no one was better prepared and that this was a new beginning in my career. Though I questioned myself, I did not doubt Evelyn or Maggie, whose job it was to hire the right people for these roles and who were true friends—they would not have encouraged me to do something I wasn't ready for. Putting my faith in them, I accepted the offer.

Mentorship

Mentorship is the ultimate in collaboration, and one of the most important ingredients for a successful career. Mentors are especially vital for women, who may not have as clear or accessible a route to the next level as male counterparts. Studies have found a solid link between being mentored and receiving promotions and salary increases, as well as improved job satisfaction. A mentor—who is usually perched on a higher branch that allows a better or alternative view—can lift you up by sharing her experience, resources, and relationships. I received so much from so many and have in kind passed on the advice to many young people throughout my career. This final section is not only about mentoring a new generation of women, but a request to the many women (and men) who have received the gains from others to pay it forward to the next generation.

What makes a good mentor? Someone who is invested in your success, not just as an employee but in a holistic way, taking into account your life goals as well. If you have a difficult time finding an official mentor at work, try to establish a mentorship network through universities, clubs, and organizations. I've also found the best mentorships grow organically out of preexisting relationships. In fact, some research finds that informal mentoring can produce stronger benefits than formalized mentoring.

Mentors aren't always in a supervisory position, but they can be. Mine was. It's no secret to anyone who knows me that the most formative relationship of my career was with Hillary Rodham Clinton. She saw my potential before I saw it myself. In December 1992, after Bill Clinton had just won the White House, I found myself at a crossroads. I'd been working as Hillary's advance person—preparing everything "in advance" for her visits as she toured the country speaking as (we hoped) the soon-to-be First Lady of the United States. Once the election was over, I figured it was the end of my time with the Clintons. Susan Thomases, a longtime friend of the Clintons and a mentor to me and many of the young woman on the 1992 campaign, thanked everyone for their service on the campaign and encouraged them to return home, but pulled me aside and told me to stand by, that Hillary was impressed with me and had a plan. About two weeks before the first family moved to DC, Hillary called me to the governor's mansion. I recalled Susan's comment but thought this was more likely a farewell meeting. "Capricia," she started, "I've watched you over these hard few months working for me and Bill, and I want you to join us at the White House." I was genuinely surprised and admitted that I was almost on the next bus to

Cleveland. Hillary—thankfully—had other ideas. She looked at me intensely and gave me a classic Hillary-ism (one that I've quoted for many bright people I've mentored): "You need to plant yourself where you can grow." Meaning: Learn your strengths so you can root yourself in a place that grows your talents. She added, pointing at her legs, "I could never be a marathon runner with these legs, Capricia. I'm just not built that way. I'm built for other things." I understood. Sometimes we dream outside the boundaries of what we are capable of doing—or sometimes we don't dream in ways we *should*, not recognizing our own talents. A good mentor points these things out. Ever since I had interned in DC as a college freshman, I had dreamed of returning and working in government, but never did I think that I, the Cleveland daughter of immigrants, would be working in the White House. Yet someone else held that dream for me and could see that it was exactly the right place for me. I soon believed that for myself, too.

Find an Excellent Mentor

We should all be so fortunate to have Hillary Clinton guiding our trajectory—and, in fact, she mentored the whole nation by becoming the first female presidential nominee in US history, showing every girl and woman what is possible—but the best mentor for you is someone in your sphere, or adjacent to it. I've had several incredible mentors over the years—men and women—and they've all had these attributes:

- **They're discreet.** How does the person talk about others? If they share negative gossip, they may not invoke a code of silence in their interactions with you either. One of my longtime male mentors, Doug Sosnik, a senior adviser in the Clinton White House, is a locked box, and many people lean on Doug. His advice to me: Be discreet and be humble. When I became social secretary, he mentored me on how to approach my new role, telling me, "Do not seek the spotlight for your own purposes." Many people in high-profile positions use a role to further their own agenda, often to their and their team's detriment.

- **They're honest, but not judgmental.** If I feel as if someone is judging me, I know I won't feel comfortable being honest with her. That said, it's important that a mentor can deliver honest criticism and steer you away from decisions or behaviors that aren't in keeping with your goals. Terry McAuliffe, the forthright former governor of Virginia, who has always been there for me, will often tell me straight out, "Why are you wasting your time on that? Think about these other options." (He also gave me one of my live-by credos: "I will sleep when I die." Live your life to the fullest through your best choices.) Minyon Moore, a principal at Dewey Square Group, and a friend who lifts my spirit every time I am with her, has a delivery of hard news that is cool and calm. The day after Hillary's loss in 2016, when we were all still incredulous, she asked a small group of us, "Did we do our part? Did we help enough? Perhaps we will never know those answers, but we need to ask the questions." She wasn't judging, but in her almost minister-like manner, she compelled us to take ownership and stop the blame game.

- **They are admired by others.** What's the watercooler conversation about this person? Does he seem to have a wide network of positive relationships? That person's contacts will (hopefully) become your contacts, so the more far-reaching and solid those relationships, the more they'll be able to give you a leg up.

- **They look for opportunities for you.** A good mentor knows what assets you have and what you need to develop. I've benefited from so many greathearted people from my time working in the Clinton and Obama administrations, people who generously offered their time, advice, and office space. After I left government, I had a posse of exceptional people helping me determine my next steps. Tom Nides, former deputy secretary of state and managing director and vice chairman of Morgan Stanley, spent hours advising me on career options. Clyde Tuggle, cofounder of Pine Island Capital Partners, a firm that combines an experienced investment team with highly specialized Washington DC–based partners, suggested I seek out opportunities in the financial arena and join his firm as an advisory partner. I never look at life as a straight road, and you never know who will open up a new door for you. Some mentors can serve as sponsors. Sponsorship is becoming a bigger focus at companies these days, especially for women and minorities who are still underrepresented in senior and VP-level positions. When you sponsor people, you essentially give them a seat at the negotiation table with you, recommending them for assignments and projects and taking a direct role in facilitating their upward movement at the company.

- **You have a real connection with them.** This is so individual, and you must determine what that special ingredient is to feel supported. I've always gravitated toward mentors who are go-getters (I tend to take chances and need help weighing out the cost/benefit of a risky move). When I left my position as chief of protocol in 2013, my path was open, though I wasn't sure where to head next. Resigning was the hardest decision I've ever had to make. (I actually cried in President Obama's office as he kindly asked me to stay, telling him between sobs, "I'm so sorry, sir." My son was just entering junior high, and I needed to be more present for him.) Hearing about my departure, the trailblazing Adrienne Arsht, who had single-handedly taken her family-owned TotalBank business and grown it into a billion-dollar entity, took me to lunch. She had just launched the Adrienne Arsht Latin American Center at the Atlantic Council and asked me, "What's next? You have a piece of marble in front of you, how are you going to carve it?" I said I wasn't exactly sure, but that I found it rewarding to work with the international community, especially in diplomacy. She continued, "Once you know what you want to sculpt, you should chip away at pieces that hinder you and have nothing to do with where you want to be. What's left is what you want to be." She then offered me a way to chisel my sculpture: an ambassador-in-residence position at her new center. She told me, "Men always help other men find a place to land while they work through their next steps, and I want to do that for you." She created that perch for me to write and research, and I've been there ever since, paying it forward to other young people, Hillary- and Adrienne-style.

- **They are talented in the very areas you need to enhance.** Kristin Mannion recommends building a personal "board" of people who can round out areas where you have deficits. "Know where you most need to grow, and select six or so senior people who will give you constructive feedback and who authentically will be invested in promoting and supporting you." No need to formalize the board— just decide who you will reach out to when the need arises. And I would add: Make your main mentor the "chairperson."

Be a Great Mentee

The other side of the coin: How can you be a fantastic mentee? I've mentored dozens of young women (and men) who have a wide range of potential—and to whom I am deeply grateful for teaching me so much, as well—and these are pivotal qualities that make the relationship more fruitful:

1. **Hunger.** I love mentoring junior staff who are passionate about learning all facets of the office, not just the ones in their lane, seeing every assignment as an opportunity for personal growth. Thomas Corrigan, who came to the Office of Protocol from my beloved Cleveland, Ohio, embodies this balance of enthusiasm and openness. He arrived with an impressive comprehension of international affairs and elegant writing abilities, allowing him to quickly learn how to utilize protocol to affect diplomacy. He was eager to learn more about policy, so he joined me at the Atlantic Council, where he impressed so many so quickly that soon recruiters were at his door, landing him at Gates Ventures.

2. **Honesty and communication.** If you cannot truthfully share with your mentor what you're wrestling with, they won't be able to help

you. Trust me: Mentors would much rather know what you're struggling with than have you suffer silently and be told after the fact. A good mentor will not use this against you but will find a way to make this a teaching moment—we *all* find ourselves in over our head from time to time. Rachel Salerno, a former protocol officer who hails from a career diplomatic family, is one of the most genuine individuals I know. She is blessed with a compassionate heart and exceptional talent, and we connected immediately. She is a textbook example of someone whose straightforward and honest approach opens lines of communication and opportunity. Most young people experience difficulty expressing their concerns or doubts about their career advancement. Not Rachel. Her forthright approach with me and Cheryl Mills about her concerns and what she needed help with landed her a whole new career in the investment trade, and she is now parked in the bullpen of the financial world as a VP at Artemis.

3. **Being open to criticism.** When a mentor redirects you, think of it as an alternative suggestion rather than disapproval. A criticism from someone invested in your future is a form of support, a vote of confidence that says, "I want you to succeed, and this is how you can do it."

4. **Being team-oriented.** I look for mentees who not only do the job they are asked to do, but never stand by idle, stepping in when someone—anyone—needs an extra hand. They recognize they're part of the squad and are working to achieve an overall goal. Ana Bedayo, a campaign aide during Hillary's 2008 run, was the epitome of a team player, one with hustle and good judgment. Her spirited nature got the work done in a satisfactory and fun way, making her a popular pick for group projects. And let me tell you, the network she created during the campaign was her bridge to a new career. After the loss, she reinvented herself and is now a powerhouse talent manager in Hollywood at Grandview Automatik.

Final Thoughts

When you reach a perch where you are setting policy and tone, you are a powerful force for who gets heard and nurtured. Your style of managing and running a meeting can offer critical openings and invitations for those who need encouragement or simply an opportunity to contribute. Christine Lagarde says it best: "We often assume that all voices in the room are being heard because our teams are so talented, outspoken, and accomplished. But we may miss a key voice, hiding in the back, who could offer a key insight or an important dissent, if only we had asked, or enabled them to speak up." She goes on to explain that this talent is especially critical when collaborating with different cultures, whose style of communication may be different than ours. "Understanding different cultures is key. Why do people speak in meetings and when do they speak? Oftentimes listening is far more important than speaking. Good leaders should look out for the missing voice, making sure that everyone feels part of the team. And then listen to that voice. Not only will this empower your team, it can also help you become a more successful leader and diplomat."

Madame Lagarde's words ring so true, and who would dispute a woman of such great accomplishment and intelligence? I have been fortunate to have had tremendous support networks throughout my life, helping me to find and express *my* voice. From my parents and school professors to my work mentors, managers, colleagues, and friends—they guided and empowered me along a path that I could not have imagined for myself or achieved alone. And that path continues, as there is always more work to be done and more to achieve for women, disenfranchised groups, or anyone who feels left behind. Help someone find her voice, and search for those openings where you can make a difference. Our single voice and our collective power—even with the occasional fall—have the power to improve life for ourselves, our contemporaries, and future generations.

Fortunately, my work engaging with other countries and cultures continues forward; I am always exploring ways to bring people together on an international scale and here at home, a country where so many different cultures—political, religious, generational, ethnic, gendered—exist together and seek to thrive. Diplomacy does matter, today more than ever. We are all global ambassadors. Through every one of us—with the power of protocol—we can do our part to create bridges of understanding and shine a bright light on the potential, achievement, and endless possibilities of *all* people.

APPENDIX: WHAT WOULD CAPRICIA DO?
A HANDBOOK OF PROTOCOL AND ETIQUETTE

The following is a selection of supplementary material for some of the insights shared in this book—definitions, tips, and references for domestic and international exchanges that I have learned and relied upon during my years of walking the diplomatic tightrope. Please use this appendix as a guideline and always check with host countries for the most current etiquette rules and cultural rituals.

1: HIDDEN SUPERPOWER OF PROTOCOL

Definitions

Ambassador: The highest-ranking representative sent by one country to another to represent its government. Ambassadors often have the qualification "extraordinary and plenipotentiary," which indicates that they remain in the foreign capital for an indefinite length of time and that they have been given full power by their home government to act on its behalf.

Bilateral: A meeting between representatives or leaders of two countries. These intimate engagements contrast with multilateral engagements, like the annual opening of the United Nations General Assembly or the NATO summit.

Diplomacy: The conduct of international relations or engaging with other countries in order to achieve a foreign policy objective.

Diplomat: A person designated to establish or maintain political, economic, or cultural relations with a foreign country and to represent the interests of their national government in another country, often through diplomacy and negotiation.

Protocol: Generally, protocol refers to the rules that govern interactions, whether in social exchanges or professional industries. In government, protocol is the framework within which diplomacy takes place, the structure that houses the dignitaries as they have the crucial conversations and negotiations that affect the people they represent.

Soft Power: Influence defined by mutual benefit and cooperation. In diplomacy, it can be wielded by nations to curry favor. Examples of soft power include food diplomacy; cultural influencers such as entertainment; economic development; and establishing educational institutions overseas. This type of power contrasts with the hard power of military intervention.

Smart Power: Smart power means developing an integrated strategy, resource base, and tool kit to achieve American objectives, drawing on both hard and soft power. It is an approach that underscores the necessity of a strong military, but also invests heavily in alliances, partnerships, and institutions at all levels to expand American influence and establish the legitimacy of American action, as defined in CSIS, "Commission on Smart Power."

Visits: In the world of diplomatic protocol, invitations for visits are issued by a chief of state or head of government to a counterpart for an official function, and the visits are defined based on the level of formality and interaction that will take place. While all visits include bilateral meetings between principals, they each encompass different elements.

STATE VISIT: The highest level of formal visit, which can only be offered to a chief of state. In the United States it often includes a public welcoming ceremony on the White House South Lawn that consists of a twenty-one-gun salute, review of the military troops, and opening remarks by the host and visitor; a state luncheon usually hosted by the vice president and secretary of state; an international press conference by the leaders; a state dinner (a dinner hosted by the chief of state for a counterpart); and an invitation to use the president's guesthouse for overnight stays. It may also include a multicity destination tour and a cultural exchange, such as a visit to a war memorial or attending a sporting activity.

OFFICIAL VISIT: A visit that maintains the same ceremonial elements as a state visit, with the exception that the visitor is the head of government (such as the prime minister of the United Kingdom), and therefore receives a nineteen-gun salute as opposed to a twenty-one-gun salute.

OFFICIAL WORKING VISIT: A visit that is inclusive of a bilateral discussion and some form of formal meal between the leaders and delegation, such as a bilateral luncheon.

WORKING VISIT: The lowest level of formality for a visit by another head of state or government, which may not include any public element.

2: THE ETIQUETTE ADVANTAGE

Handshakes

Handshakes are ubiquitous as greetings around the world, but they vary from country to country in their applicability, duration, and firmness. When visiting another country, it's always a good idea to see if your counterpart will signal a preferred greeting and act accordingly. Always shake with the right hand, even if you are left-handed (the left hand is seen as unclean in some countries).

Usage:

In predominantly Muslim countries in the Middle East and Asia, it is generally best for a visiting man not to shake hands with a resident woman unless she offers her hand. A slight nod and verbal greeting will suffice. A visiting woman should also await the extended hand of a male host.

In East Asian countries like China, South Korea, or Japan, a handshake may not be used at all and instead may be replaced with a nod or a slight bow. Wait for your counterpart to offer a hand before extending your own and nod slightly while shaking hands.

In Turkey, men shake hands while kissing on the cheek and women will touch the other woman's shoulder while shaking hands.

In Thailand, the handshake is often replaced by the "wai," which includes placing palms together at chest level and bowing. In India, the gesture is accompanied with saying, "Namaste."

Firmness:

A firm grip signals confidence in the United States but may seem rude or aggressive in some cultures.

It is best to lighten your grip in France, China, Japan, South Korea, the Philippines, and most of the Middle East, Africa, and South America. In East Asian countries, the handshake is often more of a handclasp, and it may last ten or so seconds longer than the American handshake.

Duration:

Let it linger: In Latin American countries, extended handshakes may lead to a hug or a kiss on the cheek between friends. In the UAE and Turkey, the handshake may last long enough to feel like handholding (typically between those of the same sex). As noted, handclasps in East Asia may last several seconds longer than the American handshake.

Do it quickly: In France and Australia, speed is imperative. A quick shake is all it takes.

Royalty:

When greeting royalty, protocol is varied around the world. For meeting members of the British Royal Family, the official code is that there is none, believe it or not. The Royal Household (the administrative staff who serves the Royal Family) advises, "There are no obligatory codes of behavior when meeting the Queen or a member of the Royal Family, but many people wish to observe the traditional forms." Those traditions include a nod by men and a subtle curtsy by women for Her Majesty (except for representatives of the US government, who should not show a subservient curtsy before the British monarch, given the American Revolution). While US citizens are not expected to curtsy, it tends to be somewhat of a knee-jerk—or, rather, knee-*bend*—reaction, especially for royal enthusiasts. A proper curtsy involves crossing the right leg behind the left, allowing the left foot to angle outward; place your weight on the ball of your right foot and bend both knees slightly, all while bowing your head. Don't go too deep (you may not get up!), though the deeper you go and the longer you hold it, the more respect you confer. Slowly return to standing.

Members of the Royal Family should be addressed as Your Royal Highness upon greeting and then "sir" or "ma'am" (the "a" is a short "a" like in *jam*) thereafter. The Queen should be addressed as Your Majesty and then "ma'am" thereafter. It is also advised to not touch the Queen unless and until she extends her hand, not to turn your back to her, and to wait to stand or sit after she does.

These general guidelines can be followed for most monarchies (full list below). The region with the highest concentration of monarchs with ruling power is the Middle East. Jordan, for example, is known as the Hashemite Kingdom, meaning that members of the royal family are said to be descended from the Prophet Mohammed. Monarchies like Jordan, Morocco, and the United Arab Emirates are increasingly modernizing.

Ruling monarchies

Bahrain
Brunei
Kingdom of eSwatini (formerly Swaziland)
Kuwait
Morocco
Oman
Qatar
Saudi Arabia
United Arab Emirates

Monarchies with some political power

Bhutan
Liechtenstein
Monaco
Thailand
Tonga

Constitutional monarchies

Belgium
Cambodia
Denmark
Japan
Jordan
Lesotho

Luxembourg
Malaysia
Netherlands
Norway
Spain
Sweden
United Kingdom

4: CULTURAL IQ: WHO IN THE WORLD ARE THEY?

Business Card Rituals Around the World

Print one side in English with full information and the other side in the language of the country in which you do business (e.g., Mandarin, Japanese, Arabic).

- In Japan, present your business card after the handshake or bow, making sure that the information in Japanese is displayed faceup.

- In South Korea, make sure that you never present your card with your left hand as it is a sign of disrespect. Passing your card with your right or both hands is appropriate. In most other Asian countries, present the card with both hands slightly holding the outer corners.

- Upon receiving a card, read it closely and handle with great care. Do not put the business card into your pocket or into a wallet. Keep the card on the table in front of you during the meeting or place it, after a minute or so, into your portfolio (if you have one) or your front jacket pocket.

Bows

- In some Asian settings, a head nod may serve as a perfectly functional greeting.

- In Korea, participants often bow at the beginning and end of a meeting. A departing bow that is longer than the bow at the start of the meeting indicates a sign of respect and perhaps that it was a productive meeting.

- In Japan a bow can range from a small nod of the head to a deep bend at the waist. A deeper, longer bow indicates respect and conversely a small nod with the head is casual and informal. Bowing with your palms together at chest level is not customary in Japan. If the greeting takes place on a tatami floor, people get on their knees to bow. Bowing is also used to thank, apologize, make a request or ask someone a favor.

Gestures

Remember that hand gestures may have different meanings in different cultural context, so it's always best to take care when you raise a hand or point a finger.

- **The okay hand gesture** usually refers to money in the Japanese culture and can be considered vulgar in Russia, Brazil, Turkey, and Germany. It means "zero" or "worthless" in France.

- **Avoid making the thumbs-up gesture** in the Middle East, Australia, and Greece where it's an offensive expression.

- **Pointing** at people is generally considered rude in most cultures. And the "stop sign" with the palm out is considered offensive in Greece.

- **Curling the index finger** with the palm facing up is a way of beckoning someone in the United States, whereas in the Philippines it indicates you are calling a dog and is viewed as so offensive that you may even get arrested for using it. It's best to beckon with palms faced downward.

- **The "V for victory"** sign can have a negative meaning if the palm is facing inward vs. outward in countries such as Australia.

Kissing

Upon greeting a close acquaintance, one needs to take care of the number of kisses and the side on which one begins. The number of kisses on each cheek can vary significantly even within the same country. The following list is a collection from embassies on how many kisses it takes to render a proper greeting primarily for social greetings. In most countries, kisses are not appropriate in business unless you have established a personal relationship.

Albania: Two kisses, right to left, usually not in business; hugs are acceptable and are coupled with a cheek placed on the forehead.

Belgium: One kiss with friends; two with family; never with business; in Ghent male friends will kiss one another.

Belize: Never in business, and the number of kisses with family and friends depends upon familiarity.

Brunei: Two or three kisses depending upon how personal the relationship is; start with the right; handshake only with business.

Bulgaria: Two kisses, right cheek then left; usually not in business. Men do not kiss other men in social greetings.

Chile: Once on the right; business handshake is preferred.

Costa Rica: One for the opposite gender; right cheek only; acceptable for both social and business relationships (once the relationship is more familiar).

Croatia: Two kisses with family and friends; usually starts on the left; no kisses in business.

Cyprus: Two kisses between friends and family; start on the left; no kissing in business.

Czech Republic: Not the norm in business but if rendered: two kisses, left to right.

Equatorial Guinea: Two kisses, one on each check, left to right; never in business.

Fiji: Depends upon the relationship—for less formal interactions, one; for more formal, two; and always hug after a kiss. The iTaukei traditional greeting with a VIP, such as a head of state, starts with a handshake, after which the visitor kneels down and claps the host's hand three times as a mark of respect.

France: Two kisses between friends and family; start on the right; kiss greetings are not the norm in a new business relationship but are acceptable once familiarity is established.

Georgia: One kiss on the left cheek for both business and social relationships.

Germany: A handshake is the standard greeting when meeting someone new. Female friends will kiss once or hug; no kissing in business.

Japan: Cheek kissing is not a practice in Japan; the bow is the preferred greet; shaking hands is uncommon, but nowadays people shake hands when meeting people from foreign countries, so exceptions are made.

Jordan: Two kisses, one on each cheek; not between men and women; in business always use a handshake; men who are familiar commonly kiss on the cheek.

Luxembourg: Three kisses is the norm for personal relationships between women and women and women and men but not between only men; begin on the right.

Mexico: One kiss on the right cheek.

Morocco: Two kisses between friends and family; start on the right; no kissing in a new business relationship—shaking hands is preferred.

Oman: Kisses are only between women; the number depends on the relationship–more, the closer you are.

Spain: Two kisses between friends and family; start on the right; no kissing in business unless very familiar.

Turkey: Two kisses between friends and family; no kissing in business unless very familiar.

UK: Kissing as a greeting is new in the UK; not typical for the British, yet more acceptable in London; two kisses if you are familiar; start with the right; acceptable in business (with familiarity), as it has become more so in Europe and all is adjusted according to the situation.

Dressing Abroad: Colors in Other Countries

White: Avoid wearing white in East Asian countries, where several cultures associate it with unhappiness, death, or mourning.

Blue: Generally blue is a safe bet, given that it has neutral or positive connotations in most cultures.

Green: Always a good choice in Ireland, the Emerald Isle. Similar to blue, it is generally fine to wear.

Red: Red is the color of prosperity and good fortune in China, and is generally a color of passion in European and Latin American countries. Be careful, however, as it is associated with death in some countries in Africa.

Black: Black often symbolizes sorrow or grief and is worn at funerals in the United States and most Western countries. Alternatively, men and women of power usually wear black, as in judges' robes.

Introductions

Introductions are tricky, but by abiding by a standard, you can feel more certain in that instant when you are charged with making a first impression.

- Start with the most senior (by rank) person in the group—for instance, the CEO—and then continue in accordance with the rank of the other individuals.

- If two CEOs are present and this is an informal introduction, introduce the person closest in proximity. If this is formal, use alphabetical order by either last name of the individual or company.

- At social functions, you do not have the luxury of time to think through how to make the introductions as you would prepare before a business engagement. In those instances, first introduce the eldest person in your presence, honoring their age (no one will be offended), then those in closest proximity from your left to right.

To Smile or Not to Smile

The following are generalizations, and in most other countries, it's perfectly acceptable to share your agreement or joy.

Smiling big makes you seem significantly less intelligent in: Japan, India, Iran, South Korea, Russia, France, Israel, Mexico, Greece, Poland, and South Africa.

Smiling big makes you seem *more* intelligent in: Germany, Switzerland, Malaysia, China, Austria, Egypt, the Philippines, Denmark, Australia, Brazil, Pakistan, Nigeria, Portugal, Turkey, Canada, Zimbabwe, and the UK.

6: THE SOCIAL NETWORK: DIPLOMACY AT PLAY

Tech-tiquette

Today's communications are moving at light speed. If protocols aren't evolving along with the technology, relationships are weakened, information gets misinterpreted or overlooked, errors get introduced, and deals become jeopardized.

When establishing a new relationship, you should clarify your counterpart's preferred mode of communication right away, as there may be regulations that govern how you communicate. At cabinet meetings, US presidents are known to have rules requesting advisors, some of the most powerful people in the federal government, to kindly leave their electronic devices at the door. Similarly, during meetings with foreign leaders there is a no-tech approach. Even in an age of unprecedented connection, there is an unparalleled power in an in-person engagement. But the demands of modern economy and government don't always make your own version of a bilat possible. These new rules of the digital realm will help you establish tech protocols for your business and personal life. Importantly, these frameworks still hew to the principles of good etiquette: clarity, respect, and smart persuasion.

Email: Normal updates, quick questions, or missives that you want on the record—details of a contract given verbally or confirmation of a change in plans, for example—are best for email. "Bottom line up front" is a good rule of thumb for a formal email. Summarize the main topic in the subject line. And if an email is getting too long or requires a lot of explanation, request a phone call or set up a meeting. It rarely serves your mission to litigate important issues over dozens of threads. In addition, abide by these guidelines:

- **MESSAGE FORWARDING:** Not only is forwarding an email or sending a screenshot of a message disrespectful to the original sender (unless you get their permission), but it can land you in hot water by accidentally sharing something not meant to be seen by the recipient. Be wary of shortcuts that can create greater headaches in the long run.

  If you need to escalate a message to someone, consider how much of it they need to see to understand the issue. Long threads without context makes more work for them and might include information that they don't need.

- **A SMARTER SIGNATURE:** To protect your threads, it's good practice to include text in your signature that discourages dissemination, especially if you are communicating on behalf of your company. Many companies have a signature rule, but if not I advise adding something along the lines of: "If you are not the intended recipient, please notify the sender by replying to this message and then delete it from your system. Thank you."

- **THE "REPLY ALL":** Before "replying all," consider whether it might be prudent to reply to one or two people as a first step to finding a resolution. Or, after a sensitive note is sent, it might be time to propose a group call or pick up the phone and talk directly with the sender.

Face-to-face and video calls: If you and your counterpart are at odds on an important issue or if you are uncertain of their position, push for a face-to-face or video call. Otherwise, you'll miss out on the facial nuances—pursing of lips, furrowing of brows—which can speak volumes.

If you are conducting a meeting or an interview over video, behave as if it's an in-person, private meeting in all respects. Log in a minute or two early to resolve any technical issues before the meeting starts. If you are using a device other than a computer, make sure you can keep it in a steady position on a mount or against a wall. And consider what your viewer will see. Dress as you would for an in-person meeting and make sure there is nothing in the background that could distract or project a less-than-professional image.

If the video call requires you to reference written or electronic material, make it easily accessible. If you have to look at a printed sheet, consider placing it on the wall behind the device with the camera. Better yet: keep it as an open document on your device (if you are using a laptop or tablet).

If you have to share your screen, be careful! Before the meeting, close all windows, browser tabs, and programs that are not relevant. Keep open only the material that you want participants to see during the call. If you use an instant messaging service on your computer, set your status to "Do not disturb" so that a message does not pop up for everyone to see during the call or presentation.

Texting: In professional relationships, I reserve texting for close colleagues or day-of communication with an external counterpart. Even if you are careful, others may blur the lines of the intended meaning, and the result could end a hopeful business relationship. It's all too easy to make assumptions in a medium that lends itself to informality.

And remember that once it's out there, it's out there. When you're using email or text, words take on an extra weight since you must account for the lack of tone and facial expression. Never put anything in writing that would embarrass your mother or that you wouldn't want on the Internet.

Emojis: Keep the flames, lols, and GIFs out of your professional communications. Emojis usually require a ton of context or are simply not suited for the workplace—often both. Older folks will appreciate things being spelled out, and people of all ages will know exactly what you mean if you keep language standard.

Social media: Everyone—I mean *everyone*—googles a person before interviewing them, pitching to them, or inviting them to an event. Do a weekly social media scrub to ensure that nothing on any of your platforms sends the wrong message. Better yet: Don't post it at all. Unless your career involves frequent posting from a personal account (e.g., you're an Instagram model or YouTuber with millions of followers), keep potentially sensitive material off the Internet. There are ample news stories of people in the public eye losing opportunities (e.g., Academy Awards hosting, *Saturday Night Live* casting) due to social media posts. And guess what? "Private" accounts are not as private as you think. Once you post it, you've given away the right to control where it goes.

How Not to Have Sender's Remorse:

I have a quick three-step process I go through before I press Send on anything.

First and most important, I ask myself: Is this information that would cause me or anyone harm or embarrassment if it landed on the front page of a news site? If I can answer yes, I delete or reword it. (And I pick up the phone instead, if I have to.)

Second: Is everyone who receives it intended to receive it? I make a quick check of everyone in the "To" or "CC" category.

Third: I pause again before hitting Send. Do I truly want and need to send this email? This step also saves me from emailing unnecessary info, even if it's not harmful. No one needs miscellaneous info piling up in their inbox.

9: HUNGER GAMES

American Table Setting and Eating

I love setting an elegant table. Since I was a young girl, I would pull out my Miss Manners book and with great reverence open Nonny's crystal and "fine" china cabinet, especially on Christmas Eve, which was always extra special, and she served fish, so the table setting included the rare fish fork. Most people have a difficult time with proper table settings. Where does the napkin go? Is the fork placed to the left or right? And does it really matter? It does. The rules of table settings are to assist the guest in consuming their meal in the most appropriate and efficient manner. Emily Post is a great guide (check out EmilyPost.com for some helpful diagrams), but know that certain customs have gone by the wayside, including fingerbowls—too many people were mistaking these cleansing bowls for soup. Here are some basic rules to set the table by:

Utensil placement: These are always set in order of use from the outside in, with forks to the left of the plate and spoons and knives (blades facing the plate) to the right. So the salad fork is set to the outside of the entrée fork, and the soup spoon is set to the outside of an entrée spoon. The exception: The butter knife is usually placed diagonally across the bread plate, and the dessert spoon is often (but not always) placed at the top of the setting. A word about the fish fork: I'm a huge fan, even though many people have stopped using it. The fish fork has a lovely flat side so you can easily scoop a flaky fish onto your fork without it sliding off. And if seafood is an appetizer, do not expect people to suck the meat out of the shell—instead, present a pick or small fork for ease of use.

Glasses: The closest, innermost glass, which is usually the largest, is the water glass; then the white wine glass, which is often higher and with a slenderer cup; and lastly the red wine glass—a bit more bulbous to allow the wine to breathe better. I do not like the coffee cup placed at a formal dinner with the original setting, as the table can feel jammed and appear less elegant. I believe it should be placed on the table after the main course is removed and dessert is served. If you're setting the table for a quick luncheon, the dessert spoon can be pre-placed above the main course plate and the coffee cup to the right of the plate. I'm not a fan of this place setting.

Plates: The main plate goes, obviously, in the center, with the bread plate positioned to the upper left. Why to the left? First, the glasses are all positioned on the right, so placing the bread plate on the right would render that area quite crowded. Additionally, from a purely functional perspective, you hold your bread in your left hand and butter with your right. Preset courses, especially salads, have become more common. (Preset soup is appropriate only if it's chilled.) I am, again, not a fan of presetting courses, particularly dessert, but understand—having lived in the campaign world—that meals sometimes need to move at a steady pace, and presetting the salad and dessert allows for expediency and reduces interruptions from clearing (something you don't want when there is a speaking program during the meal).

Napkins: Under the forks? On the plate? The napkin can be placed under the forks or to the left of the forks; alternatively, the napkin can be placed in the center of the plate if you are using a napkin ring or the napkin is folded in a creative design.

Now you're ready to dig in! Follow these dining dos and don'ts to keep your tablemates, host, and waiters happy:

Soup etiquette: Dip and scoop away from instead of toward yourself, and softly tap the underside of the spoon against the inside of the bowl to remove any excess before bringing the spoon to your mouth (don't lean over the soup bowl if you can help it). And no slurping unless you're in Asia, especially in Japan and China, where it's advised to slurp to fully appreciate the tastes of the various noodles. I also found that eating the noodles with a chop stick is preferable to the fork: as you place them in your mouth you can catch the ends you bite off and have your next bite ready.

To signal you are still eating: Place your fork at the 4 p.m. position with tines down and the knife across the top of the plate with the edge facing you.

To signal you are finished: American style requires you place the tines of the fork up, parallel to your knife and across your plate diagonally; Continental style is with tines down (I prefer this style to hide bits of food that may be left on the tines).

When leaving the table temporarily: Many etiquette experts state to place your napkin on the cushion of your chair, but because this is where my seat just was, I prefer to fold it neatly and place it on the right side of the plate. Some waiters will place a used napkin on the backside of the chair. When you are completely finished with the meal, place it on the left or on the center of the place setting if your plate has been removed.

How to eat steak gracefully: Request a steak knife to avoid sawing your meat, and position the serrated edge of the knife perpendicular to the grain of the steak and a bit at a diagonal to retain the juices of the meat.

How to eat pasta with ease: With your fork in your right hand, lift a few noodles with the tines and, with a spoon in your left hand, place the end of the fork onto the spoon and twirl the noodles onto the fork. This is the best way to avoid splattering your face and clothes with sauce.

How to butter your bread: First, use the bread plate if it's provided as opposed to the table or your main course plate, which should be used only if a bread plate is not on the table. Place a small tab of butter onto the bread plate and then pinch off a bit of bread and butter that with your butter knife and then eat. Do not slather butter onto the whole bun, roll, or slice.

Toast Advice Around the World

The toast—when given—is intended to honor the guest at the table for a special occasion. Customs may vary not only within country but within households. My rule: Always ask the host! Each country—and sometimes each region within a country—has its own toast traditions. Here are a few guidelines to keep in mind when querying your host.

- **When to toast:** In Russia, toasts are usually done at the top of the meal, and typically the person being toasted returns it. In Japan, the host toasts visitors, but visitors are not expected to return the favor. In China, the host starts and the guest returns the toast right away. In Greece and Italy, the host gives the first toast, and the guest returns it later on in the meal. In Hungary, the guest of honor will raise their glass and toast the host, and then at the end of the meal, someone will raise a glass to thank the host for the hospitality. In Nordic countries, sipping is important. Do not sip until the host says, *Skoal*, which is the cue to raise your glass; then wait for the host to say, "Welcome" before taking your sip.

- **Stand or sit?** In the United States you should always stand when making a toast and remain seated as the person receiving the toast. In Poland, you are to stand if the host stands to make the toast, even as the recipient. The host in Ecuador will stand to make the toast and remain standing until the first sips have been taken. The person being toasted is then expected to do the same.

- **Clinks:** In some countries, you clink glasses only with your neighbors, whereas in others—such as France—you clink everyone at the table . . . without crossing arms and maintaining eye contact! In China, you touch the belly of your glass to others with the initial toast, whereas subsequent toasts involve tapping the base to the table. In the Netherlands, you clink glasses for an informal gathering; for business or more formal occasions, you just raise your glass and glance at the person you are toasting. In South Korea, you always raise the glass with your right hand and then support your right arm with your left hand to confer more respect. And there's no clinking of glasses, but do know that if you drain your drink it will be filled instantly. Never clink in Sweden.

- **Eye contact:** Almost every country encourages or requires the person making and receiving the toast to make eye contact, but there are variations. In Hungary, make eye contact with the person you are toasting, then raise your glass to eye level, state the toast, take a sip and then make eye contact again before setting the glass back down. In the Czech Republic, it would be considered rude not to make eye contact with every person you clink your glass with. In Sweden, you raise your glass to the level of your third button, make eye contact at the top of the toast and once you sip . . . and just before you place your glass down, you make eye contact again and nod.

Finally, here's a cheat sheet of how to say "cheers!" around the world. One note: In some countries, depending upon who you are toasting—man, woman, or group—the word changes slightly. With the rest of the country examples, I give the most basic word for cheers.

Brazil: Saúde—*Sah-oo-jee*
China: Gān bēi—*Gahn bey*
Croatia: Živio, for male singular—*Zheev-e-oh*; Živjela, for female singular—*Zheev-yay-la*
Estonia: Terviseks—*Ter-vee-seks*
Fiji: Bula—*Boo-lah*
Finland: Kippis—*Keep-is*
France: Santé—*Sahn-tay*
Germany: Prost or zum wohl—*Prohst*
Greece: Yia Mas—*Ya-mas*
Guam: Biba—*Bee-bah* (long live)
Hungary: Egészségére—*Egg-esh ay-geh-dre*
Ireland: Sláinte—*Slahn-cha*
Israel: L'chaim—*Le-hi-em*
Italy: Cin-cin (formal)—*Chin chin* or Salute (casual)—*Saw loo tay*
Japan: Kanpai—*Kan pie*
Kenya: Maisha marefu—*MY-sha mar-eh-foo* (Swahili for "long life")
Latvia: Priekā—*Pre-eh-kah*
Malaysia: Yam-Seng—*Yham Sahngu*
Morocco: Bsaha—*Bah-shay* (with health)
Netherlands: Proost—*Prohst*
Philippines: Mabuhay—*Mah-boo-hi*
Poland: Na zdorowie—*Nah zrov ee eh*
Romania: Noroc—*Nah-rawhk*
Russia: Za vashee—*Zda-ró-vye* (to your health)
Spain: Salud—*Sah-lud*
Turkey: Şerefe—*Sher-I-fe*

Know that there is no or limited toasting in most Muslim countries, as alcohol is usually not consumed.

Chopstick etiquette

If you are planning to visit a country where chopsticks are used and you are not accustomed to using them, practice! In China and Korea, chopsticks should be placed parallel across a bowl, not crossed which is considered bad luck. When placing your chopsticks down, do not stab them into the rice: it resembles the placement of incense, which is used at funerals. Never stick your chopsticks straight up into a bowl of rice, which is considered inappropriate. In addition:

Don't lick the chopsticks.

Don't play with your chopsticks.

Don't rub your chopsticks together. While many do this in restaurants that provide inexpensive wooden chopsticks to ostensibly smooth any splinters, it's considered rude, as it implies the host/restaurant has given you subpar chopsticks.

Don't feel the need to use them when offered. Your host will always want you to be comfortable and enjoy the meal. If you need a fork, just ask.

10: SECRETS OF A GIFT WHISPERER

Thank-You Cards: The Three-Point Plan

After a gift has been received or a benevolent deed has been performed, the thank-you note is the indispensable follow-up. Email and text are fine to immediately convey gratitude, but nothing makes a lasting impression like a handwritten note. Whether you've received a graduation present, a bottle of fine Champagne to mark a new business deal, or the favor of a neighbor who pet-sat, the exchange is not complete until you've written the note. Here is my three-point plan for composing the perfect note:

1. **Make it sincere.** No matter the size of the gift or the occasion, every gift has a thought behind it. Your expression of gratitude may demonstrate similar sentiment. Simply write from the heart and your appreciation will shine through.

2. **Make it unique.** The best thank-you note is more than a perfunctory necessity of duty—it reinforces a special connection and represents a specific moment between client and contractor, friends, or relatives. Acknowledge the connection that the gift has to your relationship.

3. **Make it soon.** Your appreciation should be expedient: It shows the sender that it made an impact. I travel with notecards and stamps to send immediately after an engagement. For business gifts, send your note no later than five days after the engagement. For social exchanges, send a note within two weeks to a month (depending on the occasion, however—such as wedding gifts—you have a bit more flexibility).

Gifting situations with examples from several countries

Belgium: fine chocolates or good wine

England: chocolates or wine

India: a small gift of chocolates or flowers

Germany: chocolates or yellow roses

Mexico: chocolates or flowers (white are considered uplifting)

Spain: chocolates or fine wine; flowers in an odd number for special occasions

United States: Instead of a bottle of wine or flowers, I prefer gifting scented candles for friends; for diplomats I like to give Washington, DC–related items, like presidential bookmarks or White House historical association bookends.

Vietnam: trinkets for small children for a social occasion

Countries where gifts are expected for business

France: Something from your home country is most appreciated.

Mexico: a token item for the first meeting, then a more elaborate gift as the relationship develops

South Korea: Gifting is a common practice as the relationship builds. Gifts should represent your home country and be moderately priced. When gifting to a group, make sure the most senior (by rank) receives a better gift than the others.

Spain: There's no expectation of a gift for the first visit, but thereafter a moderately priced gift is appreciated (and don't give anything with logos).

Countries where gifts are not expected for business

Australia
Brazil
Canada
England

Gifts to avoid in international relationships

- Steer away from knives, scissors, and umbrellas. Sharp objects imply you are severing ties and in some countries they are considered bad luck.

- Do not give Muslims anything made of pigskin (pork is prohibited) or alcohol (most Muslims do not drink).

- Don't give nonkosher food in Israel.

- In Singapore, avoid gifts associated with funerals.

- Do not give wine in France, as the host generally prefers to select the wine for the occasion, and they will not want to offend you by not opening your wine. In Argentina, a gift of wine is considered too common.

- Don't give anything extravagant (like flowers) in the Czech Republic.

Where *not* to open the gift in front of the host (it will appear greedy)

India
Singapore

Flowers

Petals have power depending on the country and the type of flower. Keep in mind:

- Stick with an odd number, as even numbers are unlucky in almost all countries.

- Generally, avoid lilies, chrysanthemums, and carnations, as they are associated with mourning and funerals.

- Red roses could inadvertently express a romantic intention.

- Give bird-of-paradise flowers in Chile, as they symbolize freedom and joy.

- Yellow roses are perfect to give in Germany . . . but symbolize death in Mexico

Interesting Rituals:

Czech Republic: It's appropriate to refuse the gift at first and then accept it when it's offered again.

England: Buying a round of drinks at a pub is seen favorably.

Singapore: Small gifts should be presented to all present and are usually not accepted when first presented, requiring you to offer until they are accepted.

South Korea: They may send back gifts that seem too high in price to avoid the appearance of bribery.

Wrapping:

India: Do not wrap a gift in black or white—the colors represent bad luck.

Singapore: Always wrap a gift.

South Korea: In Seoul, blue is a preferred color for wrapping. Avoid green, black, and white, which are unlucky. And do not sign a card in red, as it symbolizes termination.

China: A Gift-Giving Country

- Business practices may prevent some businesses from accepting gifts.

- Occasionally a gift may be declined up to three times before accepted (keep offering until they accept).

- For business exchanges, hard-to-find, high-end gifts are becoming popular, but I find that gifts that are meaningful are sure winners.

- Gifts should be presented after negotiations and with some care.

- As with the business card exchange, the gift should be presented with two hands.

- Wrapping a gift in red is best; gold paper is also acceptable.

- Groupings of eight, a lucky number, are viewed favorably.

- Avoid any groupings of four, as it is an unlucky number.

- Avoid gifting clocks or watches, which mean "time's up!" Also avoid gifting anything white, blue, or black.

- Avoid handkerchiefs, as the Chinese word for it also means a farewell.

- Avoid images of storks—they symbolize death.

Egypt: A Country with a Rich History in Gift Giving

- Traditionally, gifts of gold and silver were given to gain favor with the royals. Today the traditions continue: You must bring a hostess gift, such as fruit or dessert, when visiting someone's home.

- Gifts should be wrapped and opened at a later time.

- Gifts for children of the house are appreciated, but avoid praising the children as it is thought to bring bad luck.

- Never give the Quran as a gift.

- Give the gift with the right hand only when possible.

The Middle East

- Avoid pictures of people, as Islam prohibits images of the human likeness.

- Avoid images of dogs, which are considered unclean.

- Use the right hand (or both hands, if need be) to give a gift. Do not use the left hand only, as it is considered unclean and would be an offense.

- A compass is considered a good gift—it indicates the giver wants the recipient to always know where Mecca is while he is traveling.

Latin America

Avoid gifts until the relationship is developed, and be careful of male-to-female gifts (and vice versa)—this could imply an unintended romantic interest. If visiting a home with children, token gifts for them are appreciated.

11: KEEPING UP APPEARANCES

Casual vs. Business vs. Formal Wear

The applicability of a dress code can differ from region to region and culture to culture, but there are a few basics to keep in mind:

- The host selected a style of dress to complement the level of the engagement and your selection should align with the wishes of the host. Plus, you will enjoy the event more and your participation will be more fruitful if you feel suitably dressed. *Always* call the host or event coordinator to get a clear understanding of the expected attire. When you can't get a clear answer, err on the formal side. I tell friends who are fearful they dressed up too much for an event, "As long as you look great, own it."

- **"Black tie" or "black tie optional"** is reserved for events that are very high level and punctuate a celebration. State dinners, the Oscars, proms, or fiftieth employment anniversaries fall into this category. For men, this means a black tuxedo, a bow tie, a cummerbund, and formal shoes. Men may also wear dark suits with a black or silver tie and a vest with their tux or suspenders. Women should wear a long formal dress with adorned jewelry to accent. Gowns are reserved for galas (a gown has a fuller skirt than a long formal dress and a more intricate style). Many women may also wear a silk tux pantsuit or very fancy shorter, cocktail dresses (see below). And for hosts: I am not a fan of "black tie optional"—you should either make it black tie or not.

- **Cocktail Attire:** For men, cocktail is a simple dark suit and creative tie, and allows for a less business-y style. For women, you can flex your creative muscle, wearing a fancy pantsuit or a shorter dressier dress or jumpsuit (one of my favorites), as long as the material is of a quality that heightens the outfit to suit the dress code. If this is a business event, I would lower the level of creativity, depending upon the industry, to avoid a workplace snafu (a slit too high or neckline too plunging).

- **Business:** This is the easiest dress code to get right: a suit for men and a business dress or pantsuit for women.

- **Business Casual:** This dress code is the one people have the hardest time figuring out, because you have to distinguish it from merely "casual wear." I find that the event is the best starting point for guidance. If it's a club luncheon or an after-work event, a dress and polo top without a jacket will work. Hosts should absolutely assist the invitee with clarification, such as "boots and jeans or sundresses and polos welcome" or "no tie," which indicates that it is not quite business.

    Hosts are becoming more creative in their dress codes on invitations. Recently, "Festive" or "Holiday" has become more commonplace. These are still vague descriptors, so again I advise hosts to provide some guidance within the invitation: "Favorite holiday reindeer sweaters welcome" is a great cue, for example. A new one I have enjoyed using is "business with bling," indicating you can take the tie off and that women can have fun with jewelry and wear a bold lipstick.

13: THE MAGIC OF EXTREME PREPARATION

US Flag Protocol

Every country carries a fierce pride for their national flag, taking care to display and handle it in a way that honors what it represents: the history, struggles, triumphs, and symbols of a nation and people. In the United States, the treatment of our Stars and Stripes—as our flag is often called—is encoded into law and spelled out in the congressional publication *Our Flag* (go to www.govinfo.gov and type "our flag" into the search bar). It's a great resource for anyone wanting to learn about its history and protocol (along with how to fold it properly). Here, a few important points for displaying the flag so you don't offend or breach US code at your next event, parade, or picnic.

- Display the flag "on its own right." A good rule of thumb we used at the State Department is that, on US soil, the flag of the United States should always be displayed "on its own right." In other words, when observers are facing a stage or a podium, there should be no other flag—and no podium—to the left of the United States flag, so it gets its own prominent position.

- When flags of two or more nations are displayed, they are to be flown from separate staffs of the same height. The flags should be of approximately equal size. International usage forbids the display of the flag of one nation above that of another nation in time of peace.

- When on US soil and ordering flags on a stage or displaying flags after the US flag, the flags should be presented in precedence order, usually alphabetical order in English. For example, at the United Nations in New York, the flags are organized in English alphabetical order from north to south.

- US flag protocol dictates that no person shall display any other national or international flag more prominently than the United States flag at any place within the United States. (The headquarters of the United Nations, which is not technically on US soil, treats the US flag as it would any other nation and elevates the United Nations flag to a special place of prominence.)

- The lowering of the US flag to half-staff is subject to executive oversight by the US president, a governor, or in some cases, a mayor or local chief executive. The president will order the flag to be flown at half-staff upon the death of principal figures of the United States government or state governments as a mark of respect to their memory. There are varying guidelines for the duration of the order based on rank.

   Thirty days for a president or former president

   Ten days for current vice president, chief justice, or a retired chief justice of the United States, or Speaker of the House

   Day of death until interment for associate Supreme Court justice, secretary of an executive or military department, former vice president, or governor of a US state or territory

Day of death and the following day for member of Congress

The flag, when flown at half-staff, should be first hoisted to the peak for an instant and then lowered to the half-staff position. On Memorial Day, the flag should be raised to half-staff until noon and then raised to full peak thereafter.

- During inclement weather, flags should be taken down unless they are all-weather.

- The flag should never be draped over a vehicle, train, or boat, but it can be displayed from a staff on the right fender. And it should never be used to carry anything.

- The flag should never be used as apparel, bedding, or drapery, nor should it be used in advertising or printed on anything that will be discarded, such as a box or napkin.

What to Pack in Your Mary Poppins Bag

- A mini-stapler. I can't tell you how many times I stapled a tablecloth, a hemline, a waistband, or a scarf. (Safety pins, bobby pins, paper clips, and binder clips play important supporting roles as well: They can keep cords from unraveling, secure tablecloths in place, or pull hair back in a pinch.)

- Rubber bands. I used them to adjust too-big tablecloths or flags that were drooping on the floor.

- Scissors.

- A ruler. I would sometimes use it as a straight edge to cut paper if I lacked scissors and to measure the distance between table settings.

- Sharpies in various colors. They double as polish for shoes (heel marks, toe scratches) or bags. I also used them to color in a nick on a chair that a VIP would be sitting in. (*Pro tip:* Have a gold or silver sharpie on hand if you need to write on black paper stock or poster board—often our dignitaries were asked to sign things and only metallic would show up.)

- A sewing kit. Not only do I pack a kit with lots of different threads, but I pre-thread the needles so I can whip it out and start stitching immediately.

- A pick comb. Nothing works better for volumizing on women and especially men. Picks are so much better at fluffing underlying hair to create shape and the right amount of volume—or to cover a bald spot.

- Hair spray for breezy days on the tarmac or to stop a run in stockings.

- Dry shampoo. It's a game changer. If you don't have any, run out this instant and buy some and thank me later. My favorite is the original Psssst! ($2.99) and it comes in a travel size. If you invest in a good blow-dry before a big trip or meeting (I always get one before a long trip), you can get at least two more days out of your blow-dry with dry shampoo.

- Lip balm. Men's lips can get so dry and cracked, and because they aren't as cognizant of lip care they tend to have chapped lips more often than women. I advocate for lip balm with a hint of color for men—because otherwise their lips can look a bit dead. I even suggested it for President Obama (whose body guy took it—but I could never quite tell if he used it). I tried it out on my husband first (Rob's lips are sometimes super-dry—Fresh is the best brand I found) to make sure I wasn't giving the leader of our nation a clownish look. Lip balm is great for women as an extra layer over lipstick that's so matte you can see every little feathery line.

- Hand cream. Hand cream is a must—when you shake hands, you don't want someone to pull away with an "ew" reaction to scaly skin.

- Deodorant and a small bottle of perfume. No explanation needed. (*Pro tip:* They freshen up shoes, too!)

- Tide To Go Sticks and Shout Wipes. Invaluable when you don't have time to change out of a stained blouse or pair of pants.

- Downy Wrinkle Release. No iron? No problem.

- Nude and clear nail polish. Works for runs in tights, glossing over a chipped nail, and keeping laces or clothing thread from fraying.

- Small erasers. They can act as earring backings in a pinch.

- Ballet flats. If you need to scramble up four flights of stairs or dash across a parking lot or convention floor (which I did on the regular), you'll shave off time and save yourself some pain by having a pair in your bag.

- Reading glasses. Men especially always seem to need an extra pair.

- Extra pantyhose or tights in neutral and black (we frequented remote parts of the country where we couldn't even count on a supermarket that would carry L'eggs eggs, the brand du jour in the 1990s).

- Power bars for the go-go-go pace.

- Emergen-C or Zicam. We traveled with packs of these immune boosters as a preventive strategy, mixing them into water bottles, which also kept us drinking more. Summits and general assemblies were ground zero for whatever seasonal germ was floating around. I can't say for sure if they worked, but I rarely got sick on planes when we traveled. Or if I did feel symptoms of a cold, I would pop a Zicam every three to four hours, which claims to lessen the severity of the virus.

Overnights and Overseas

When I traveled with First Lady Hillary Clinton, we always packed backup outfits for her. Open Sharpie pens during greetings with a crowd along a rope line always seemed to leave their mark on her silk suits—accidents happened, so we needed to swap out the blouse/pants quickly and learned to pack an alternate outfit for her to change into each day. Having taken countless domestic and international trips—and having packed for America's First Lady for years—I've become a phenom at travel prep and rarely end up in a situation lacking something. My process is unusual (I drive my husband nutty), but it checks all the necessary boxes:

Prepacking:

- I check temperatures for all cities I'm departing from and arriving to and review my schedule—all events—and confirm the attire with the host if there's a special event.

- I collect my packing materials: clear plastic dry-cleaner bags to layer between clothes and prevent wrinkling; shoe bags for shoes that are delicate; paper shoe inserts for the toes of pumps.

- I have two prepacked, clear toiletry bags in my bathroom that I can grab in an instant. One is for the carry-on bag (taking care that all products are under the three-ounce limit) and the other, with more and larger quantities of products, for longer trips when I check my bag. I will take only one on whatever length of trip it is. I regularly refill the bottles.

For my main suitcase:

- I lay the outfits on the bed according to the schedule, sometimes trying them on to make sure they fit and to check for stains or holes.

- I make sure I have all items needed for each outfit—shoes (a neutral dress shoe for day and a black dress shoe for night), jewelry (plus an extra necklace or earring set in case one breaks or gets lost), belt, and pantyhose (which I rarely wear but always pack just in case). I also go through each outfit to determine what undergarment I'll need for each.

- I wrap each outfit separately in plastic. Additionally, I use soft-sided luggage (it has a bit more give) and because water can penetrate the material, the plastic protects my outfits if it is raining and the luggage handler is slow to load baggage onto the plane. I make sure that both inner sides of the luggage—the bottom and top—are covered with the plastic.

- I add my workout clothes and pack workout shoes that are more flexible than my usual at-home larger, firmer ones.

- I always pack one or two nice shawls/pashminas—many venues are naturally cool or overly air-conditioned—and a baseball cap for a walk.

- I bring one casual pair of pants or jeans in case I want to hang out in a lobby and read.

For my carry-on:

Compression socks for the plane to prevent swelling—your feet will love you when you land—and blood clots; a pashmina (an old one so it doesn't matter if it pills or if I spill something on it); sanitizing wipes for your area; my favorite fleece jacket; flats to change into; a neck pillow; soap to wash my face; and an extra toothbrush. If I'm heading to a meeting immediately after arrival, I have the outfit packed in a hanging bag with shoes (and jewelry) to easily change into.

Tricky social Qs

1. I don't want someone vaping in my home. Can I ask them not to even though there's no smoke involved?

Declaring your home a no-smoke zone for guests is socially acceptable and rarely challenged—the dangers of secondhand smoke are well known, and the odor clings to furniture and walls. Plus, smokers are used to having to go outside to light up since most public venues are nonsmoking these days. However, vaping can be more challenging to control, especially when people insist there is no smoke, so "it's no big deal." While it's true that vaping is smokeless, it's not harmless. The chemical soup of aerosol released by e-cigarettes—including nicotine—have been found in secondhand aerosol, according to the surgeon general. So next time a vaper wants to "light" up, lay out the facts and kindly ask them to step outdoors.

2. How do I apologize for being a no-show at an event?

Having a doctor for a husband means last-minute emergencies are a possibility, so I have been in this situation more than once. I first attempt to let the host know we will be delayed. Often, I end up arriving alone, so I need to make amends as there will be an empty seat at the table. (Fortunately, having a hospital emergency is generally considered a forgivable excuse for not showing up.) If the event is a larger gathering and it is impossible to get in touch with the hostess, I always call and apologize the next day. If the event is special—a holiday party, an engagement party—I also send flowers to apologize: If anyone knows how much work has gone into the planning for an event, it's me. I've seen people go through the RSVP list at the end of the night and cross no-shows off the list saying, "Never again." As for changing your RSVP from yes to no at the last minute, I try never to do that, even if it means going to all extremes to stop in for thirty minutes. I have also committed this tragic social faux pas—sometimes, I just forget! I am mortified and immediately let the host know how horrible I feel (and accept that I may not be invited to his next event).

3. My good friend wants to bring her children to my cocktail party/ wedding, but I really don't want children there. Am I a terrible person?

No, you're not. And it's certainly your prerogative, especially when alcohol is being served and it's a nighttime affair. It's always up to the host, so don't let anyone tell you otherwise. That said, there are circumstances where you might consider bending your rules. If you're inviting someone in the military, remember that many military families are separated for months at a time and they cherish every moment together when the parent is on leave, especially during the holidays; allowing these couples to bring their kids is a thoughtful gesture (and you can explain this to other couples you've invited, they'll understand). The same goes for new parents who are crazy nervous about leaving their babies but also dying for a night out. I was one of those parents, and I'll never forget the generosity of a friend who, upon learning that I was declining her dinner party invite to stay home with my young son (I brought him everywhere with me and was heartsick to decline her invitation in particular), insisted that I bring him. She set up a special place for him to sleep in her bedroom and even encouraged me to bring him to the table when he woke up in the middle of dinner.

4. I'm afraid my cousin Susie will show up to my birthday party with Lulu, her adorable shih tzu, but we have invited a few guests who are allergic. What should I do if she brings her?

Hopefully you can avoid the awkward moment by giving everyone advance notice that someone attending the event is really allergic to pets, thus letting Susie know that Lulu has to stay home. But when a guest doesn't pay heed (yes, pets are people, too, and considered family), the rule is that the person who didn't ask permission or who has ignored your ground rule has to leave. As sweetly and as apologetically as you can, let Susie know that as much as you love her and Lulu, you can't compromise the health of a guest who has already alerted you to his allergy. If a guest shows up with an unannounced emotional support animal, I would try to accommodate them by keeping the animal and the allergic guest in separate spaces. If you know a guest will arrive with an emotional support animal, pre-inform guests on an invite.

5. My party guest's child shattered a family heirloom. Shouldn't the parent be held responsible?

If a friend's child bumps the table and the Lalique crystal vase your aunt gave you tips and chips (can you tell this example is personal?), your job as the host or hostess is to put the guest at ease, no matter how upsetting it is to watch a family heirloom kick the dust. Part of the social bargain of hosting is expecting that things will happen when you open up your home. If *you* are the person who has spilled or cracked something, offer to fix or replace it. If they say "no need," and refuse to divulge any details that would allow you to track down a replacement, buy them something similar anyway. (For the record, I would never expect someone to replace a Lalique vase.) I've often found that a gift with a little humor—like unbreakable stemware—helps ease the ouch.

6. *My dinner conversation went off the rails the other night. Too much of the good stuff was served, and I may have said too much. How do I check in to see if I offended anyone? And if I did, what do I do?*

You have no idea how many DC dinner parties I've attended that have turned ugly and the political fangs of many guests come out. It happens. Immediately call—don't email or text, but call. Start by thanking them for the dinner and let them know that you were aware the conversation got "interesting" and then offer a full apology. Doing so takes the air out of the anger bubble.

7. *I was introduced to a small group by the host of a party and he mispronounced my name and got my title wrong. What is the best way to correct him without embarrassing him? And is there ever a moment when you should let the error stand?*

These moments are cringeworthy. If this is a new group of individuals for business purposes, it is essential that your name and title be conveyed properly. My name is mispronounced about 75 percent of the time when someone new introduces me. I try very hard in advance to pronounce it for them in nonchalant ways. Upon meeting someone new, I often talk about how my parents named me, adding, "Capricia is unique but difficult." It has been a great opener for some interesting conversations. And when they got my title wrong, I would restate my title in my response to a query or comment. If I missed hearing someone's name or title, I ask them to repeat it for me. Relationship building begins with that first introduction—getting it right is really important.

8. I sent out an email to a potential employer with a huge typo. Should I have followed up with an email pointing out the error and correcting it? And is there any way to do that gracefully?

When speaking, emailing, or writing a letter, proper grammar and punctuation should always, always be top of mind. And yet, we are human, and on occasion we mistype or misspeak our communiqués or dash a note off quickly and miss an error. You must correct it as soon as you discover it: "Please allow me to correct an email I sent earlier which had an error."

ACKNOWLEDGMENTS

- **Tula Karras,** my collaborator, advisor, and friend.

- **Denise Oswald,** my editor.

- **The Ecco team:** Meghan Deans, Allison Saltzman, Sonya Cheuse, Dominique Lear, and Norma Barksdale.

- **Rebecca Gradinger and Christy Fletcher,** my agents, and the team: **Elizabeth "Liz" Resnick, Melissa Chinchillo, and Brenna Raffe.**

- **Heather Samuelson** (vetting) and **Thomas Corrigan** (research).

- **President Bill Clinton and Secretary of State Hillary Rodham Clinton**

- **President Barack Obama and Mrs. Michelle Obama**

- **President Joe Biden and Dr. Jill Biden**

- **Secretary of State John Kerry**

- **Former chiefs of protocol of the United States:** Lloyd Nelson Hand, James Symington, Tyler Abell, Evan Dobelle, Edith Dobelle, Marion Smoake, Abelardo Valdez, Selwa "Lucky" Roosevelt, John Weinmann, Molly Raiser, Mary Mel French, Donald Ensenat, Nancy Brinker, Natalie Jones, Peter Selfridge, Rosemarie Pauli, Sean Lawler, Mary-Kate Fisher, Cam Henderson and the Blair House Restoration Fund, and the State Department Fine Arts Committee, Marcee Craighill.

- **The Office of Protocol,** (2009–2013)

FRONT OFFICE: Lee Satterfield, Ali Rubin, Dennis Cheng, Natalie Jones, Mark Walsh, Rachel Salerno, Thomas Corrigan, Carl Gray, Amanda McTyre, Sterling Watts, Rayda Nadal, Grace Garcia.

VISITS OFFICE: Asel Roberts, Penny Price, Paul Hegarty, Shilpa Pesaru, David Solomon, Kamyl Bazbaz, Jason Rahlon, Mimi Reisner, Shawn Lanchantin, Kimberlin Love, Connolly Keigher, Tanya Turner, James Infanzon, Jessie Johnson, Willodean Lewis.

GIFTS: Katie Jack, Liza Ballentine, Jennifer Romano, Tracy Bernstein, Sarah Henning, Jennifer Wham, Leigh Garland.

CEREMONIALS: Jessica Zielke, Alisa La, April Guice, Kim Townsend, Myrna Farmer, Jennifer Nicholson, Kristin Burkhalter, Sheila Dyson, Lauren Bernstein, Jeannie Rangel.

DIPLOMATIC AFFAIRS: Gladys Boluda, Chenobia Calhoun, Angie Young, Julia Huber, Jordan Hird, and SA 33: Holly Coffey, Alexis Olive, Jennifer Weronski, Abigail Aponte-Vasquez, Aloysius Ahimbisibwe, Gametta Perry, Sandy Foster, Timothy Beckler, Victorino Flores, Murat Obek, Susan Higgins, Johanna Wright, Ian Meyerhoff, Sally Claibourne.

BLAIR HOUSE: Randell Bumgardner, Tabitha Bullock, Jose Fuster, Yael Belkind, Rod Waters, Dario Santos, Alfonso Diaz-Gonzalez, Ian Knox, James Sinopolli, Terezinha Dias, Jemma Rennie, Weozelange Xirocostas, James Irby, Sixto Mercado, Jerry Richardson.

DIPLOMATIC PARTNERSHIPS: Sarah Nolan, Nick Schmit, Thomas Moran, Forest Harger, Jessica Andrews.

MANAGEMENT: Rosemarie Pauli, Shirley Stewart-Coates, Thomas Rathburn, Dee Lilly, Walter Rhinehart, Emory Webb, Laura Wills,

Judy Swapshire, Sharon Luden, Leslie Teague, Janet McDonald, Jason Larkin (chef), Chris James (chef).

- **Former Social Secretaries:** Nancy Tuckerman, Bess Abell, Lucy Winchester, Maria Downs, Mabel "Muffie" Brandon, Gahl Hodges, Linda Faulkner, Laurie Firestone, Ann Stock, Catherine Fenton, Lea Berman, Amy Zantzinger, Desirée Rogers, Julianna Smoot, Jeremy Bernard, Deesha Dyer, Anna Cristina "Ricki" Niceta Lloyd.

- **The Clinton Social Office:** Dwight Cramer, Sherry Daniels, Tracy LaBrecque Davis, Helen Dickey, Robyn Dickey, Tutty Fairbanks, Sarah Farnsworth, Emily Feingold, Dick and Nancy Flood, Dee Horsley, Eric Hothem, Michelle Houston, Elizabeth Jones, Sharon Kennedy, Bari Lurie, Ann McCoy, Debby McGinn, Rick Muffler, Rick Paulus, Diane Sappenfield, Laura Schwartz, Jamie Schwartz, Shereen Soghier, Alison Stein, Tibby Turner, Claire Turner, Setti Warren, Kim Widdess, and all of Hillaryland.

- To the great foreign service, career civil service, and military officers who serve our country with honor and distinction.

INDEX

ABOUT THE AUTHOR

CAPRICIA PENAVIC MARSHALL served as White House social secretary in the Clinton administration and as United States chief of protocol in the Obama administration. In her posts, she advanced the presidents' agendas, using new tools and innovative protocol methods to build relationships between dignitaries and industry leaders worldwide. She oversaw the diplomatic details of state visits and summits such as the G20, the Nuclear Security Summit, APEC, NATO, and the Sunnylands Summit. She is president of Global Engagement Strategies, LLC, which advises global organizations and companies on issues relating to the nexus of business and cultural diplomacy. Her clients include Bloomberg, 3M, and other Fortune 100 corporations. As a first-generation American, she has brought an understanding of the importance of culture to her posts and consultations. Marshall is an ambassador in residence at the Atlantic Council in Washington, DC, and a partner in Pine Island Capitol Partners.